Carole Landis

ALSO BY E.J. FLEMING

*The Fixers: Eddie Mannix, Howard Strickling
and the MGM Publicity Machine*
(McFarland, 2005)

*The Movieland Directory: Nearly 30,000 Addresses
of Celebrity Homes, Film Locations and Historical Sites
in the Los Angeles Area, 1900–Present*
(McFarland, 2004)

*Hollywood Death and Scandal Sites:
Sixteen Driving Tours with Directions and the Full Story,
from Tallulah Bankhead to River Phoenix*
(McFarland, 2000)

Carole Landis
A Tragic Life in Hollywood

E.J. Fleming

McFarland & Company, Inc., Publishers
Jefferson, North Carolina, and London

LIBRARY OF CONGRESS CATALOGUING-IN-PUBLICATION DATA

Fleming, E.J., 1954–
Carole Landis : a tragic life in Hollywood / E.J. Fleming.
p.   cm.
Includes bibliographical references and index.

ISBN-13: 978-0-7864-2200-5
softcover : 50# alkaline paper ∞

1. Landis, Carole, 1919–1948. 2. Motion picture actors and actresses—
United States—Biography.   I. Title.
PN2287.L27F64   2005   791.4302'8'092—dc22   2005009583

British Library cataloguing data are available

©2005 E.J. Fleming. All rights reserved

*No part of this book may be reproduced or transmitted in any form
or by any means, electronic or mechanical, including photocopying
or recording, or by any information storage and retrieval system,
without permission in writing from the publisher.*

Cover photograph: Landis at the pool at her Sunset Boulevard house, 1942

Manufactured in the United States of America

*McFarland & Company, Inc., Publishers
Box 611, Jefferson, North Carolina 28640
www.mcfarlandpub.com*

For Barb
Still and always there

Acknowledgments

As I began researching Carole Landis' story, I had no idea the impact that she had on people whose lives she touched, even briefly. All I knew about her was that she had killed herself because Rex Harrison wouldn't marry her, and that awful picture of her body on the bathroom floor. But as her remarkable story unfolded through my research, it became more and more puzzling to me *why* the story remained untold.

Each time I was lucky enough to speak with someone who knew her, it seemed more important to tell her story. But I couldn't have done so without their stories, their pictures and the love they still feel for her memory. They had two things in common. They embraced a stranger to help write her story, and they all still remember Carole Landis. Fifty years later. For that I want to thank all of them.

Thanks to Bill Starke, United States Air Force (retired), for sharing his stories and photos of Carole's wartime visit to Guadalcanal. To Noonie Forten, United States Army (retired), for her photos and reminiscences of Carole's travels with Martha Raye, and for keeping "Col. Maggie's" torch still aflame and her memory alive. Clarence "Korky" Korker, United States Navy (retired), shared his fabulous photos from Carole's 1945 visit to the U.S. Navy Armed Guard Center in Brooklyn, and Tom Bowerman shared his remembrances.

A special thanks to Don Esmond for sharing his photos and introducing me to the 26th Photo Squadron. Don and his comrades roamed the war zones with their 4 × 5 Speedgraphic cameras risking their lives so that we might better remember what World War II was really like. And to Gary Gray for sharing his photos and connecting me with other members of the 90th Bombardment Squadron—the legendary "Jolly Rogers."

Thanks to Bonnie and Jason Dilworth, who are instrumental in keeping the memories of the "Jolly Rogers" alive and who helped me get one of the final copies of the unit history. They also arranged introductions to many of the men who spent time with Carole during her visit. And thanks also to all of the men of the 90th who shared their stories through Bonnie's incredible message board.*

Dan Brigham shared his rare copy of the 1948 *Movie Times* featuring an article written by Carole's mother Clara after her death. Nick Bougas—my fellow Hollywood history fanatic—dug the coroner's photos out from within his voluminous

---

Thanks also to Pam Johnson for sharing her father's photographs of Carole's visit to the 38th Bomber group on Owi, New Guinea.

archives. Thanks also to Barry Ralph for his information about Larry Adler and Carole and for sharing his photos, and to Paul Nichols for sharing his remembrances of Bob Hope's visit to Owi Island with Jerry Colonna and Francis Langford.

Thanks to Patricia McKlintock Schmidlapp, the last wife of Carole's ex-husband Horace, for taking the time to respond to a stranger's letter and for sharing even a little of her life with Horace. Also thanks to her assistant Elsie Maki. And, as usual, a special thank you to the staffs of the Herrick Library at the Academy of Motion Picture Arts and Sciences, the U.S.C. and U.C.L.A. libraries, and the Los Angeles Public Libraries. And to my other L.A. friends—Scott Michaels and his wonderful website findadeath.com, Kevin Apodaca and his *Titans of Hollywood*, and Gary Hamann—thanks for your help and friendship.

A very special thank you to my brother Tony (who was instrumental in my earlier books but received no credit because I'm a moron) for his ongoing assistance with all things data-related. And another special thank you to Phil Tufts, who keeps my computers alive. His technical expertise is only matched by his ability to resurrect 60-year-old photos from the grave, always under deadline.

Lastly to my good friend Gerry Tax, thanks for your office, your country club, and your friendship. And as always, thanks to my friends who pretend I'm a writer, and allow me to pretend the same.

E.J. Fleming
March 2005

Table of Contents

Acknowledgments	vii
Introduction: Someone Worth Remembering	1
ONE * Fairchild and Two Fathers	3
TWO * San Bernardino Dreams	10
THREE * San Francisco and Hollywood	18
FOUR * Hollywood Comes with a Reputation	25
FIVE * The Edge of Stardom	63
SIX * War and Love, Again	106
SEVEN * The South Pacific	147
EIGHT * Coming Home, but to What?	185
NINE * Rex	213
TEN * July 4, 1948, Independence Day	229
Epilogue: Ghosts	258
Appendix A: Filmography	263
Appendix B: Radio Appearances	272
Chapter Notes	275
Selected Bibliography	281
Index	289

Let me tell you this: Every girl in the world wants to find the right man, someone who is sympathetic and understanding and helpful and strong, someone she can love madly. Actresses are no exception; the glamour and the tinsel, the fame and the money mean very little if there is hurt in the heart.
— Carole Landis

I have no intention of ending my career in a rooming house, with full scrapbooks and an empty stomach.
— Carole Landis

The first time I wore a bare midriff gown, Hollywood noticed me. Hollywood didn't discover me, I discovered it.
— Carole Landis

The most dramatic Hollywood stories are not filmed, they are lived.
— Jimmy Fidler, October 18, 1955

Introduction:
Someone Worth Remembering

Before she was a glamorous actress, before becoming a wartime pin-up star, even before she was Carole Landis, she was Frances Lillian Ridste, an insecure young girl from Wisconsin. Frances was beautiful, she was talented, and she would become a movie star. Yet she still spent her entire life searching for love, only to be cast aside by every man she did manage to love.

One man said to have been her father left just a few weeks before she was born. Within a month, her mother was living with another man who may actually have been her biological father, a man who abandoned the family when she was barely two. There would be no more fathers for young Frances and her brothers and sisters—siblings that she raised with her sister, as much as her working mother did. Frances grew up quickly. Frances was never a child. She never had time.

At 15, she married the first man who told her he loved her. After an annulment and remarriage, the union predictably failed within months. When she first became a little well-known years later, he would sue to get some of her money. At 16, but looking a decade older, Francis was living alone in San Francisco as "Carole Landis," singing in cabarets and cafes in the city's jazz district. She was said to have supplemented her income working as a call girl.

When she came to Hollywood at 18, she was passed around from movie executive to movie executive trading sex for small roles; she ended up doing roles far below what her enormous talent and breathtaking beauty should have earned her. Although it was a common practice, an industry rite of passage faced by girls with little or no choice, she earned the enmity of other actresses and the fury of the "studio wives," further stunting what should have been a glorious career.

But, not strangely, Carole was universally beloved by almost everyone else who crossed her path. She quietly learned the name of every person who labored on every set she ever worked on, and treated them as friends. She called them all "Honey." She wrote personal letters in her own hand to thousands of fans thanking them for *their* letters and support, often offering support of her own.

She was generous with her money and her time. She spent more time visiting troops during World War II—traveling hundreds of thousands of miles and coming near death not once but twice—than any other Hollywood star. The illnesses she contracted — pneumonia, malaria and dysentery — never left her, torturing her for the remaining years of her life.

Everyone, it seemed, loved Carole Landis, but it's doubtful *she* really loved anyone. She meant to. She wanted to. But she never learned *how* to, growing up in the dysfunctional surroundings in which she did. By her mid-twenties she had married three more times, always on whims, and always with the predictable outcome. Yet another divorce. Laughing at her own failures, she wore her four wedding rings at once to remind her not to marry again. But she cried about it more than she laughed.

Probably predictably, the man who she thought her one true love, the one man who promised her everything, was a pathological liar and womanizer who would, inevitably, break her heart. With tragic results.

This is the story of Carole Landis, one of the most fascinating women in Hollywood history. Fascinating, yet somehow virtually forgotten. An incredible talent somehow ignored by movie history. It's difficult to find an adjective or term *not* used to describe Carole: generous, sweet, liberated, femme fatale, amoral, call girl, victim, gay divorcee, ambitious, independent, casting couch victim, tragic icon, lovely, generous.... Perhaps the real tragedy is that she has indeed been forgotten.

Independence Day, July 4, would have a coincidental and repeating significance during the life of Carole Landis. On July 4, 1934, she left home at 15 for San Francisco. On July 4, 1940, she entered into one of her four failed marriages. One of the most independent actresses in Hollywood from the 1930s to the 1940s, she celebrated her country's independence by tirelessly working for the military during World War II. And on July 4, 1948, she killed herself by swallowing 25 pills. Dead on Independence Day. But she was never really independent. That is part of the tragedy that was Carole Landis.

But who was the *real* Carole Landis? Why did she kill herself before reaching her thirtieth birthday? During her life, writers and fans focused on her astonishing beauty and almost perfect body, seldom mentioning her acting ability and comedic timing. After her death, writers and fans remember only promiscuity and suicide. Her death has become her defining attribute — a photo of a young woman curled up on a bathroom floor in a gingham dress. Even learning just a little bit about her reveals the unfairness of all of that.

In his book *Fallen Angels*, Kirk Crivello described Carole as "streaking into stardom like a comet ready to burn out — and a few years later, she did. The legend is that Carole Landis was playing herself; a bright and bouncy girl, with an undertone of occasional sadness, searching for something even she wasn't sure of."[1]

Carole once said, "Hollywood didn't discover me. I discovered it." But her short Hollywood life is the cautionary tale of the perils faced by actresses during the Golden Age of Hollywood. Her tragic 1948 death — the *Los Angeles Times* described her in death as "one of the brightest careers in the film world" — highlighted the inequities of the studio system, the treatment of actors versus actresses, and the almost impassable road to stardom faced by the "six-month option girls." For those thousands, stardom was most likely a fantasy, unattainable. But nobody would tell them.

Carole Landis was much more than Crivello's fallen star or the promiscuous actress from the rumors of her day. More than any of this, Carole Landis was an interesting woman, a person worth remembering. Her life should be celebrated, not her death.

★ ONE ★

Fairchild and Two Fathers

At the dawn of the twentieth century, the upper Midwest — with its long cold winters, isolation and distance from big city troubles — was a haven for northern European immigrants. As World War I raged in Europe, millions of refugees from Sweden, Norway and Denmark fled the conflict for the tranquility of America. Thousands settled in Wisconsin and Minnesota, already heavily populated with Scandinavians.

They filled towns large and small, scattered throughout central and northern Wisconsin and Minnesota. They packed hundreds of logging camps and worked at dozens of the paper mills squatting along the rivers dissecting the woodlands and low-strung hills. They farmed the rich soil and kept the railroads moving. If there was difficult or hazardous work to be found, Scandinavians seemed to find it, and thrive on it.

Today, Fairchild, Wisconsin, is still a tiny village squatting in the far southeast reaches of Eau Claire County, in the center of the state. Eau Claire County lies 100 miles east of the Mississippi River and the riverfront towns of St. Paul and Minneapolis. Fairchild is another 20 miles further east from Eau Claire. In the late 1800s it was a full day's ride over the rutted dirt roads to Fairchild from Eau Claire. It's almost as remote today as it was in the early 1900s.

Fairchild was founded just after the Civil War and named for Lucius Fairchild. He was a Civil War hero and one of the first governors of the state. The first settlers — the Hobarts, the Pettises, and the Livermores — arrived in 1865 and began clearing acreage in the beautiful and pristine Diamond Valley.

Soon the lowlands were dotted with several dozen rough-hewn log cabins and the beginnings of Victorian farmhouses next to dozens of small creeks with names like Harmony, Coon Pass and Whippoorwill aside. Descendants of those first families continue to farm the land today.

In 1868, the West Wisconsin Railway Company brought their rails through Fairchild from St. Paul by way of Eau Claire. John Van Auken, one of the original settlers, built a large steam-powered sawmill next to the tracks. Soon an actual village of Fairchild had sprung up around Van Auken's mill. But the first general store wasn't built until 1870, when the railway company began building a depot.

Over the next two decades, Fairchild grew with the lumber industry and with money from N.C. Howard. Howard came to Fairchild in 1876 from Fort Howard, where he already owned the largest lumber and paper company in the state. Soon after his arrival in Fairchild, he built a huge saw mill that by 1880 employed 260 men. In the 1880s he built a hotel and paid to build 45 miles of track to connect Fairchild with his lumber mills in Mondavi. His "Mondavi Line" would later be sold to the St. Paul, Minneapolis and Omaha Railroad. During the early 1890s he had an opera house built and opened the large McKinney Hotel. He also built yet another short line railroad, this one connecting Fairchild with the nearby village of Owen.[1]

But even Howard's generosity and largesse could not jump-start Fairchild. In 1890 the population — just over 1,250 souls — was the same as it was a decade earlier (the population today is still just over 1,300). In 1895 his investment stopped after the entire downtown — save his opera house, a church and a small home — were reduced to ashes by a fire ignited by a overturned kerosene lamp inside the Arnold Drug Store.

Howard's railroad sustained Fairchild into the 1900s, but the sleepy hamlet stubbornly refused to grow. The railway depot was a major interchange for the trains carrying lumber, cattle and grain through Wisconsin. But most of the 30 trains that passed through Fairchild every day by 1915 did not stop.

In 1910 there were about 150 families calling Fairchild home. Half of them lived in the village and worked in some fashion for the railroad. The other half worked the dairy and grain farms filling the nearby valleys. Most of the farmers and dairymen were European immigrants. There were families from Austria, Hungary, Poland, Germany, Norway, Sweden and Russia. There were a few from England and Scotland as well, but the village had a distinctly Scandinavian feel.

Ludvig Louis Zentek and his wife Frances Lillian Gronowska lived on a small farm a mile or so outside of Fairchild. Both were born in Poland and had immigrated to the United States in 1890. The neighboring farms were also owned by Polish and German immigrants; most of the Poles were Catholic and the Germans Lutheran. There were half a dozen churches in and around the hamlets surrounding Fairchild. Like Ludvig Zentek, the other residents were rough-hewn men like Anton Polzak, Peter Zingeheim and Ole Olson.[2] Also like many of his fellow immigrants, the Zentek family name was often misspelled, listed as "Sentek." It was "Sentek" on the census forms, but on personal documents and formal historical records the spelling was "Zentek."

The 1910 census lists the family of Ludwig and Francesca, who would later become known as "Frances." Their children included 18-year-old Agnesica (born in 1892, she became known as Agnes), 13-year-old Martha (born in 1897), 12-year-old Harry (born in 1897), nine-year-old Albert (born in 1900), seven-year-old Maria (born in 1903) and five-year-old Barbra (born in 1905). All of the Zentek children were born in the family home. It has always been assumed and written that Ludvig Zentek was a farmer, but the recently-unearthed 1910 census lists his occupation as "section hand" for a "railroad" company, while Francesca was a "farmer" on a "family farm." Later census records (1920 and 1930) describe Ludvig as a farmer, but in 1910 he was working for N.C. Howard's "Mondavi" Line railroad.

Like most European families at the time, the Zentek clan spoke Polish at home. Little — almost no — English was spoken in the house. The children spoke English haltingly until their teenage years, when they left home to work on their own. In the first several decades after Fairchild was settled, the Europeans held firmly to their customs, their language and their heritage.

Surprisingly, one child was not listed with the family when the census taker walked away from the Zentek farmhouse on April 16, 1910. There is quite a bit of confusion regarding the whereabouts of 15-year-old Clara Lillian Zentek from early 1910 into early 1911. Clara was born to Ludvig and Frances in 1894 but was absent from the 1910 census when she would have been only 15.

We do know that Clara was strong-willed and fiercely independent and later that year met a Norwegian railroad mechanic named Alfred Ridste. Ridste, just 19, had only recently arrived in Fairchild from St. Paul, Minnesota. He was born on October 10, 1891, in Dawson, Minnesota, the youngest of four children and the first son born in the family. As late as the spring of 1910 he was working in St. Paul as a welder for a refrigerator company and living at 1518 Charles Street, a working class neighborhood in West St. Paul.[3] He was a handsome Midwesterner with piercing blue eyes and brown hair.

During the summer of 1910, Ridste went to work for the St. Paul, Minneapolis and Omaha Railroad. It is probable that Ridste worked alongside Ludvig Zentek, which led to his meeting Clara. Alfred and Clara met in late 1910 and were married in Fairchild in 1911. Not long after the wedding, the newlyweds followed Alfred's railroad work and moved to western Minnesota, where on March 26, 1912, their first child, a boy they named Lawrence Bernard, was born.

The railroad work that was Alfred Ridste's livelihood was dangerous and the pace grueling. Worse for the family, it could also be sporadic. If a local industry faltered, the need for rail service ended. And even though it did not pay very well, Ridste had to go where the work—and the railroads—sent him. For the better part of the next eight years, Ridste and his family moved to whichever company town that the railroads sent him to.

Ridste did enjoy the protection that the far-flung company towns offered. As the United States was suffering through World War I, more and more immigrants began distancing themselves from their histories, fueled in part by the rampant anti–European sentiment in the bigger cities. Many of the mostly European railroad workers lived in secluded railroad towns throughout the Northwest. In these small towns they were safe from the random acts of violence sometimes occurring in the larger cities.

Ridste went to work for the Burlington Northern Railroad and in 1913 the family found themselves near the tiny central Montana town of Lewistown. Lewiston was at the end of a railroad spur line that connected the tiny settlement with a main north-south trunk line that dissected the state. It was a company town. The nearest big city was Helena, still over a hundred miles to the southwest.

The family lived in a tiny house—little more than a cabin—in the little Fergus County burgh of Denton, about ten miles farther into the wilderness from Lewistown. Denton has not changed much since the Ridste-Fenner clan lived there. Seven-block-long downtown Denton in bordered on the south by Main Street and on the north by Broadway (in 1920 called the old State Route 81). Once they exit "downtown

Denton," the two streets dissolve quickly into farmland that stretches for miles up into the mountains. To the east the nearest town is Danvers, to the west Coffee Creek. The entire area of Denton is less than two square miles. The same Central Montana Rail tracks on which Albert had worked still run along the southern edge of the tiny town.

Clara bore three more children while she and Alfred lived in Montana—two sons and a daughter. Lewis was born in early 1914, Jerome (Jerry) in July or August 1916 and Dorothy on July 8, 1917. Clara tended to her growing family while Alfred continued his railroad work, which may have become somewhat sporadic. When he filled out his World War I Draft Registration form in June 1917, he listed his occupation as "farming."[4]

Tragedy struck the family later in 1917 when 17-month-old Jerry was severely burned after his bedclothes caught fire as he slept next to the fireplace. He died of his burns several days later, on December 20, 1917. In early 1918, just a few months after little Jerry's death, Clara found herself pregnant again. For reasons not entirely clear, Clara, Alfred and their three remaining children left Denton and returned to Wisconsin. With nowhere to live and apparently no specific job prospects for Alfred, the family moved in with Clara's family outside Fairchild. By then, Ludvig Zentek was no longer working for the railroad. He was tending the family farm with Frances and son Harry, the only remaining Zentek child living at home at the time.[5]

There could have been any number of legitimate reasons for Alfred to move his family back to Wisconsin so abruptly. Perhaps the stress of the death of a child or the nomadic and challenging life that characterized his railroad work led to the hasty move back to Wisconsin. Or perhaps he moved his family from Montana to break up a burgeoning relationship between his wife and a Montana neighbor, farmer Charles Fenner. Whatever the real reason for leaving Montana and returning to Fairchild, it is a mystery why he left as soon as he and his family got back there. It appears that almost immediately upon their return in the late fall of 1918, Alfred left his pregnant wife and three children and departed into the night.

Alfred was not in Fairchild when his divorce from Clara was finalized, nor was he there when his fifth child, a daughter, was born in the tiny house in the farm fields outside of town. She was named Frances Lillian, after her maternal grandmother, in whose large four-poster bed she had been born.

In a later article ghost-written for Clara after Carole's death for *True Story Magazine*, "The Heartbreaking True Story of Carole Landis," Clara excused Alfred's exit, noting, "Her father was not with me at the time. He was a man whom life had given too much responsibility too soon. A restless boy. Carole inherited this quality. He had left home several months before the new baby was born."[6] Perhaps coincidentally and certainly conveniently, no mention was made about the baby's obvious conception in Montana.

She was such a beautiful baby that she was nicknamed "Baby Doll." Her mother called her that for the rest of her life.[7] Growing up, young Frances developed the same independence and strong will of her mother. But she also seemed to inherit her mother's wanderlust and an inability to successfully navigate relationships with men.

Like many of the details of the Clara Zentek-Alfred Ridste relationship, there is confusion surrounding the actual date of Frances Lillian's birth. Legend has it that Frances was born on New Year's Eve, 1919, but circumstantial and verifiable evidence leads this author to believe that she may have been born some months later, as late as March or April 1919. There is a birth certificate on file in Eau Claire County, Wisconsin, for "Frances Lillian Ridste," and it is dated January 2, 1919. But that conflicts with the 1920 census taken on January 28, 1920, that lists Clara Ridste and her children Lewis A. (listed as age six), Dorothy A. (age "3 & $^6/_{12}$ths") and Frances L. (described as age "$^{11}/_{12}$ths").[8] Her age is a clear conflict.

If she had indeed been a New Year's Eve, 1919, baby, she would have to have been listed as a one-year-old on a census taken on January 28, 1920. But Clara evidently told the census taker that Frances was 11 months old, not one year. I tend to believe that Clara was telling the truth in 1920; that her daughter was indeed 11 months old on January 28. There would have been no reason for Clara to lie about her child's age, and if she was really one year old, Clara undoubtedly would have said so.

Regarding the birth certificate on file in Wisconsin, it is often challenging to determine the accuracy of vintage birth records. Relying on the accuracy of the formal birth records from that era can be a notoriously risky business, because the records were typically not filed for weeks or even months, depending on the distance from the family home to the county offices.

Unlike today, when birth certificates are filed at that moment, in rural areas like Fairchild, Wisconsin, in 1919, births and deaths were recorded when the family found time to get to the county seat and provide the information. The best source for actual dates were and are the family Bibles, which were appended with birth, death and marriage dates as a matter of course. Also, at that time many people living in remote rural areas were often in doubt about the exact date anyway.

Whatever the reason, it's difficult to speculate on why an obviously incorrect date was given for Frances. But it was. It does appear that Frances was born during the late winter or early spring of 1919, and not January 1 or 2. She was more likely born in February or March. When and why she was later described as a New Year's baby may have had more to do with movie studio publicity.

In any event, soon after the birth, Clara learned that Alfred was in Chicago. He had enlisted in the Navy after leaving the family, and his records were uncovered at the Great Lakes Naval Air Station in Glenview, Illinois, north of Chicago.[9] He was listed in the January 1920 census as an "aviation student" but he was in fact training in aviation mechanics. He was one of the oldest students in a class of 650; only eight students were above the age of 27. Almost 620 were under 21.

While Alfred was in basic training, Clara was heading back to Montana. Without telling Alfred of the birth of his daughter, the ever-independent Clara returned to Montana within two months of the birth. The hot and dusty train ride must have been difficult for a 25-year-old woman traveling alone with a newborn and three young boys aged three, six and seven. Strangely by the summer of 1920 the Ridstes had moved into old friend Charles Fenner's remote farm outside of Denton.

One has to wonder why a 33-year-old Montana farmer would invite a woman and four children — including a newborn — into his home already crowded with his own two sons. Apparently the two had a relationship prior to Alfred taking his family back to Wisconsin, since immediately after Frances' birth Clara packed up the children and headed back to Denton and Charles Fenner, and he welcomed them "home." There seems no other logical reason for Clara to do that. She may have offered a clue in the *True Story* piece when she mentioned that "in a few months I was able to take baby Carole and the four older children to Montana and establish a home where we could be with my husband."[10] She was not speaking of Alfred.

Knowing what we know, this author tends to think that the Fenner-Clara relationship was the reason for Alfred's abrupt departure from Montana and ultimately the abandonment of his family. It may have been that little Frances was Fenner's child. That may also explain the obvious discrepancy concerning Frances' actual birth date. Nobody has ever asked these questions before, and they're obviously impossible to answer now, but the circumstantial evidence offers an interesting situation.

Further circumstantial support for the theory that Frances was Charles' child arose when the 33-year-old Fenner and 25-year-old Clara were married in Fenton on December 19, 1919, within just a few more months of her return. The extended Fenner-Ridste clan included his children, eight-year-old Edward and three-year-old Floyd, and the four Ridste children, Lawrence, Lewis, Dorothy and Frances. The Ridste children were all listed on the 1920 Federal census as Fenner's stepchildren.

Listed in the 1920 census records, the small Fenner farmhouse was located outside of town on an "un-named country road." It was — and still is — a dirt and gravel country road that ran off of Placer Coulee Road. The boxy wood-frame house was crammed with the couple's extended family. The couple and their six children — all under the age of eight — were crammed into four tiny rooms. Charles Fenner eked out a hardscrabble living off the rocky soil.

Even as an infant, Frances showed an independent streak far beyond her years. When she was just 18 months old, Clara got her dressed to go for a walk near the family's farm. Clara left the room for a few minutes, returning to discover that the child had left the house. An hour later a group of neighbors and Clara found young Frances nonchalantly picking flowers a mile away. She looked up and said, "Look, Mommy, pretty flowers."[11]

In yet another strange twist in the life of Clara Ridste and her young children, she and Fenner divorced after just 17 months. They split in April 1921, and he remarried another local woman (she also had several children) a few months later. Clara spoke of that period, saying only, "my husband [having] left us again."[12] In her interviews and writings she never publicly distinguished between Alfred Ridste and Charles Fenner. She always inferred that she only had one husband during that period in her life. That omission is telling given the circumstances.

Charles Fenner became the second husband to leave Clara and the second father to abandon young Frances and her siblings. She was a newborn when Alfred Ridste exited, and though she remembered nothing of him, she was probably exposed to a steady stream of invective from her mother. By the age of four she had become familiar with abandonment by men. Although she was only an infant, Frances would be deeply affected by Jerry's death, followed so soon afterward by her stepfather's departure. The three-year-old had to be filled with confusion. Confusion that never really left her.

Rather than return — yet again in failure — to Wisconsin, Clara took Lawrence, Lewis, Dorothy and Frances to dusty San Bernardino, California. Coincidently, her ex-husband Alfred and his second wife were already living there. Ridste was working as a machinist at the Navy Yards in San Diego, and to his credit he had tried to keep in touch with his former family after his initial disappearance. He also sent small amounts of money whenever he could. It may have been his suggestion that Clara brought the children to California.

⋆ Two ⋆

San Bernardino Dreams

When the Ridste family arrived in San Bernardino in 1923, the town was a two-hour car trip from downtown Los Angeles but was years away in lifestyle. Most of the distance between the two towns was empty. It is unknown where Clara and the children — nine-year-old Lawrence, eight-year-old Lewis, six-year-old Dorothy and three-year-old Frances— lived, but she doubtless rented either a small house or rooms in one of the town's many boarding houses. Perhaps Clara rented the small house on Bryant Street where the family would still be living in 1930. Family stories and written records place the family there as early as 1925 or 1926. Some historians have mentioned the family in San Diego first, but I can find no support for that assertion. Clara herself said she went directly from Montana to San Bernardino.

Almost everyone on working-class Bryant Street was renting, paying between $15 and $50 a month for their four- or five-room bungalows. It was not a glamourous street at all, but it was clean. The Ridste house at 175 Bryant Street was one of the largest on the block.

At the end of the street, a seemingly endless stream of Union Pacific freight trains chugged toward Arizona. Just a few blocks further east, the Santa Ana River meandered past. It was just a short walk away, and the children spent lazy summer afternoons along its bank or jumping in on a dare.

The Bryant Street neighborhood could never hide its unglamourous personality. It was a distinctly blue-collar, working-class area, even by Depression-era standards. To a person, Clara's neighbors struggled to scratch out a living.

There was not much money on Bryant Street but there were plenty of kids to play with. Next door at 159, the Watsons had a son the same age as Dorothy and a daughter the same age as Frances. At 120, George and Willie Hill, the neighborhood's only black family, shared a tiny bungalow with their children. George was a porter, his wife cleaned houses, his son Linell was a caddy at the San Bernardino Golf Club and his daughter Beatrice was a maid for a white family in town. Perhaps a sign of the times, they paid the highest rent on the block —$15 a month — even though their house was the smallest.

The family of carpenter Allen Schaggs rented their little house for $10 a month. Fireman Robert Praster and his family paid $10, as did blacksmith James Gordon. Almost across the street at 159 lived the Watson family, the only other family on the street beside Clara's that owned their home. Howard Watson worked at an auto

Sleepy — and dusty — San Bernardino at the time the Ridste family lived on Bryant Street in the 1920s.

salvage yard, and 12-year-old Elizabeth was Dorothy's best friend. There was also a cement worker, a mechanic, a fruit farm-hand and a truck salesman.[1]

Across the street at 170 was Lucy Brumbelow, almost 80. Everyone in the neighborhood called her "Grandma" and she helped watch the Ridste children during the day while Clara worked. Lucy lived with her son Ronny and three orphaned children that she had taken in, 17-year-old William Parsons, five-year-old Johnnie Kelly and three-year-old Carrie. The Brumbelows rented their four-room bungalow for $12 a week. Ronny was a carpenter. They were of Native American descent, and Lucy was described by Carole's mother as "a sweet old Cherokee Indian lady."[2]

Just two blocks away, where Bryant Street dead-ended onto Brook Street, sat the grubby Brook Street Auto Camp. There, a half-dozen families lived basically in small tents on platforms next to their cars, or in one of a few small bungalows. The residents shared communal bathrooms and showers. Mainly, they lived out of their cars. These were the friends of the Ridste children.

The Auto Camp was cheap. Taxi driver Theodore Massey and his family lived in one tiny room and a bath that cost $30 a month. City park worker Wil Smoot and his wife lived next door. House painter Marty Hogan and his family, and waitress Lena Walter, lived at the Camp as well. It was an interesting contradiction, as these hard-working families were among some of the few people living in that part of San Bernardino who actually owned cars.

Interestingly, Alfred Ridste lived just a few miles away, at 1271 North K Street in San Bernardino.[3] He had remarried, to Ann, an Indiana divorcee five years his junior. He was no longer working for the Navy, but had returned to the railroads, working as a machinist at the Sante Fe Railway machine shop and round-house (about three blocks from his home). His wife was a secretary for a lawyer. Unlike Clara, Alfred and Ann rented their home.

Clara supported her family by working a number of menial jobs, at different times cooking, cleaning houses and nursing. Needing to work full-time to support her brood meant that the children had to fend for themselves during the day. A group of children between four and ten took care of themselves when Clara was unable to bring any of them to work.

In Clara's revealing 1948 *True Story* interview, there were telling details hidden inside a story of a family she described as really having "a home, with it all, and a close-knit family life." She described the "the big ones looking after the little ones, and all four looking after Mommie, who was sure to come home from work tired. I would get home to find the table set, the vegetables prepared, and all the children bathed and sweet, already in their night things."

It's no wonder Frances grew up to be such an independent woman, even as a teenager, and also so insecure. She never had a father whom she could remember, and was probably in doubt as to who her *real* father was. And for all intents and purposes, she and the other children were actually raising themselves as their mother worked. Clara offered a glimpse into the future as she described the impact the lifestyle had on the children:

> [The children] knew from the beginning what my problems were, what the obligations were that I had to meet. They shouldn't have had to know so much, really. It was too much brutal reality for little heads to cope with, but they knew and they tried to help. It's not good for children to know so much of their elders' worries and fears; it robs them of the security without which real self-confidence is impossible.

Reading Clara's stories describing the childhood of Frances and her siblings, a clear picture emerges of a family where the support came not from a parent or parents to children, but from the children to the parent! The Ridste children — all under the age of ten — provided the emotional support for Clara and, one hopes, for each other, while receiving almost none from their mother.

Frances and all the Ridste children grew up in a completely dysfunctional family, without obtaining any of the emotional tools necessary for psychological survival. It's no wonder that the older Frances had such a problem with relationships and important life decisions. Of Francis specifically, Clara mentioned, "Carole was so young during those hard years. She, more than the others, had only the vaguest recollections of a father, of a man's authority, and support, in the house. All of her life, I think, she looked for security, based on the love and understanding and support of a man she loved, without ever finding it." It's no wonder. Clara never taught her how to look.

When Frances was only four, Clara suffered a ruptured appendix at the house and had to be rushed to a local hospital. The four children stood in a row as she was bundled into the ambulance and carted off to the hospital. Clara remembered that the only one who wasn't crying was Frances. With some help from the neighbors, the children took care of themselves for the two weeks that she remained hospitalized.

If raising themselves was not enough of a challenge, real tragedy struck the Ridste household in 1925 when Frances' older brother Lewis, then 11, was accidentally shot and killed at the family's kitchen table. While Clara was at work on the afternoon of July 15, Lewis and some friends were playing cards after spending the morning shooting tin cans down near the Santa Ana River near the house. Lewis and his friends used a pistol that a neighbor, 16-year-old Harry Montgomery, had taken from his own home.

When the boys finished playing cards, Montgomery placed the pistol on top of the card table like the boy's western heroes did in the movies. But the pistol discharged, and the bullet tore into young Lewis' stomach. When police investigated the shooting, it was discovered that the pistol would discharge with just the slightest movement, a fact unknown to the boys. Interestingly, the newspaper story under the headline BOY WOUNDED AT CARD GAME described Montgomery as the dead boy's "half-brother."[4]

Adding to the tragedy, the mortally wounded young boy lingered at the hospital for over a week before dying. Typically, Clara said she cried out, "I shouldn't have left him." Frances told her, "You had to, Mommy. You had to, and you mustn't cry." She was not quite six years old.

During the day, the children took care of themselves and the house, with its small garden and backyard hutches holding rabbits and chickens. Frances took particular interest in the garden, learning to love flowers even as a child. She would never lose the feeling for flowers. When she was only nine, her friend and neighbor Elizabeth Watson walked through her garden and trampled Frances' flowers. Frances told her to stop and, when Betty continued, punched her in the mouth. Neighborhood "Grandma" Brumbelow walked across the street and handed 25¢ to Frances, who said, "*Nobody* can stomp on my Mommy's flowers!"

Young Frances was a beautiful child with an angelic face framed with beautiful brown hair. She also loved to perform from an early age. But her first public performance did not go very well. In 1926, seven-year-old Frances attended an amateur night at the local Strand Theater (they were free so it was a cheap night out) with her mother and older brother Lawrence. The moment the master of ceremonies walked on stage, little Frances shouted "I want to sing," and sprinted down the aisle before her mother could grab her.

She bounded on to the stage and began to sing the then-popular Bud Green love song "That's My Weakness Now." After belting out the final verse, she bowed to the crowd. Unfortunately, only her mother and Lawrence were applauding. The rest of the crowd sat in stunned silence before offering subdued applause for the little girl. But Frances did not even notice, so excited was she that she had actually performed.[5] According to family members, from that moment on, when an adult asked Frances what she wanted to do when she grew up, she told them "I'm going to be a movie star."

At the dawn of the Great Depression in late 1929, Clara was working as a waitress at a local restaurant. In the interim years she had somehow cobbled the money together to purchase a small frame house at 175 Bryant Street for $1,800. Lawrence, then 18, worked at a local grocery store and Dorothy, 12, and Frances, 11, attended a local elementary school, the Jefferson School. It was an indication of Clara's independence that she eventually purchased the house she had been renting. Likely the children helped pay for it.

Referring to 1930 San Bernardino a "suburb" would be too handsome an adjective. New Highway 66 had just come through, connecting St. Louis with the ocean and bringing with it droves of tourists; this led to new restaurants and stores and a few small motels. But San Bernardino was still a working-class town, and no amount of tourist cars and drive-ins could camouflage that fact.

San Bernardino was an inland melting pot; a well-defined grid of a variety of ethnicities each living in a specific area. The whites had carved out the biggest section with the nicest little bungalows, the southeast side of town, where the Ridstes lived. Other sections of San Bernardino housed blacks, Latinos and a large Asian population. The Asians—Chinese and Japanese laborers and gardeners—themselves further sectioned their own piece of town.

The racial separation of the town's neighborhoods was not mimicked in the schools. The Ridste children attended classes with a mix of children from dozens of ethnic backgrounds. Their Midwestern roots and the teachings of their independent mother would engrain in the Ridstes a level of racial tolerance far above most people at the time. Little Frances learned as an infant to be particularly accepting of people of other races and colors. She lived that creed her whole life.

The family attended mass every Sunday at nearby St. Bernardine's Church, just a few blocks from the Bryant Street house. After Jefferson elementary, the Ridste children attended the David Sturges School, about a mile away at the corner of 8th and E Streets. The mission-style school, originally built in 1885, still stands, unchanged, but is now the David Sturges Center for the Fine Arts.

Frances entered San Bernardino High School in the fall of 1932. If Clara had 5¢ from her tips, Frances had to walk only a few blocks west to E Street to catch a bus up to the High School at 18th and E Streets. If not, Frances walked the two miles or so to school every day.

Growing up, Frances was a contradiction. From her earliest years in school she was a very smart student, always on the honor roll. But at the same time she was a gregarious and vivacious young girl. She also inherited her mother's independence. She had a wonderful personality and made friends easily; most of them called her by her mother's favorite, "Baby." Friends would call Carole "Baby" until she died. Her friends were not just the pretty white teenage girls that she hung around with most of the time. Frances hung out in public with the blacks and Latinos who were typically ignored by her friends.

One thing she did share with her friends was their childlike obsession with boys. She had her share of crushes on the high school football stars and collected pictures of the movie stars and singers popular with the kids. She was a typical teenage girl. Beautiful, but she was also a dyed-in-the-wool tomboy. She belonged to her school Girl's Athletic Association, and played on the field hockey and softball teams. Most afternoons she could be found either in the schoolyard or on Bryant Street playing catch with her male friends.

During her high school sophomore year, she approached the principal and asked

Two * San Bernardino Dreams

that she be allowed to form a girl's football team! There was no such thing in the state of California at the time and likely nowhere else in the United States either. But to Frances, the idea of a girl's football team seemed appropriate. She actually convinced a dozen of her friends to try the game, but during their second day of practice, the principal came outside and told Frances that the school was disbanding the team. Football was just "too rough and unwomanly," she was told.[6]

Though she and older sister Dorothy were still pretty much responsible for the family and Lawrence during the day, she lived the life of a pretty typical teenager. Though Clara was obviously far from wealthy, there was enough money in the house to allow Frances to hang out with her friends after school at one of the local drive-ins. Just like the young kids in the wealthy towns, the kids in San Bernardino spent their afternoons gossiping and drinking sodas at Ruby's Drive-In, Haywood's Ice Cream or the Big Bear Creamery.

One of Frances' childhood friends described those years. "We didn't really have rowdy students. We didn't have anyone in jail or juvenile hall or anything from our class. Most of the kids liked school, although there were a few — like Frances — who were boy-crazy."

Frances knew by 13 that she wanted to be a singer in the movies. It was not hard to see why a young girl in San Bernardino would so love the movies in the early 1930s. Even though San Bernardino was a dusty three-hour drive by car to Hollywood, at the time when Frances was living on Bryant Street, the city was the motion picture preview capital of the world. More new movies were previewed for audiences in and around San Bernardino than in any other Southern California locale.

It was Irving Thalberg, the youthful Number Two man at Metro-Goldwyn-Mayer, who first began previewing movies before live audiences. He was one of the most creative men in early Hollywood, but Thalberg believed that his audiences were never wrong. He felt that they would offer the truest comments or criticisms of his work. He never trusted the Hollywood studio "yes-men." To get an honest opinion of his work, he began showing his films to real audiences in real theaters before 1920.

Although almost every studio relied "sneak previews," MGM's system was the most organized. Thalberg purchased an over-sized electric rail passenger car almost as big as a Pullman sleeper car. The European-style Interurban car was then retrofitted to house several lounging areas with overstuffed couches and chairs, four card tables and a wet bar.

The Pacific Electric Railway Company had laid a spur from their tracks on Washington Boulevard right into the MGM lot so the executives could walk directly from their offices to board "Big Red." Bill and Charlie — the two headwaiters at the studio commissary — served caviar, sandwiches and other delicacies during the trips to the remote movie houses.

Besides Thalberg, each film's director and producer would come along; usually the cameraman, too, and the writer in case revisions might be suggested. Eddie Mannix, the studio General Manager, often rode along also. Depending upon how much the studio had invested in the film, studio chief Louis B. Mayer might join the group as well.

Movie previews were always unannounced until the last moment. At 4:30 P.M.,

Thalberg's secretary called the theater manager to inform him that he could advertise a preview that evening. The larger suburban theaters had electric signs on their rooftops to let the neighbors know that there would be a "Preview Tonight!!!"

When that sign was illuminated, it meant a full house. Where else could a blue-color family from San Bernardino attend a world premiere? Not only that, but they also got to see the regular feature after the preview was shown. The titles and the stars were never announced before the curtain went up. Thalberg favored San Bernardino and the surrounding towns of Ontario and Riverside for the audience mix. Questionnaire cards were handed out to the people attending and collected after the preview.[7]

Though not as glamourous as a Hollywood premiere, they may as well have been to starry-eyed Frances Ridste. The local previews still fueled her fixation with everything Hollywood. If the Ridste girls saw the "preview" sign on top of the California Theater and Clara's tips allowed, the family walked the mile to 4th and E Street. Frances loved the previews. She particularly loved the musicals. Forgetting her inauspicious debut as a seven-year-old at the Strand, Frances still wanted to sing in the movies.

She grew into a beautiful teenager. By the age of 14 she had competed in, and won, several local beauty contests. She lied about her age to get in, and used the makeup tricks she had learned from reading movie magazines to look even older. Even without it, at 12 she looked 18, and by 14 looked to be in her twenties, already fully "developed," as they might say in 1930. She got the first pair of stockings she ever owned when she won a bathing beauty contest at the age of 12. At 14, she won an electric heater for the Ridste house in another competition.[8]

By then, she had also taken up smoking, which completed her older look. Seeing 14-year-old Frances walk down the sidewalk in her makeup, sandy blonde hair floating in the breeze and a cigarette in her mouth, one could easily mistake her for a 25-year-old.

Her contest successes made her Hollywood dreams even more real, but Clara was insistent that Frances continue with her schooling. Young Frances, physically in her twenties but still an immature 14-year-old, was growing increasingly disenchanted with school, and with her life helping to run the house on Bryant Street.

Frances was a typical "boy crazy" teenager. She was in love with Ross Columbo, Gary Cooper and Clark Gable. She bought second-hand movie magazines so she could read about all of the stars that she watched in the previews. She lay on the floor in the family living room for hours in the evening listening to Hollywood radio programs. She hated school and began skipping classes. Her older sister wrote notes to her teacher and signed Clara's name, dropping them off herself on the way to her own classes. As Frances prepared to enter her sophomore year at San Bernardino High School in the summer of 1933, all she could think about was boys and singing.

During that summer, Frances was working part-time at a local hamburger stand, one of those old indoor-outdoor setups popular in the 1930s and '40s. Even though she was still only 14, she began attracting the notice of older men. She loved the attention and acceptance and eagerly returned their attention. Once, a group of local pilots who frequented the restaurant asked Frances to present the trophy to the winner of a local air show meet at the San Bernardino Airport. There she was, 14-year-old waitress Frances — looking 25 — presenting the trophy and the kiss to the winning pilot.[9]

A psychologist would probably say that it was only natural — probably even preordained — that Carole would find herself attracted to men, usually older. Surviving the abandonment of not one, but *two* fathers, one could easily guess that she was no doubt searching for one. With her beauty, and her body even as a young woman, finding them would never be a problem. Trying to keep them would eventually kill her.

Then she met Jack Roberts, or Jack Ryan, depending on whom you asked. Jack was almost 19 when they met just before Christmas 1933. He lived with his mother and stepfather at 1544 8th Street, not too far from San Bernardino High School. Roberts called himself "Irving Wheeler" and told the starry-eyed 15-year-old that he was a writer. He had indeed written a few short articles and stories that had appeared in the local newspapers, but calling himself a "writer" was supreme self-aggrandizement. He was mainly a part-time movie extra and general sleaze. Wheeler told Frances he loved her; for Frances, she thought she was truly in love for the first time. Seizing the opportunity to get away from school and Bryant Street, she agreed to marry him.

On Saturday, January 14, 1934, Wheeler borrowed — or stole — his father's car and drove with Frances to Yuma, Arizona, where the two were married by a justice of the peace. When they arrived back for Sunday dinner at Bryant Street, they did not tell immediately Clara that they were married. Frances hid the marriage certificate in the bureau in her bedroom until Clara was serving dessert. She was so stunned at first that she said nothing, but by that evening was so angry that she threw Wheeler out of the house and told Frances she had to go back to school. She had the marriage annulled a few days later.

In later articles and interviews, Clara attributed the annulment decision to Frances, but in reality her daughter was furious. She and Wheeler set about scheming for a way to re-marry. No doubt Wheeler's primary motivation was the sex that had been denied him after their first ceremony.

Clara and the children had remained on somewhat good terms with their father Alfred, who was still living about a mile away with his second wife. The children often visited Alfred's house, and Frances began working to convince her father that she should be allowed to marry Wheeler. It took three or four months, but Frances wore him down and, against Clara's wishes, Alfred signed the papers. On August 25, Frances and Wheeler were married again.

Wedded bliss did not last very long. On September 19, during an argument at his parents' home (where they were sharing his childhood bedroom), Wheeler threatened to throw her out. She beat him to the punch by walking out and trudging back to the Bryant Street bungalow and her mother.

The couple never went through the formality of divorce, they just went their separate ways. Their lack of action would cause Frances problems later, but for now Wheeler went back to Hollywood to look for extra work and forgot about his child bride. In 1940, Frances would describe the break-up, saying that the couple only "lived together for three weeks and then had an argument. I've only seen him once since then, when he asked me for a divorce."[10] Frances set about making bigger plans.

✦ THREE ✦
San Francisco and Hollywood

For a short time after leaving Wheeler, Frances returned to San Bernardino High School. Predictably, she soon bored of the class work and went to work. She had always worked, from the age of 12 or 13; a succession of after-school jobs to help Clara make ends meet. She worked in a dressmaker's shop, as a clerk in a department store and as a waitress in a dozen different restaurants. She was also an usher at the California Theater. Watching movies and attending every "preview" at the theater added more fuel to her fire to become a star.

Later studio biographies would indicate that young Frances put the youthful marriage behind her and went back to finish high school. But there is no record of Frances Ridste graduating from San Bernardino High School in 1935 or 1936 when one would have expected her to do so had she remained. When she first began working in Hollywood, press stories mentioned that she was going to Hollywood High School five nights a week to get her diploma.[1] Given her film and social schedule at the time, that was probably studio publicity department fiction.

Almost immediately after walking away from Wheeler in September 1934, Frances set her sights on San Francisco, in the early 1930s the center of the California music world. Chock full of jazz clubs, bars and dance halls, it was *the* place to pursue a music career. Frances figured (correctly, as it would turn out) that it would be easier to make a name for herself musically and then use that fame to get into Hollywood. She would find work as a lounge singer on her way to becoming a star. She was only 15 when she set about finalizing her plans.

Frances had always given most of the money she earned to her mother to help with the household expenses. She did so without complaint, but she managed to keep $16.82 from her tips and secretly bought a $4.50 Greyhound bus ticket to San Francisco.[2] Becoming aware of the plans, Clara begged her to stay in San Bernardino, but while Clara was working on a fall day in 1934 Frances boarded a bus to Los Angeles and another on to San Francisco. Arriving there, she rode a trolley out to the Pacific Heights area and rented a room in a small rooming house. She was not quite 16.

Clara would later tell a much different story, saying that she and Frances talked it out at length, and that she had $100 when she left. She also said Frances was 16, not 15. The truth may lie somewhere between the two versions, but Frances had nowhere near $100 when she left San Bernardino. It's doubtful Clara even had $100. We do know though that for the two and a half years she lived in San Francisco,

Frances did not write a single letter home, nor did she visit once. She had had enough of Bryant Street.

The reality of her life during those first days and months in San Francisco is a testimony to her personality. Obviously, she had no fear. She had no job, very little money left from $16.82 stake, and had never sung professionally before. But her biggest concern wasn't finding work; she just *knew* she would find work. No, what she needed first was a name. She spent hours poring through the San Francisco phone books looking for just the right name. She needed the perfect name since she was going to be the world's greatest torch singer.

She knew that her real name didn't have the right ring. She wasn't going to become a star as Frances Ridste. She always liked the name Carol, and added the extra "e" *a la* one of her favorite actresses, comedienne Carole Lombard. Choosing "Landis" after baseball commissioner Kennesaw Mountain Landis—she was after all still a tomboy at heart and a huge baseball fan—she became "Carole Landis."

She also decided that "Carole" was a better name for a blonde, so she became a blonde as well. Blonde bombshell Carole Landis was born sitting on a tiny bed in a windowless room in a dirty boarding house in San Francisco during the fall of 1934.

San Francisco was one of the most vibrant cities in the U.S. in the 1930s. It was not crowded at all. In 1930, over 7,500,000 people lived in and around New York City and almost 2,500,000 folks called L.A. home. At the same time, less than 645,000 people lived in San Francisco. The small population and the startling geographic beauty gave the city a folksy, almost artsy feel. It had a reputation as an open-minded and ethnically diverse city, but even so, 95 percent of the population was white. There were about 25,000 Japanese and Chinese inhabitants, and less than 4,000 blacks. Perhaps it just *felt* diverse.

Pan American World Airways had begun China Clipper service to Hawaii the previous autumn, and one of the greatest construction projects of the early twentieth century was near completion in 1935 and 1936. The same month that Carole arrived in San Francisco, the main suspension cables for the new Golden Gate Bridge connecting the city and Marin County were attached to the massive towers at either end. A suspension structure of that size had never been attempted before. The bridge would open the next spring.

Carole's rooming house was only a short trolley ride from the Pacific Ocean and miles of pristine beaches. At the western tip of the peninsula, minutes from downtown by rail, the Cliff House Restaurant and the massive Sutro Baths stood overlooking the beach. Owner Adolph Sutro, who owned most of the land on the western side of the peninsula, built his own railway system to bring people from town out to his grand baths. He charged 5¢ a ride.

Sutro's five pools held almost 1,700,000 gallons of seawater and covered almost three acres. The main pool could be filled or emptied in an hour with the tides and was large enough to allow 25,000 people to swim together (at 25¢ apiece). Other pools of smaller sizes were kept heated and 20,000 bathing suits and 40,000 towels were rented a day. Carole loved to swim at the Sutro baths. The massive ruins and foundations for the pools are still visible today.

The social fabric of the city was shaped in the entertainment district, home to hundreds of restaurants, clubs and bars catering to every imaginable taste. The most famous area was the old Barbary Coast section, next to Chinatown and just a few blocks away from the wharves lining the city's eastern shoreline. The heart of the "Coast" was roughly near the intersection of Pacific, Columbus and Kearney Streets. The area was home to dozens of the most famous jazz clubs in the U.S., and some of the most popular bars and dance halls on the West Coast.

Pacific Street was an endless string of clubs, with almost 50 in a three-block stretch. The musicians called that part of Pacific "Terrific Street" because of the quality of clubs and the musical talent working there. The Turkish Café, Zasa Café, the Squeeze In Club, the Oregon Dance Hall, the Monterey, the Iowa, the Bear Café, the Belvedere, the Hippodrome, the Tivoli Café, the Red Mill, the Moulin Rouge. There was one great club after another. Bars like the Ivy, Spider Kelly's and So Different Café (later called Purcell's) welcomed "Coloreds."

Purcell's was world-famous, a black jazz club founded by two former Pullman porters, Lew Purcell and Sam King. Blacks from all over the U.S. came to Purcell's to listen and dance to some of the most famous singers of the day. The lights above the bars lining Terrific Street could be seen for miles. At night, cars could not pass, so crowded were the streets. Sophie Tucker sang at Purcell's, as did Al Jolson. Mary Lewis worked at Tait's Bar, and jazz legends like Lee Lloyd, Baby Ruth and Jimmy Blyler and Fred Brown could be found at the clubs in San Francisco.

One of the most popular clubs in 1930s San Francisco was owned by Agostino Giuntoli, an Italian immigrant from Tuscany who began working at the famed Palace Hotel restaurant as a janitor at the age of 19. He became a cook at a nearby club and in the early 1930s he and his boss opened the 365 Club on Market Street. The club was soon crowded with movie stars and celebrities from across the country. Of equal interest to the nightly crowds were the beautiful chorus line dancers—Rita Cansino performed there before she became Rita Hayworth—and the antics of Dolfina, the Girl in the Fishbowl. She apparently swam nude in the huge enclosed fish tank behind the bar.

Carole tirelessly made the rounds of the city's nightclubs trying to get a singing job. During her first few weeks she worked as a hula dancer at the popular Royal Hawaiian restaurant while she looked for work during the day. She really did have it all. She was beautiful, she had a perfect figure (even at 15 she was 36½-23-35), and possessed a lovely singing voice.

Carole's first jobs were reminiscent of her first singing experience at the Strand Theater in San Bernardino a decade earlier. She approached the manager of the Royal Hawaiian and asked for work. When he asked her if she could do a hula, she said "certainly" and was hired. She was actually posing as a singing and dancing sister act with a friend, Kay Ellis.

Later, she was unable to get an interview or audition at the upper-class St. Francis Hotel bar because she didn't have an agent. The St. Francis, a stately old building in the heart of the city on tree-lined Union Square, was the nicest hotel in town. It had been the site of Roscoe "Fatty" Arbuckle's famous 1921 Labor Day party that resulted in actress-whore Virginia Rappe's death and the end of Fatty's career.

In typical Carole fashion, she simply barged into the hotel bar and demanded that the manager let her sing. When he saw her and heard her sing, he hired her on the spot. Within just a few weeks of her arrival in town, she had several jobs singing on different nights at a few clubs, a regular spot at the St. Francis, and was singing at a few other local places as well. She became a regular performer at the Rio del Mar Country Club in nearby Santa Cruz, and guested at the Pacific Avenue bars. Carole fancied herself a torch singer, belting out show tunes and jazz melodies in a husky, smoky voice. And that body. The men loved her.

At one time or another, every big band played the St. Francis Hotel Ballroom. Carole worked in one of the smaller, more intimate bars there. It was a good singing job but hardly top tier. The big bands fronted by musicians like Tommy Dorsey, Duke Ellington, Artie Shaw, Anson Weeks and Tom Coakley were playing the main ballrooms there during the early 1930s.

Coakley's 20-member orchestra was one of the most popular big bands in California. They toured up and down the length of the West Coast, playing three-month engagements at swank venues like the Roosevelt Hotel in Hollywood and luxurious Palace Hotel in San Francisco. In March 1935, Coakley's featured lead singer was a young man named Carl Ravazza, who happened upon Carole on a night he wandered into the St. Francis and heard her voice from within the bar as he stood outside the lounge.

Following the voice inside, Ravazza was captivated by Carole's looks and voice, and tried to convince his bandleader Coakley to hire the beautiful blonde singer. Coincidentally, at the same time Coakley was getting ready to go back to law school, and instead of hiring another singer simply handed over his orchestra to young Ravazza. Coakley would become one of the most respective California jurists, a Superior Court judge who served until retirement in 1972. Ravazza took over his former band in April 1936.

The first thing he did as the new leader of the Carl Ravazza Orchestra was to hire Carole. He had no confirmed contracts except for the St. Francis gig, but even so Ravazza offered Carole $50 a week to appear with his orchestra on Friday and Saturday nights (close to $1,000 today). The new Carl Ravazza Orchestra and its lovely female lead singer were soon one of the most popular orchestras in San Francisco, and were attracting fans from across the country with their radio performances. She had been working just over a year, and was barely 17.

During 1936, Carole and the Ravazza orchestra played at some of the country's top hotels and ballrooms. In addition to their regular appearances at California clubs like the St. Francis and the Del Mar Club, they headlined at the Lexington Hotel in New York and the world-renowned Aragon Ballroom and Trianon and Blackhawk Hotels in Chicago. But she only worked for Ravazza for five or six months before deciding to go to Hollywood.

Carole liked her life as an orchestra singer in 1936. She sang three or four nights a week, doing at most two performances a night at high-end establishments. Almost every afternoon, she went to the beach. She frequented the beaches out past the Sutro Baths and the Cliff House, and the smaller spots south down the coast. When the Ravazza Orchestra returned to the St. Francis during the summer of 1937, Carole told her boss that she was going to try the movies.

It was not just a personal drive that prompted Carole's move to Hollywood.

Everyone, it seemed—from bandleader Ravazza to the club manager at the Rio del Mar club to her boss at the St. Francis—nagged Carole to go to Hollywood. Everyone told her that she was too beautiful and talented *not* to be in the movies. So in the late summer of 1936, Carole left San Francisco for Hollywood. But this trip was not on a hot and crowded bus like the one she had taken north just a year before. She was returning to L.A. by train. And she was traveling in a first-class berth.

She had only been in San Francisco for about a year and a half. It's hard to pinpoint arrival dates, but she may have lived there only a year. But during a very short period of time she had accomplished a lot. Arriving penniless, she had become one of the city's most popular performers, earning more money than anyone in her family ever had. No doubt about it, the former Frances Lillian Ridste was a success.

Carole's rapid career success in San Francisco gave rise to rumors that still survive today, although there is obviously no substantive confirmation. She began earning a good living within weeks of arriving in San Francisco, working at a variety of small music and jazz clubs, even before working at the St. Frances and for Carl Ravazza. Even so, rumors followed Carole that she had worked as a call girl in San Francisco. She may or may not have. It's impossible to determine fully, but it appears that she did, in some fashion, "use" men for money.

It would have been difficult for Landis to have been a call girl in 1935 San Francisco. There was an unlimited supply of high-priced prostitutes working in San Francisco at the time. It still had a reputation as the Barbary Coast. But it would be unlikely that a newcomer—a 15- or 16-year-old newcomer—from Los Angeles would be able work as a high-priced call girl. Any beautiful young girl could certainly have become a prostitute in San Francisco at the time. But the typical street prostitutes did not work for high-end establishments in 1935; they frequented the bars and brothels in the seedier parts of San Francisco.

Also, she was working almost from the moment she arrived in San Francisco. She could probably not have been able to work as a prostitute while also singing in the lounge at the St. Francis Hotel. Nor would she have needed the money, earning what she did. Particularly after Ravazza paid her to front for his orchestra.

Carole was certainly not the first, nor will she be the last, actress to be accused of prostitution or of having questionable morals. During that same era, Jeanette MacDonald was said to have been an escort in New York and Lupe Velez a brothel whore in Mexico City. Grace Kelly's morals were maligned, deservedly so, as were those of Lucille Ball and Ingrid Bergman, probably less deservedly. But in Carole's case, it does not appear that the San Francisco stories had a grain of truth. And most of these stories are impossible to conclusively prove or disprove.

The "San Francisco call girl" stories were cultivated, expanded upon and passed on after Carole went to Hollywood in 1936. The keepers of the Landis rumors were the studio wives and the ladies of L.A.'s café society who did not know Carole during her San Francisco days. But they did have plenty of reason to be jealous of the gorgeous actress.

It appears that Carole arrived in Hollywood some time during the late summer or early fall of 1936. We know that she was in San Francisco in 1935 and working for Ravazza as late as June 1936 when she was barely 17. Later studio biographies put the

L.A. arrival at a later date, some as late as 1938, but those were no doubt efforts to better match arrival dates with a more "appropriate" age.

But we know that she had small uncredited roles in several films that were shot during the late summer and fall of 1936, so she was there by then. Though her first *credited* roles would not come for a year or two, she was working in Hollywood in the fall of 1936. The assumption is that she probably arrived in Hollywood in August or September of 1936.

The studios would have had to fudge on her age in their bio materials. It would not have been "proper" for a 17-year-old to be living on her own in Hollywood walking the sidewalks looking for work in the movies. It makes a great movie plot, but real-life movie fans were far less accepting of Horatio Alger–like qualities if they were attributed to a gorgeous young girl on her own. They would never find out — nor did anyone ever seem to do the simple math — that Carole had gone to San Francisco at 15 and come to Hollywood at 17. She looked 25.

The teenager took a small apartment in the Bronsonia Apartments at 1933 North Bronson Avenue. The five-story building was in the middle of Hollywood, just two blocks north of Franklin Avenue on the edges of Beachwood Canyon. One- and two-room apartments rented for between $30 and $75 a month. Landis picked a good-sized one-bedroom that cost $45 a month.

The Bronsonia was far from glamourous, but certainly not the "$5-a-week flophouse" that studio biographers described in later press releases. It was clean and well-kept; it is to this day. The tree-lined neighborhood had small bungalows, mansions and apartment houses of all sizes. Writer L. Frank Baum's "Ozcot" estate was a block or so away down near Franklin. Writer Adela Rogers St. Johns lived next to Baum. Actor and silent star Jack Mulhall lived at 1808 Bronson, just a block away.

That part of Hollywood was dotted with large apartment buildings like the Bronsonia. Just two blocks away on Franklin were the Villa Carlotta and El Capitan apartments, and down the street was the Chateau Elysee. Apartments at these more upscale buildings cost over $100 and some up to $250 a month. For that reason, while the Carlotta boasted Adolphe Menjou, Louella Parsons and David O. Selznick on its tenant rolls, and Clark Gable and Humphrey Bogart lived at the Elysee, no such stars made the Bronsonia home.

Landis' building was decidedly less high-brow. Scattered among the fifty or so apartments were a number of minor actors and low-level studio employees. People like actors Catherine Alexander and Leo Harwood, studio singer Grayce Andrews, and directors William McCool and Frank Beal all lived at 1933 North Bronson. With the exception of Beal — a relatively successful 1920's director — and Landis, nobody from 1933 made much of a go of the movie business. The people at the Bronsonia tended to remain unknown.

Just as she did when she first arrived in San Francisco, Carole dedicated herself to making the rounds of the studios looking for work. The first months were a bit of a comedown for her. In San Francisco, not only had she been successful and popular, but she had also been something of a local celebrity. She was a "someone" there. But in Hollywood, she was just another nameless, anonymous actress trying to find work. The difference was that she was almost breathtakingly beautiful and had a stunning figure.

Later biographies paint a picture undoubtedly at odds with the way it really was. According to a 1940 *Life* magazine biography Carole's first months in Hollywood were "a round of cheap rooms, skimpy meals, and an endless attempt to look glamorous and 'sexy.' She posed for hundreds of cheesecake pictures."[3]

She allegedly spent several months posing for these "leg art" pictures before she got her first actual movie job. That's difficult to believe. We know she had a good bit of money from her San Francisco work with the Ravazza Orchestra, and none of these allegedly early cheesecake photographs seems to have survived.

Somehow, Carole found work in the movies. Almost immediately and against all odds. The hows and whys of that would forge a reputation she could never escape.

★ Four ★

Hollywood Comes with a Reputation

Carole's first 12 months in Hollywood set the tone for the rest of her career. It actually set the tone for her reputation in Hollywood and, unfortunately, for the rest of her short life. Carole had basically been on her own since she was under ten. Her own mother Clara described how a 12-year-old Carole had to help raise her brothers and sister in San Bernardino while she worked at menial jobs. At 15 she was living totally independently in a big city 350 miles away from her family. Perhaps remembering, certainly echoing, the abandonment of two fathers, Carole abandoned her siblings to strike out on her own while not yet 16. Carole always did what she had to do to survive. She didn't complain, she didn't wither; she just survived. And she would survive in Hollywood, albeit at a terrible price.

Before postulating on *how* Carole earned all the work she got during that first year, we need to look at the world in which she was working. While thousands of pretty, often beautiful young women came from all parts of the country to Hollywood every day to "become a star," almost none did. Almost none found any work at all. Not anything. Not a single small role in a single film.

When she arrived in Los Angeles, the thousands of women trying to find work invariably ended up dropping their photographs and résumés off at the Central Casting offices. In 1936, there were over 8,000 actors and actresses registered there. Their average earnings for the year were about $350 ($7,000 today).[1] Almost none of them worked very much. But Carole did. She worked a lot. "Why?" is the question that haunted her career and memory.

Carole had small roles in 20 or 21 films between the fall of 1936 and late summer of 1937, her first 15 months in Hollywood. Most of the roles were uncredited but she was working at an astonishing pace for someone in her position. And within six months of arriving, she had been signed to a long-term contract. As contracts went back then, it was not a stunner. Just your average six-month option contract. But it was a contract with a major studio.

Even the writers took note of her rapid ascension. Robbin Coons, who wrote the syndicated "Hollywood Speaks" column, noticed Carole's rise by the early fall of 1937. His piece, which appeared on October 1, described what "little chorines"—a term for pretty young starlets filling chorus lines during the 1930s—were made of

One of the earliest of the Landis studio cheesecake photographs, probably 1937–38.

and how they got work and maybe a career with all of the competition in Hollywood. He noted that these young woman would obviously be beautiful, and would be wholesome types; probably athletic (perhaps a swimmer or a tennis player); and certainly smart. She might have come from the Broadway stage, or perhaps from national advertisements, or from a wealthy family. He ended his piece by stating, "But she very probably won't get a movie contract right away ... like Carole Landis ... Carole came out with a long-termer after six months in pictures!"[2]

We can only guess if Carole's later reputation for trading sex for roles began during those first months, but it is not too hard to imagine that she would have had to.

Four * Hollywood Comes with a Reputation

At the time it was routine procedure for casting people, directors—really, *any* man working at a studio—to offer work for sex. Even if he couldn't provide the work.

We certainly would not begrudge Carole the work. In 1936 that was perhaps the only way a beautiful woman could get the work. And it wasn't reserved simply for extra and small roles. The studio heads routinely demanded sex from even their biggest stars, and almost always received it. Unless the woman was a true super-star, the request (demand) could typically not be declined. It is not implausible that Carole traded sex for the bountiful amount of work she did. And given what we know of her personality, she would have done so without complaint, understanding that it was just part of the price she had to pay. That being said, let's look at the roles.

Carole's first role was supposedly a bit part in the Warner Bros. movie *The King and the Chorus Girl*, which was filmed in October and November 1936. Directed by Mervyn LeRoy and written by Norman Krasna and Groucho Marx, the stock piece starred Fernand Gravey, Joan Blondell, Edward Everett Horton, Jane Wyman and Alan Mowbray. It is a contrived piece about an alcoholic former King Alfred (Gravey) who spends every day of his life in a Paris apartment drinking himself stupid. But when he meets a beautiful American chorus line dancer (Blondell) at the Moulin Rouge, he stops drinking and falls in love. After the expected misunderstandings amidst the semi-royal trappings, the couple is wed aboard an ocean liner on their way to America. In the final scene, ex–King Alfred orders the captain to take the liner to Niagara Falls. The film was originally re-released in the U.S. on March 31, 1937, and later released in the U.S. as *Grand Passion* and *Romance in Paris*. In the United Kingdom it was called *Romance Is Sacred*.

According to legend, Carole's independent streak showed itself during the rehearsals when she loudly expressed her displeasure at not being put at the front of the chorus line. Director LeRoy reportedly liked the beautiful youngster with the sparkling personality, and he and Berkeley moved her to the front row. It is in these scenes that she is apparently visible.

In several scenes—particularly the Follies Bergere Moulin Rouge set—a beautiful brunette dancer bears a striking resemblance to a young Carole, but there seems to be no independent confirmation that she indeed appeared in this film. Her name is not included in the archival records relating to the film, nor does it appear in the "uncredited cast" list. After the "name" roles were listed and the stars identified in a film's credits came all of the actors with the anonymous roles that Carole would have been begging for in the summer and fall of 1936. Among the uncredited extras in this film was an unknown and untalented actor named Jack Roberts—in reality, Carole's first husband Irving Wheeler.

Several biographers and early newspaper reports include this film among Carole's work.[3] Beth Renner was a dancer and chorine whom Berkeley hired numerous times. She confirmed several of the Carole rumors said to have arisen during *King* filming, saying, "I danced with Carole in several musicals, but the one that stands in my mind is *The King and the Chorus Girl*. She was having marital problems with her husband [Wheeler], who was an extra and always about. In one routine, she was upset that our choreographer, Bobby Connolly, didn't put her up front during the rehearsals.

When it came time to shoot the number, Carole had her way. The director Mervyn LeRoy liked her, and I remember Buz [Berkeley] just adored her. Carole was ambitious, independent and wanted it all."[4]

"Uncredited" actors were usually either just starting out — like Carole — or their careers were just dying out. They were not usually even contract actors. Instead, they could be daily hires, plucked out of the long lines outside the studio gates because they looked like a needed character or caught someone's eye. Most of the females were hired for their non-acting talents. The casting offices at MGM had windows and doors that opened on to Washington Boulevard so the casting agents could pick beautiful women out of line and escort them into their private offices.

Over the next year, Carole would work almost continually, no small feat for a struggling actress in 1930's Hollywood. During the rest of 1936, Carole worked on two big pictures, *A Day at the Races* at Metro-Goldwyn-Mayer and *A Star Is Born* for David O. Selznick. *Races* was shot between early September and late November, and *Star* between October 31 and December 28. It is likely that Carole's work on *Races* was done in September and for *Star* possible November.

A Day at the Races was the second Marx Brothers movie produced by Irving Thalberg and MGM. The first — *A Night at the Opera* — had grossed an impressive $3,000,000 ($100,000,000 today) after its November 1935 release. Thalberg was possibly the most creative manager in the history of MGM, perhaps of any studio, a man whose imprint was quite literally on everything Metro did during its first dozen years. He chose stories, he hired actors and actresses, he edited film, he designed sets and costumes and he wrote and edited scenarios. Thalberg personally convinced Louis B. Mayer to hire Groucho and his brothers away from Paramount, even though their films had been undistinguished at the box office, and MGM was known for more highbrow titles and lavish production quality.

Thalberg loved the Marx Brothers, going back to the first time that Groucho, Chico, Harpo and Zeppo came to a meeting at Thalberg's formal and formidable MGM office. The group was shown inside and asked to wait a few minutes for Thalberg, who was habitually late. When Thalberg — then the Number 2 man at the studio and arguably among the most powerful men in Hollywood — walked into his office, the Brothers were seated around a roaring fire in his fireplace cooking potatoes held over the fire on sticks. They were sitting on the floor in their underwear. He hired them on the spot.

A Day at the Races had a profound impact on MGM, apart from the financial success. During the script development of the movie in the late summer of 1936, Thalberg took a Labor Day weekend vacation to Monterey with the movie's director Sam Wood and close friends Chico and Helen Marx. During their stay at the Del Monte Lodge, Thalberg held an evening *Races* story conference with Marx and Wood on the hotel veranda despite the coolness of the late summer evening.

Thalberg had been born with a congenitally weakened heart and was particularly susceptible to colds and ill health, illnesses that would inconvenience most but could easily kill him. His wife Norma Shearer repeatedly warned him to put on a sweater and come inside, but he ignored her as the group sat for several hours on the porch talking about the film. He caught a cold, and by the time they returned to L.A.

on September 8, Thalberg would be mortally ill with pneumonia. He would die on September 15, 1936.

Carole was filming when Sam Wood was called off the *Races* set and told of Thalberg's death. When he returned, he tearfully said, "The little brown fellow's dead" and shut down the set.[5] In an unprecedented show of grief that has never been repeated, the studio shut down for an entire day.

The completed film was typical Marx Brothers fare. Dr. Hugo Hackenbush (Groucho), Tony (Chico) and Stuffy (Harpo) try and save a farm owned by a beautiful young girl (Judy, played by Margaret O'Sullivan) by winning a big race with her horse. Unknown to the townspeople — among them the omnipresent dowager Margaret Dumont — Hackenbush runs a high priced clinic for the wealthy who don't know he is actually a veterinarian. The film grossed over $4,000,000 after its release in June 1937.

Carole was uncredited. Among the other uncredited players was the 14-year-old black singer listed as "Performer in the 'All God's Children Got Rhythm' number." Her name was Dorothy Dandridge.

As soon as *Races* filming was completed, Carole was given a small role in the David O. Selznick production *A Star Is Born*. Ironically she would be filming back at the Santa Anita Racetrack, where she had filmed her *Races* scenes. Her walk-on spot was in a film which would be a full-scale studio blockbuster with a budget of almost $1,250,000 (over $25,000,000 today) and an all-star cast including Janet Gaynor, Fredric March, Adolphe Menjou and many other name stars.

Shot in color, the movie is the classic Hollywood tale of the sudden rise and equally quick fall of a movie star. Gaynor plays a young actress who becomes an instant star by a quirk of fate and then marries March, an alcoholic in the twilight of his career. As her career continues to soar, the bitter March's career dwindles to nothing. The story — written by a "Who's Who" of movie writing heavyweights included William Wellman, Dorothy Parker and Alan Campbell, Ben Hecht, Adela Rogers St. Johns and Ring Lardner, Jr.— was based upon the real-life romantic saga of Barbara Stanwyck and Frank Fay.

Stanwyck was a 22-year-old rising star in 1928 when she married Fay, an abusive ex-vaudevillian nearly twice her age. The wedding was rumored to have been forced upon the two by the studios to quiet the rumors of her lesbianism. Stanwyck went on the road for five months within an hour after exchanging wedding vows with the homosexual alcoholic. Fay was one of the world's most popular song-and-dance men, once commanding almost $20,000 a week for his stage work. But after a promising movie career faded, their marriage evolved into a series of drunken brawls, physical abuse and finally, mercifully, a 1935 divorce.

Wellman's first drafts of the *Star* screenplay were so similar to the real lives of Stanwyck and Fay that the movie almost did not get made. Lawyers hired by Fay listed over 20 pages of similarities between events in the scripts and the real-life Fay-Stanwyck marriage. Most of the more specific instances were absent from the final draft, but all of Hollywood knew who the movie was really about.

The movie began filming at the Culver City studios on October 31, 1936, and over the next two months scenes were shot all over Los Angeles. Locations included

A young Carole sits for a very early studio photograph session, likely 1938 or 1939.

the Ambassador and Biltmore Hotels, Grauman's Chinese Theater, the Hollywood Bowl, the Trocadero Club, and Santa Anita Park in Arcadia. Carole was an extra in the scenes shot at Santa Anita.

She was only in one or two scenes, and is listed in the credits as "girl in beret at Santa Anita bar." She is barely visible and then only for perhaps five seconds. The beret is perhaps more evident than Carole, who is seated facing away from the camera.

A Star Is Born was Carole's first close-up glimpse of big Hollywood moviemaking. While *Races* was a full-scale MGM production, Marx Brothers films tended to be somewhat haphazard affairs because of the personalities of the brothers. The supporting cast was not full of huge stars. And *The King and the Chorus Girl* was a "B" feature.

Star on the other hand had an all-star cast and crew. After director Wellman, his all-star writers, and actors Gaynor, March and Menjou, the supporting cast included May Robson, Andy Devine, Owen Moore and Edgar Kennedy. Even the list of Carole's fellow uncredited actors was impressive: Clara Blandick ("Auntie Em" from *The Wizard of Oz*), Helene Chadwick, Herbert Evans, Marshall "Mickey" Neilan, Dennis O'Keefe, Franklin Pangborn and Vera Steadman. Another young actress who appeared as an extra in the Santa Anita scenes who wasn't lucky enough to remain in the final version of the film was a 16-year-old head-turner named Lana Turner.

Filming was completed just after Christmas 1936. Carole attended the April 20, 1937, premiere at Grauman's Chinese Theater, her first touch of celebrity. She did not walk down the runway with Gaynor, March or Menjou. Her name was not in the credits yet. She was let in later with the rest of the real fans, but she got to see herself on screen. At least for a few seconds.

The movie was a critical and industry success. It earned Academy Award nominations for Best Picture (Selznick), Original Story (Wellman), Lead Actor (March), Lead Actress (Gaynor), Director (Wellman) and Screenplay (Campbell and Parker). Coincidently, one of the other Best Actress nominees that year was Barbara Stanwyck for her work in *Stella Dallas*. *A Star Is Born* would be remade in 1954 and again in 1976.

Carole's next role was another unbilled bit part in a bigger film, MGM's *Broadway Melody of 1938*. The Roy Del Ruth–directed musical featured Robert Taylor, Eleanor Powell, George Murphy, Binnie Barnes and Sophie Tucker. Kind of a musical within a musical, the film is less about plot and more about showcasing MGM talent for the moviegoers.

Besides a solid cast, the movie featured MGM's biggest technical talent. The music was arranged by Arthur Freed, the art direction by Cedric Gibbons, costumes were by Adrian and sound by Douglas Shearer. It also featured one of the most-remembered movie scenes of the 1930s: 15-year-old Judy Garland's singing fan letter "Dear Mr. Gable, You Made Me Love You" to a picture of Clark Gable. The scene was a re-enactment of a studio-designed birthday party for Gable, when Louis B. Mayer had Garland sing a song for Gable.[6]

Carole probably only spent a day or two on the set during filming, which due to the format was filmed in bits and pieces between February and July of 1937. The film was released in August.

Her small role in *Broadway Melody* was followed with an equally small role in another MGM film, *The Emperor's Candlesticks*, which was filmed between March 11 and April 22. Again, her role was almost invisible. The film was a stock piece with William Powell and Luise Rainer as secret agent–spies smuggling messages through Russia hidden in candlesticks, but the cast and crew were again filled with name stars. George Fitzmaurice directed, Harold Rosson filmed, Adrian did the costumes and Shearer again handled the sound. Supporting roles were played by the likes of Robert Young, Maureen O'Sullivan and Frank (*The Wizard of Oz*) Morgan. Although filmed after *Broadway Melody,* the film was released a month earlier, in July 1937.

To work as an unbilled extra at any studio, Carole would obviously have had to sign employment paperwork. That is not to say that she had an acting contract with Warners, which listed her as an employee as early as May 13, 1937. But the studio listed her not as an actress, but as a dancer. Studio employee records list Carole as a "dancer—Varsity Show." She lied on her employment forms, listing "Chicago, Ill." as her birthplace, her age as 19, and that she was single.[7]

Berkeley had seen her on the set of *The King and the Chorus* Girl and been sufficiently impressed to put her at the front of the chorus line for the final scene. But it is unlikely that they were formally "introduced" until March or April 1937. It was fairly well-known that Berkeley pulled strings to get her the contract she got, probably soon after her "introduction" to Berkeley.

Her first formal audition with notorious womanizer Berkeley took place in March or April 1937. He was one of the most creative directors in Hollywood, but tortured by alcoholism and haunted by failed relationships with women. He had a serendipitous entree into Hollywood. He was a marching instructor in the Army.

Berkeley enlisted in the Army during World War I and was trained as an aerial observer. Too late in the war to find any battlefield service, he instead found himself a lieutenant in the artillery, assigned to choreograph and conduct special parade drills to as many as 1,250 servicemen. After the war he was assigned to direct large camp shows held for returning veterans, after which he went to Broadway to work as a choreographer. By 1930 he was in Hollywood working for Goldwyn Studios.

The advent of sound propelled film musicals to the heights of popularity in the early 1930s. Berkeley's first film for Goldwyn was the Eddie Cantor vehicle *Whoopee!* (1930). Filming the largest dance number, Berkeley reverted to his Army aerial experience and trained the cameras on the dancing Goldwyn Girls from above. It would become his trademark.

After leaving Goldwyn, Berkeley worked at Warner Bros. for the rest of the 1930s. He co-directed hits like *42nd Street* (1933), *Gold Diggers of 1933* (1933) and *Dames* (1934). His routines got bigger and bigger, and the effects more elaborate. He choreographed dancing skyscrapers in *42nd Street* and an array of 60 white pianos in *Gold Diggers of 1935*. The 1937 version of *Gold Diggers* featured 75 helmet-wearing dancers carrying drums and flags and 50 oversized white rocking chairs, each large enough for two or three people.

Also noticeable in his choreography was a humorous sexuality, almost voyeuristic in its core. The 1933 *Gold Diggers* features a hundred dancers clad only in oversized gold coins, singing "We're in the Money." A young Ginger Rogers is buried among the chorines. Later during the same film, Dick Powell uses a can opener to open Ruby Keeler's metal clothing.

Berkeley's creative innovations carried over to the other side of the camera when he began directing films as well as choreographing them. He used only one camera to film his dance sequences. To film his massive overhead shots, holes had to be drilled in the roofs of the studio soundstages and cameras mounted outside. He also featured closeups of his anonymous chorus girls. Studio executives disliked "wasting" film on faces unknown to the public. He told them, "We've got all these beautiful girls in the picture; why not let the public see them?"

He was obviously a creative force in the movie industry in the 1930s, but Berkeley had a somewhat controversial personal life. His reputation as a flagrant womanizer was well-known even outside the studio and in the press. He had a serious drinking problem and likely suffered from depression as well. Between 1929 and 1935 he was married and divorced three times, and would eventually marry twice more. But more recently he had barely escaped going to prison for his involvement in a fatal September 1935 car accident in Malibu.

Berkeley was returning from a party late on the evening of September 8, 1935, when he crossed the median on the Pacific Coast Highway north of Sunset Boulevard, bounced off a car driven by a local college student and collided head-on with a second car. Killed in the second car were 64-year-old Monterey Park widow Ada Von Briesen, her 26-year-old son and her son's 19-year-old girlfriend. Von Briesen's 20-year-old daughter survived with serious injuries.

According to the crash survivors, other witnesses and a service station attendant who had spoken with Berkeley just moments before the accident, the director was clearly drunk. And it appeared that he was speeding when he slammed into the other cars. He called MGM studio police chief Whitney "Whitey" Hendry, who called celebrity lawyer Jerry Giesler.

Berkeley was charged with second degree murder and during the next 18 months Giesler navigated through three trials. He orchestrated the trials like Berkeley would a dance number. For the early court appearances, Berkeley was carried into court on a gurney covered with a sheet. His head was heavily bandaged, and his leg in a cast.

During the trials, Giesler hired dubious "tire experts" who testified that defective tires on his car caused the accident. He had a parade of a dozen Warners stars, headed by Pat O'Brien and Guy Kibbee, who each lied under oath and testified that Berkeley was sober when he left the party they all attended. On January 1, 1936, shortly after the third and final mistrial, Warners quietly paid the family of the dead woman $95,000. Carole arrived at his office for her audition a few months later.

When Carole met Berkeley, musicals featuring his dance numbers were among the top box office hits for the studio. He was "interviewing" actresses and dancers for the finale of his musical *Varsity Show*. The film would be the longest musical produced at Warners, over two hours in length. It featured Dick Powell and paid homage to America's leading colleges and universities.

Berkeley always cast his chorus line girls the same way. He first picked a group of what he called his "old girls," women who had worked with him before. Depending on the size of his production numbers, there could be from 15 to 50 of these "old girls." He then had the studio casting directors put a call out for 250 to 300 young unknowns. To a girl, they were barely legal and beautiful. And by the nature of the business they would be desperate for work. From this huge group of hopefuls Berkeley chose perhaps a dozen of what he called "new faces."

Berkeley's cattle calls took place on a studio sound stage. If one of the unknowns caught his fancy, a private interview was moved to Berkeley's office. Once his office door was closed behind the young girl, Berkeley would command her to stand in front of him and tell her to "raise your skirt." The request was ostensibly so he could check her legs for his dance numbers, but once the initial request was complied with, he would suggest, "Oh, I need to see more than that."

The little charade would continue until the young woman was standing cross-legged with her skirt over her head. Berkeley would tell the humiliated woman that she had the job already; it was all just a joke. The tension gone, he would usually then have sex with them.

Carole caught Berkeley's eye from among the hundreds of dancers auditioning for *Varsity Show*. According to Madison Lacy, a still photographer at Warners and friend of Berkeley, he was present during the audition when Berkeley chose Carole from the line of dancers snaking across the sound stage. Lacy's wife Adele was a dancer who had worked for Berkeley before and the two were good friends. According to Lacy, Berkeley not only never made Carole strip, he did not even request a private audition. More likely, he was taken with what artist James Montgomery Flagg once described as "her startling physical silhouette, bordering on the magnificent."

Lacy said that the moment Carole began swaying into her dance routine, Berkeley exclaimed, "Oh yes, we want her." Lacy said, "She had on this tight sweater, and when Carole started to swing and to dance, why, she was a cinch."[8] Lacy's version was a little sanitized though, probably because he and Adele would become good friends with Berkeley and Landis over the coming months. It is more likely that Landis did indeed strip for Berkeley, and according to other studio contemporaries the two began a sexual relationship during their first meeting.

Whatever happened during their private meeting, Berkeley hired Carole on the spot, and even gave her a line of dialogue. It did not make the *Varsity Show* final release print, though. Doing that was another Berkeley ploy with the women he was trying to bed. He'd have them film extemporaneous dialogue that he knew would not be included in the final print. They felt like a star. Whether or not Landis was sleeping with Berkeley is impossible to confirm, but it appears that she was.

Berkeley's dancers rarely if ever moved from his chorus lines to acting roles, but Carole began acting immediately. It was as if Carole was an "old girl" from the first day. Not only that, within a few weeks Berkeley himself got Carole her seven-year contract.

It was a standard six-month option contract, offering $50 a week to start, with studio options to increase to $500 a week. It guaranteed her work and regular pay increases as long as the studio continued to re-sign her. But the standard studio contract was far from favorable to the actors. The studio could assign her to any movie it wished and any role they demanded she play. The studio could loan her to another studio for whatever amount of money they desired for any role being offered. If they loaned her out for more than they were paying her, they kept the difference. If she refused any demand, she risked being suspended without pay. Warners could cancel the contract at any six-month anniversary. She had no rights at all. But Carole was working.

There was nothing special or unusual about the contract she was offered and that she signed. What was unusual was that she was offered a contract at all. Clearly she would not have gotten one without Berkeley's help. What was equally clear — to everyone at Warners— was that the beautiful but unknown blonde from San Francisco was Berkeley's protégée. And sexual partner.

Carole's contract was quite standard. All she needed to do was sign it. But she was only 18, and under California law still a minor. She could therefore not legally sign any contract. Further complicating matters, even though she and Irving Wheeler had been estranged for over three years, she was still legally married to him. That made her an adult.

Her lawyer Sidney Wetzler could not find Wheeler. He was still calling on all of the studios trying to find acting work as Jack Roberts, as he had been when he supposedly worked on *The King and the Chorus Girl*. It's not definite that Carole even saw Roberts during filming, though it could have happened and her friend Beth Renner inferred that it did.

With Wheeler nowhere to be found, she was forced to petition the court to approve the contract on July 28, 1937. It was then that her early marriage became public, but it's not likely anyone at Warners gave it much thought. She declined to tell the court her husband's name or even when the marriage took place, but Superior Court Judge William Wilson observed that since she was married that she was "probably not a minor any more and this whole matter is unnecessary." She was allowed to sign the contract, and went to work. Nobody paid much attention to the early marriage, probably because of her lowly status within the studio caste system.

The studio rumor mongers had a field day with Carole's personal life and her relationship with Berkeley. It would not be the last time that she got involved with a man with a soiled public reputation. Unknown to her, a reputation was being forged in the foundry of studio gossip, one that she would never outlive. News traveled quickly inside the studio walls, and her rapid ascension from unknown chorus girl to working actress, and her confirmed relationship with her director, left her the butt of inside jokes, stories and rumors.

Some of the rumors about Carole were undoubtedly true. Carole knew how to play the game, and play she did. The basic story was probably true — Carole slept with Berkeley and worked more than most actresses — but from that basis most of the stories became exaggerations or were outright untruths. Unfortunately for Carole she always somehow managed to put herself into a bad position. She just picked the wrong men. Even though their casting couch partnership would evolve quickly into a legitimate relationship, the rumors were etched in stone.

Exacerbating Carole's problems was the tendency for the men she met to fall in love with her. It's impossible to find a man who did *not* doggedly pursue Carole once he went out with her. The combination of Carole's typical bad judgment and the normal response from men was a terrible one. She was often pursued by the worst possible candidates.

One of a series of bathing suit photographs taken of a 19-year-old Carole, one of which was published in the July 12, 1938, edition of *PIC* magazine, an early tabloid.

For the rest of her career — which would also be the last decade of her life — Carole Landis lived under the shadow of the reputation that began during those first days with Berkeley. Like a shadow, she could never outrun the stories. Carole's reputation as a studio whore began almost from the day she began working.

But work she did. Her first recorded line of dialogue had found the cutting room floor, but over the next year Carole worked in over 20 pictures. She often filmed three different movies in a single month. That is a staggering number of movies for a newcomer like her.

Carole and Berkeley were mentioned regularly in gossip columns as a couple, their evenings out at Hollywood clubs and premieres were regular items. In late 1937, it was in the tabloids that "Busby Berkeley and Carole Landis have 'that old feeling....'"9 They made no attempts to hide the fact that they were a couple at the time.

Within days of landing at Warners with Berkeley's help, Carole befriended Diana Lewis, another young actress. Known to her friends as "Mousie," the tiny Lewis was also a teenager, barely 18 at the time. The two youngsters became immediate pals, and Lewis gave Carole a little gold necklace with a cross for her birthday the following March. Carole wore the cross every day for the rest of her life. "Mousie" starred in three dozen mostly forgettable films and would later marry actor William Powell in 1940. They stayed together until his death in 1987.

Like the rest of the option girls, Carole was assigned voice and acting coaches and attended daily classes in both. Warners' acting teachers were well-known and respected: Malvina Dunn and Sophie Rosenstein, who grouped Carole with another newcomer Peggy Moran. Peggy was the daughter of artist Earl Moran (who would later hire unknown Norma Jean Baker as a model before she became Marilyn Monroe) and, like Carole, was a headstrong youngster.

One day Peggy simply walked up to the Warners gate and told the guard she was there to become a star. She walked past, wangled an introduction to a producer and began working. She no doubt had to pass the same sexual initiation that Carole endured, but she was given a contract and began working as an option girl as well. The other youngster in Carole's group was teenager Lana Turner.

Though Berkeley hired Carole for *Varsity Show*, it would not be the first film she worked on at Warners. Almost immediately after her contract was processed in May she went to work on *Fly-Away Baby*. The film was the sequel to an earlier 1937 release, *The Smart Blonde,* and would be among eight "Torchy Blane" movies released between 1937 and 1939 with titles like *Blondes at Work* (1938), *Torchy Runs for Mayor* (1939) and *Torchy Plays with Dynamite* (1939).

The series starred Glenda Farrell as crime-fighting writer Torchy Blane and Barton MacLane as her policeman boyfriend Lt. Steve McBride. Farrell was perfectly cast as the fast-talking reporter; in real life she was able to speak at an incredible 390 words per minute. In *Fly-Away,* Carole has yet another forgettable and uncredited role as "blonde at airport."

But she is on screen, looking for the entire world like a movie star in a fur wrap and matching hat, standing next to her playboy boyfriend, singing. During filming, she even ad libbed a line ("A picture?") to some photographers in the extras crowd. Her time on screen is less than a minute. The film was released on June 9, 1937.

Varsity Show filming began at Warners in mid–May. The studios had begun to realize that musicals were loving fan interest. Like any other fad or object of popularity, movie genres come in and out of vogue in cycles. Musicals were all the rage in the early 1930s, driven to popularity in part because sound itself was so new. But by 1936 or 1937 the public appeared to be growing tired of the type.

Varsity Show was the longest musical made at Warners but shortest on plot: A group of kids at Winfield College asks a down-and-out producer to help them put on their annual talent show. It was also light on cast. Dick Powell starred, playing a college student though he was 33 at the time. The second credits belonged to a band— Fred Waring and his Pennsylvanians— and a has-been— Ted Healy, the alcoholic founder of *The Three Stooges,* in one of his final roles, just months before he would be beaten to death by Wallace Beery in a drunken bar fight.

The highlight of the film was one of Berkeley's signature production finales, but that too was stiff and uninspired by Berkeley standards. He was given an Academy Award nomination for dance direction, but that was likely because there were so few others that year. Carole played an uncredited bit part.

During the last six months of 1937, Carole worked on somewhere between eight and 12 films at Warners. All were solidly B in type and quality. Some of her roles can be confirmed, some can not. Studio records indicate that she was assigned to several— perhaps half a dozen—films where it's impossible to find her among the crowds of extras. In June and July, Carole worked on three films, the first a formulaic prison piece about an unjustly convicted man, starring John Litel and Ann Sheridan. Litel is sent to Alcatraz on a tax evasion charge and then framed for the murder of an inmate who once tried to kidnap his daughter. Litel would work on four films with Carole; in *Alcatraz Island* she is noted as "extra, uncredited," but finding her is impossible. She is perhaps hidden in some of the crowded courtroom scenes.

On the *Alcatraz* set, Carole befriended another young actor, New York–born Worster Von Eps. Just a few years older than Carole, and another struggling Warners contract actor doing tiny roles, the two became fast friends. Von Eps was a one-time New York City meter reader who turned professional tennis player, but in 1937 he changed his name to Willard Parker and came to Hollywood. Parker and Landis would remain close friends for the rest of her life.

Both Carole and Parker went right to work in *Adventurous Blonde,* a (slight) upgrade from *Alcatraz. Blonde* was another of the *Torchy* movie series, like Carole's *Fly-Away Baby.* But she is not visible in this film. Next up at Warners during that summer was *Hollywood Hotel,* directed by her friend Berkeley. Carole's *Torchy* star Glenda Farrell appeared in a cast led by Dick Powell, Lola Lane and Rosemary Lane. The film is pretty much forgettable except for the swing music, provided by the Benny Goodman Orchestra and written by Johnny Mercer.

Like the rest of the Warners "Bs," it has a simplistic plot: A talented but unknown singer (Powell) gets hired and fired while falling in love with the double (Rosemary Lane) of a temperamental movie star (Lola Lane) who has disappeared. Carole appeared briefly on film as a hat-check girl, looking stunning in a gorgeous dress, helping the star's father (Hugh Herbert) on with his coat.

The film is actually more memorable for the rest of the supporting and unbilled

Another early studio bathing suit photograph, from the late 1930s.

cast than the plot, the acting or the stars. Another actress with a small role was Susan Hayward, appearing in her very first film as the "starlet at table." She was only 19, a year older than Carole. In one of his first film roles, a young Ronald Reagan appears as a radio announcer.

Edgar Kennedy, a long-time foil of Stan Laurel and Oliver Hardy and renowned for his famous "slow burn," has a small role. Ted Healy plays a photographer, working on his final film set. Former silent screen stars in the cast included William B. Davidson, who appeared in 325+ films from 1915 through 1949, Hugh Herbert (who appeared with Carole in her scene), who worked on over 100 movies, and Harrison Greene, who appeared in almost 150. Playing themselves in cameos were musicians Harry James, Gene Krupa, Lionel Hampton, writer Louella Parson and makeup legend Perc Westmore. Other than the people involved, the film was totally unremarkable.

During the fall of 1937, Carole worked almost non-stop in small roles. She appeared in ten films, six that can be confirmed and another four that are likely but impossible to definitively confirm. One film is missing several reels, one of which probably contained her footage; in another film, it is impossible to pick Carole out of the various crowd scenes. But it appears that she did indeed work on a minimum of eight or nine films in three months. Occasionally she worked on two or three films simultaneously, but the roles were not taxing and would not take much time.

From early September through mid–October, Carole is confirmed to have worked on *Women Are Like That* and *Over the Wall*. At the same time, she was supposed to have appeared in *The Patient in Room 18*. During October she did appear in *The Invisible Menace* and allegedly in *Blondes at Work*, another *Torchy* movie that filmed through mid–November. Also in November she began work on *A Slight Case of Murder* and *Love, Honor and Behave*. She was also supposed to have worked on *He Couldn't Say No* in November. In December, Carole appeared in *Penrod's Double Trouble* and *Men Are Such Fools*.

It is difficult to confirm that she worked in *The Adventurous Blonde*, *The Patient in Room 18*, and *Men Are Such Fools*. But it would make sense for Warners to assign her to *The Adventurous Blonde*, since she had already worked on two previous *Torchy* films, *Fly-Away Baby* and *Blondes at Work*. It was common studio practice to assign contract performers like Carole to similar films because they were familiar with the direction, the crew and the cast, so it makes sense that she would indeed be on the *Adventurous Blonde* bit part assignment list.

Men Are Such Fools is another likely assignment for Carole since the film was directed by her old boyfriend and supporter, Busby Berkeley. Coincidently, the two leads, Wayne Morris and Priscilla Lane, also starred in *Love, Honor and Behave*, which was filmed just a month earlier and was another of Carole's films. Carole's role is well-described in the records: "June Cooper, Girl with Jimmy's School Chums." Her best friend Diana "Mousie" Lewis also had a small role in this movie.

The problem confirming this appearance, even with all of the circumstantial evidence, is that two of the original eight reels of film are missing from the Warners archives. Carole's appearance is likely on one of those films.

The single role that is impossible to confirm among Carole's ten films is *The Patient in Room 18*. She is allegedly clearly visible in several scenes, but does not appear in any cast or assignment records relating to the film. Also, none of the production staff—directors, producers, etc.—worked with Carole previously, so it's hard to say with any sense of finality that she did indeed appear in this film.

Her first assignment during that very busy fall was *Women Are Like That*, one of several of her fall 1937 films; it began filming on August 29. Directed by Stanley Logan and starring Pat O'Brien and Kay Francis, *Women* was based on a same-name 1929 novel by E.M. Delafield (written under the pen name Edme Dashwood). The battle-of-the-sexes comedy has an uneven plot and so-so writing, though there are some entertaining moments.

Claire Landin (Francis) tries to help salvage her husband Willie's (O'Brien) advertising agency, and is doing a credible job until Willie's expected insecurities threaten to torpedo the whole thing. There is the expected happy ending. The only memorable performance was by Thurston Hall as Kay's father. He steals the movie as a lewd and eccentric old rogue. The only other interesting elements are several truly awful outfits that Francis was forced to wear.

Co-stars included Melville Cooper, Grant Mitchell, Sarah Edwards, Joyce Compton and Ralph Forbes. Carole is not listed in the credits but is visible in one party scene wearing a lovely black dress and hat. Asked about the whereabouts of one of O'Brien's clients, she utters her single line, "I think he's in the bathroom with the hostess." The film was released on April 23, 1938.

Also filmed in September was the lightweight prison picture, *Over the Wall*, that starred Dick Foran, June Travis and John Litel. Directed by Frank McDonald, *Wall* is possibly the most predictable, cliché-ridden film ever made at Warners. It offered a pugnacious boxer (Foran) unjustly accused of murder and sent to Sing Sing where he becomes a singer. Also featured are a prison chaplain (Litel) who just *knows* Foran is innocent (and helps prove it), a brutal guard, a lovely girl on the outside (Travis) who objects to his boxing, a killer named "Ace" and on and on.

When the former street tough-boxer-inmate sings "Ave Maria" with the prison choir, it's hard for viewers to stay in their seats. By the time Travis and Litel are visiting the warden and then the Governor with the evidence to win Foran a pardon, they're running for their cars.

The film did offer an impressive cast along with the clichés, including Ward Bond, Eddy Chandler, Dick Purcell and George E. Stone. Carole had a small role as the real murderer's girlfriend Peggy, and appeared in perhaps four scenes. It was released on March 27, 1938.

The Patient in Room 18 was filmed at the same time as the first two films, beginning on August 29. It was directed by Bobby Connolly and starred Patric Knowles and Ann Sheridan. *Patient* was well-written by Eugene Schlow and Robertson White, crafted from a story by Mignon G. Eberhart.

Police detective Lance O'Leary (Knowles) is recuperating in Room 18 of the Thatcher Hospital from a work-induced nervous breakdown when a wealthy patient brings to the hospital $100,000 worth of radium to be used for his own care. He is murdered later that same evening and the uranium is stolen. Rapidly "cured" patient Knowles and his nurse Sarah Keate (Sheridan) must solve the crime, as bodies pile up, without the help of inept Police Inspector Foley (Cliff Clark).

Hollywood seemed terribly interested in this character for some reason. The story had earlier been shot at Warners as *While the Patient Slept* (1935) starring Aline MacMahon as Nurse Keate, and again at 20th Century–Fox as *The Great Hospital Mystery* (1937) with Jane Darwell. Warners would feature the character again in

Mystery House (later in 1938), again with Sheridan. *Patient* was released on January 8, 1938.

October began with *The Invisible Menace*, which featured Boris Karloff in a typically sinister role in this murder mystery set on a fog-bound Army base. When a young private (Eddie Craven) smuggles his new bride (Marie Wilson) onto the post for an illicit honeymoon, they uncover a murder. The Army detective (Cy Kendall) directs his attention to the obvious suspect—Karloff—while ignoring the real culprits. *Menace* could have been a quality and scary film, but almost every performance except Karloff's was wooden and uninspiring.

Carole appears briefly in the beginning of the film, begging "Can't I go with Johnnie?" as her husband heads off to the base. Also playing small roles were her good friend Willard Parker and Anderson Lawler, a New York actor who came to Hollywood with his boyfriend, Cary Grant. Soon after they arrived, Grant left him for Randolph Scott. The film was released on January 22, 1938.

At the same time in October, Carole worked on *Blondes at Work*, the third of the *Torchy* films that she appeared in. It was a vague remake of a 1935 Bette Davis film entitled *Front Page Woman*. A wealthy department store owner is missing and reporter Torchy Blane (Glenda Farrell) finds him dead but somehow ends up in jail for contempt of court. Even incarcerated, she is able to solve the crime and to free the man unjustly accused of the crime.

The *Torchy* series was probably beginning to run its course, though there would be four more films. Both Farrell and Barton MacLane, as Torchy's detective boyfriend, offer uninspired—often boring—performances. Co-stars Tom Kennedy and Betty Compson in a bad-girl role were the most interesting characters in the film. Carole had a small role as a department store model named Carole who speaks with Torchy about the man suspected of the killing. *Blondes* was released on February 5, 1938.

Carole's next October film was *A Slight Case of Murder*, based upon a failed play by Damon Runyon and Howard Lindsay. Directed by Lloyd Bacon, it offered an impressive starring cast of Edward G. Robinson, Jane Bryan, Allen Jenkins and Ruth Donnelly. The film is a funny skewering of the mob and Prohibition.

Robinson plays Remy Marco, a bootlegger who decides with the end of Prohibition to go legit. Marco was making a fortune during Prohibition, but only because none of his toadies bothered to tell him his beer tasted terrible. But given the times, it sold. Unfortunately, once it's legal, nobody will drink it. The film evolves into a farcical comedy of errors that climaxes with a family gathering at Marco's summer house replete with a visit from his daughter's policeman fiancé, the hidden bodies of four dead gangsters who died in a shootout that was (of course) their own fault, and $500,000 in hidden money that Marco needs to save his brewery.

Ruth Donnelly, Margaret (*The Wizard of Oz*'s Wicked Witch) Hamilton, John Litel and Carole's old friend Willard Parker also appeared in the film. Carole, playing "the blonde who talks to Whitewood," can be seen during a party scene standing in a white dress and dancing next to a piano. The comedy, remade in 1952 as *Stop, You're Killing Me* with Broderick Crawford and Claire Trevor, was released on February 26, 1938.

Carole's next credit was *Love, Honor and Behave*, an interesting—but confusing—

film that asked the question whether it is better to lose gracefully than fight, or always fight and win. Adapted from a story by Stephen Vincent Benet by Clements Ripley and directed by Stanley Logan, the film featured Wayne Morris, Priscilla Lane, Dick Foran, Thomas Mitchell, John Litel, Mona Barrie, Dickie Moore and Audrey Leonard.

Young Ted (Morris) has been raised to be a good loser by his mother, who forces him to give up football for medical school and tennis, which he hates. By the time he finishes school he is unable to assert himself. Even after marrying his childhood sweetheart Barbara (Lane) and becoming a husband and provider he won't even fight for her respect, which he quickly loses. When she starts stepping out on Ted, the inevitable family clash ensues; seemingly everyone is arguing with everyone and, a Casper Milquetoast no more, Ted ends up spanking Barbara to get her in line. That type of chauvinism played well to 1930s audiences but would not be very well-received today.

Not all early studio photographs were cheesecake, and when the photographers concentrated on Carole's beauty, it showed, like this studio still from the late 1930s.

The film veers chaotically between comedy, drama and farce and arrives at a much too coincidental ending; the only thing that stands out are the performances of Morris and Lane, both of whom were wonderful. Carole had a small role as a girl playing with young Ted (also described as "wheel watcher at Ted's party"). The film was released on March 12, 1938.

During November and December, Carole did another three films beginning with *Penrod's Double Trouble*, one of four "Penrod" films Warners adapted from the Booth Tarkington stories. *Double Trouble* was directed by Lewis Seiler and starred Billy Mauch as Penrod Schofield, Billy's brother Bobby as Danny and the real-life husband and wife team of Gene and Kathleen Lockhart as Mr. and Mrs. Schofield. Supporting cast members included Dick Purcell, Hugh O'Connell and Charles Halton.

This film is pretty typical *Penrod* fare. Young Penrod costs his father a chance at a raise by getting into a fight with the boss' obnoxious son. Though it was not his fault, he is locked in his room while everyone goes to the carnival. But he sneaks out, somehow gets stuck in an escaping balloon and ends up being held for ransom in an abandoned house by two crooks. Penrod's dog Duke saves the day, leading the rest of Penrod's young friends on the expected rescue mission.

Double Trouble filmed from the second week in December until the third week in January. Carole worked during the carnival scene, looking lovely in a coat with a fur collar. Those scenes were filmed during December. Standing by one of the barkers, she says to Gene Lockhart, "Give him the 25¢ you skinflint ... come on!" The film was released on July 23, 1938.

Carole's next movie was filmed during the same mid–December to mid–January time-frame. *Men Are Such Fools* was a Busby Berkeley–directed effort featuring Wayne Morris and Priscilla Lane — the same lead couple Carole worked with in *Love, Honor and Behave* just a few months earlier.

Fools is a poorly written film with a weak plot adapted by Faith Baldwin from her own magazine article. The alleged comedy explores the conflict when an ambitious 1930s woman wants a career and a family at the same time. Linda (Lane) works for an advertising agency and is newly married to ex–football star Jimmy Hall (Morris). Advertising big shot Harry Galleon (Humphrey Bogart) offers to help Linda's career if she'll be "nice" to him and tries to convince her to leave Jimmy. The inevitable separation of the Halls and their battles and eventual reconciliation are all very predictable.

Co-stars included Hugh Herbert, Penny Singleton, Mona Barrie, and Gene and Kathleen Lockhart. Carole is listed in studio production records and cast lists as "June Cooper, girl with Jimmy's old school chums." However, no complete print of the film seems to survive, and the available film does not show Carole. Her friend "Mousie" Lewis is also missing from the available version of *Fools*. In some sources she is listed as "telephone operator," while in others it is noted that her scenes were deleted. *Fools* was released on July 16, 1938.

Carole's final filming in 1937 may have been done some time between late October and late November. *He Couldn't Say No* was adapted from a story in the January 1936 issue of *Hearst's International Cosmopolitan* by Norman Matson and movie was produced by the team of Bryan Foy, Hal Wallis and Jack L. Warner. It was directed by Lewis Seiler. Frank McHugh played timid office worker Lambert T. Hunkins alongside Diana Lewis as Iris, the surprisingly beautiful object of his affections. This was "Mousie" Lewis' first major role, and Carole was thrilled for her best friend. Jane Wyman is her competition Violet Coney and Cora Witherspoon is Violet's battleax mother (Mrs. Coney).

Timid advertising office worker Hunkins buys a nude statue of Courage at an auction because he recognizes his dream girl Iris was the model. Like most Warners comedies from the 1930s, an unlikely series of events leads to the expected happy ending. Iris' prudish Senator father wants the statue destroyed to save his political career, Mrs. Coney is trying to force Hunkins to marry her daughter Violet, three gangsters— with the unlikely names of Slug, Hymie and Dimples—try to kidnap the statue, etc.

But the audiences seemed to identify with the common man's battles and the film was fairly well received after its March 19, 1938, release.

Carole was said to have appeared in an uncredited bit, but it is impossible to find her in the final print. There are plenty of crowd scenes where she could be hiding. For the second film in a row, Carole worked with her best friend "Mousie," but this time Lewis' role was a major one.

Carole had been in Hollywood for just a little over a year. She was still living in her apartment at the Bronsonia and still in a serious relationship with Berkeley. The couple were routinely mentioned in the tabloids and photographed during their evenings out at the Trocadero, Mocambo or Ciro's. He was always the "director," she the "Berkeley chorine." But she didn't mind; by late 1937 she was in love with Berkeley and they had begun talking about marriage.

Carole also had an-ever growing circle of friends at Warners. Her closest pals were "Mousie" Lewis and Willard Parker; like other young Hollywood actors in 1937, they spent their weekends at the beach or exploring the Hollywood club scene.

Gold Diggers in Paris was another Warners song and dance spectacle that began filming on January 15, 1938. The movie was directed by Ray Enright and written by Jerry Horwin and Jerry Wald, all Warners heavyweights. Berkeley was to direct all of the dance numbers. It featured an all-star cast that included Rudy Vallee, Rosemary Lane, Hugh Herbert and Allen Jenkins, and supporting players Melville Cooper, Mabel Todd and Fritz Feld. Filming lasted on and off until mid–March.

This film is something of a lightweight musical by Warners standards, but by early 1938 the budgets for musicals were being drastically reduced. *Gold Diggers* offered Vallee and Jenkins as the owners of a nearly bankrupt nightclub, the Club Ballé. When their dancers are mistaken for ballet dancers and invited to the Paris International Dance Exposition to compete for money, they jump at the chance to save their club. A ballet teacher is hired to teach the girls ballet aboard the liner taking them to France, followed on another liner by the real New York ballet company that was supposed to be invited.

There is much song and the expected comedic hijinks, but the story lacks punch. However, the light plot allowed Berkeley more opportunity to present his dance numbers, which were impressive though on a much smaller scale than previous films. Carole is cast as one of the "Gold Diggers," along with her pal "Mousie" Lewis and Peggy Moran. In the film she is the first dancer shown on film and the third credited. The movie was released on June 11, 1938.

Four's a Crowd, offered perhaps the most impressive cast of any film she had ever worked on. Directed by Michael Curtiz and written by Wallace Sullivan, *Crowd* starred Errol Flynn and Olivia de Havilland, backed up by Rosalind Russell, Patric Knowles, and Walter Connolly. Even the supporting cast was impressive, featuring Hugh Herbert, Melville Cooper, Franklin Pangborn and Herman Bing. Filming took place between mid–February and mid–March.

The problem wasn't the cast; the problem was that Errol Flynn — as tongue-in-cheek amusing as he was in real life — was virtually incapable of doing comedy. The studio had tried an earlier comedy, 1937's *The Perfect Specimen*, which bombed, and *Crowd* would suffer the same fate.

Wearing one of her trademark fur coats, Carole listens as her director and then-lover Busby Berkeley (right) chats with *Gold Diggers in Paris* production manager Frank Mattison. Their relationship was not a secret, but Carole is described by studio writers as simply "one of the girls."

The comedy is a story of a public relations man's (Flynn) ongoing battles with his largest but most difficult client (Connolly) as he tries to help a reporter (Russell) save her newspaper. Along the way he falls in love with the client's daughter (de Havilland), the only reason he offered to help in the first place. The stale plot and Flynn's absolute inability to be comedic doom the picture, although almost every other actor performs admirably.

Carole played Flynn's second secretary and is on film for a little less than a minute exchanging secretarial chatter with Flynn. The film was released on August 4, 1938, and also offered another beautiful young actress in an uncredited role: Lana Turner, who celebrated her seventeenth birthday during filming.

When Were You Born? was filmed at the same time (February and March) as *Crowd*. Directed by William McGann, *Born* offered Anna May Wong as an astrologist helping police track down a murderer, along with Margaret Lindsey, Lola Lane, Anthony Averill and Jeffrey Lynn.

Fortune-teller Wong tells one of her fellow passengers on a ship that he will die within two days. When he turns up dead the next day, police suspect her so she agrees to help them to clear herself. The movie is a pretty basic whodunit without much excitement (or plot or acting). Carole is one of the ship's passengers, appearing on screen and smiling for about ten seconds. The movie was released on June 18, 1938.

Her next film, *Boy Meets Girl*, was beset with problems even before it began filming. Adapted by Sam and Bella Spewack from the successful Broadway play of the same name, it was about two studio writers and an unwed mother; the original stars were to be comedians Olsen and Johnson, and the female lead Marion Davies. But Olsen and Johnson were committed elsewhere and Davies did so much complaining about her dressing room and the script that the producers finally replaced them all.

By the time filming began during March and April, the two reporters were being played by James Cagney and Pat O'Brien and the unwed mother by Marie Wilson. When Cagney and O'Brien, two lazy screenwriters who need a story for their failing studio's only star (Dick Foran), discover their friendly studio waitress (Wilson) has become an unwed mother (the baby's name is "Happy"), they write a similar story for their cowboy star.

The plot revolves around Happy's rise to stardom but the film seems more a swipe at moviemaking and studio life than a comedy about a baby. Most of the acting is awful; Cagney talks a mile a minute, and Wilson takes her voice to such high places she is barely audible. But audiences loved the film, as did the critics.

More interestingly, the script is littered with studio inside jokes and little potshots at the movie business, all of which are funny. But if the viewer isn't looking for, and ready, for them, they are lost and the downside of the movie is all that is visible. Carole had a small role as a cashier in the studio commissary, answering the phone and saying, "No, they're not here." A young Ronald Reagan also had a small role in this, his eighth film. It was released on August 27, 1938.

In *Girls on Probation*, which was filmed during April and May, Reagan and Jane Bryan played the leads in this somewhat silly film about a pleasant but dense girl (Bryan) who not once, but twice, allows herself to be arrested because of her bad-girl best friend (Sheila Bromley). She ends up in prison, but of course a kindly parole officer helps her get out and back into the arms of boyfriend Reagan. It's almost painful.

Carole is listed along with four or five other young actresses as "prisoners" but she is not findable on film. Another extra prisoner was a young Susan Hayward. The film was released on October 27, 1938.

By the end of April 1938, Carole had appeared in 21 films—a stunning amount of work for an option girl. The rumor that Landis was sleeping her way to work had already begun circulating. Even though her relationship with Berkeley was far more serious than sexual, that is clearly how the rumor began. To co-workers it would never be serious, never be a "real" relationship. It would always be the young starlet sleeping with the man who got her roles.

Worse yet, she was becoming a target of an even more powerful industry group—the studio wives. The spouses of actors, directors and studio executives were all well aware of the readily available stable of young women willing to trade sex for fame. They were even more catty and ultimately more vindictive than Landis' fellow studio employees and actresses. Carole's love life became a common topic of conversation among the studio wives, and the rumors intensified.

The studio wives, and their well-organized cliques in Hollywood, were perhaps the most hypocritical of any group in Hollywood. Most of these women had taken a similar route to their positions. They had slept their way to their roles as industry wives. Adding to their jealousy of Carole was her immense likability. She was a genuinely nice young woman, pleasant to crew and fellow actors alike. Her tomboy background made her a potential friend to everyone.

It was at that time that a persistent rumor was born, likely started by the studio wives club. The rumor that Carole worked as a call girl in San Francisco became one of the more long-lived of the negative stories about her. There is no concrete proof, but acquaintances from her San Francisco café days who later ended up in Hollywood perpetuated the story as fact.

Carole was likely prone to trading sex for work. Her comment "I have no intentions of ending my career in a rooming house, with full scrapbooks and an empty stomach" would seem to bear it out. But she was also independent enough, and feisty enough, to be less bothered by the seemingly uncomplimentary nature of her numerous affairs.

From 1937 through early 1939, Carole and Berkeley enjoyed a relationship that was much more than simply sexual. They were a public and private couple, and she was deeply in love with him. Even though they had openly spoken of marriage, the relationship and the four films she did with him at Warners fueled the rumors.

In the latter part of 1937 and early 1938, Berkeley and Carole were talking about marriage, and the rumors were in the tabloids. However, it was spoken at Warners that Berkeley backed out of his promise to marry because of interference from his mother. Apparently, she had heard the rumors about Carole including the San Francisco stories and did not feel Carole appropriate for her son.[10] Their well-reported parting was noted in a *Los Angeles Times* story just before year's end; it was noted that the two were seen "at Sardi's appearing much happier after their spat."[11]

Carole and Berkeley were back together during the early part of 1938, appearing in public numerous times, but the last public mention of the two as a couple was in the March 16, 1938, edition of the *Times* when they attended a costume party at the Hawaiian Paradise Café. By early May 1938, as Carole was beginning work on *Girls on Probation*, the tabloids were announcing that the relationship was over. *The Hollywood Reporter* noted in early May that the "Berkeley–Carole Landis relationship had gone cold...."[12] By that time the relationship may have been cold, but it was certainly exposed for all to see.

Whether or not the events that played out during the middle of May *caused* Carole and "Buzz" to break it off, or the events *were* the cause, can only be guessed at. But within a few short weeks their relationship was over. So was her relationship with Warners. And Berkeley's as well. And it was all played out very publicly.

On May 13, Warners informed Carole that her contract, up for renewal on June 1, would not be picked up. Strangely, just a week earlier she had been chosen from among all of the contract girls to make a publicity appearance at the new Burbank Post Office, riding up to the new building on horseback.[13] At the same time another young option girl was also dropped, the beautiful Susan Hayward,[14] who appeared in *Hollywood Hotel* alongside Carole in a similarly tiny role.

The reason that Carole was dropped had less to do with her work than with her tumultuous private life: the ill-timed re-emergence of first husband Irving Wheeler. Within a few weeks of Warners' decision not to renew her contract, the now-unemployed Carole was involved in a lawsuit filed by Wheeler against Berkeley. It is probable that Warners knew of the suit before it was formally filed—Wheeler's lawyers would have approached Warners looking for a payoff before going to court—which led them to release her on May 13.

Warners obviously refused to pay Wheeler off. On May 20, 1938, Wheeler announced that he was suing Berkeley for alienation of affections, alleging that Berkeley "stole" Carole from him. It was a patently obvious attempt to extort money from Berkeley, who had been openly dating Carole. Their photographs had appeared in dozens of newspapers during their many very public dates, but now headlines were screaming BUSBY BERKELEY NAMED IN $250,000 LOVE THEFT SUIT!!![15]

One might have expected such a suit to be a minor inconvenience for both, but when the "Queen" of the Hollywood gossip writers jumped on the story, it was apparent that it would be played out front and center. Louella Parsons covered the story extensively, and surprisingly sided with Carole when she wrote,

> Chatter in Hollywood is that Carole Landis, whose husband, Irving Wheeler, is suing Busby Berkeley for alienation of affections, has told friends that if and when the case comes to court she will testify for the dance director. Miss Landis, a Berkeley chorine, says that for three years she has tried to locate her husband without success. The first she heard of him was when he cropped up with the lawsuit. She and Buz haven't been seeing each other for weeks, so the willing gesture on her part is not caused by any romantic feeling, but simply because she thinks it is the right thing to do.[16]

Under a headline ACCUSED OF TALKING WAY INTO HER AFFECTIONS, newspapers across the country ran front-page photographs of Berkeley and Carole at a table (probably at Mocambo or the Trocadero). The text noted that, "Busby Berkeley, big Hollywood dance man who stages those dizzying girl spectacles, is charged by the husband of lovely 19-year-old Carole Landis, movie chorine, with turning her affections from her husband to himself. Berkeley and Miss Landis are shown above chatting gaily over a café table. Miss Landis' husband, Irving Wheeler, asks $25,000 for his wife's affection in a legal action begun in Los Angeles."[17]

Wheeler's lawyer Alexander L. Oakley argued that, "since last August, Berkeley carried on a campaign to win the affections of Miss Landis, finally succeeding and destroying the actress' love for her husband." Wheeler demanded $150,000 actual damages for the "love theft" and $100,000 more as punitive damages (about $3,000,000 today). Berkeley counter-filed with a demurrer requesting the case be thrown out.

From August 15 through the 19th all of the parties met in Superior Judge Kenney's court. Carole was forced to lie in the press and in court, probably at the direction of Berkeley's and Warners' attorneys. She told the court, "There has been neither affection nor consortium between myself and Mr. Wheeler since September 1934." She claimed that her association with Berkeley was strictly platonic. Even though their relationship was not secret (witness the reference in Louella Parsons' column), had she told the truth; that she and "Buzz" were a couple who at one point considered marriage, Wheeler would have had a much stronger case and perhaps could have prevailed.

Carole told Kenney, "I didn't think anyone knew I'd ever been married. Mr. Berkeley and I are good friends but we certainly aren't in love. I thought Irving had forgotten our marriage too." She added that she was only 15 when she married Wheeler and that their marriage lasted less than a month, adding, "We lived together for three weeks and then had an argument. I've only seen him once since then, and that was when he told me he wanted a divorce. I can't see how he figures anyone stole me from him."[18]

Berkeley described Landis as a protégé and star pupil and that there was no romance between them. That same day, Wheeler's suit was rightly thrown out as Judge Kenny sustained a demurrer filed by Berkeley's lawyers.[19] Unfortunately, what had been at least somewhat of a private affair became fully public.

Berkeley left court with his new girlfriend, a young actress who had allegedly appeared in *Gold Diggers of Paris*. She would have worked with Carole on the film, and her name was said to be Eleanor Bailey.[20] However, no such person is listed—even among the uncredited bit players—in that film's cast. Arkansas native Eleanor *Bayley* appeared in a half-dozen films around that time; it is more likely that the woman with Berkeley in 1938 was that actress.

Landis was represented by Gregson "Greg" Bautzer, a Hollywood attorney and sometimes agent with a reputation for bedding his clients, almost all of whom were female. The list included Joan Crawford, Ava Gardner, Paulette Goddard, Dorothy Lamour, Ann Miller and Ginger Rogers, all of whom were seen being escorted by Bautzer at one time or another. It was rumored that he also slept with Carole, fresh off the failure of her relationship with Berkeley. During Hollywood's next generation, he represented, among others, Zsa Zsa Gabor and Jayne Mansfield.

Carole's dismissal was also affected by Berkeley's diminishing status at the studio. It was remarkably bad timing for him to be caught in the middle of a love triangle while he was working his way back from his car accident problems *and* directing in a film genre that was rapidly losing favor with the fans.

Berkeley finished up at Warner Bros. directing a non-musical, *Hollywood Hotel* (1938), and the forgettable *Calling All Girls* (1939), which was little more than a rehash of a half-dozen songs from Broadway. Just after Carole left Warners, Berkeley too was gone, to MGM. There he had small responsibilities on a number of films, beginning with *Broadway Serenade* (1938), where he choreographed the final production number.

By 1939, his work was so unimpressive that the original Scarecrow's dance that he choreographed for *The Wizard of Oz* was scrapped from the final version of the film. He had limited work on perhaps ten films during the 1940s, after which he faded from Hollywood memory.

But for Carole, Berkeley represented yet another failure by a man she loved. Not only had he reneged on a marriage promise, his lowly status (by that time) at Warners left him unable to protect her as he was on his way out. She was let go more because of Berkeley's problems than anything she did.

After she left the studio, Carole signed with agent Louis Shurr, a well-known New York theatrical agent who was known for finding actresses on stage and bringing them to the movies.[21] In Carole's case he did the opposite, suggesting that she do some stage work while he cast around for a studio. At least she would be getting paid while he found her another studio home.

Shurr did arrange an offer from Paramount, but he and Carole decided to turn it down. Shurr landed her roles in several plays around Los Angeles, both with only middling results. From June 6 through June 21 she appeared in *Roberta*, playing one of the female leads opposite Bob Hope. She then did a play entitled *Once Upon a Night* with a small theater company; it was a failure. She was not a "name" actress and would not have been a significant draw, but she had a problem with live stage versus filming and was let go after three performances. The play itself apparently closed soon afterwards.

She also got back into the public dating scene, appearing several times with agent Vic Orsatti and with actor Alexander D'Arcy. Orsatti was a graduate of the University of Southern California who played professional baseball with the St. Louis Cardinals. During the off season he worked for MGM, hired primarily so he could play on Louis B. Mayer's studio league baseball team (Mayer liked to win his games). D'Arcy was a young actor who appeared in films like *The Prisoner of Zenda* and *The Awful Truth* (both 1937). He would later work at 20th Century–Fox.

It was noted in the tabloids that she was also taking classes at night. Harrison Carroll told movie readers that "here's something that Hollywood doesn't know about the beauteous Carole Landis. She goes to school at Hollywood High five nights a week."[22] She did take some classes, but most certainly not five nights a week. She also took classes in voice, diction, dramatics and languages. And she earned extra money modeling clothes.

Even though she had been released, Carole still attended the Warners Christmas party a week before Christmas 1938. It was there that she met Kenny Morgan, a newspaper columnist who would later become a studio public relations executive. In the 1940s he married Lucille Ball's cousin Cleo and ran the P.R. Department for Lucy and husband Desi Arnaz's Desilu Productions when they began filming *I Love Lucy* episodes in the early 1950s.

Morgan's reporting experience made him familiar with the men involved in the founding of Republic Studios, and he suggested that Carole leave the Warners party and go to the Republic party with him. She said "yes," a fortuitous decision on her part. Republic was a small studio located in North Hollywood, and Morgan's introduction and efforts got Carole a contract there.

Just a month later, in early February 1939, she signed a three-picture deal with Republic. She would start work on her first film, *Three Texas Steers*, in early March. In the month since their meeting at the Warners Christmas party, Carole had been seeing Morgan privately. It was probably at his urging that she legally shed Irving Wheeler.

Carole would later say that the real advantage of marriage was that it helped to keep "the wolves at bay." She still wore her wedding ring for that reason; if men assumed she was married, more of them would leave her alone. It wasn't foolproof — Carole was much too beautiful for that — but it did help. She knew, however, that before she began working at Republic she needed to divorce Wheeler. On March 6, 1939, Carole went to court and sued for divorce, charging mental cruelty. Her court date would be two months hence.

She was losing an old husband and gaining a new boyfriend and she also decided to move to a new home. Sometime in late 1938 or early 1939 Carole left the Bronsonia Apartments and rented a small bungalow at 1130 South Clark Drive in Los Angeles. In the 1930s the South Clark neighborhood was a quiet neighborhood full of studio employees and young actors just starting out. It was a clean, working class area full of nice little bungalows. It was also close enough to both the Culver City and the Hollywood studios.

Morgan's relationship with Carole followed a pattern that would be repeated dozens of times during the next decade. Something seemingly happened to every man in Carole's life once he got to know her. They all wanted a more serious relationship with her, all (except maybe Cesar Romero and Cary Grant) wanted to have sex with her, and almost all of them wanted to marry her. Morgan, like Berkeley, fell in love with Carole almost immediately.

I don't believe that it was something that Carole consciously "did." I don't think she "reeled men in" to use men. Indeed, most of the men in Carole's life helped her *before* they became involved. It was as if they proved themselves to *her* and then she allowed them in. Unfortunately, as much as she wanted love, as much as she wanted marriage, she had no idea how to successfully accomplish either.

But she had a new studio. Republic was most certainly a B movie mill, one of the last studios making serial westerns.

Under the headline COW OPERAS MAKE MONEY, an article in the *Hollywood Citizen News* described how Republic was able to make money. George Sherman, a mainstay director there (he worked his way up from an office boy to their top director by the age of 25), described the environment;

> The reason we can make [films] so cheaply is that we really work. On a big production [at a big studio] a director thinks he's doing all right if he puts four or five scenes a day in the can. We finish 65 or 70 scenes in ten hours and think nothing of it. We have fun on our sets, but we don't waste a minute. We know what we're going to shoot before we shoot it, and we don't do any masterminding as we go along. Fact is, we never experiment. All our actors are old hands at the game. They know what they're doing. And if we give a guy $200 a week [a very low salary at the time for a star] he'd better be Paul Muni.[23]

Sherman's films typically cost about $35,000 and never netted the studio less than $100,000 (several million dollars today). One day, when five writers left their writing room for lunch, Sherman had the furniture removed and the room was used as a stable for John Wayne's horse.

"The Three Mesquiteers" were Western characters created by novelist William

Colt McDonald. Republic's first venture into the Mesquiteers franchise was 1936's *The Three Mesquiteers*, starring Bob Livingston, Ray Corrigan and Syd Saylor. The studio would make 51 Mesquiteer movies from 1936 to 1943.

The films were incredibly popular given their simplicity. *The Motion Picture Herald* and *Box Office* magazine each ranked the Top Ten Western Stars every year. At a time when Westerns were extremely popular, the poll results meant millions to the studios. Every year between 1937 and 1941, the Mesquiteer series—not the stars, but the series itself—was voted among the most popular.

In 1938 Livingston wanted a break after 29 *Mesquiteer* films. His replacement was contract player John Wayne.

His first film in the series would be 1938's *Pals of the Saddle*. He would appear in eight *Mesquiteers* movies during his year or so at Republic.

His only film with Carole was her first Republic film, *Three Texas Steers*, filmed between March 17 and March 31. Wayne (Stoney Burke), Corrigan (Tucson Smith) and Max Terhune (Lullaby Joslin) live next to a ranch that's been in the family of circus owner Nancy Evans (Carole) for generations. Her nasty business manager wants her to sell because he knows the state is planning to build a dam on the site, making the land worth millions. So he burns her circus to force her to mortgage the land.

Predictably, the *Mesquiteers* manage to save both the ranch and her circus when Terhune drives one of Carole's circus horses to a surprise victory in a rich trotter race. Carole is beautiful though miscast as a circus owner, and handles her role with charm. Her athleticism is evident throughout the hour-long film as she rides horses and throws herself around the set. The film was released on May 12 to strong reviews.[24]

Carole's next Republic film was *Daredevils of the Red Circle*, which began filming barely a week after the completion of *Three Texas Steers*. Filming was done near Rincon in San Diego County and Sea Cliff out in Ventura, and ran from March 28 through the end of April. *Daredevils* was a typical 12-part Republic serial. Its entire $126,118 budget was dwarfed by the budgets of single films at other studios.

The plot was straightforward. Escaped criminal Harry Crowel (Charles Middleton) takes his revenge on the man who put him in prison, Horace Granville (Miles Mander), by trying to destroy all of his various business holdings. Carole is the lead as Granville relative Blanche.

When Crowel targets an amusement park owned by Granville, he comes up against an unlikely group of heroes: the Daredevils of the Red Circle, athletes (Charles Quigley, Bruce Bennett and David Sharpe) who perform dangerous stunts for the park crowds. As the episodes play out full of action and carnage, dozens of innocent townsfolk die as Crowel is seemingly able to replenish his bandit horde at will. Crowell even kidnaps Granville and (wearing a mask) replaces him before Carole helps the Daredevils thwart the plot. *Daredevils* is known as one of the best serials ever made. The first episode of *Daredevils* was released on June 10, 1939, less than a month after the final day of filming.

Around this same time, Carole was finally able to legally shed Irving Wheeler. When she arrived at L.A. Superior Court with her attorneys Greg Bautzer and G. Bentley Ryan on May 10—after the requisite two-month waiting period—she was far from the schoolgirl Wheeler married. She appeared for all the world a movie star; she wore a fur jacket, black velvet dress and fuchsia accessories.

In court, Landis told Superior Judge Thomas C. Gould about her annulled first marriage to Wheeler and their subsequent 25-day second union. She testified that Wheeler stayed out all night, that he screamed at her constantly and that he eventually abandoned her.

She testified about their long estrangement: they had hardly seen each other in a year and a half, a convenient half-truth, since they may have seen each other at Warners. Though Wheeler thought that she was worth $250,000 when he sued Busby Berkeley, Wheeler didn't contest the action and Carole was granted an uncontested interlocutory decree of divorce. It would be her first. Of four.

As far back as San Francisco, Carole wore her wedding ring although she told people she was single. "To keep the wolves at bay," she liked to say. She would eventually take to wearing her wedding bands on her thumb, first one, then two, finally four, a personal reminder "never to marry again." But even with her ring like a bow tied around a finger as a reminder of something, she never seemed to remember. Kenny Morgan was already asking her to marry him!

But at least she was doing bigger and better roles: In August, Shurr negotiated a contract with a bigger and better studio for Carole. She would leave Republic and sign with Hal Roach Studios on August 25. It was clearly a step up from the Republic operation to the established Roach Studio. She had to fulfill the rest of her Republic contract, which required a loan-out to RKO Studios for a small role in the Western *Reno* and one more Mesquiteers film.

She would film *Reno* first, at the RKO lot. The movie was a better-than-average B production that actually featured a pretty strong cast, led by Richard Dix as a Nevada mining town divorce lawyer and Gail Patrick as his wife. Anita Louise co-starred as the female protagonist. The movie was filmed between late August and late September, and released on December 1. Carole joined the cast on September 10, playing one of Dix's divorce clients, "Mrs. Humphrey."

At the time, the movie Production Code prohibited the studios from portraying divorce in a positive light, so all of the female characters are greedy and unhappy women looking for revenge. Most also stereotypically try to bed the married lawyer. Carole's small role was little more than her flirting with Dix during a short visit to his law office. The film was pretty forgettable, actually.

After *Reno,* she went directly to the set of *The Cowboys from Texas,* another Mesquiteer movie and her final commitment to Republic. While she was away, John Wayne had exited the series and Livingston had returned to the Stoney Burke role. Carole barely missed any time away from her new studio (Roach) since the filming only ran from October 10 to October 18. Carole plays June Junes, the female lead. Smaller roles were filled by the likes of Raymond Hatton, Ivan Miller, Betty Compson, and Yakima Canutt.

Cowboys is typical *Mesquiteers* fare; during a Texas land rush, badman Clay Allison (Miller) wants the homesteaders' land and with his gang goes about terrorizing the locals until they are ultimately stopped by the boys. Carole is gorgeous as Allison's main target. The film was released on November 29.

Four * Hollywood Comes with a Reputation

Her Republic and loan-out commitments now complete, Carole turned her attention to her new studio in late September. Hal Roach Studios was founded by Hal Roach, Sr., who after only two years as an extra decided to make his own movies in 1914. Using a small inheritance, he hired as his first actor Harold Lloyd, filming and directing the star himself. By the 1920s Roach's studio was one of the most successful in Hollywood. The list of Roach's studio successes is mind-boggling: the *Our Gang* and Laurel & Hardy series (both Roach's idea), Charley Chase, Will Rogers and dozens of others.

By the mid–1930s, comedy series had become fiscally undesirable with the advent of double features. Instead of the long-standing program of one or two shorts and a feature, moviegoers, particularly post–Depression moviegoers, wanted two features. Hence the birth of the double feature. By the late 1930s Roach had expended his offerings with the likes of *Topper* (1937) and *Of Mice and Men* (1939). *One Million B.C.* would be among the studio's newer-style offerings.

It was Shurr's suggestion that led Hal Roach, Jr., look at Carole. Roach suggested that she be tested for an upcoming role in a film set in prehistoric times. Entitled *One Million B.C.*, the movie was to be principally directed by Roach's father Hal, Sr., Hal, Jr., and (allegedly) the legendary D.W. Griffith. The film, though improbable in plot, would be a star vehicle.

Roach had been having a difficult time casting the lead female — Loana — who had to be equal parts beautiful, athletic and sexual. She also had to have a good figure, because her one and only costume was an animal-skin sarong. When Shurr arranged for Carole to meet Roach, she wore a tiny beach coverall. Given the inequities of their positions in 1939 Hollywood, approaching such a respected studio head in such a way was a bold move. But Roach had no problem recognizing her physical attributes.

As part of his *B.C.* casting call, Roach sent the actresses — there were upwards of 25 "finalists" — for a private meeting with Griffith. Carole was terrified; she was meeting a legend. D.W. Griffith was truly one of the groundbreaking filmmakers in the medium's history. Many credit him with inventing modern filmmaking. He directed over 500 films between 1908 and 1941. He wrote another 250 and produced 100 more. He and his cameraman George W. ("Billy") Bitzer also developed new camera techniques and filming innovations still in use today. It was the Griffith-Bitzer team that first used flashback, the iris (opening and closing the lens) shot, the mask and others.

He was also unparalleled at developing talent. At Biograph Studios he discovered almost all of the screen's earliest stars, among them Florence Lawrence, Mary Pickford, the Gish sisters, Mae Marsh, Robert Harron and Henry B. Walthall. He also gave a young Canadian pipe-fitter named Mack Sennett his first jobs as both an actor and as a director.

But Griffith did not adapt well to sound. His first sound film was *Abraham Lincoln*, filmed in 1930, a full three years after the first talkie. It was one of his last films. By 1931, he was forced to retire. Not a single studio in Hollywood would hire him, even in minor directorial positions. Bitter with an industry he felt had abandoned him, Griffith retreated to his tiny stucco bungalow at 201 South Peck Drive in the distinctly unglamourous streets south of Wilshire Boulevard. He spent his days walking the sidewalks and visiting the neighborhood taverns, drunk most of the time.

Roach, Sr., directed his son to pull Griffith out of the Wilshire Blvd. bars in 1939 with an offer to help direct *One Million B.C.* His strongest qualification for the job was that Roach, Sr., felt sorry for him.

But Carole would not know that as she approached her appointment. All she knew was that it was D.W. Griffith. Walking into his little house on South Peck, she was terrified. It was, after all, *D.W. Griffith*! He obviously enjoyed the audition process, which he ran in a kind of test structure. First, he gave her a pantomime scene, leaving the room to giving her time to think it over and come up with something. When he returned and began to direct Carole, she dutifully reacted to every command. They ran through some lines, and it was over.

Leaving, Carole thought that Griffith had seemed pleased with her work. The next morning, Shurr called to tell her that Griffith wanted to make a screen test of her. Griffith was clearly enjoying being back in the process and his series of tests lasted from August through October 1939. The good news was that actresses were paid for this type of ongoing screen-testing. The Roaches were a tad annoyed at Griffith's extended processes, but glumly allowed the one-time giant his whims.

After being called back dozens of times for screen tests, line readings, costume fittings, more pantomime sessions and just to talk, Carole was given the role. Hal Roach remembered,

> One day [Griffith] said, "I found your girl." It was Carole Landis. "Come out. I want to show you something." We went out on the back lot where there was street scenery and, on the corner, a telephone post. He looked at the girl and said, "Take your shoes off. Now run to that post as fast as you can. Then run back to me as fast as you can." She did. I wasn't particularly impressed. That's a hell of a way to pick our leading lady. We know she can run. He said, "I've had fifty girls run to that post and back. She's the only one who knows how to run. You're not going to make a believable girl in a picture of that kind who runs like an average girl. She's got to run like an athlete, a deer." And she could. Her rhythm was really beautiful. In the picture, you never noticed it. But if she ran like most girls, you would damn well have seen the difference.[25]

On October 20, on Griffith's recommendation, Roach gave Carole her first real lead role in a major film because she could run fast. But she didn't care. She had the lead in a major film. Griffith was correct; Carole's athleticism would be a great benefit to the film. For most of the actors in this film, there would be no dialogue at all, just running, climbing rocks, gesturing and grunting. Hollywood legend has Griffith directing numerous segments of the film, but the reality is that after original casting, he had virtually no participation in the project.

The male lead was to be played by Victor Mature, recently signed by Roach to a big contract at $250 a week as the studio's next male star. Four writers—Mickell Novak, George Baker, Joseph Frickert and Grover Jones—went to work on a screenplay designed to keep him in front of the cameras as much as they could. The film would be a Victor Mature showpiece. But as usual, Carole would steal the show.

Mature grew up the son of an Italian knife sharpener in Louisville, Kentucky, and ended up in California performing at the well-known Pasadena Playhouse. It was there that Roach found the outdoorsy actor and signed him to a contract during the summer of 1939. Mature was still a Kentucky boy at heart, and in fact lived in a tent next to a small river in the San Fernando Valley. At first he refused Roach's demand that he move into more suitable lodging, as he had also refused to change his name.

Roach made a deal with him: Keep your name but move out of the tent. Since he wouldn't look for a house on his own, Roach moved him into one being shared by Jules Seltzer, a Roach press agent, and two fan magazine editors, Carl Schroeder and Walt Ramsay. Mature had his own live-in publicity staff.

As *One Million* began filming on October 16, Carole and Kenny Morgan's relationship was reaching a crossroads. Within months of meeting Carole, Morgan began talking of marriage. By June, the rumors

Carole, already an acclaimed beauty, in her breakout role in 1940's *One Million B.C.*

were in the papers. Erskine Johnson's column noted that "Carole Landis and Kenny Morgan are planning an early marriage" as early as June![26]

But this time it was Carole who uncharacteristically put the brakes on the relationship. When Morgan's pressure to marry became too strong, she broke off the relationship in October.[27] Not surprisingly, there was another man waiting in the wings to take his place, another man who had only recently met her but was captivated none the less. Hal Roach, Jr., had only met Carole during the audition process and was barely 21 years old, just like her. They hit it off immediately and, as filming began, so did their relationship.

Within a week of the start of filming, newspapers were noticing Carole and her new escort. Before the official newspaper "funeral" of the Morgan relationship, Carole and Roach were seen at a Steffi Dunn opening at La Conga Café.[28] The next night, Jimmy Starr noted that after "arriving late at La Conga, Hal Roach, Jr., and Carole Landis made their own music."[29] By December the two were a well-known Hollywood couple. Writer Ed Sullivan confirmed the breakup with Morgan, noting that "Carole Landis, the shapely, and Hal Roach, Jr., carrying on since her bust-up with Kenny Morgan."[30]

Most of *One Million B.C.*'s exteriors were filmed in the Valley of Fire in Overton,

Another view of Carole in *One Million B.C.,* with young co-star Mary Gale Fisher.

Nevada, just northwest of Lake Mead. It could be an uncomfortable set; even in November, it was still in the nineties every day. Other exteriors were filmed at the Vasquez Rocks area of Aqua Dulce, northwest of Hollywood. Roach, Sr., was the first unit director, and Jr. the second unit director.

It was a typical Hal Roach set. According to Mature, "At ten of one every day … Hal Roach would turn to his assistant director and say, 'I don't want to miss the second race at Santa Anita. You direct this afternoon.'" Roach never let go of the *laissez faire* filming attitudes that were the hallmark of the earliest years of filming, even as the movies got more technical.

The film was to be a showcase for Roach's new star Mature. Like Carole, he spent the entire movie wearing animal skins and loincloths. Almost 6'3" tall, with a 205-pound body literally chiseled in muscle, he played Tumak, the leader of a tribe known as the Rock People. The plot seems almost laughable today. After fighting for a piece of meat, Tumak tumbles over a cliff and somehow gets tossed from a tree into a river by a mammoth. He floats into the land of the Shell People and meets the beautiful Loana (Carole).

As they inevitably fall in love — somehow communicating their names among the grunting and groaning—Tumak teaches the Shell People some fascinating survival skills. First, he shows that by shaking a tree, fruit will fall down. He also saves the village from a man in a dinosaur suit. But even with all his good deeds he gets thrown out of the Shell camp for fighting and heads back up the hills to his Rock people. Loana, of course, goes with him.

During their trip, they encounter any number of photographically enlarged "dinosaurs," including a slurpasaurus, which was actually an iguana with obviously false fins glued to its back. They watch a giant mongoose eat an equally giant snake, and get chased up a tree by a huge armadillo. Arriving back at the Rock People camp, Tumak and Loana manage to foster peace within the group. After surviving a final volcano-induced dinosaur stampede, Tumak and Loana—and a recently added orphan Rock child—end up together, tied up in a perfect prehistoric love story bow.

From the fall through the film's release, stories and photograph spreads on the movie ran in every film magazine, from *Pic* and *Pictureplay* to *Hollywood* and *Photoplay*. Fans loved the movie, but critics were at a loss for what to think. Was it camp? Comedy? Serious science fiction? Roach never clearly indicated what he was trying to accomplish, seemingly waiting for the public reaction to tell *him* what kind of movie it was. Most legitimate critics good-naturedly ribbed the film. *The New York Times* labeled it a "bargain counter excursion into paleontology."

The *Hollywood Citizen News* asked Roach what he was doing, noting that "Roach ... fails to indicate for whose entertainment *One Million B.C.* was especially intended ... junior fans ... or adult customers...." The writer also described the film as "virtually plotless and dialogless."[31]

Other Los Angeles newspapers were more forgiving, though it's difficult to understand why. The *Hollywood Preview* noted that the film offered "one of the most terrifying, electrifying storms the screen has known ... [with] rivers of burning lava and to add to the horror an earthquake opens wide gaps in the earth, into which giant animals and humans go to their death."[32] But reviewers were consistent in their praise of both Mature and Carole, who was described as "ideal for the role."

It's hard to fault critics who poked fun at the film. It is indeed hard to figure this film out, Roach's obvious indecision aside. In any case, there were ridiculous problems and contradictions with the film work. Carole's hair is always perfect, even as she and Mature spend most of a day and night hiding up in a tree. And she never gets dirty. Mature is always clean-shaven while every other male has a beard.

Additionally, technical problems abounded. Roach imported hundreds of expensive flowering plants from Australia and New Zealand but they withered and died in the lights within hours, so expensive—but obviously fake—rubber reproductions were made.[33]

Roy Seabright and Frank Young actually *glued* fins on various crocodiles, lizards, and iguanas and then photographically enlarged them for the screen. They filmed numerous lizards fighting each other in brutal fights to the death. After one such fight, real blood can be seen pouring out of the neck of the (real-life) losing lizard as Tumak (Mature) walks by. The obviously cruel treatment of the creatures in the film inspired the American Society for the Prevention of Cruelty to Animals to permanently ban almost everything that was done for the film. But the scenes would be recycled in dozens of later *Tarzan* films and B pictures like *Untamed Women* (1952), *King Dinosaur* (1955) and *Valley of the Dragons* (1961).

Carole always had her tomboy side and it was in evidence during the *Million* filming. Among the "extras" in the film was a 15-foot-long Burmese python name "Pete" who was trained to slither menacingly down around a tree trunk toward Carole and co-star Mature, who were sitting in a prehistoric treehouse. Mature was terrified of the python, which took a dozen takes to slither down the limb and poke its huge head into the tiny space occupied by the two stars.

Carole was nonplussed as the snake slowly crawled toward her and, as it got within inches of her face, even flicked its long tongue angrily at her cheek. At that point, Mature — per the script — seized the animal and thrust him away, visibly shuddering as director Roach yelled "*Cut!*" Mature hated filming the scene, but Carole said, "It wasn't so bad after all. I've never really been afraid of snakes anyway. But the kiss was more than I bargained for."[34]

Carole knew that spending two hours on screen dressed in skimpy animal skins would do nothing to dispel her reputation as just a pretty face and body. The role of Loana was a double-edged sword for her; it would make her famous, but would probably further stereotype her. Writer Donald Hough of the *Los Angeles Times* visited the set and all he saw was Carole. He wrote, "She was dressed in a leopard skin ... blond and pretty and looks nice in almost anything." These were the types of compliments that only made it tougher for Carole to be taken seriously.

In an interview after the film's release, she gamely told writer Virginia Vale, "I'm studying English, French and Italian, and I've studied voice for years. I sang with orchestras before I entered motion pictures. Honestly, I can do a few other things besides wearing a skimpy fur costume. This picture is a lot of fun and I'm tickled that I got the part. But after it's over I want people to sort of forget that I was the girl in the animal skins."[35]

The movie's main attractions in 1940 were the special effects and Carole. Still today, those are the only two reasons to watch the film. The special effects because they seem so campy, and Carole because she, as usual, steals every scene. It was a recurring theme: Carole overwhelms the supposedly bigger star of her film with her beauty and talent. She had done it before. This time she stole the picture from Mature, for whom the role was designed as his Roach Studios "coming out party."

Her performance and clear talent convinced Roach to restructure her contract during filming. Her tendency to outshine her co-stars was part of the reason that she never got the real plum starring roles that less talented and perhaps more demure bombshells like Rita Hayworth and Rhonda Fleming were given. Here it was rising star Victor Mature. Just after filming ended, she was given a bigger and longer — now seven-year — contract with Roach.

Carole agreed to attend the studio's premiere of their movie *Of Mice and Men* on December 21.[36] Even though Roach, Sr., wanted her for his studio for another seven years the relationship with Roach, Jr., was starting to fall apart. Carole was unable to avoid relationships. She was enchanting and almost universally desired, so the opportunities were endless.

Problematic for her was her apparent inability to say "no." All of her bosses coveted her, and she ended up somehow — by coercion or choice — sleeping with them. Some of the "boss" relationships, like Roach, were relatively normal. Some, like Darryl Zanuck, were simply sexual for one or both. Still some, like Berkeley, were a strange hybrid of the two. Most should never have been allowed to even start.

When the Roach relationship began to crumble, Pat DiCicco — a friend of Roach — turned his sights on Carole. Pasquale DiCicco was a sometime agent who came to Hollywood when Charles "Lucky" Luciano arrived in Los Angeles to take over the drug trade in 1929. DiCicco had no movie clients of any substance but had ties to both the Chicago and New York mobs and was also involved in bookmaking and gambling. He was also cousin to Albert Broccoli and an heir to the fortune that came from the family's development of the food. He was a handsome playboy with a violent temper.

DiCicco was the front man for Luciano's invasion of Los Angeles in 1929. Within weeks, the bullet-riddled bodies of local drug dealers unwilling to join the new team started showing up on sidewalks and alleys all over Los Angeles County. Within a month, Luciano "owned" Los Angeles, including the police and the District Attorney's office.

In 1932 DiCicco married Thelma Todd, an actress very similar to Carole: feisty, independent and loved by all. After the marriage ended in 1934 amid beatings by DiCicco, he introduced Todd to his boss, also known as "Charlie Lucifer." Luciano pursued Todd aggressively. When Todd approached a corrupt district attorney about Lucky's dealings in late 1935, she was unaware that Luciano had the office in his pocket. She was found dead a week later.[37] DiCicco probably helped arranged the murder.

Just two years before he began dating Carole, DiCicco, his cousin Broccoli and Wallace Beery beat comedian Ted Healy to death outside the Trocadero restaurant. The murder was covered up by Eddie Mannix and Howard Strickling, the MGM "fixers." Broccoli and his wife were given jobs at MGM (he would later produce the James Bond movies under the name "Cubby"), Beery was sent out of the country for six months, and DiCicco left for New York. He returned shortly before he was introduced to Carole. The two dated for several months in late 1939 and early 1940.

DiCicco obviously had a violent temper, and had a reputation for beating the women in his life. Coincidently, in the middle of her relationship with DiCicco, Carole spent a week in the hospital to have a nose reconstruction. It was reported in the tabloids on January 15 that she had just been released from a hospital after having "plastic surgery on her nose." But interestingly, photographs of Carole from 1939 and later in 1940 show no even noticeable change in her nose structure.

It seems that Carole's need for nose surgery was not cosmetic; it was more likely due to a beating administered by DiCicco. If the nose work had been cosmetic, it would have taken longer and had a more visible result than was seen when she reappeared in public just three days after leaving the hospital (incredibly, with DiCicco). If it was medical, for instance to repair damage from a beating, the results would be more in line with what was evident.

When that question was posed to Hollywood correspondent Col. Barney Oldfield just before his death, he told this writer, "I had heard something about her being beaten up, but nobody ever knew who did it."[38] The coincidental timing of the medical care and the end of her relationship with DiCicco would indicate that it was him. Just after her hospital stay, Carole ended the relationship with DiCicco. It was a tough way for Carole to start a new year.

The relationship with DiCicco was an example of the bad judgment that Carole often showed. Certainly inexperienced, but Carole still should have known better than to have her name linked to DiCicco in Hollywood. No fans outside of Hollywood would have thought anything of a beautiful movie star dating a handsome "agent," but within movie circles the couple would have been easy grist for rumor.

Everyone knew that DiCicco was a gangster, was involved in one way or another with Thelma Todd's murder, and it was rumored that he was among the men that murdered Healy. To accept a date, let alone endure even a short — albeit tumultuous — relationship, played right into the hands of the people that were continuing their verbal assaults on her character. One can almost *hear* the studio wives saying, "See. I told you. Look at her."

Carole made bad decisions that hurt her image — like dating someone like DiCicco — even on smaller levels. Giving a later (1943) interview to Sidney Skolsky, she gave him a tour of her beach-front house. As she led the writer through her gorgeously appointed and tastefully decorated bedroom, she told him that she always slept in the nude. Unless she was sleeping with someone, when she wore sheer nightgowns, usually trimmed in black lace. She also told him that her dreams were "something Freud would love to analyze."[39]

The column should have and could have been a nice bit of positive publicity for Carole, but her off-the-cuff and unnecessary embellishments lessened the positive impact. This was the kind of self-destructive behavior that haunted Carole her whole life.

★ Five ★

The Edge of Stardom

Carole began 1940 by attempting a make-over with the goal of a more glamourous image. She felt that she had too much of the "girl from Wisconsin" and not enough sex appeal. She was the only one who felt that way, but she went on a diet and lost 15 pounds, dyed her hair blonde, at the same time she endured the January nose surgery. This was all part of the contradiction that *was* Carole Landis. Arguably one of the most beautiful women in Hollywood, she was still insecure enough to think that blonde hair would make her more attractive. But to whom?

After dumping DiCicco, Carole repeated her usual practice of almost furiously dating after the end of a relationship. In February and March she was photographed at different times with a dozen different men. Clearly, many of the photographs were staged by her studios, but many were not. The roll call of names and locales is like an honor roll of Hollywood partying during the 1930s and 1940s. During those few months Carole was photographed at Ciro's with Ed Gardner, at a movie premiere with Kenny Morgan, did the rumba at La Conga with Harry Seymour, was at Sardi's with Dave Sigal, danced to Guy Lombardo with Harry Crocker at the Ambassador, attended a fashion show with Harry Seymour and was at the Trocadero with Myron Kirk. That doesn't include the variety of other appearances where her date was not identified!

On February 1, 1940, Carole drove her sister Dorothy Ross, who lived in Long Beach, to the hospital to give birth to her daughter. It must have been disheartening for Carole to watch her sister have the child that Carole longed to have. She would play the doting aunt, showering gifts on the little girl.

As Carole's career slowly inched upward, she became more and more used to the price she would have to pay. She had already had her personal life splashed all over the tabloids and newspapers, had already begun dealing with a reputation she probably didn't fully deserve, and was fighting for legitimacy as an actress. In early January 1940, she learned about stalkers.

A 30-year-old chauffeur named Stanley Campbell mailed Carole an obscenity-laced tirade. It disturbed Landis enough to call the police. They investigated Campbell, discovering that he had already served two years in prison on a morals charge.

There were no stalking laws in 1940, and since no direct physical threat had been made against Carole it looked as if nothing could be done. But when she personally appealed to a young assistant district attorney to do *something*, Campbell was charged in Federal Court with misusing the mails. As a judge read the disturbing letter, Campbell blurted out that when he saw magazine pictures of Landis it "did something to him." Federal Judge Ralph E. Jenney was sufficiently worried that, on February 28, Campbell received a three-year term in federal prison for harassing Carole.[1]

As Campbell was heading to Folsom Prison, Carole began filming *Turnabout* for Roach on February 19. It would be a challenging role for her. *Turnabout* was based on a novel by Thorne Smith, who also wrote the *Topper* movies. Carole's role meant playing a man opposite John Hubbard as a woman. Hal Roach produced and directed the film, which was adapted for the screen by writers Mickell Novak, Berne Giler and John McClain.

Carole plays the wife of advertising executive Hubbard. Both are bored with their respective roles and dream of trading places. The opportunity comes when they both mutter angry complaints about their lives near a wish-granting statue named "Renavent," an Indian god resembling Buddha that stands in their bedroom. When they wake up the next morning they discover their personalities, voices and mannerisms have changed bodies. She is now in his role and he in hers. The situation comedy gets complicated when he, as she, becomes pregnant. Also appearing in the film were Adolphe Menjou, William Gargan and Mary Astor.

The film would not make its official premiere until mid–May, but was previewed at Grauman's Chinese Theater on April 30. Some of the critics were lukewarm, but most loved the movie. *Screen Guide* described it as "the funniest idea ever filmed."[2] In every theater, audiences howled at the film, laughing at Roach's bizarre situations. (Such a sex-change was a radical idea in 1940; critics called the idea "startling."[3]) They especially loved Carole.

She was absolutely marvelous playing the difficult role of a 1940's chauvinist male who realizes he/she is pregnant. She was able to mimic Hubbard's every mannerism and

Carole and co-star John Hubbard in 1940's *Turnabout*.

voice inflection, and portray a man perfectly. It was an incredible performance in a minor comedy. Unfortunately, fans also loved her because she spent a good deal of the film in pajamas. Reviewer James Francis Crowe describe the film and Carole: "The whole production is handsomely mounted, and plentifully peopled by pretty and provocative girls, of whom the prettiest and most provocative is Carole Landis herself, the feminine lead." The film was extremely successful for Roach and the studio.

The Roach-inspired twist at the end of the film — the statue relents and switches the duo's personalities back to their original bodies — also created quite a stir. The statue realizes too late that it has made a mistake — the husband is still going to have the baby. It was almost too bizarre for 1940 audiences to handle.

When Carole exited her limousine in front of Grauman Theater's famous Forecourt of the Stars, she had an escort who had already been introduced to the photographers and reporters flanking the red carpet. Just a week earlier, Willis Hunt and Carole had been photographed together at the Coconut Grove watching the dance team of Fay and Gordon.[4]

The 28-year-old Hunt was a wealthy member of Southern California society circles who told people he sold yachts for a living. He lived in a richly appointed apartment in the impressive art deco Sunset Towers Apartments at 8358 Sunset Boulevard in Hollywood. During the 1930s and '40s, the Towers were home to dozens of members of Hollywood's "A-list," including Errol Flynn, John Wayne, director Howard Hawks, studio head Joe Schenck and mobster "Bugsy" Siegel, who owned the penthouse. Hunt was known by all of his neighbors for his raucous and well-attended parties.

Some researchers believe that Carole lived at the Towers in mid- to late 1939 and met Hunt during that time, but this has never been confirmed. She spent most of 1939 living in a bungalow at 1130 South Clark Street in Hollywood. The confusion may have come because the Sunset Towers are at the base of Sunset Plaza Drive. Carole had an apartment on Sunset Plaza later in 1943. There is probably confusion because she spent so much time at Hunt's apartment while they dated and briefly after they were married.

At the time she met Hunt, she had just spent two months searching for her first home. After looking throughout Hollywood and Brentwood, she purchased the first home she ever owned herself, at 1816 Prosser Street near Culver City. The typical Southern California bungalow was just a block below Santa Monica Boulevard in a quiet neighborhood just minutes from the studios.

Hunt, a daredevil, loved speed. He was so well-connected politically and with the Los Angeles Police Department that he often spent his weekends filling in for Hollywood motorcycle cops. He was a common sight flying over the curving streets in the Hollywood Hills, dressed in his policeman's uniform, complete with gun and handcuffs. He even pulled drivers over and handed out tickets.

Hunt and Carole seemed an incongruous match. He, the wild, wealthy playboy who loved speed and parties. She, the fun-loving but far-from-wild actress who liked to read, decorate her houses, play tennis and relax outside. Her parties were also quite a bit more reserved; she had only recently purchased her little Prosser Street bungalow. But she was captivated by the adventurous Hunt, spending time with him cruising around Beverly Hills in his Lincoln Continental convertible. Carole loved convertibles, and had purchased a 1939 Cadillac version just six months earlier.

Hunt was also a pilot, and Carole also enjoyed spending time with his flier friends who flew out of nearby Baker's Field. Baker's was used as a fighter pilot training center by the Royal Air Force. The R.A.F. maintained a fleet of six two-seater AT-6 fighter planes and an equal number of instructors to train American pilots who had volunteered to fly for Britain during the "Battle of Britain," before American entered the war.

One of Hunt's best friends was Major Howard W. Hively, known as "The Deacon," and as wild as Hunt. The Carole, Hunt and Hively threesome was almost inseparable. They spent nearly every weekend together, partying at Hunt's apartment, cruising in Hunt's Lincoln or partying at the Mocambo or the Trocadero.

The R.A.F. AT-6 trainers had no markings on the outside of the aircraft, so there was no way for authorities to identify them, particularly at night. The Baker's Field group — including Hunt — had a deserved reputation for taking advantage of that benefit. People up and down the California coast often saw flights of five or six AT-6s cruising up and down the coast at night. What they didn't see was that the rear seat usually held a young girl in an evening dress being flown to some distant date location by a young R.A.F. pilot.

Whenever they returned from one of their night flights, the pilots invariably buzzed their favorite bar, The Ritz, located in a building next to the control tower. They flew right at it, buzzing the buxom pianist, Millie, a favorite of the men. Carole later took flying instruction from pilot Hively.

For reasons known only to her, when Hunt asked her to marry him just two weeks after the met, she said "yes." By May 4, she was photographed with Hunt "wearing his diamond."[5] Perhaps she had was motivated after attending a party with Hunt just a few days prior at the home of her producer and former boyfriend Hal Roach.

Roach gathered a large group of cast members, crew and movie folk to celebrate the success of Carole's film *Turnabout*. It must have been an interesting gathering. Carole had previously dated Roach, who was at the time of the party dating Hunt's ex-wife, socialite Alva Consuelo Brewer. "Dolly" Brewer grew up in a mansion at 414 North McCadden in Hancock Park,[6] the only daughter of an oil millionaire. She and Hunt had been married just a year when they divorced in 1939. Just three weeks after the party, on May 27, Roach and Dolly would get married.

Another reason might be found in a short notice in the June tabloids. Jimmy Fidler noted on June 6, 1940, that "Carole Landis wants her mother to live elsewhere, but she likes Hollywood."[7] She was no doubt tired of supporting her mother and sharing the Clark Street bungalow with her, and did not want to move into her new Prosser Street house with her. Also, Clara had begun to set herself up as Carole's self-described aide-de-camp and assistant, a fact that certainly riled Carole.

We don't know why she married Willis Hunt. Whether she was trying to escape her mother (yet again) or was feeling bad about losing Roach to Dolly Brewer, she was again marrying someone with little prospect of helping her, or even making her happy. At the same time she announced her engagement, Carole threw herself back into filming: Her next effort, *Mystery Sea Raider*, was to start in late May. Roach loaned her out to Paramount to do the film, but she got some good news when Roach rewarded Carole for her successes at the studio by renewing and increasing her contract on May 29.

While Carole was at Paramount, Roach and his publicity director Frank Seltzer decided to bestow yet another nickname on Landis. Since the late 1920s and doe-eyed Clara Bow's nomination as "The It Girl," studios believed that their starlets needed nicknames. There were hundreds of post–Bow monikers. Warner Bros. dubbed Ann Sheridan "The Oomph Girl" after an offhand comment by writer Walter Winchell. Perhaps the worst was Paramount's dedication of young actress Jean Phillips as "The Woodie Girl."

Carole had earlier been dubbed "The Sweater Girl" and "The Pin-Up Girl" (names years later conferred on Lana Turner and Betty Grable) so it's hard to understand why Roach and Seltzer would publicize her as "The Ping Girl" other than to embarrass her. In 1940's Hollywood, the word "ping" was a slang reference to a male erection. There were more snickers from the studio wives club.

But Roach knew Carole's personality well; he had to know that she would respond negatively to such a derogatory name. This was surely a Roach ploy to punish Carole for breaking off their relationship just a month or so earlier. To make matters worse, Roach had become romantically involved with socialite Hunt. Her ex was getting ready to marry Carole.[8] So Hal decided to make Carole's life miserable for a while.

With Landis away on loan-out, Seltzer sent a press release announcing her as Hollywood's new "Ping Girl" and planned a gala reception to present Carole with her new nickname. Hundreds of Hollywood news correspondents received a handsomely engraved invitation to a reception "in honor of Miss Landis tomorrow at Ciro's, Movieland's most fashionable supper club … on her selection as America's Ping Girl…." For no good reason, Seltzer's press agents added that she was the "Ping Girl" "because she makes you purr."

Carole was furious, and shocked Roach when she refused to have anything to do with the nickname at all. She would not accept the name and she would not attend any receptions, "gala" or otherwise, to publicize it. Nor would she speak to the press about the nonsensical name.

She then herself paid for advertising space in all of the trade papers—from *The Hollywood Reporter* to *Variety*—very clearly announcing that she was most definitely *not* "The Ping Girl." She denounced the nickname and said

> I have just learned and with great dismay that invitations have been extended. The plan is an obvious attempt to publicize my role in *Turnabout* and while I know that many things are endured in the name of publicity, this mental blitzkrieg carries things a little too far.
>
> I was never consulted about the scheme, nor do I approve the appellation they would like to inflict upon me. For these reasons I will not be present at my own reception to ping, purr, or even coo.[9]

Roach and Seltzer were left with 100 prepaid dinners at Ciro's and a dozen cases of Scotch. On top of that, Carole would speak to nobody at the studio. In addition to her newspaper advertisements, she sent letters to the 100 largest newspapers in the U.S. Her letter was a plea.

> This is the lament of a fugitive from a leg art career. I want a fair chance to prove myself something more than a curvaceous cutie. I want to get out of bathing suits and into something more substantial. Unfortunately, the publicity department of my studio does not agree. They have conceived the brilliant idea of selling me to the public as "the Ping Girl — because she makes you purr." This flash of genius is to be illustrated with a series of pictures out of their files, suggestive of anything but acting talent.
>
> I haven't any legal redress. There isn't, I am advised, any way to stop the publicity department. Therefore I am asking you to help me nip the scheme in the right place — in the pages of your newspapers.

She concluded the letter by asking that editors refrain from publishing anything referring to "The Ping Girl," and asked them to please "consign all bathing suit photographs of her to the waste basket."[10] Most writers ignored the nickname but not columnist Robbin Coons, who wrote, "Carole Landis, the 'Ping — she makes you purr — Girl' may live that down but she still looks like Loretta Young when she puts on a brunette wig. Ping Landis has more oomph that Oomph Sheridan or IT Bow, but not as much as Mary Martin."[11] Martin was the waifish star of the stage version of *Peter Pan*.

Carole standing up to the studios was a huge gamble. No actress at her level had ever told the studio "no" to anything. Although newspapers described her as "having her picture taken in bathing suits perhaps more than any other actress," they noted that she had "shattered a Hollywood precedent and left the high-powered publicists at Hal Roach Studios biting their fingernails."[12]

But the "Ping" episode not only showed Carole's feistiness and independence. It also showcased her intelligence. Never able to shed the image of a vapid blonde, Carole was actually extremely intelligent and well-read. The advertisements and the letters to the newspapers were written not by studio publicists, but by Carole herself.

Unfortunately, her loud and vocal protest resulted in another round of nationwide publicity, making it appear as if it were all a publicity stunt. A June 17, 1940, *Life* magazine article mentioned that it was "fully aware that Actress Landis and Publicity Director Frank Seltzer have thus pulled out of the dustbin one of the hoariest of publicity gags." Some writers incorrectly thought that the entire affair was planned by Roach and Landis, which was patently false. Again, Carole would not get credit that she deserved, and again outside influences would even further diminish her message and legitimacy.

The fact was that the studio did not care about her "Ping" protest one way or the other. To them, any publicity was good publicity. As one writer put it, "it was all ink." But a large bathing suit manufacturer did care. Since November 1939, Calcraft Knitting Mills contracted Carole to model its bathing suits and appear in their advertisements. They were indignant that, in her well-publicized letter to the newspapers, she said she wished to "get out of bathing suits and into something more substantial."

According to a lawsuit filed in Superior Court on June 11, if Carole "wanted to maintain her attitude of dignity which precludes her from posing for photographs in scanty attire," she would have to pay them $50,000. The company's lawsuit also asked for damages from Carole, and an injunction to prohibit her from any further attempts to "influence newspaper editors" not to use the hundreds of her cheesecake photographs floating around. A good percentage of those photographs featured Carole in Calcraft bathing suits.

The Calcraft suit was another example of Carole's personality winning the day. At a meeting between Carole, her attorneys and the Calcraft representatives, she was able to simply tell them she didn't mean to harm Calcraft and would do anything she could to make it up to them. She *loved* their product, and would certainly continue to work for them. Calcraft dropped their lawsuit.

The "Ping" episode would eventually fade away but it died a slow death. Months later (January 1941) *American Magazine* would dredge up the "Ping" story that had been mostly forgotten. They did however note that Carole had been "dubbed by columnists from coast to coast as Hollywood's top glamour girl, with the most gorgeous figure in moviedom, a distinction she said she hates."[13] I tend to believe that she really did hate the image, although it got her everything she had, bad and good.

Carole was winning these outside battles but clearly losing the war to earn respect as an actress. In her last three films, she was chased by badly faked prehistoric monsters in *One Million B.C.* and supposed to climb a flagpole at the top of a building in *Turnabout*.

In *Topper Returns*, she was asked to stand almost directly beneath a 250-pound chandelier rigged to fall next to her. Since the chandelier cost the equivalent of about $20,000, only one take was allowed, so it had to be set up to fall almost on top of her. The light fixture grazed her arm as it crashed to the floor. Her image as a beautiful body doing physical comedy was overtaking any ability to be accepted as a serious actress.

Part of Carole's difficulty was her looks and her body. From her earliest days in Hollywood — indeed, from her teenage years when she was fully developed at 13 — Carole's body was the subject of discussion, innumerable comments, jokes and conjecture.

During the 1940s her chest measurements were somewhere between 37" and 38", and her hips 35". She was also tall for an actress in the 1940s, listed in various studio forms as 5'5½" or 5'5¾". Most of the popular actress were two or three inches shorter; the silent screen stars were all barely 5' tall.

Columnist Sidney Skolsky noted in 1945 that "her chest measurement is 36½ inches and that's without taking a deep breath ... she fills more of a sweater, naturally, than any actress in town."[14] Erskine Johnson noted that "a dress designer confided to us that Carole Landis measures 38 inches around the bust and 35 around the hips." He ended his note with the amusing, "No comment."[15] Even the usually dry Ed Sullivan offered an interesting Carole comment in his gossip column: "Why rave about the performance of Luise Rainer in *The Good Earth* ... why not rave about the performance of Carole Landis in her (most recent) publicity still?"[16]

Carole's body would actually become grist for movie dialogue. William Wellman's 1945 film *The Story of G.I. Joe* is often described as the most realistic view of the drudgery and discomfort of G.I. life during World War II. In this story of writer-cartoonist Ernie Pyle's travels with the 18th Infantry across North Africa, Wellman cast Burgess Meredith (one of Carole's best friends) and Robert Mitchum in the lead roles, but filled the infantrymen's roles with actual veterans of the unit. During one brief scene, one of the G.I.s asks Pyle (Meredith) about Carole. The answers to his questions, each beginning with phrases like "Does she really..." or "Are they really..." are obscured by loud explosions. Pyle's answers are non-committal. It is doubtful that Carole would ever truly escape the image that her own body offered. So she just kept working. Her next project would be *Mystery Sea Raider.*

Originally entitled *Mystery Ship*, the movie may have been the best technically made film Carole ever worked in. It was one of the first films directed by Edward Dmytryk, who spent most of the 1930s as a film editor before turning to direction. He became one of the finest directors during the 1940s, earning an Academy Award nomination for *Crossfire* (1947). But the long-time political activist was one of the "Hollywood Ten" who refused to cooperate with the HUAC. His career was ruined and he spent six months in jail before bowing to Committee pressure to "name names." His experience as a film editor made him a wonderful technical director, always getting the most out of every scene.

Dmytryk and cameramen Harry Fischbeck and Dewey Wrigley were noted by critics as "the best part of the picture," but the movie itself was something of a mess due to an unbelievable plot and uneven writing. Carole received top billing, starring as June McCarthy, who somehow becomes involved with a Nazi naval officer (Onslow Stevens) searching for a supply ship for a group of German submarines. She also accidentally helps him acquire a ship from her fiancé (Henry Wilcoxon) that becomes the "mystery ship" and she is kidnapped and brought along by Stevens. But good wins out when Carole figures out how to use life preserver flares to alert companion ships and end the damage caused by the mystery ship.

The gloomy and misty sets take away from Carole's beauty, but cannot completely hide it. She carries off a role written without much depth, stuck inside a poor plot, with her natural talent. Somehow, her beauty shines through all the darkness and water. Critics noted that she "was the motivating character of the story"[17] although she didn't "have much to do."[18] The highlight for fans and writers was "the curvaceous Carole Landis [doing] a swimming scene ... believe it or not ... in a full-length evening gown."[19]

It was not an easy shoot, but Carole never complained. For almost two weeks she was forced to spend between four and eight hours every day in the cold water tank at Paramount. When reporters asked her if it bothered her, she told them, "Not at all. I had ten years of cold showers before we lived in a house with hot water, so I'm used to it."[20]

On the morning of July 4, just after filming wrapped on *Raider*, Carole and Hunt chartered a Paul Mantz plane and told reporters they were "running away to get married." As they boarded the plane at the Union Air Terminal at Burbank Airport, they asked pilot Bob Perlick for speed and headed to Las Vegas.

Five ✳ The Edge of Stardom

Their engagement had taken everyone in Hollywood by surprise; the marriage turned surprise to shock. Nobody expected the two to marry so quickly. From the time she broke up with Roach in November 1939, to the first sighting of Hunt in April 1940, Carole had been linked with or seen publicly with no fewer than a dozen other men.

Even so, just after they arrived in Las Vegas on the evening of July 4, Carole and Hunt were married by Justice of the Peace George E. Marshall in the Nevada Gretna Green Hotel. Pilot Perlick and a deputy county clerk were the only witnesses. Some newspapers reported Hunt to be a "stock broker ... prominent in Los Angeles society."[21] *Time* magazine described him as a "yacht broker" and her as a "cinemactress."[22] Most of the stories also noted that Hunt's ex-wife Dolly had only recently married Carole's ex-boyfriend Roach.

The couple stayed in Las Vegas only for the rest of the night, flying back in Perlick's plane early the next morning. Arriving in Burbank, they were met by a horde of reporters. They confirmed that they had gotten married and that they had told none of their friends. Hunt added, "It was all so sudden, we had no time to make honeymoon plans."[23] That evening, the couple went to the La Conga Club to see singer and dancer Chiquita rather than spend the time alone at home.

There would be no honeymoon, since just four days later Carole embarked on a month-long personal appearance tour promoting *Turnabout* and *Raider*, which would open on August 5. These publicity tours were grueling and were a job requirement, but they not only had to attend press meetings and showings of their own films but those of other fellow studio stars as well.

On August 17 the tour was in Denver and Carole had to attend the premiere of the film *Kit Carson* though she had not appeared in the film. In addition to the actors in that film — Jon Hall, Lynn Bari, Ward Bond and Dana Andrews— Carole was also forced to attend with Mature, Anita Louise, Fay Wray, Simone Simon and Jack LaRue.[24]

When *Raider* opened during her tour, she hadn't seen her new husband since July 8. Hunt had been extremely displeased when she left, throwing a major tantrum. It would be the first of many during their short relationship.

During the tour, Carole unhappily saw evidence that her Ping mutiny had effectively done nothing. Seemingly everywhere she went, theater marquees displayed PING in big letters in lights, theater ads filled copy with it, and mobs of college boys around stage doors yelled at her, "What's Ping?" When she was forced to answer the question, she would reply, "I looked up the definition of 'ping.' Do you know what it means? According to the dictionary, it means 'the sound made by rifle bullet as it cuts the air!'" Unfortunately, that was not the definition that anyone remembered.

After the *Turnabout*–*Sea Raider* publicity tour, Carole returned to Los Angeles and Hunt, and then went to work filming *Road Show* on her home lot. *Road Show* was pretty typical Hal Roach screwball comedy fare. Carole plays Penguin Moore, the owner of a traveling carnival who befriends two escapees from an insane asylum. One is a millionaire (John Hubbard) who accidentally ended up in the asylum after feigning insanity to avoid marrying a gold digger. The other is glib-talking eccentric Col. Carleton Carroway (Adolphe Menjou). The two hitch a ride with Carole's carnival.

A night out with husband Willis Hunt and Carole's mother Clara, 1940.

The plot is predictable, with authorities—and the gold digger's family—chasing the men as they hide out among Carole's carnival sideshow performers. Among them is Patsy Kelly, playing an Indian medicine woman being pursued by a Harpo Marx–like Indian (George E. Stone). The supporting cast included Charles Butterworth, Florence Bates, Polly Ann Young and Edward Norris.

Road Show fails to deliver on what should have been a promising and funny premise. After its February 6, 1941, premiere at the Warners Hollywood Theater, reviewers charitably described the end result as "light-hearted and rollicking merriment"[25] and "an amusing comedy"[26] but even with a talent-laden cast and any number of interesting situations within the carnival milieu, the film failed to deliver. It was just an average comedy when it should have been sensational.

Carole and Menjou offered standout performances and were regularly singled out for praise in reviews. She also offered a beautiful song, singing Hoagy Carmichael's "I Should Have Known You Long Ago" in a shower cap. Somehow she still looked beautiful. According to the *Film Daily* reviewer, the combination of the song and Carole was "bull's eye stuff."[27]

Road Show was a chance to showcase her silky contralto voice but Carole was serious about wanting more as an actress. She spent many of her days off at movie matinees watching women she thought of as "real actresses." When she worked at Warners with Bette Davis, she routinely snuck onto her sets so she could watch her work and learn from her.

During filming, Carole was lucky to escape serious injury when she was struck on the head with a vase. Unbeknownst to her, the prop man neglected to replace the real ceramic vase with a studio break-away version and she was knocked unconscious. But she gamely finished shooting that day, sitting between takes with an ice bag on her head.[28] The film features the accidental version, which explains the noticeable realism of the shot.

She also met a woman who would become one of her closest friends on the *Road Show* set. The two shared a coincidental history: They both knew Pat DiCicco. Patsy Kelly was a masculine-looking character actress who had been in Hollywood since 1933 working for Hal Roach. In 1933 she replaced Zasu Pitts in a comedy serial alongside Thelma Todd. The Todd-Pitts series had been enormously successful for Roach, but Pitts demanded a huge raise and a percentage of the films and he fired her and replaced her with Kelly. Kelly and Todd made 21 films together from September 1933 to December 1935. They were as popular as the earlier Pitts versions.

Kelly's last film with Todd was the William Terhune–directed *Top Flat*, which was filmed during the first week of December 1935. On December 16, just a few days after filming wrapped, Todd was beaten to death by associates of her boyfriend Charles "Lucky" Luciano. Todd's ex-husband Pat DiCicco was widely thought to have been involved in her murder. Roach rushed the *Top Flat* release up to December 21, two days after Todd's funeral.[29]

Kelly knew that DiCicco often beat Todd during their marriage, that he allowed Luciano to get Todd hooked on drugs and then had her killed, and no doubt knew DiCicco arranged the murder. She also knew about Carole's aborted relationship with DiCicco, and of Carole's phantom "nose job." The two became fast friends. They would appear in only one more film together (Carole's next, *Topper Returns*) but remained friends for the rest of Carole's life.

Back at home with Hunt, Carole tried to make a home of the little Prosser Street bungalow. She tried to be a good wife, pampering her new husband—fixing his drinks, rubbing his back (even though her own was sore from a difficult *Road Show* filming; she spent days on a high-wire) and even lighting his cigarettes. But it was all for naught as Hunt grew more and more combative, rebelling against her career, her success and her fame. He was little more than a spoiled, insecure, unsuccessful boy from a rich family.

Less than two months into their marriage, he became verbally—and reportedly physically—abusive. After a particularly vicious September 4 fight, Carole simply walked out of the house and into the seclusion of the Beverly Wilshire Hotel. As she got into her car, he screamed at her, "You're a damn fool, like everybody else in motion pictures."[30]

She left Hunt at her 1816 Prosser Street bungalow. Friends called Roach and told him that she would not be able to work for a few weeks. On September 18, she came out of seclusion with her attorney Greg Bautzer and filed suit for divorce in Superior Court, charging Hunt with extreme mental cruelty. She stated in her complaint that "Hunt objected to her film career."[31] The filing continued, "Such conduct on Hunt's part came about without any provocation on her part and caused her so much embarrassment and humiliation that it became impossible for her to continue marital life."[32]

At the time the divorce was in process, Carole was featured in a newspaper article describing the failures of three high-profile marriages. Under a headline TRIO OF HOLLYWOOD ROMANCES BROKEN, DECIDE ON PARTING, the John Barrymore–Elaine Barrie, Gene Markey–Hedy Lamarr and Carole–Hunt splits were autopsied for the world to see. For her part, Carole told the writer that it hadn't taken her anywhere near the full 60 days the marriage lasted to realize she should divorce Hunt, and that it took "exceptional forbearance" just to make the 60.[33]

At the same time, an article appeared in the September issue of *Screen Guide* magazine that had been prepared some months before. Entitled "Saturday Date with a Starlet," the story detailed a typical Saturday evening with Carole, with several photographs of her attending a party with Hunt.[34]

After an absence of a few days, she quietly returned to the set and finished *Road Show*. Roach had shot some scenes around her, but still her absence had thrown the studio schedules into disarray. Because of that, she would have to start her next film, *Topper Returns*, without her customary break.

What little time off Carole had between her divorce announcement and working on *Topper* was spent on a promotional tour of the East Coast with Ken Murray. On September 26 she flew into Cleveland to meet up with the group and continued with them for stops in Akron, Indianapolis, and on October 4, Chicago.

When she was back in Los Angeles she seemed intent upon making a point to Hunt, as she was out almost every night. It would become a routine that Carole would follow after every failed relationship. It had occurred first just after she and Busby Berkeley went their separate ways. Whenever a relationship ended, even an obviously poor one like the ill-fated marriage to Hunt, Carole dated almost obsessively for several months. It seemed like she did not want to be alone; wanted and needed the reassurance that she was still desired by men.

This obsessive need for acceptance, or proof of her own desirability or beauty, seems to be insecurity as its worst. Within a week of Bautzer's original divorce announcement, Carole was spending intimate evenings with Ken Murray during their publicity tour of the Midwest.

Her excessive dating often involved overlapping boyfriends. During October she got quite serious with actor Franchot Tone. They attended the October 15 premiere of Chaplin's *The Great Dictator*[35] as a couple and then were photographed at Ciro's twice in early November.[36] Between those dates, Tone and his pal Spencer Tracy hosted a large birthday party for Carole's close friend Burgess Meredith which Carole attended. Unfortunately, in typical drunken Tracy fashion, he had forgotten to invite Meredith!

In between those appearances with Tone she dated MGM art director Cedric Gibbons and young agent Bentley Ryan. Carole's power dating typically lasted about two or three months post-breakup. In a typically unfounded opinion, Hedda Hopper accused Carole of divorcing Hunt because she knew that she got more press when she was dating than when she was married.[37]

After her return from the Midwest publicity trip, Carole went to work on *Topper Returns*, which began filming on November 4. The film continued a series begun with 1937's *Topper* and the 1939 follow-up *Topper Takes a Trip*. The films starred

Ca. 1940.

Roland Young as Cosmo Topper, a stuffy bank president who has an affinity for coming upon ghosts, and Billie Burke as his fluttery spouse Clara.

In *Topper Returns*, the latest phantom to torment poor Cosmo is the lovely and sexy ghost Gail Richards (played by Joan Blondell). Accidentally murdered while visiting wealthy friend Ann Carrington (Carole), who was supposed to be killed instead, she enlists Cosmo to find her murderer. It's fairly typical madcap comedy fare but funny even by today's sophisticated standards. The cast also included Patsy Kelly and Eddie "Rochester" Anderson.

On November 14, in the middle of the *Topper* shoot, Carole received a request from the family of child actress Mary Gale Fisher. Four-year-old Fisher had appeared as an orphan cave child in Carole's *One Million B.C.*, and the two had become attached to one another. The child adored Carole.

During the fall, the unfortunate child contracted a virulent form of pneumonia and lay near death in a hospital some hours from Hollywood, asking to see Carole. When her mother left a message at the studio switchboard asking if Carole would come see the child, Carole had shooting shut down for two days so she could go visit her young friend.[38]

A week later, on November 20, Carole returned to the Superior Court to sign her final divorce decree. Surprisingly, Landis wept as she told the judge that the breakup had caused her to suffer a nervous breakdown.[39]

She looked every bit the tortured and aggrieved wife but every bit the movie star as well, wearing a black dress and veil along with a three-quarter length silver fox fur jacket. For months after their divorce though, Hunt appeared regularly trying to get Carole back. She ignored his entreaties. After the divorce, she wrapped *Topper Returns*, and finally had some time off. *Topper Returns* premiered on April 23, 1941, at Loew's State Theater and Grauman's Chinese Theater in Hollywood.

As 1940 was about to end, she found herself single and alone yet again. But she had a new studio, and a big raise. Just before Christmas, Carole was hired by Darryl F. Zanuck and 20th Century–Fox Studios. The deal was allegedly instigated and driven by Zanuck himself, probably for personal reasons.

But whatever the reason for her hiring, she received a new seven-year deal, but this time she was guaranteed $400 a week (perhaps $10,000 today) with annual raises that would top out at over $2,000 weekly by the seventh year. Carole was thrilled with the opportunity to work at a new studio. After the business details were worked out between Zanuck and Roach, Carole was expected to go to work for Fox just after the holidays, in January 1941.

Heading into the new year after divorcing Hunt, in the middle of a brief hiatus from filming after *Topper Returns,* and armed with a new high-paying contract, Carole continued her dating and social whirlwind. She dumped Tone in December, and during the next two or three months was linked at different times with Gene Markey, Ivan Goff, Cedric Gibbons, Phil Armidon, Eddie Norris (who also gave her flying lessons), Conrad Nagel, Tim Durant and Robert Stack. She was rumored to have been dating Charlie Chaplin after the two were seen together having dinner.[40]

At the same time, Carole went looking for a new house. She did not want to return to her lovely little Prosser Street bungalow in Culver City. It must have been disappointing though. She had spent months finding the place, the first home she actually owned herself, and now it was gone. Hunt stayed there after the divorce, and she had no interest in returning, so did not fight him for the house.

Not wanting to stay in her hotel digs any longer either, in January 1941, she set about looking for another house. After much searching she found a lovely mansion at 12424 Sunset Boulevard. The ten-room colonial style house was hidden amid tall trees, behind large gates and stone fences covered with bougainvillea. It had bars on all the windows, courtesy of the previous owner, and was as secluded a place as could be found on Sunset Boulevard. It was also in the heart of a movie star neighborhood.

Five * The Edge of Stardom   77

Zanuck on the deck of his yacht, ca. late 1930s, at the time that he was becoming one of the most powerful men in Hollywood.

Dozens of the most famous stars in the movies lived nearby around Bristol Avenue neighborhood on the other side of Sunset, and just to the south the Brentwood Country Club area. Director Clarence Brown lived next door on Sunset and Francis Langford and Jon Hall a few houses further down.

She rented the house from Edna May Oliver and moved in late in January. Oliver was an early Broadway and silent film actress who appeared in the classic films *Little Women* (1933), *Romeo and Juliet* (1936) and *Drums Along the Mohawk* (1939) for which she received Academy Award nomination for her supporting role. Oliver was heading to New York to do a play when she rented it to Carole.

Unfortunately, mother Clara moved in with her, but Carole did her best to ignore her and set about redecorating the dark mansion. She filled the library with her collection of classic books—works like Storyville Henderson's *The Failure of a Mission,* Will Durant's *The Life of Greece* and Elizabeth Russells' *Mr. Skeffington.* Included in her collection was a housewarming gift from Ernest Hemingway, a complete set of autographed books.[41]

Her shelves were also filled with hundreds of music albums. Almost all of them were classical, her favorites being Debussy and Sibelius. The same month she moved in, she began taking piano lessons.[42] She was serious about it; as her teacher she hired Jacques Rachmilovich, the renowned conductor of orchestras around the world. In

Carole in her Sunset Boulevard house, 1942.

California he conducted the Los Angeles Philharmonic and founded the Santa Monica Symphony Orchestra.

Carole's tastes were much more bookish than any of her fans and most of her friends would have guessed. Only her close friends knew of her varied interests.

Carole enjoyed the privacy of the Oliver house and the quiet relaxation offered

Five ✭ *The Edge of Stardom*

At the pool at the Sunset Boulevard house, 1942.

by the backyard swimming pool. When she wasn't filming, she spent her afternoons in the backyard reading and swimming. Carole described the house in a tour offered to the readers of *Silver Screen Magazine* that ran in June 1941. It was noted that, "Carole Landis, whose film career has been going up by leaps and bounds, has rented the house formerly owned, and lived in, by Edna May Oliver. She definitely gives it a 'something' that Edna May never gave it. When someone commented on the bars on all the windows, Miss Landis said, 'I didn't put them there. I like people coming in. Miss Oliver put them there.'"[43]

The first month she lived there she had a bombproof shelter dug under the cellar. It was reportedly large enough for eight people.[44] The installation of such a refuge is a good indication of the level of "war fear" surrounding the United States even before December 7. At the same time, papers reported that child star Deanna Durbin had also installed a similar facility underneath her nearby Brentwood house.[45]

Carole's new neighbors were not thrilled to have a movie star living in the neighborhood. Just a few weeks after she moved in, she had to hire lawyers to fight a Brentwood ordinance limiting homeowners to keeping three dogs. Carole had four — her Great Dane Donner, a German shepherd, a small poodle and a spaniel — and her neighbors tried to force her out. But she spent thousands of dollars in legal fees so she wouldn't have to get rid of any of her beloved pets.[46]

Carole's favorite dog was Donner, who rarely left her side when she was at home. Donner had been a gift from old boyfriend Gene Markey, and she was virtually inconsolable when the dog died on May 12, 1942, just after she returned from her first Camp Tour. *Motion Picture* magazine featured an article about Donner entitled "My Dog Is Dead."[47] Just a week after Donner's death, she was walking down a sidewalk in the San Fernando Valley and saw a cocker spaniel puppy peering out at her from inside a pet store window. Predictably, she brought the dog home.

She also indulged her hobbies of photography and flying. She had a fully operational darkroom installed in her cellar, similar to the rooms at the studio. Studio film technicians were used to finding Carole working on her own inside the workplace darkrooms. She was quite a talented photographer. She also snuck over to Baker's Field to continue her flying lessons with ex-husband Hunt's old flying pals, but that was kept secret from the studio.

Carole's one extravagance was clothes. She spent liberally on clothes, particularly hats and shoes. If she was having a bad day, her solution was to go shopping. January was spent getting used to her new house, and the casting competition for a film that she really wanted: a movie about Belle Starr, a female version of Jesse James, being made at her new studio. The film would be directed by Irving Cummings, an interesting choice since his specialty was the flamboyant musicals for which Fox was known. Randolph Scott and Dana Andrews would co-star.

Carole was among the many name stars considered for the role, which would seem to fit Carole's personality perfectly. Myra Belle Shirley was born in 1848 in Carthage, Missouri. Her father was a wealthy hotel owner and her mother Elizabeth Hatfield was descended from the Hatfield side of the famous Hatfield–McCoy feud in Kentucky. She was very bright, attended private schools and excelled at a variety of pursuits including Latin, Hebrew, mathematics and music.

After her family moved to Texas and her brother was killed by Union troops in the Civil War, she began spying for the Confederacy. Her closest childhood friends were Cole Younger and his three brothers, who joined Frank and Jesse James after the war robbing banks, stagecoaches, and wealthy farmers and cattlemen. They used Belle's family home in Sycene, Texas, as a hideout.

In the late 1860s, Belle and her husband Jim Reed fell in with the Starr clan, a notorious Cherokee family roaming Oklahoma and stealing cattle, whiskey and guns. Jim and Belle broke off on their own and in 1873 robbed a wealthy Creek Indian farmer of $30,000 (about $750,000 today) in gold coins. By then she had taken to dressing like a man in buckskins and moccasins topped with a man's Stetson hat, or in black velvet skirts, high-topped boots and twin holstered pistols. She spent her evenings in Texas saloons and often charged through towns on horseback firing her pistols into the air.

Reed was killed during an 1874 robbery so Belle married one of the Starr sons, Samuel, in 1880. She had a reputation for paying bribes of cash or sex to obtain freedom for her fellow gang members. For the most part her celebrity reputation kept her out of prison. President Grover Cleveland was even enamored of her exploits, pardoning her son and overturning a seven-year prison sentence.

Just short of her forty-first birthday, Belle was murdered outside a general store

Carole, ca. 1939–40.

near her home in Eufaula, Oklahoma, killed by a shotgun blast to the back. Her killer was never found and she was buried on her ranch. Starr's fascinating life would seem to have been a perfect match for Carole. Writers agreed, weighing in during the casting which took place in early 1941. Paul Harrison noted for the role of "she-bandit Belle Starr ... life outside the law will look much more attractive when such a role is played by oomphy Carole Landis."[48] Jimmy Fidler noted that "although Alice Faye was slated for the lead, producers wanted Carole."[49]

The role went to Gene Tierney. Carole was extremely disappointed. She would have been a much better choice than Tierney, who was horribly miscast, and unable to fake a passable accent. Randolph Scott — who did not want to do the movie at all — and Dana Andrews also both acted poorly in the film. It was awful.

Instead of the true story of the real Belle, writer Niven Busch offered a watered-down tale of a Southern family losing their land to northerners and forced to become outlaws. *Belle Starr* was little more than a blatant attempt by Zanuck at a ripoff of *Gone with the Wind*. What should have been a good story about an interesting woman turned into a horribly staged imitation of a different film. Cummings even cast a black woman as a maid named "Mammie." The film was a bomb at the box office. Who knows how it would have fared with Carole as Belle?

Carole had a bit more power at Fox and was able to flex her muscles somewhat in terms of roles she took or avoided. It was reported in several of the trade papers that she was offered a romantic lead in a musical entitled *Sis Hopkins*— and a $10,000 bonus— but turned it down.[50] She was probably holding out for the Belle Starr role at the time.

Carole's post-divorce maelstrom of dating continued from the fall of 1940 into 1941 and she begins spending more time with Gibbons. He was an interesting choice. He had just divorced his wife of a decade, the beautiful Dolores del Rio, and was 48 years old to Carole's 21. Every few days, Carole and Gibbons' names could be found in the tabloids. On January 20, Louella Parsons noted that "Carole Landis, who does get around if I do say so, is now concentrating on Cedric Gibbons."[51]

Her new studio was not pleased with the press that their new star was getting, and they let her know it. The May–December nature of the relationship with Gibbons was a problem as much as the volume of dates. On January 10, Kenny Morgan's gossip column noted that fans should "look for our two 'energetic' youngsters, Lana Turner and Carole Landis, to become strictly the home type."[52] At the time, Turner was rebelling against what she thought were her childish roles. *Photoplay* magazine had earlier offered advice to an unnamed "blonde starlet," warning "against any more silly or hasty marriages. One more such step and she's out."[53]

Carole arrived on the Fox lot the second week of January 1941, after all of the negotiations between Roach and Zanuck were completed. During her first few days at Fox, Carole was Carole. She spent two or three days walking the halls of the Administration Building dressed in blue jeans and a sweater just walking into offices and introducing herself.[54]

As an employee of 20th Century–Fox, Carole's reputation would now be merged with that of her new boss, Darryl Zanuck. Within just a few months at Fox, Carole would be known as "Darryl Zanuck's mistress." The description may or may not have been accurate, but there was certainly a ring of truth to the stories.

Five ★ The Edge of Stardom

Zanuck walks the Fox back lot during the time of his affairs with Carole Landis in the early 1940s. (Photograph purchased from the Darryl F. Zanuck Estate.)

Zanuck was a product of his childhood. His father was an alcoholic night clerk in a tiny hotel in equally tiny Wahoo, Nebraska, a nothing town 60 miles west of Omaha. His mother was the promiscuous daughter of the hotel's owner. By the time he was a teenager, both parents had abandoned him, so at 15 he enlisted in the Army and by 16 was an infantryman fighting in the World War I battlefields of Belgium.

He was thought to be barely literate, leaving school at 12, but he still always fancied himself a writer. So when he returned after the War, he headed for Hollywood and found a small apartment on Gardner Street. He dreamt up scenarios for Mack Sennett, Sydney Chaplin and Carl Laemmle before joining Warners in 1920.

Zanuck and his daughter Susan.

As young writers for Warners, he and his partner Jerry Wald were thought of less as writers than men whose minds "bubbled with story ideas ... torn from front pages or borrowed from cocktail-party shoptalk or twists of ideas already sold. Hungry and without shame...."[55] Zanuck ground out unimpressive scripts until he got lucky with an idea for a series of police-dog movies. Although most of his contemporaries believed that it was anothr partner, Malcolm St. Clair, who was the real idea man, Zanuck always took the credit for *Rin Tin Tin*. The success of the series led to his promotion to head of production in 1925. He was only 23.

With financial backing from Louis B. Mayer and Joe Schenck, Zanuck left Warners and formed Twentieth Century Pictures in 1933, two years later taking over the bankrupt studio Fox Pictures. Initially he was Vice-President in charge of production. Never without his foot-long Cuban cigar, he lorded over every aspect of his studio's production, putting out classic films like *The Grapes of Wrath* (1940), *How Green Was My Valley* (1941) and *Twelve O'Clock High* (1949).

He was known as the most "hands-on" of the studio bosses, and that characteristic was no better evidenced than his treatment of the women who worked for him. And often under him. According to Maurice Rapf, Zanuck was a "pig ... he slept with every one of his stars ... one every day."[56]

Carole, at her loveliest in the early 1940s. It was easy to see why Darryl Zanuck found her so attractive.

Zanuck's first reaction to a woman was always to size her up physically. Often before he even said hello, a comment was made about something physical. When he was introduced to talented teenaged black singer Dorothy Dandridge in 1941, he looked her head to toe, said, "You're very pretty," and walked away.[57]

Producer Milton Sperling was quoted in the Steven Farber–Marc Green book *Hollywood Dynasties*: "As with so many other moguls, extramarital encounters were practically a daily ritual with Zanuck. Headquarters would close down every afternoon between 4:00 and 4:30. That was Zanuck's playtime. He had a constant stream of women eager to award their favors because he had so many favors to give in return."

Many of Zanuck's guests were "option girls" on shorter contracts who had even less power than Carole. Biographer Alexander Walker described these women as being put "on the payroll, put into parts that kept them busy—but not too busy ... until age or a change in the studio management caused them to 'retire' ... given moderate attention by the publicity department, which usually advertised in a softer, more generalized way the same attributes that had made them welcome on an executive's office couch."

According to Sperling and dozens of Zanuck contemporaries, employees and the women themselves, every single day at four some beautiful young girl on the lot was led into his office like a Christian to the lions. The door was locked. Once the young girl was in his office, Zanuck simply turned away, and when he turned back around to face her, his penis was exposed.

The first time Carole was called in, the ink on her new contract was probably not even dry. It was early in 1941. In a Zanuck biography, wrote, "It was usually a starlet who was chosen for this daily assignment, and it was rarely the same one twice. The only girl who ever seems to have been called in more than once was a Fox contract feature player named Carol (sic) Landis, who was casually referred to by Sperling as 'the studio hooker.' Otherwise, any pretty extra was picked for the daily session."[58]

Sperling is undoubtedly accurate in most of his descriptions; there is no doubt that Carole was indeed called into Zanuck's office regularly. But she was clearly not the "only girl who ever seems to have been called in more than once." Sperling is hardly an objective source; one of his closest friends was Lilli Palmer, wife of Rex Harrison, the man who would ultimately drive Carole to suicide. Sperling worked with Palmer on several films he produced just before Carole's death, and according to a 1948 Louella Parsons column, "Lilli Palmer and Rex Harrison arrive tomorrow on the Queen Elizabeth II. Lilli is to accept an award on behalf of Milton Sperling from *Parents Magazine* for *My Girl Tisa*, as the 'outstanding family picture for February.'"[59] His friendship with Harrison and Palmer makes everything suspect; to be viewed in the context of that quite clear agenda.

In any case, the fact that Zanuck found Carole so attractive that he repeatedly requested her presence was the ultimate back-handed compliment. Unfortunately, she was quickly branded as "Zanuck's mistress," the "studio hooker," or worse. Sadly, there was nothing she could do about it. Few actresses could refuse Zanuck's request (demand). Only major stars could do so, even though Zanuck did his best to include them on his list as well, often with comic results.

When he invited Betty Grable in one afternoon, he turned around and asked her if she thought his exposed penis "was beautiful." Grable laughed at him and said, "Yes, Darryl, it is. You can put it away now." But this episode took place when she was a major star and could say "no" if she wished. Early in her employment for Zanuck, she was not as disagreeable.

Corinne Calvet, a Paramount player on loan-out to Fox for *What Price Glory* (1952), described her encounter in her autobiography *Has Corinne Been a Good Girl?* Once the door was locked, "Dramatically, he turned on his heels and stood a few feet away from me with his erect penis standing out of his unzipped pants," offering to take her to "Palm Springs for a weekend of sunny sex play." She simply laughed and walked out, convinced that he was just a flasher. Since she didn't actually work for him, she had the luxury of declining his offer. Most did not.

Carole clearly had no choice when she was called in by Zanuck. Her career was just starting to gain momentum and she had only recently signed a contract with Fox — a contract that Zanuck could cancel at any time for any reason. Effectively, her only options were sex with the boss or lose her job. It is very likely and probably true that Carole surrendered to Zanuck's repeated demands for sex. The fact that she had no choice did nothing to stop the rumors from gaining momentum.

At Fox, Carole was forever branded with a scarlet "M," for "mistress," and for using her body to get ahead. Sadly, Landis was prohibited from becoming the star that she could easily have become had she not been painted with the brush of promiscuity. Other, more successful actresses, envious of her public persona outside of the studios, which was impeccable, were guilty of fueling the rumors about her.

In a later tabloid column, Jimmy Fidler described a "naughty dancing Carole Landis" and her date Woolworth Donohue leaving Mocambo Café customers with their "eyebrows merging with their hairlines."[60] No doubt enjoying the moment, she would typically be unaware or uncaring about what was "showing." She was comfortable with her body, and with the public perception that her attitude amplified. She once said, "The first time I wore a bare midriff gown, Hollywood noticed me."[61]

Unfortunately it was *that* perception, innocent or not, that would eventually stifle Landis' career and take her life. Not from the public. The fans accepted almost anything from their stars and Landis went out of her way to endear herself to them. Not for publicity. She was indeed a genuinely nice person and did not need to be publicly "nice."

But the "studio wives" had every reason to be fearful of Carole and efficiently ensured that the San Francisco rumors along with the probably true stories about Berkeley and Zanuck were kept alive. The wives were afraid of Carole. She was well-liked. She also had an independent streak that they lacked, a bravery they would never have, and the ability to ignore the rumors. At least publicly.

The press agents, and Carole herself, attributed her high profile to the work of the publicity department. And the public loved her, scaring the wives even more. Director H. Bruce Humberstone, who worked with Carole on *I Wake Up Screaming*, said of her, "She had an energy that the camera picked up and transmitted to an audience." Female fans loved her personality. Men loved her shape. And the wives hated her.

Rex Harrison, who would later pursue Carole with tragic results, described the work of the wives in his autobiography, noting that "those were the days of the drawing rooms of Beverly Hills and Bel Air, the wealthy 'Hollywood ranchers' and the so-called ladies, none of whom considered Carole a lady."[62] Writer John Austin described the wives as "those 'ladies' of Hollywood were attending social events, afternoon teas at the Riviera Country Club, volunteering a few hours a week at the U.S.O. in Hollywood, all the while bemoaning the fact that they couldn't find any good servants ... Japanese domestics had been interned."[63]

Austin, who knew Carole well after meeting her during one of her English U.S.O. visits and liked her, continued on this subject, describing how the wives worked:

> [T]he wives spreading these rumors had followed the same road to stardom, or into those drawing rooms, or ranch houses as the wives of executives or actors they were accusing Carole of following. Hypocrisy at its Hollywood worst. They were also

jealous of Carole's popularity with the press, the crews and with fellow actors. They were envious that Carole could tell a good joke, often on herself.... It was these women who had used their influence with their husbands—the movers and shakers of the industry—to wind down Carole's career. That drawing-room crowd forever prevented Carole from becoming the great star she could have been under different circumstances. She was the right girl at the wrong time and was well aware of those rumors and accusations and that she could not overcome them. To have denied them publicly would have made it worse. They were well aware of this and capitalized on it—to Carole's detriment.[64]

Carole took the high road and never publicly addressed the rumors, knowing full well the activities going on behind her back. She even took jabs at herself, telling *Silver Screen Magazine* writer Kay Proctor, "I'm a fire-eating, bomb-throwing regular old rip-snorter, ready to trade punches with man, woman or beast." But Proctor found when she interviewed her co-workers that if you "talk to prop men, electricians, carpenters and directors ... to hairdressers and dressmakers[:] 'Landis?' they say. 'She's an angel!'"[65] Later, as her career would begin to stall due to Zanuck's machinations, Carole would become terrifically depressed about the stories and the callous mistreatment. But for now she just lived with it.

It is interesting to note that Carole was not the only actress about whom such rumors were spread. The same things were said about Linda Darnell, Maria Montez, Simone Simon, Gene Tierney, Loretta Young and the soon-to-be royalty (although virtually amoral) Grace Kelly. When Dorothy Dandridge became a Zanuck protégé in the 1950s, she was said to be one of his regular afternoon guests.

In these cases, the stories were undoubtedly true as well, and probably more true than those told about Carole. Also interestingly, the typical victim of these rumors were all from backgrounds similar to Carole's. Darnell was one of five children of a female postal clerk raising the family alone. Like Carole, at 12 she was modeling and lying about her age. It was said at the studio about her that "she didn't usually even know who was on top of her." Simon was an illegitimate child who handed out gold keys to her bedroom to the men she slept with. Editor Mary Loos said of her, "She looked like a peach blossom, and everybody knew what a tramp she was." For her part, Simon said, "If you do not do as they say, they treat you like dirt. They try to break your spirit."

Frances Farmer, said to have been victimized by producer Howard Clurman, ended up lost in the California mental health system, suffering years of electro-shock treatments that she did not need, as well as repeated sodomization by brutal asylum guards. Betty Hutton, allegedly forced onto the couch of producer B.G. DeSylva, disappeared into drug and alcohol addiction until someone later stumbled upon her working as a hostess at a jai alai fronton. The almost surreally beautiful Veronica Lake, immortalized in the film *L.A. Confidential*, was passed from couch to couch by producers William Dozier, Raymond Hakim and his brother Robert. She died forgotten, of hepatitis, at only 53.

In every case where an actress stood up to the studios, they were branded as "rebellious" or "difficult" or "hard to work with." The reality was that they just didn't want to be raped any longer. Zanuck tried to have Carole labeled with similar monikers, but was unable to effectively do so because everyone outside of the circle of wives and executives knew the truth. So he responded the only way he could, by giving her lousy roles.

Forgotten in all of the Carole-bashing was a little-recognized fact that also led to problems for her: She was more talented than all of the actresses and some actors that were among the bashers. And her beauty was un-matched by any of them.

A recurring theme in her career was Carole's ability to play a supporting role and make it look bigger than the star's. She out-played Betty Grable in *Moon Over Miami* and *I Wake Up Screaming*, Victor Mature in *One Million B.C.*, even Rita Hayworth in *My Gal Sal*. Even so, she repeatedly lost plum starring roles to lesser talents like Hayworth, Rhonda Fleming and Gene Tierney. And the rumors never, ever went away. Even after she was dead.

Zanuck during a visit to the New York offices in the late 1940s.

Even given the developing rumors, it's difficult to validate the studio treatment of Carole. She was apparently keeping Zanuck happy in whatever form that took. And she was obviously very talented and beautiful. So it makes it hard to comprehend the often contradictory treatment that Carole received.

As early as the first month after she joined Fox, columnist Jimmy Fidler wrote, "20th Century biggies are boasting that if any of their singing stars go temperamental, they have an ace in the hole — Carole Landis, who's been improving her fine natural voice by industrious study these past months."[66] Carole had a better singing voice than almost every other 20th actress — remember her popularity in the notoriously tough San Francisco club scene — yet was rarely given a chance to showcase her talent.

The same month, *American Magazine* noted, "Though Carole has appeared in big roles in only four pictures, she has been dubbed by columnists from coast to coast as Hollywood's top glamour girl with the most gorgeous figure in moviedom."[67]

Zanuck had a reputation for pitting one star against another, ostensibly to keep the higher-ranked star in line with the threat of replacement. Zanuck believed that the studio was always bigger than the stars — he used the phrase as his personal motto — and Carole's hiring may have had something to do with keeping Alice Faye in line. He would repeat the procedure with Betty Grable.[68]

Writers and studio people took note of her talent, wondering aloud why she wasn't better-used. In February 1941, Kenny Morgan noted in his column that Carole would sing in *Moon Over Miami* and mentioned "people will be surprised."[69] But her Fox "debut" was less than auspicious.

On studio orders, Carole attended the 1940 Academy Awards dinner, held at the Biltmore Hotel in Los Angeles on February 27. She was obviously awestruck at all of the glamour and glitz, but managed to make a spectacular *faux pas.* According to film historians Mason Wiley and Damian Bona, "spectators missed the evening's most dramatic entrance when Carole Landis descended the grand stairway into the Biltmore Bowl only to have her slip drop from beneath her gown and land at her ankles."

She just laughed and went on her way; she told that story to friends for years. Typically Carole, she asked a soldier friend, Major General J.O. Mauborgne, to escort her to the awards ceremony. He was an officer she had met at the British War Relief benefit she attended in Palm Springs in February.

Carole seemed to be at the right studio at the right time. Fox was not known for the type of blockbusters that came out of Warners, or the intellectual properties from MGM. Rather, Fox was known for glamour films and for tirelessly promoting their films and their stars' images. The image they wanted for Carole was not to her liking. Out of the blocks, Fox painted Carole as a single girl looking for the right man. Their first press release described her as having "only one cloud that hovers on the horizon. She's afraid of romance, fearful that she may fall in love and Cupid may play a trick on her."

The studio orchestrated a half-dozen magazine stories during the first few months of 1941 after Carole signed, all designed to offer Carole as searching hopelessly for love. *Modern Screen* offered Landis' advice on "How to Handle Wolves with Kid Gloves."[70] John Reid's interview with Carole in *Silver Screen* was entitled "No Advice to the Lovelorn."[71] *Movie-Radio Guide* offered a "Spotlight on Carole Landis; Hollywood's Most Dated Starlet."[72] But according to all of the stories, she still couldn't find a man.

In April, Carole sat for an interview with writer Kyle Crichton for *Collier's Magazine*. Knowing the truth about Carole's popularity with men, and indeed her effect on men, Crichton asked Carole how she could be afraid of romance, having been married twice before, and with all of the relationships and dates she'd had. He tried to get Carole to admit that the entire image offered up by Fox publicity was a sham, a concoction, miles away from the truth. As Crichton drilled her with questions trying to get her to admit something, she laughed and said to him simply, "What are you trying to do, my dear friend, get me killed?" She knew she had to play the game.

But her response was exactly the type of honesty that endeared Carole to people, especially writers. Crichton had gone into his meeting with Carole with a preconception; by the time he walked out he had a true understanding of the girl. The title of his piece? "Carole Landis—Determined Lady."[73]

Carole allegedly described her needs in a later *Screenland* article "What Carole Landis Demands of Men!,"[74] one of two articles about Carole written by Gladys Hall during the fall of 1941. The other, entitled "Interview: Glamour Girls Are Suckers," ran in *Photoplay*.[75] The articles offer no better idea of what she really wanted in men, rather serving up the standard movie star fluff. Among her alleged "demands" were that men be well-mannered and attentive to a fault. They must offer flowers for dinner—flowers that match her dress—and give thoughtful and well-chosen gifts.

The one demand that has an interesting ring of truth, and offered a clear view into Carole's psyche as far as men were concerned, was her wish for a man who wanted to be with her *without* needing to be seen with her. Almost sadly, she also added that all she wanted was a man "who wouldn't make her suffer."[76] Carole really did want little more than a man who loved her and wanted to be with her. The rest, the trappings of stardom, were unimportant to her.

On the personal side, Willis Hunt had been begging Carole for a reconciliation after their 1940 separation, and as 1941 got underway was still trying to wear her down and get her back. But she was smart enough to know that Hunt's dark side meant the mental and physical abuse would never really end so she rightly ignored his entreaties. She probably also figured that the uptick in her career prospects, the new contract and more money, made her that much more appealing to him.

His childish response was to try to make her jealous. Given Carole's ability to date almost anyone she wished, that would not seem the smartest strategy, but Hunt went about it anyway. During March and April he seemed hell-bent on dating every beautiful woman he could find, and made sure to have their photographs run and names in the tabloids.

Hunt's siege began after the March 11 tabloids reported that Carole had "given the final 'no' to ex-husband Willis Hunt's reconciliation plea."[77] She would officially have nothing to do with him. He was first linked with Martha O'Driscoll, a beautiful and talented singer and dancer who appeared in B movies for Paramount and Universal and was the ad face for Max Factor cosmetics.[78] The following week he began dating Eleanor Frances, a young actress from New York who, interestingly, was a dead ringer for Carole.[79] While he was dating O'Driscoll and Frances, tabloid writers also linked Hunt to Carol Gallagher, a young contract player for Howard Hughes and RKO Studios.[80]

Hughes personally selected young unknowns and put them on the RKO payroll. Almost all were well-endowed brunettes. They were then sent to a small group of Hollywood portrait photographers whose studios were equipped with two-way mirrors so Hughes could personally direct the photo shoots. Hughes' signees were put up in one of two dozen Hollywood apartment buildings that Hughes owned, and they were allowed to date only with his permission.

All of Hunt's efforts to get Carole back went for naught. She would not speak to him again. She went to work on her first film for Zanuck and Fox, *Moon Over Miami* on the Fox lot on March 3. *Moon* was a remake of the 1938 Fox film *Three Blind Mice* that featured Loretta Young and Pauline Moore. Carole and Betty Grable reprised their roles.

The Technicolor production was framed against the lush backdrop of pre-war Miami and offered an excellent cast. Starring with Grable were Don Ameche and Robert Cummings, and supporting cast members included Charlotte Greenwood, Jack Haley and Cobina Wright.

Carole in the early 1940s.

Carole and Grable played two sisters who talk their aunt (Greenwood) into taking $15,000 they've just inherited and traveling to Miami. Grable decides to invest the money in clothes and a lavish hotel suite, intent on hooking a millionaire husband by pretending to be a millionairess. Carole poses as her private secretary and Greenwood her personal maid. But instead of hooking just a single millionaire, she also entices a fellow *faux* millionaire (Ameche), falling in love with him before she realizes he's as poor as she is. The ending is predictable, but the film has its funny moments, and Carole is flawless in her portrayal.

Grable and Carole were both newcomers to the Fox lot, but Grable was being given the full star build-up while Carole was still viewed as an apprentice. Just two years older than Carole, Grable had signed with Fox a year earlier but had only two film assignments during the 12 months.

It would be an interesting pairing. Carole, the apprentice, was much more beautiful and a much better actor. Grable, the supposed star-to-be, was not an actor as much as a singer and dancer. *Moon* would be another opportunity for Carole in a supporting role to outshine a star in a lead role. The competition between the two erupted into a feud that filled Hollywood tabloid columns for years. There was almost instant animosity from the moment Grable met Carole.

Betty Grable was an average actor more famous for a photograph of her derriere than for her talent. She was the product of a bizarre upbringing. She was born in St. Louis in 1916, the youngest of three children of an obsessive stage mother known for stubbornness and greed. A brother died at two just after Betty was born and just as mother Lillian began an unsuccessful effort to get a three-year-old sister interested in acting. When that failed, she turned her attention toward Betty. Lillian Grable became fanatical in her efforts to see her daughter in show business.

Lillian talked her husband into taking the family to California for a 1929 vacation, knowing in advance that she was going to stay there with Betty and never planning to return to St. Louis. Betty was enrolled in the Hollywood Professional School, took dancing lessons at the Ernest Blecher Academy and took acting lessons at the Albertina Rosch School. Lillian also dragged Betty to auditions, telling the casting people she was 15 instead of 13.

Betty had bit parts in two dozen films between 1930 and 1933 but no roles of any substance. Her problem was that, although she was beautiful and could sing and dance, she couldn't act. With her career going nowhere, she moved to San Francisco to sing with the Jay Whidden Orchestra at the Mark Hopkins Hotel, but Mother brought her back to Hollywood in 1934. She still had nothing of a career. But then she met and married former child star Jackie Coogan.

The publicity from their relationship — and the studio contract and roles that he got for her in spite of her inability to act — made Grable a household name. She was at Paramount for two years, but even Coogan couldn't stop the studio from dropping her in 1939 after about 20 films. At the time, Coogan was in an ugly litigation to recover childhood earnings stolen by his parents. He was no longer able to help her career, and was fighting with his own family for his own money; Betty divorced him.

Once again it appeared that her film career was over. With not a single other offer to do anything in films, she went on a vaudeville tour with bandleader Phil Harris and Eddie "Rochester" Anderson, and did a few small plays. During this period, Darryl Zanuck saw her and did what he usually did when he saw a pretty girl without a studio contract. He gave her one and slept with her.

She signed a Fox contract in July 1939, just a few months before she divorced Coogan. Typical Zanuck, he gave her a contract — and invited her in for his afternoon meetings — but didn't assign her to any films. She sat idle (except for most of her afternoons) until June 1940, when she was assigned to *Down Argentine Way*, a musical co-starring Don Ameche and debuting Carmen Miranda. With European film markets gone due to the war, Zanuck made a shrewd decision to target South American markets. Miranda was already a huge star there.

Grable was given the assignment only because reigning Fox star Alice Faye had been hospitalized for an emergency appendectomy. After *Argentine*, Grable worked on *Tin Pan Alley* with Faye in September–October but would not work again until the *Moon* shoot began in March of 1941. Grable is almost invisible in *Down Argentine Way*, which was a huge coming-out for Miranda, and Faye got most of the credit for *Tin Pan Alley*.

How or why Carole and Grable didn't get along is lost, but there was an immediate dislike between the two. It isn't likely that the problems began with Carole. She never begrudged anyone their successes, nor did she bear any animosity toward Grable although the preferential treatment she was receiving from Zanuck might have grated against her. And no doubt Carole could relate to Grable's afternoon calls from Zanuck, which would have elicited sympathy rather than disdain.

It's far more likely that Grable realized the threat posed by her beautiful co-star. According to Col. Barney Oldfield, at the time Grable was "awful ... so full of herself it was a wonder she didn't explode. She really thought she was a star."[81] Even though she couldn't act.

Filming began with no obvious tension between the two. They were often seen lunching together at the studio commissary during the first weeks of filming, usually with mutual friend Alice Faye.[82] Faye was newly married to bandleader Phil Harris, whom Grable had worked for briefly.

The first hint that something was amiss — aside from the rumors flying out of the studio that the two women hated each other — was the studio's obvious attempts to put the two together. Every day or so a gossip writer would be given a tidbit themed on their friendship. On March 12 they "shared a date" with writer Kyle Crichton.[83] That same week Sidney Skolsky mentioned that the two shared lunch every day, and were often seen "sharing a comb."[84]

Grable was smart enough to see that Carole was prettier and a better actor, and insecure enough to feel threatened by her. Also, while Grable invariably aroused universal apathy from the crews she worked with, they loved Carole. During the *Moon* shoot, she showed up on the set on Good Friday with candies she had made for them herself.

Grable got upset over a minor incident that highlighted the power of Carole's looks. Critics of the film described both Grable and Carole as "eye-stopping." They were; during one scene both actresses wore equally skin-tight, revealing evening gowns. During a break, Carole mentioned that some of the sequins were falling off of her gown, saying to writer Harrison Carroll, "Hey, these beads are dropping. I think I'm coming apart." Without missing a beat, Don Ameche looked at both women and said to Carole, "I know I am."[85] Grable stalked away from the table.

By the middle of April, the two weren't speaking to one another. Writer Skolsky noted that during a visit to the studio commissary he visited Grable at her table eating lunch with her stand-in, while Carole sat "at the opposite end of the lunchroom with hers."[86]

Surprisingly, the problem with Grable did get to the point that Carole got involved with the one-upsmanship. During a scene filmed in a water tank during the first week of filming, she suffered nasty cuts that required stitches, but gamely went on with filming.[87] But the ongoing tension with Grable got Carole to the point where she demanded a better dressing room, the size of Grable's. After she left filming for two days with the "flu," she was given the better quarters she demanded.[88] It was the only time during her entire career that Carole acted the part of the difficult movie star.

Carole and Grable had to form an uneasy alliance in the middle of filming however, when the Hays Office announced to the studios on March 25 that it was considering a ban on what it referred to as "sweater art." Sweaters would have been prohibited in both studio stills *and* films. Carole had been known as a "sweater girl" for years, but there were other, more important actresses taking advantage of their attributes, like Rita Hayworth, Grable and a young Lana Turner.[89] They and their studios reacted to the proposed prohibition with horror.

Unfortunately — or fortunately, depending upon your perspective — the Hays people knew Carole all too well. She was known through the studios to have the highest "kill" rate of any actress in Hollywood, referring to Hays edicts banning particular photographs. Writer Jimmy Fidler noted that "It's Carole ('watafigure') Landis whose publicity stills rate the highest per censors ... referring to 'kills' from the Hays office censors."[90]

The sweater flap created a major buzz in Hollywood. Grable and Landis spoke to columnists together in a united — albeit frosty — front until the Committee backed off on its threat. Carole's publicity photographs would have undoubtedly suffered. During the *Moon* shoot, she was posing for a Fox still photographer in one of her trademark sweaters. He had to ask her, "Please Miss Landis, don't inhale while I'm taking your picture."[91] But her off-camera activities weren't limited to studio fluff.

But filming continued with an aura of tension between the two that is evident on the screen. At one point during filming, the tabloids reported that Bob Cummings had to step in to stop a hair-pulling fight between the two.[92] A November 1941 *Screen Guide* magazine offered a cover headline "The Betty Grable–Carole Landis Feud." In January 1942, another film magazine published an article begging the two to put an end to their fight for the good of the movies and the fans under the title "An Open Letter to Betty and Carole."[93] Barney Oldfield confirmed that the two really did hate each other, and that Grable was the instigator of the ongoing battle.[94]

During the first week in May, Carole asked for and received two days off the set so she could take part in the filming of a *Meet the Stars* short film that featured a group of stars touring the naval base in San Diego. Appearing with Carole were Richard Barthelmess, Carmen Miranda and a half-dozen other well-known movie stars.[95]

She and Grable managed to get through filming, which concluded at the end of the second week of April. Next up for Carole was the Irving Pichel–directed *Dance Hall*, which was to start filming on April 21. Also that week was the annual Fox Studio employee gala, held on April 28. Zanuck had studio decorators transform the Biltmore Bowl at the Biltmore Hotel for the 20th Century–Fox Studio Club Spring Fiesta. It was an dinner party and musical evening open to every employee from Zanuck down to the janitors, allowing the working employees an evening of mingling with their stars. Milton Berle served as the emcee.

Carole particularly enjoyed the events that included her crew friends, and she spent most of her evening chatting with them rather than the executives or the other stars. Grable sat at a head table with Darryl Zanuck and his wife, which for anyone other than Zanuck might have been an uncomfortable situation. With them was a crew of studio heavyweights like the Bill Goetzes, the Walter Wangers and the Tyrone Powers.

Meanwhile, Carole took a table near the back, sitting and chatting with her friends and the dozens of crew members who stopped by the table. She was with her boyfriend at the time — actor George Montgomery — and her close friend Cesar Romero, who had to attend with a studio-assigned female, singer Janis Carter.[96]

Even with all of her filming and military-volunteering, as well as the personal problems with Hunt and Grable, Carole still found time to take care of her friends. Florence Jones had been her stand-in and closest friend for five years, and was about to marry her young golf professional fiancé, Lou Wasson. Wasson was the head professional at the Riviera Country Club in Pacific Palisades. When Carole discovered that the young couple could not afford a honeymoon after their March nuptials, she gifted the couple with a two-week trip to Florida as a wedding present.[97] She also paid for most of the wedding.

Just a few months later, Carole arranged for a special fan to visit her at her studio. Five years earlier, in 1936, a young teenager from Oak Park, Illinois, named Peggy McKenna wrote her a fan letter after seeing her in a studio photograph. It was the first fan letter that the unknown young actress received, and she wrote a personal letter back to young McKenna. A friendship developed and Carole traded letters with the youngster, who became the self-appointed president of Carole's first fan club.[98]

When Carole visited Chicago in late 1940 on a publicity junket, she arranged to meet her young fan. Carole invited her to come to Hollywood for a private visit. In April, Carole hosted McKenna at the Sunset Boulevard mansion she also brought her along for her studio work and to social events as her guest and friend. On her own, Carole took four days off and took the youngster on a tour north up the California coast in her Cadillac convertible.[99] Most of the visit went unreported and, at Carole's request, un-photographed.

Certainly some of the visit was used by the studio for publicity purposes — noted in an extensive *Life* magazine article entitled "Carole Landis' No. 1 Fan Gets Vacation with Star," but clearly Carole went above and beyond what was required by the studio. The trip, after all, was her idea, not the studio's. She was simply doing what she did most of the time; she was being nice. The studio told the press that McKenna became Carole's stand-in for several years, but given her relationship with Florence Wasson and the dates of her work with Florence, this was probably studio fiction.

On April 23, Carole attended the premiere of *Topper Returns* at Grauman's Chinese Theater, alongside her co-stars Joan Blondell, Roland Young and Billie Burke. Her escort was her good friend and frequent "date" Cesar Romero.

The studio offered Carmen Miranda as an encore for each showing of the film, and she was brilliant at getting the audience worked up. Miranda, whose career was just taking off after two films, sang songs like "Mamma Equero" and "South America Way." She had to do her samba-singing, hip-wriggling show six times. The audiences loved her fractured English, ending her performance with, "Sank you, you nize peepul."[100]

Topper received so-so reviews, mostly because of Roach's tendency to repeat gags (one of his directorial tendencies). Reviewer Carl Combs noted that the film "begins to pall — after Miss Blondell has manifested herself ... half a dozen times ... after Eddie Anderson has been dumped out of a trick rocking chair three or four times.... [M]atters continue to be boringly repetitious right up to the end."[101] Among the bad reviews, Carole's was the only positive; "Landis, without much to do here, still shows her star possibilities."[102]

Dance Hall began on April 21, in the middle of the various social engagements Carole was committed to by the studio. But she was also in the middle of another dating frenzy. During March and April she spent time with George Montgomery, Alexis Thompson, Raymond Hakim, Matty Fox, her pal Romero and her old boyfriend Kenny Morgan. Even the magazines had taken notice of her social calendar. The April 19 issue of *Movie-Radio Guide Magazine* featured a cover article entitled, "Carole Landis— Hollywood's Most Dated Starlet."[103]

Her work was getting Carole noticed outside the

This photograph of Landis was taken during a photograph shoot staged while she was filming *Dance Hall*, in March 1941.

studio. On April 23 she was one of 350 guests invited to attend the Mack Sennett Bathing Party at the Beverly Hills Hotel. The guests included everyone from studio executives to movie stars. Milton Berle emceed the afternoon and evening affair, to which the guests were required to wear turn-of-the-century bathing suits and participate in all manner of lawn games.

It was quite a coup for Carole to receive an invitation to the affair, included in a celebrity guest list of top movies stars like Mickey Rooney, Judy Garland, Lana Turner, Cesar Romero, Alice Faye, Cary Grant, Tyrone Power, Linda Darnell, Robert Taylor and Barbara Stanwyck.[104]

Dance Hall was a classic Fox B picture assignment for Carole. It was directed by Irving Pichel, a veteran of the Pasadena Playhouse who had played ethnic–European villains in a string of 50-plus forgettable movies in the 1930s before becoming a director at Fox. He was a minor director best-remembered for later discovering Natalie Wood.

But bad B film or not, Carole enjoyed the shoot, sharing the lead with her close friend Cesar Romero. Romero played soft-hearted but roguish Duke McKay, owner of the Danceland honkytonk. He is constantly at war with his top dancer, the independent and feisty Lily Brown (Carole). They engage in an hour's worth of bickering before ending up pals after he introduces Lily to his piano player Joe Brooks (William Henry). McKay and Lily unite to get Joe to Broadway.

It was an uneventful shoot of an unimportant movie, so unimportant that it wasn't formally released for almost a year, not until March 12, 1943. The studio pulled it from theaters after preview showings in July when early reviews came in. One reviewer noted, "*Dance Hall* is a picture which the people at 20th Century–Fox decided was better than the B- product rating it was given at the outset. Some even thought it was grade A-. As a matter of fact, it isn't that good at all."[105]

Most reviewers suggested that the only reason to see the film was because Cesar Romero—then the most popular star at Fox—and Carole were in the leads. Carole's singing was received well by critics as "especially appealing" and most reviewers were almost apologetic for the two stars; one mentioned that both were "hobbled by the so-so screenplay." Another noted that the "weak story stops efforts of the cast," while asserting that Romero and Carole were the only "redeeming factors" to the film.[106]

Just after *Dance Hall* wrapped, Carole was invited by the Department of the Navy to attend a private party at Ciro's in Hollywood. The guests of honor at the May 17 event were officers from various South American Naval forces.[107] Her attendance was not just to add a pretty face to the proceedings; she was asked to offer suggestions regarding morale-boosting and civilian volunteerism.

Two weeks later, on June 9, Carole left on a week-long tour of a half-dozen Army bases in California, from Camp Hunter Liggett to Fort Ord. Along with Marlene Dietrich, Kay Francis, Linda Darnell and the Kay Kyser Orchestra, Carole performed for over 60,000 troops in six concerts. She was clearly the crowd favorite. One infantry group, knowing of Carole's love of dogs, gave her a Great Dane puppy after her performance.[108] She returned to Fox on the 12th in time to begin her next assignment.

Meanwhile, Zanuck told reporters that he thought one of the problems with the

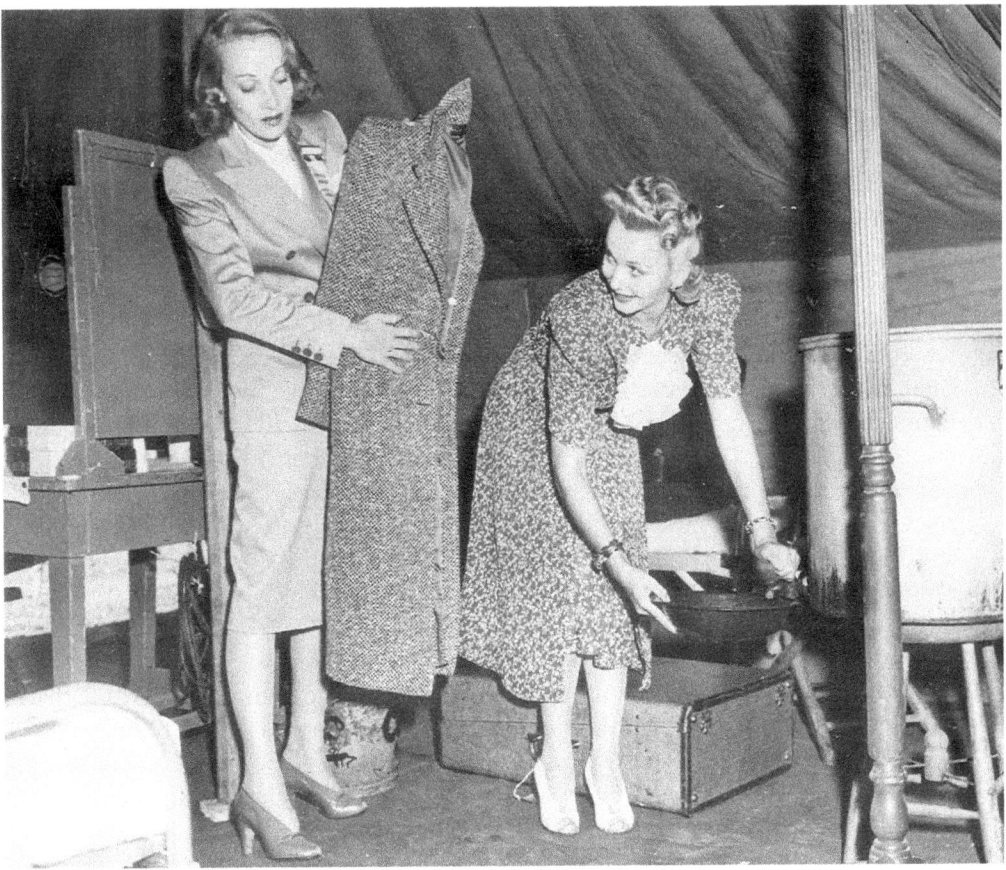

Carole and Marlene Dietrich (left) in their improvised "dressing room" during their June 1941 visit to Camp Hunter Liggett, where Carole performed for over 25,000 troops.

movie business was that studios spent too little time and effort developing new faces. He notified the 20th Century–Fox producers and directors that a select group of new players were to be given top priority. Among them were Carole, Gene Tierney, Anne Baxter, John Sutton, Dana Andrews, George Montgomery and Laird Cregar.[109]

He then assigned Carole to *I Wake Up Screaming*, which was as good a movie as *Dance Hall* was bad. In yet another contradiction, though, she was also assigned to *Cadet Girl*, as boring a film as *Screaming* was thrilling. Both films were to begin filming during the third week of July; *Screaming* was scheduled to run through the end of August, *Cadet Girl* the end of September.

Before *Screaming* began filming on July 12, *Moon Over Miami* was previewed on June 18. The reaction of most critics was summed up by a *Film Daily* reviewer who wrote that it would be "difficult to imagine anything more delightful than a good story, Technicolor, Betty Grable and Carole Landis for the gentlemen, and Don Ameche and Robert Cummings for the ladies."[110] The film would be a financial windfall for Zanuck after its formal debut on July 16 at Grauman's Chinese Theater.

I Wake Up Screaming was an H. Bruce Humberstone adaptation of the Steve

Fisher book of the same name. The original movie title was *Hot Spot*. *Screaming* was a fine thriller and has become something of a film noir classic. It was produced by Milton Sperling, the Fox executive who first dubbed Carole the "studio hooker."

There was plenty of opportunity for tension on the set. First, Carole was paired with two actors whom she had clearly out-played in their previous work, her *Miami* co-star Grable and *One Million B.C.*'s Victor Mature. Mature was openly complaining that Zanuck would not renegotiate his contract. He was still making only $250 a week, and told a writer visiting the *Screaming* set that he "could get a couple of thousand dollars a week just to stroll through a department store and attract the girls who would rush to get my autograph."[111]

Grable was openly upset at the attention that Carole was getting from Zanuck's "new faces" edict. She was also upset that Zanuck had cast Carole himself, telling Humberstone that he wanted her character to be "sex-loaded." The feud was back on.

Zanuck first ordered the two to present a friendly image to reporters and writers. On July 21, the first week of filming, Sidney Skolsky reported that "Betty Grable and Carole Landis were supposed to be feuding during the filming of *Moon Over Miami*. Today they start work together in *Hot Spot*, and they have already arranged for this sign for their portable dressing rooms; 'WE'RE NOT FEUDING.'"[112]

Their public protestations aside, it was obvious during the first day's filming that little had changed. Within a week, Skolsky had amended his story, writing that "the Betty Grable–Carole Landis feud on the set of *Hot Spot* is really beginning to sizzle."[113] The next day, Harrison Carroll wrote, "[T]he feud between La Grable [an obvious jab at Grable's haughty demeanor] and Carole Landis is on the level. And it's all the more ironic because they play sisters in *Hot Spot*."[114]

Again, it appears that the instigator was Grable. Skolsky noted in his August 13 column that "just what Betty is angry with Carole about is not known, but the girls do not speak to each other." Then, referring to a possible event hat every writer in Hollywood was hoping would happen, he added, "This seems to be another George Raft–Edward G. Robinson fight, and it might even end in a nice hair-pulling match, with a cameraman handy."[115]

In the film, Mature plays a promoter who, along with actor Alan Mowbray and writer Allyn Joslyn, chooses waitress Vickie Lynn (Carole) to glamourize and transform into a darling of café society. Their plan works and she gets a Hollywood contract that she accepts without first checking with her three backers. The next day she is murdered. Betty, as her sister, falls in love with Mature even though he is suspected of the killing, and she hides evidence that apparently makes him look guilty.

But love and justice prevail and Mature and Grable eventually find the real killer from among the cast of suspects. Zanuck was worried about casting Grable in such a straight role, and probably secretly knew that she would not be able to keep up with Carole. Director Humberstone noted, "Carole was extremely easy to work with and really underrated as an actress." Of Grable he said that she could become a good actress "with a little coaching and a lot more self-confidence...."[116]

In her first big role at Fox, Carole took the role as the "plain" sister and clearly outdid Grable's work. One writer described Carole's performance as "outshining the woman who won World War II." That might have been an overstatement but through a combination of looks and her ability to let her true personality show through the camera lens, Carole stole the picture.

Carole's character Vicky Lynn was a model and singer who wanted to be a star, murdered on the eve of her departure for Hollywood stardom. It is difficult to watch the film without making the comparison to Carole's own tragic life.

Screaming was the last Grable–Landis pairing. During the early 1940s, Grable dated George Raft, an incorrigible former New York street tough who had first asked her out when she was only 14 (he was in his twenties). Whenever he wanted to make Grable angry during their relationship, he called her "Carole Landis."

The film was previewed during the fall as *Hot Spot* before the title was changed to *I Wake Up Screaming*. Zanuck knew that he had a hit with *Screaming*. One review noted that the film was "sock entertainment slated for strong grosses ... it has been a long time since a melodrama has come this way which packs the suspense that this production does...."[117]

Carole steals the film from Grable, although she dies early in the film and appears in flashback scenes. Grable's performance, like many of her dramatic efforts, was labeled as just "satisfactory."

The cliché-ridden *Cadet Girl*, which began filming on July 14 (just two days after *Screaming* commenced), was described in reviews as "undistinguished" and "moderately entertaining." But almost all of the reviews were similar the opinion in *Film Daily* that noted the high points were "the stunning beauty of Carole Landis and the music."[118]

She is described as "captivatingly beautiful" in her role as orchestra singer Gene Baxter, and she sings three songs in the film. Her singing is lovely, particularly on "She's a Good Neighbor" and "I'll Settle for You."

The story is pathetically predictable as bandleader Bob Mallory (Shepperd Strudwick) gets a visit from his West Point brother Tex (George Montgomery). He falls in love with the beautiful Gene (Carole) and is ready to throw his Army career away to marry her. West Point cadets can't be married, and Tex is ready to give it all up until Bob writes a patriotic ballad for Tex to sing.

When Tex and Gene form a band, their first concert is for a large crowd of soldiers, which reminds both that Tex's real duty is to his country. Everyone realizes that the marriage between Tex and Gene must be cast aside for his duty to country.

This is one of Carole's finest performances, probably because she came so close to playing herself, particularly singing for the soldiers. *Cadet Girl* was a stunning victory—this time not over another actress but over a contrived and silly script.

Montgomery and Carole dated during *Cadet* filming. She also was seen publicly with ex-husband Willis Hunt, Bill Marshall, Randolph Scott, Marty Fox, Burgess Meredith and Tony Martin, most of whom were more old friends than lovers. Montgomery and Landis had a pretty heated coupling; one *Boston Globe* reported visiting the *Cadet* set reported that during their love scenes Montgomery was actually making love to Carole![119]

Yet again Carole shows her versatility, her acting and singing talents, and the ability to totally take over a film. This was the moment that should have been the

watershed moment in her career. But events that took place during the *Screaming* and *Cadet Girl* filming would conspire to reduce Carole to B films for the rest of her career. Some of it was her doing, but most was not. As usual, it was Zanuck pulling the strings. It all took place during the August casting of director Rouben Mamoulian's film *Blood and Sand*.

Blood and Sand was a remake of the 1922 Valentino classic of the same name, with slight modifications in the plot written in by Jo Swerling, a talented scribe who worked on *Gone with the Wind* (1939) and would later pen *The Pride of the Yankees* (1942) and help re-write *It's a Wonderful Life* (1946). *Sand* would offer an all-star cast in the story of small-town matador Juan Gallardo, who becomes the most famous bullfighter in Spain. Though graced with a loving wife, Carmen, he falls in love with rich socialite Dona Sol.

Mamoulian was a Hollywood legend fresh off the classics *Golden Boy* (1939) and *The Mark of Zorro* (1940). Zanuck himself would produce, Travis Banton did the costumes and Ben Wurtzel the set design. Hermes Pan was hired for the choreography. Tyrone Power would play Gallardo and Linda Darnell was cast as Carmen. The supporting cast included Alla Nazimova, Anthony Quinn, J. Carrol Naish, John Carradine, Lynn Bari and Laird Cregar. The big sticking point in casting was Dona Sol, the lead female role.

Carole was told by Zanuck that role was hers even though over 30 actresses were tested, including Betty Grable, Maria Montez and Gene Tierney.[120] *Blood and Sand* would be a breakout role for whoever had the pivotal "vamp" role because Fox would be investing millions into the film.

Studio wardrobe shot, ca. 1942, perhaps during the *Moon Over Miami* filming.

Zanuck wanted Carole for the role of Dona. It would have been a natural role for her and the studio announced to the press that she had been given the plum assignment. Carole desperately wanted the role and was very excited about doing the film, but somehow the role went to Rita Hayworth. Everyone wanted to know, "why?"

Mamoulian reportedly wanted Hayworth and lobbied against Carole. His desire for Hayworth made no sense. The part of Dona Sol, a Spanish noblewoman who steals Power from his wife, did not fit Hayworth at all except for her Latin lineage and appearance. It was clearly a role she would have trouble handling. Hayworth was much less an actress than a pretty face. And if Hayworth were to star, the singing would have to be dubbed, since she was tone deaf could not sing.[121] Carole was a wonderful singer.

Zanuck knew that Hayworth was not enough actress for the role. He had never been impressed with her acting ability. When he took over Fox in 1936, one of his first edicts was to deny the contract renewal of the actress he scornfully called the "Spanish girl."[122]

At first Zanuck stubbornly insisted that the role should go to Landis. He told Mamoulian that he was paying for the film, and at the time Hayworth was under contract to Harry Cohn at Columbia anyway. Arranging a loan-out for her would be expensive. So the decision to use Hayworth made no financial sense, either.

How Mamoulian would, again supposedly, prevail in such a situation is a mystery. But he did. The role went to the less-talented and more expensive Hayworth. Zanuck called a press conference and had Carole herself tell the press that she turned down the role because she didn't want to dye her hair red. That studio publicist's concoction is obviously patently false. That problem could be easily solved by Carole wearing a wig. But it made Carole look shallow and unprofessional.

There was something else at work here. Why then did Carole lose the role that would have propelled her to A roles and stardom? Why did she lose the role and get thrown back to Bs, never to resurface? Would Mamoulian dig his heels in on a whim, wanting Hayworth just for the sake of some small power play with Zanuck? Doubtful; he was smart enough to know that the best star makes the best picture, and had always fought for the best star in his films. Hayworth had just lit up the screen in *The Strawberry Blonde*, but it was a typical Hayworth role with more beauty than substance. Even so, Mamoulian allegedly said that "as soon as I saw Rita Hayworth walk I knew I had my Dona Sol...."[123] Perhaps he did think Hayworth a better actress, but it's hard to understand how.

Stories immediately surfaced inside and outside of Fox that Zanuck changed his mind and sided with Mamoulian when Carole told him that she was done giving in to his demands for sex. Deflecting the blame toward Mamoulian, saying it was *he* who wanted Hayworth—damn the cost and trouble—took Zanuck off that hook and was a typical Zanuck move. It would also explain Carole's awful film assignments that followed.

To satisfy Mamoulian's whim or because Carole demanded an end to their sexual relationship, Zanuck paid Harry Cohn and Columbia a loan-out fee of five times her weekly Columbia salary. It would cost Zanuck *15* times what it would have cost to give Carole the role! And Harry Cohn and Columbia would receive millions in free publicity for *their* star. Zanuck wouldn't have done that to satisfy a Mamoulian whim. Trade papers also reported that Zanuck had tried to wrest Hedy Lamarr from MGM to play the role before settling for Hayworth.[124]

The stardom didn't make Hayworth's life easier either; like Carole, she could never find love. Her life was a nightmare that began when her dance partner–father Eduardo began having sex with her when she was barely 13. She spent her life trying to replace him with a series of abusive older husbands. After descending into alcoholism by 1960, she was staggered with the early onset of Alzheimer's disease. By the late 1970s, she was almost helpless and died in 1987 at 69.

Just months before, Zanuck had promised to commit all of the studio's efforts to making Carole's "new face" a star; now he pulled the plug. He sent her to do a B, *A Gentleman at Heart*. It's a nice, even a quality movie, but miles away from *Blood and Sand*. She knew it too. According to Col. Barney Oldfield, Fox studio people knew that Carole's refusal to sleep with Zanuck led to her banishment to the B's.[125]

To make the exile even more obvious — and painful — the vengeful Zanuck also changed her assignment for the only other A film she was set to do. Carole was to do the lead role in *My Gal Sal* which, like *Blood and Sand*, was a high-profile A film. Instead, he took that role from her and gave her a minor, almost cameo role in the film. He then paid Harry Cohn his exorbitant loan-out rate for Rita Hayworth again and gave her the lead.

Barney Oldfield told me that it was Carole's idea to walk away from the lead in *Sal*. It was rumored at Fox that she told Zanuck to "stuff the role" after he pulled *Blood and Sand*.[126] It's impossible to confirm that otherwise, but it fits Zanuck's spiteful personality.

Carole was not afraid to voice her opinions, and she made it clear to anyone within hearing distance what she thought of Zanuck, Mamoulian and the studio after the *Blood and Sand* fiasco. Her very vocal outrage — often in front of other shocked studio

Carole, likely during the 1941 shooting of *Cadet Girl.*

employees—made Zanuck even more determined to banish her to studio Siberia. Zanuck spent a lot of time telling people that it was Carole's own fault that she had cost herself the roles, and in fact took public umbrage at her comments. He shed crocodile tears over what he told employees was a betrayal on her part. But most of the people who knew Carole knew the real reason for the entire situation.

Even with the bitter battle going on between Zanuck and Carole, he still used her whenever he could. When actors or actresses signed appearance or endorsement contracts, the studio name and the title of any current films had to be included. Often, the advertisements did more for the studio than the product.

Carole was hired to appear in advertisements for the Tappan Company's kitchen products in the late summer of 1941. She was clad in an apron and standing in front of an oven, and the ad reads, "Carole Landis, 20th Century–Fox actress starring in the current motion picture successes: *Cadet Girl* and *Hot Spot* indicates that a splendid way to offset rising food costs is to use less expensive cuts of meat, but cook them in the modern low-temperature oven of the Tappan gas range." The ovens cost between $99.50 and $169.50.[127]

To call Carole's next assignment, *A Gentleman at Heart*, formulaic studio B material would probably be too generous a compliment. Other than Cesar Romero, Carole and Milton Berle, there was barely a recognizable face in the entire Ray McCarey–directed film (McCarey directed *Cadet Girl* with Carole and would later handle *It Happened in Flatbush*). Supporting actors included the likes of Richard Derr, Rose Hobart, Jerome Cowan and Francis Pierlot.

Filming began in October and lasted less than a month. The film was based on the story "Masterpiece" by Paul Hervey Fox. It is a contrived piece about somewhat lovable loser Lucky Cullen (Berle) who works for bookie and gambler Tony Miller (Romero) and owes him thousands. When Lucky inherits an art gallery, he and Miller plan to sell it to get Miller's money back. But Miller falls for lovely gallery manager Helen Mason (Carole), and sees it as an opportunity to sell fakes painted by local artist Gigi (J. Carrol Naish).

As Miller tries to become an art connoisseur and win Carole, there are several funny scenes in the otherwise pointless script. Carole is lovely in her role, and takes over the film. She always performed well when she worked with Romero, one of her closest friends. After its January 1942 release, a reviewer stated that Carole "does not have much to do except to be herself, which is more than enough,"[128] at the same time describing the film as one of Fox's "lesser budgeted efforts."

⋆ Six ⋆

War and Love, Again

The first half of 1941 had been a hectic and stressful time for Carole. She had a busy filming schedule that included *My Gal Sal*, *A Gentleman at Heart*, *I Wake Up Screaming* and *Moon Over Miami*. She endured the protracted demise of the Hunt relationship, the *Blood and Sand* fiasco and war with Zanuck, and the attentions of a dozen potential new suitors vying for her attention.

Some of her social engagements were clearly studio-arranged. She was first paired with young heart-throb George Montgomery, star of their *Cowboy and the Blonde*. But Jimmy Fidler's note about the date revealed the *faux* nature of the pairing when he mentioned that she "may have attended the other night's party with George Montgomery, but she danced most of the evening with Cesar Romero."[1] She worked with Romero on *Dance Hall* and the two were the closest of friends. It's doubtful they had a romantic connection, though. He was gay, and a frequent "beard" for actresses who needed dates or rumors.

The war everyone in America thought imminent brought out Carole's dedication to social issues. The war would become the most important part of her life. Her volunteerism began months before the U.S. was thrust in the conflict in late 1941. Beginning as early as February 1941, she was volunteering money and time for a dozen different groups making preparations for the entrance of U.S. troops.

She was a founding member of the Hollywood Victory Committee, a group of movie people set up to organize local industry assistance to the pre-war efforts. She also volunteered for extensive junkets selling war bonds. She was a flyer with over a hundred hours to her credit, and by October 1941 qualified for her pilot's license.[2] Even before the attack on Pearl Harbor she had tried to enlist in the A.T.S., a group of female British pilots who flew reconnaissance missions. She withdrew her application when she found out that she would have to surrender her American citizenship.[3] But she became an active Civilian Air Patrol pilot, flying frequently for that group.

She earned the coveted gold earrings given to the Commanders, First Division, Aerial Nurse Corps, she was a volunteer sentry and home defender in the Los Angeles Sheriff's Rifle Auxiliary Squadron, and volunteered to become a storekeeper, one of the main organizers with the Bundles for Bluejackets program.

Later, she would spend literally every free evening visiting and dancing with soldiers at the Hollywood Canteen. And at least once a week, she quietly drove to local hospitals to donate blood. She never let her studio know; stunned nurses were almost too nervous to take her blood.

Some of the studio-arranged efforts seemed pretty lame, but she gamely allowed herself to be used for the war effort. One group of photographs of her ran in newspaper articles around the country instructing women how to dress when visiting military posts. She still managed to look lovely in a plain beige gabardine suit with a gold and red belt, pants and a matching skirt-length cape.[4] The article described the proper attire for women visiting boyfriends and husbands at their assigned posts.

She also offered her body for pin-up photographs that became some of the most popular in the armed forces. Unfortunately her efforts ran afoul of the Hays Office, which had earlier demanded approval of all of her photographs prior to their release.[5] Carole's "cheesecake" photographs were less famous than the legendary Betty Grable derriere pose, but Landis' photographs were much more prized by the servicemen.

In September, Jimmy Fidler reported that Carole had requested a film assignment in England. According to Fidler, who was obviously incorrect, she wished to go to be near her ex-husband Willis Hunt, said to be ready to join the Eagle Squadron.[6] Since there are no records of Hunt taking or even asking for such an assignment, it was Fidler fiction. She actually requested—and almost got—the assignment so she could be closer to American troops already assigned in England.

On September 19, Carole left Los Angeles for three weeks of personal appearances for the studio and for the military. She offered to go on her own to Milwaukee to attend the National American Legion Convention[7] on the 20th. The next day she flew to New York, where she stayed until mid–October.

On the 24th, Carole appeared with Joe DiMaggio on Eddie Cantor's radio program "It's Time to Smile." The show ran from 9:00 to 9:30 in the evening; Cantor's sidekick was a young female singer named Dinah Shore. It was a sign of Carole's popularity that she was booked on the show alongside America's most popular athlete. (Just the week before Betty Grable had been a guest, and Carole's best friend Burgess Meredith two weeks later.)

Carole would run into Grable the next evening when she attended the premiere of Fox's pre-war *A Yank in the R.A.F.* on studio orders. The film, which was about the famed Eagle Squadron of American pilots who flew for the R.A.F. during the Battle of Britain, was written by Darryl Zanuck under the pen name Melville Crossman. Grable and Tyrone Power starred in the poorly made film. Carole enjoyed the evening more than the film or seeing Grable again, since the premiere was held at the Roxy Theater and included a gala ball to benefit the Military Ambulance Corps.

Carole spent her free time in New York shopping and visiting restaurants with old friends, including one of her pals, Burgess Meredith. The press, always looking for Carole's latest boyfriend, quickly began spreading tabloid stories of the pair's "dates." Walter Winchell also reported that she was seeing Bob Ritchie while she was there.[8]

Again on her own, Carole returned to New York a week later to help host an October 15 Fight for Freedom Rally at Madison Square Garden. She performed before over 15,000 fans to raise money for the military. Her efforts were profiled in several

Life magazine articles during October and November.⁹ During her few days in the city she managed to have herself linked in the tabloids with singer Tony Martin and French director Raymond Hakim.¹⁰ She stayed in New York just two days, and then returned to L.A. for yet another volunteer commitment.

On October 19, Carole attended and sang at a benefit performance at the San Diego Naval Training Center, performing for almost 1,000 sailors to benefit the base Naval Family Hospital at the North Island Naval Air Station. During two evenings—the 18th and 19th—a number of movie stars made appearances, including Grable, Marlene Dietrich, Charles Boyer, Claudette Colbert, John Garfield, Chico Marx, George Burns and Gracie Allen, Jimmy Durante, Roy Rogers and Abbott and Costello. Milton Berle served as the master of ceremonies. But the biggest cheers were reserved for Carole's performance.

Her ongoing issues with Hunt and her demanding schedule finally took their toll in early November. On November 6, Carole collapsed during costume preparations for her next assignment, *My Gal Sal*. She was taken to the hospital suffering from exhaustion and did not return to the studio for ten days.

Carole obviously had no problem finding dates of her own, but the studio still required her to endure arranged outings with other actors. Fidler noted that reporters "aren't hep to the Carole Landis–Cary Grant datings, specifically to the Ocean Park fights?"¹¹ Obviously set-up dates for Grant, who was at best severely bisexual and who dated women every five years or so when his personal guilt and shame over his homosexuality peaked. If she were really dating Grant, it is doubtful that they would go to the fights anyway, but very public "dates" like that were typical of studio-arranged outings.

She so disliked the arranged but mandatory dates that as her popularity grew in the coming months of 1942 that she undertook a personal rebellion. Whenever the studio forced her to go out with someone she didn't like, she would ask a second male friend to come along, showing up for the publicity photographers with two dates. It would then be impossible for them to decide who was the studio-arranged "real date." During the summer of 1942 she was nicknamed "Double Feature Landis" in tabloids and gossip columns.¹²

Obviously, 1942 would be dominated by the impact of World War II after the Japanese attack on Pearl Harbor. From the moment the first bombs fell on the early morning of December 7, 1941, Hollywood was a major cog in the United States' military propaganda and morale machine. Writer Erskine Johnson noted correctly, "Trying to ignore the war in Hollywood is like trying to hide a Flying Fortress [a large bomber] in a phone booth. It can't be done."¹³

The War Department contacted Clark Gable's Hollywood Victory Committee as early as January 1942, to let them know that volunteers from Hollywood—high-profile volunteers—would be important to the war effort. As much as many of the stars wanted to go and fight was how much their studios wanted them to stay out of harm's way. Or just stay!

The War Department guessed correctly that such famous enlistees would be a very powerful image as they tried to boost home front morale and swell the numbers of soldiers. Hundreds of famous stars joined the fray. Washington also pressured

Hollywood to provide movie star volunteers in the technical areas of the service like filmmaking.

Washington need not have worried about Hollywood's response. Francis Marion remembered, "Hollywood was stunned. A giant foot had stepped on our ant hill. Men immediately left the studios in droves; almost two-thirds of the skilled employees from the technical crews, scores of writers, directors, cameramen and actors and even Zanuck enlisted."[14] He had earlier served in Europe in World War I as a 16-year-old; he lied to the enlistment officer to get in. Hal Roach also enlisted.

It was General "Hap" Arnold, head of the Army Air Corps, who first saw a need for professionally-made films for training, morale and propaganda purposes. He asked Jack L. Warner for help.

Warner's patriotism was a little less evident in the days right after Pearl Harbor. From the moment of the attack, people living along the coast feared an invasion because the Los Angeles area had so many aerospace facilities. Right next to the tangle of Burbank studios stood Lockheed Aircraft's largest facility, dozens of huge camouflaged hangars, runways and office buildings. From the air the property looked no different from the surrounding buildings, homes and fields.

Right next door was Warner Bros. and the very eccentric Jack L., whose first response was a bit removed from flag-waving. Worried that his large sound stages would look like the nearby aircraft hangars, he had studio workers paint the name "LOCKHEED" in 50-foot-tall letters on the roof of his biggest soundstage, along with a 100-foot arrow pointing in Lockheed's direction. When a stunned local Civil Air Patrol pilot saw the sign and it made the papers, Warner was forced to paint over his work.

After Arnold's request, Warner and producer Owen Crump went to Washington, D.C., and cut a deal with the military. Although nothing was specifically granted in exchange for the studio help, a good number of studio personnel managed to stay at the studios during the war. Part of the arrangement was that the production people—though technically and officially soldiers—avoided the same basic training as other recruits. That only made sense; many were quite a bit older.

The military took advantage of the moviemaking expertise by forming what was called the First Motion Picture Unit, known as FMPU. It was attached to the U.S. Army Air Corps 18th Air Force Base to produce training films and morale and propaganda films. The unit abbreviation F.M.P.U. was pronounced "fum-poo."

The first F.M.P.U. production was entitled *Winning Your Wings*, produced at Warner's Burbank studio to attract enlistments in the Air Corps. The 25-minute film was released in May 1942, and was credited with generating over 150,000 new recruits. As the F.M.P.U. staff expanded, Warners re-opened the shuttered Vitagraph silent film studio in Edendale and people were moved there. They soon outgrew the Vitagraph facility and were forced to move yet again.

Visiting MGM in Culver City, Crump noticed the idle Hal Roach Studio nearby. Roach had volunteered for active duty and shut his studio down, so he allowed Warners to move the F.M.P.U. people onto his lot for the duration of the war. Roach leased his entire studio to Warners for $1. This turned out to be an excellent move by Roach. Aside from the public relations bonanza and tax benefits, when the F.M.P.U. shut down after the war, his entire studio site had been upgraded for free. The location was known as "Fort Roach" for the rest of the war.

The personnel assigned to the unit were incredibly talented, some of the best and brightest in the industry. In addition to Lt. Col. Warner and writer-producer Col. Crump, Roach himself ended up working for the unit. Col. Frank Capra shot some of the finest battle footage produced during the war. Lt. Col. George Stevens, Major William Wyler and Major John Huston helped run the unit. It might have been the most talented studio in the movie business in the 1940s based upon personnel alone.

Thousands of studio employees were among the throng of enlistees rushing into every branch of the service. Included were hundreds of the most popular stars in the world, volunteering to fight and perhaps die. Most did so over the often-violent objections of their studios, which did everything they could to keep their top stars out of danger.

Jimmy Stewart tried to enlist but was initially refused entry because he was five pounds under the required 148 pounds. He talked the recruitment officer into ignoring the test. He eventually became a colonel in the 8th Air Force, flying his B-17 "MALE CALL" over Europe and earning the Distinguished Flying Cross, the Croix de Guerre and seven battle stars. He later flew B-52s and B-58s in Vietnam. He became the highest-ranking actor in military history when he was promoted to Brigadier General, but would never allow his war record to be used in movies or in his publicity records.

Robert Montgomery, Robert Taylor, Buddy Rogers and Douglas Fairbanks, Jr., enlisted. On January 16, 1942, actress Carole Lombard was tragically killed in a plane crash returning to Los Angeles from an Indiana bond rally. In August her husband, 41-year-old Clark Gable — whose friends were certain he simply wanted to die in combat — volunteered for one of the most dangerous assignments in the Air Corps.

As an aerial gunner aboard a B-17 in the 317th Bomb group, he was assigned to a base in Polebrook, England, and would fly several dozen bombing raids over Europe. Adolf Hitler put a $5,000 bounty on Gable's plane. Once, a 20 mm shell ripped through his boot. Another exploded right next to his head, but he miraculously escaped injury after several such close calls.

Hundreds of stars quietly went off to war without fanfare and returned home the same way. Sabu "The Elephant Boy" Dastigar, though Indian-born, became a U.S. citizen and flew 40 missions as a tail gunner on a B-24. Russell Johnson enlisted in the Air Corps and earned a Purple Heart when his bomber was shot down in a bombing raid over the Philippines. He is better known as the Professor on television's *Gilligan's Island*. Television producer Jack Smight (*Twilight Zone*, *Route 66*, and *Alfred Hitchcock*, among others) served in a B-24 bomber group in the South Pacific.

Jimmy Doolittle led his famous 1942 "Raiders" on an almost suicidal bombing raid over Tokyo. The planes had barely enough fuel to make their bombing runs and then (hopefully) make it to the Chinese mainland where their only option was to crash land. But when Doolittle flew over Tokyo, director John Ford was lying in the exposed nose cone of the lead bomber, filming the bombs. Unbelievably, he was also screaming at Doolittle to "fly lower, fly lower!," so he could get better shots.

Other famous "movie star soldiers" included Sgt. Lee J. Cobb, Lt. Van Heflin,

Capt. William Holden, Sgt. Arthur Kennedy, Sgt. Alan Ladd, George Montgomery, Don Porter, Capt. Ronald Reagan, Sgt. George Reeves, Kent Smith, Capt. Robert Sterling and Craig Stevens.

Carole simply continued her incredible dedication to the military after the U.S. entered the war. She volunteered to make a cross-country trip to a War Bond Rally in St. Louis just two days after the attack on Pearl Harbor. She was joined by Linda Darnell, Melvyn Douglas, Helen Gahagan and Sam Levene for the trip, scheduled to depart Los Angeles late Friday night on December 12.[15] The Navy was still trying to rescue trapped sailors aboard over-turned and damaged ships at Pearl Harbor.

Earlier that Friday, Carole appeared with a dozen 20th Century–Fox stars at a previously scheduled charity benefit at the Shrine Auditorium sponsored by the newspaper the *Los Angeles Examiner.* Carole sang a song and appeared along with Rita Hayworth, Bob Hope, Tyrone Power, Abbott and Costello, George Montgomery and a number of singing acts like Roy Rogers and the Sons of the Pioneers and The Merry Macs.[16]

But when Carole and Linda arrived at the airport for the trip to St. Louis they discovered that the military had grounded of all commercial airline traffic. Her traveling companions wanted to turn around and go home, but Carole — knowing that over 12,000 tickets had been sold for the appearance — coddled and coerced everyone to stay while she worked the phones. It took 12 hours — all the while convincing her friends not to leave the airport — before the Navy approved their flight and they took off early Saturday.[17]

In spite of Carole's efforts, they never reached St. Louis. During a re-fueling stop in Wichita, Kansas, the group was formally grounded; unable to continue. But Carole and Darnell were thrilled when they found out that their train back to Los Angeles was full of hundreds of soldiers bound for the Coast. Giving up their luxury compartments, Carole and Darnell spent the entire two days playing cards, drinking and smoking with the servicemen.[18]

Zanuck tried to ignore the war, and incredibly went ahead with the shooting schedule for *My Gal Sal.* It commenced shooting the day after Christmas and filming lasted until the end of February. The last thing Carole wanted to do was make a film — particularly this one, which was part of Zanuck's punishment for the *Blood and Sand* problem. But Zanuck forced her to finish the project.

The casting shuffle on the *My Gal Sal* set came directly from Zanuck and was meant to further humiliate Carole for refusing his further sexual demands. Like the *Blood and Sand* situation, Carole was promised the lead, and her casting had been publicized. But when filming began, Zanuck had moved her to a minor role and given the lead to Rita Hayworth. It was an example of the depths that the infantile Zanuck went to, that he again paid the exorbitant Columbia loan-out rate to give Hayworth a role she was ill-equipped to handle. Zanuck struck back at Carole by giving her a role that was little more than a cameo.

The movie was a fictionalized tale of the life of Paul Drieser, brother of the famed novelist Theodore Dreiser, who ran away from his fundamentalist Indiana home in 1873 at the age of 16 and joined a traveling medicine show selling "wizard oil." He spent several years wandering the country from troupe to troupe and in his spare time wrote wonderful songs that became immensely popular.

Dreiser, changing his name to Dresser, wrote dozens of famous songs between 1886 and 1900 but squandered his fortune and by 1902 was broke. He saved himself with a self-published semi-autobiographical book *My Gal Sal*, which sold millions of copies. Unfortunately, he never saw any of the money; he died of a heart attack in early 1906 before the royalty checks began arriving.

The movie strays from the true Dreiser biography by adding a beautiful singer, Mae Collins (Carole), to the traveling show. Their love affair ends with the arrival of big theater star Sally Elliott (Hayworth), who steals Dresser away and takes him to New York. By singing his songs she makes him famous and rich. Mae is forgotten.

The story would have been better-served with leads other than Mature and Hayworth, neither of whom could carry what is basically a nostalgic period musical. Hayworth couldn't even sing, while just the week before *Sal* filming began, Carole signed a contract with RCA to produce a series of record albums.[19] Probably because of their lack of musical talent, the movie becomes more of a love-hate relationship piece for Mature and Hayworth rather than the musical it started out to be. Even so, the highlight of the film is still songs—most written by Dresser himself—like "On the Big White Way," "The Convict and the Bird" and "Mr. Volunteer."

Carole has a touching role that she plays very well but she is gone from the screen within the first 20 minutes. When she *is* on screen, the cameramen were obviously instructed to keep her shots at a distance while keeping Hayworth in close-ups. There is obvious chemistry between Mature and Hayworth in absence of any acting talent; the two were involved in a heated affair during filming.

Mature was something of a 1940s version of a "muscle-head" when he began acting. He was variously described as "a gorgeous hunk of a man" for his physique and "the poor man's Charles Boyer" for his somewhat tentative acting ability.[20] Although they were both married to other people at the time, he and Hayworth began an open affair during *Sal* filming. The passion was obvious; several scenes had to be re-shot because their kissing and physical activities went above and beyond the script.

After the early April release, critics reacted to the obvious snub of Carole. *The Hollywood Reporter* noted on April 23 that "Carole Landis is wasted on a part much too brief for her career at this point but plays it like a trouper." Bosley Crowther mentioned in his April 30 *Herald Examiner* column, "if you look sharp you can see Carole Landis...."

Then they commented on the subpar performances of Mature and Hayworth. Mature is lauded for "strutting the strut ... and baring the torso ... helpful of selling tickets," while Hayworth is described as "Rita Hayworth for the masculine trade, filling the lens with her auburn beauty...."[21]

My Gal Sal was the last A picture Zanuck gave Carole. And she had a "D" role. But at the time, the last thing she wanted to do was make movies. There was a war on. Hollywood was still getting itself organized to fight the "battle of the home front."

John Garfield—unable to enter the service due to 4-F status—had the idea for a club exclusively for the servicemen who frequented Hollywood, and he mentioned it to his friend Bette Davis. Davis approached her agent Jules Stein, founder of the massive Music Corporation of America agency.

Stein and Harry Warner teamed up to raise money to build or buy a club in Hollywood, and ended up purchasing a former livery stable at 1451 Cahuenga Boulevard, just off of Sunset. It was called the Hollywood Canteen, named and modeled after Broadway's famous Stage Door Canteen. Davis was the president, Garfield the vice-president.

To upgrade and enlarge the facilities and equip a full-service nightclub, members of the 14 guilds and unions servicing the studios donated materials, labor and money. Carpenters rebuilt the building inside and out. Plumbers installed pipes and electricians wired. Studio artists and animator-cartoonists painted murals on the walls. The food was donated by volunteer groups and companies. During a typical week, the food cost approached $3,000 (perhaps $75,000 today).

The Canteen opened on October 3, 1942. Stein charged people $100 to sit in the bleachers that surrounded the large dance floor inside, raising $10,000 for the club. Davis said that it was so crowded on opening night that she had to climb through a side window to get inside.

The Canteen quickly became a mecca for servicemen on leave, or preparing to ship overseas. It was staffed with volunteers from the studios. On a given night, Rita Hayworth might be there to dance with the boys, the Andrews Sisters to sing, and drinks might be poured by Veronica Lake. At the Canteen, soldiers departing for battlefield assignments spent their final hours dancing and drinking with movie stars.

Publicly, Davis put on a serious face for the press about the work of the Canteen, thanking her fellow actor-volunteers and saying that she would always be grateful "for the loyalty of those who outlived the first flush of publicity and novelty and continued to work with us."[22] Privately, she was a little less solemn; she led a good number of star actresses who earned reputations for bringing servicemen home for a more private goodbye. Often, Davis simply dragged some star-struck soldier behind the stairs or into her office for sex.

During a two-month hiatus from filming, she actually followed one young conquest to his assignment at Fort Benning, Georgia. She so enjoyed the sex with Cpl. Lewis A. Riley that she rented a small house just outside the base and sat around waiting for him to come over during his off hours. She stayed there for almost two months until Riley was sent overseas.

Speaking to a young Marine about Davis, actor Jack Carson was initially upset when the young man said he "heard she screws like a mink." Carson was angry but then thought to himself, "Well, ain't it the truth?"[23] During the war, the young girls handling Davis' fan mail passed around dozens of letters from sailors and soldiers thanking Davis for her private farewells.

Davis' amorality could be considered much more offensive to common sensibilities than that for which Carole was so roundly punished during her career. After all, Carole's sexual escapades were usually at the command of her bosses. Davis' Canteen frolics were strictly casual. And while Davis is to be commended for helping found the Canteen, Carole worked much more diligently supporting the troops than Davis (in a different manner, as well). But while Carole would be vilified by women like Davis and the studio wives, Davis' behavior earned nothing but a wink and a nod from Hollywood.

Carole volunteered many evenings at the Canteen, and truly enjoyed dancing and sharing stories with the soldiers. Even so, she was adamant that she wanted to become involved in supporting the war effort somehow.

In early 1942 Carole moved again when Edna May Oliver returned from New York to her Sunset Boulevard house. Unbeknownst to Oliver, she was already gravely ill with intestinal cancer. Never knowing the true severity of her illness, she would die within just a few months of her return.

Carole had always wanted to live at the beach and found a beautiful 1920s stucco and log house on the sand in Santa Monica. She moved into 703 Ocean Front Avenue in late March. The neighborhood was celebrity-packed. The white colonial next door at 705 had belonged to Douglas Fairbanks and Mary Pickford; the magnificent Irving Thalberg–Norma Shearer Tudor-style mansion was at 707; Louis B. Mayer was a few doors down at 625; and Gilbert Roland, Paulette Goddard and Jesse Lasky were nearby.

Along this stretch of Ocean Front (now Palisades Beach Road) were and still are a seemingly endless row of garage doors, forbidding-looking gateway entrances and closed windows. But the houses are all magnificent, commanding incredible ocean vistas. Carole's house was on a little rise above the beach, with three levels of draped porches and a mosaic stairwell made of beautiful hand-painted tiles leading down to her private beach.

She set about decorating her new home, filling it with her records and books. She matched the inside to the outside, decorating in an early Spanish style. But she redid the living room in the Chinese motif she so enjoyed from the Oliver house. Her master bedroom and second floor sitting room opened onto a large porch overlooking the beach. She re-did her room in pale rose and eggshell colors with olive trim. She slept in a large double-bed with a large eggshell-quilted headboard. Her bedspread was bordered with embroidered roses.

Once again she let her mother live with her. She would remain there for two years. At the time Carole was moving in at the beach, several movie publications visited for photographs and articles. *Screenland* ran a photograph spread and story written by Betty Boone entitled "Inside the Star's Homes"; *Movie Star Parade* offered "Carole Landis at Home."[24] Both featured a half dozen photographs showing her well-appointed home, but the article was written and the photographs taken some months before, at the Sunset Boulevard house.[25]

Carole's choice of homes fulfilled a long-time dream to live by the ocean, but it was an interesting choice given the fears that gripped many at the time. From the moment of the Japanese attack, the entire West Coast was terrified that it would be the target of a full-scale invasion. The biggest fear was that Southern California would be targeted due to the large number of aircraft manufacturing facilities in the cities around Los Angeles. Carole exhibited no such concerns, and spent most evenings walking the beach in her role at Air Raid Warden, accompanied by her Great Dane Donner.[26] A visiting soldier would give Carole another Great Dane, and she was thereafter seen walking the beach at night with the two huge animals.

As America went to war, Carole continued her determined and committed volunteerism. She was so active in so many defense department units and volunteered

Carole and her beloved Donner at her Santa Monica beach house in 1943.

in so many different groups that she was forced to carry a large case in the trunk of her car. It was filled with several dozen different uniforms so she could "make quick changes."[27]

She spent almost every free night working at the Hollywood Canteen. She not only danced and drank with the servicemen, but worked. She waitressed, tended bar and most evenings stayed past closing to help clean up. But she never missed an early morning call the next day.

Her tireless volunteerism did not go unnoticed. As early as March 1942, she was recognized as one of the most dedicated actresses in Hollywood with the first of dozens of commendations and awards she would receive during the war. On March 14, she was commissioned as an honorary Colonel for her outstanding service to the American Legion. The award, offered by the Hollywood Post 43, honored Carole along with Jane Withers, Judy Canova, Dorothy Lamour and Rosalind Russell.[28]

There was almost never a weekend that Carole didn't offer her beach house to at least ten visiting soldiers or sailors. She invited groups from the various camps within driving distance of Los Angeles to spend the weekend at the beach. She and her mother got up early to make breakfast for everyone in the house. The visitors were allowed the run of the house and all of its food and liquor, and they could enjoy the beach as if they were staying at their own homes. Her mother reported that "ten or twelve boys would be sleeping on cots of the ocean house every weekend night."[29]

When she wasn't filming or entertaining troops locally, Carole made private, often unannounced visits to the military camps all over California. She was such a regular visitor at San Diego's Camp Callan that she was nicknamed "Our Blonde Bomber." She also the two-hour-long trips to Camp Callan, Camp Haan in Riverside, Camp Hunter Liggett and Fort Ord.

The men often gave Carole little mementos of her visits, usually unit insignias, patches and items like that. Michael Pearman, who before the war had been an agent with the Feldman-Blum Agency in Hollywood, later wrote, "Carole really had a lot of fun and not only was she made an honorary sergeant but by the end of the day she was covered with so many chevrons and insignias given her by the military jaws that George Jessel had to advise the General to tie down the howitzers before the boys gave her those too!"

Several times each month she made the two-hour trip into the desert southeast of Riverside to visit Army Air Corps flyers stationed at March Field, the main bomber and gunnery training site during the early 1940s. She particularly enjoyed watching movies with the men at the base's 1920s-era theater located adjacent to the large parade ground. She was also a regular visitor at the football games played by the camp's traveling football and baseball teams. A November 24, 1941, edition of the *Los Angeles Times* noted that "the March field gridders defeated the 160th Infantry team by a score of 20–0 ... maybe because the Bombers had Carole Landis as a sideline inspiration."[30]

In the years just before the Japanese attack on Pearl Harbor dragged the United States headlong into World War II, there was loud and often rancorous debate as to whether the United States should join the fray in Europe or the South Pacific. John F. Kennedy's amoral father Joseph, appointed Ambassador to Great Britain, did not want America in the war on either front. Neither did publisher and Hollywood gadfly William Randolph Hearst.

But Americans were active in their support of our allies in their country's efforts, particularly Great Britain. What became known as British War Relief began U.S. charity and volunteerism several years before the advent of the U.S.O. As the war in England became more catastrophic and the needs greater, Americans were generous in their financial and moral support. The government was also providing boatloads of munitions and equipment.

Charities to help the British people included groups like the American Committee for Air Raid Relief, the American Hospital in Britain, the British American Ambulance Corps, the British Hospital Association and Bundles for Britain. By 1941 most of these groups were administered by an umbrella organization called the British War Relief Society (B.W.R.S.).

The B.W.R.S. was primarily a central receiving office for donated money and supplies which they then parceled out to its affiliate organizations in the U.S. and Britain. Only one of the B.W.R.S. organizations raised its own money: Bundles for Britain. Bundles was begun in 1939 by Mrs. Wales Latham, a young New York society matron who began her charity work for Britain by organizing her friends to knit garments for British sailors serving on the frigid North Sea. Mrs. Winston Churchill originally put out a call for Englishwomen to knit these items and Mrs. Latham decided to answer the call from across the Atlantic. What began as her little knitting circle became a major wartime charity.

A magazine article about Latham said that "she got a license from the State Department, wheedled an empty store rent-free from a Park Avenue landlord and persuaded Mrs. Winston Churchill to become a sponsor."[31] Latham's Bundles group focused on collecting supplies rather than money. Cast-off clothing was mended or made over; if they were not usable they were cut up for woolen patchwork blankets or baby sleeping bags. Americans supported Bundles in every conceivable manner. A Mississippi sharecropper sent in nine pennies; $1.15 arrived from two sisters' Kool-Aid stand; a radio appeal by movie stars Charles Boyer and Ronald Colman raised $30,000 (perhaps $600,000 today) for medical supplies.

In Hollywood, a group of actresses banded together as they had done during World War I to found the American Theatre Wing of the B.W.R.S. They did everything from entertaining at benefits to operating a sewing room to produce items for British war refugees. It was common to see newspaper photographs of (usually, but not always) British actresses like Vivien Leigh knitting something for the B.W.R.S.

On April 11, 1942, Dixie Lee Crosby opened up the house she shared with Bing Crosby at 10500 Camarillo Street in North Hollywood to the public for a "Bundle Tea." Over 3,000 fans got to walk around the Crosby house by donating a bundle of clothing and 50 cents. Gracie Fields was known as the "Sweetheart of the British Empire" largely because of 50+ concerts she did for British war relief in 1940 and 1941. Cary Grant donated his entire salaries from *The Philadelphia Story* and *Mr. Lucky* to British war relief. The United States would form a similar domestic group in 1941 as it became more apparent that *something* was going to happen to drag us into war.

In late 1941, the American Theater Wing approached Carole with the idea of having her and some other actresses visit the military bases in Great Britain. Carole jumped at the chance, and enlisted Kay Francis, Martha Raye and Mitzi Mayfair to embark on a "Victory Caravan" tour of overseas military bases.

Francis was the oldest of the four women, but nobody knew by how much. She believed herself to be a true movie star, and was extremely vain; even at her studio, no one knew her real birth date (it was somewhere between 1899 and 1908). She married and divorced five times, and in the early 1930s she was indeed the top star at Warner Bros. By the time she was traveling with Carole and the girls, she had been forced off her pedestal at Warners by Bette Davis and had begun drifting into B movies. But she still thought of herself as a star.

Raye was born backstage at a vaudeville theater in Butte, Montana, and joined her Irish immigrant parents' song and dance act at two. She was a true comedienne, a female clown, and loved performing. She entered the movies in 1936, but her lack of schooling meant that scripts had to be read to her. She was so deathly afraid of flying that she had to drink herself into a stupor before boarding a plane. Volunteering for this type of trip was a testament to her dedication to the cause.

Mayfair was the least well-known of the group, an attractive Broadway dancer who had appeared in four or five '30s movies. The group was made up of an actress (Francis), a comic (Raye), a dancer (Mayfair) and a beautiful singer-actress (Carole). The four girls were a good mix and could put on a fine show. The tour would make the American Theater Wing the first organization to send entertainers on what soon came to be known as "camp tours." The trip was originally to commence in May 1942, just three months after U.S. troops arrived there, but would not get going until the fall.

Eventually the American Theatre Wing would join with a new domestic organization, the United Service Organizations, but Carole's little band was the first to go. The U.S.O. would not get to Europe for another year. The A.T.W. would eventually open the world-renowned Stage Door Canteen in New York, and in the following years become responsible for the theater's Tony awards.

Carole's group was not only the first group to make a camp tour but the first and only all-woman troupe to make any kind of tour. Theirs was the longest and most dangerous of any of the trips taken by anyone during the war. During the entire length of the war, Carole would be one of the most tireless volunteers in Hollywood.

The U.S.O. would become synonymous with camp tours, but it would take another year. United Service Organizations was actually an umbrella group conceived by President Franklin Roosevelt. His idea was for an organization whose only purpose was to reach out *from* the American people *to* the people serving in the military. Roosevelt, a great natural leader, foresaw a non-governmental group operated by civilian volunteers that would act as a support mechanism for no other purpose than to deliver morale-enhancing programs to the troops, wherever they were.

Roosevelt's United Service Organizations was founded on February 4, 1941, in New York and included six all-civilian agencies he personally approached to join the fold. They were the Salvation Army, the Young Men's Christian Association, the Young Women's Christian Association, the National Catholic Community Services, the National Travelers Aid Association and the National Jewish Welfare Board. The U.S.O. was (and still is) a private, nonprofit organization supported entirely by private citizens and corporations. During the war it was a channel for directing community volunteerism directly to the troops. On November 28, 1941, the first large, government-run U.S.O. club opened at Fayetteville, North Carolina. Smaller local U.S.O. centers were opened in over 3,000 towns, big and small, in every conceivable location, from museums and churches to yacht clubs and storefronts. At the same time (1941–44) the number of U.S. troops grew from 50,000 to 12,000,000. The U.S.O. effort was massive, and effective.

The main goal of a U.S.O. center was to provide off-duty or travel recreation for soldiers, to provide a "Home Away From Home" wherever they may be. Centers could be dance halls, cafes, quiet places to write letters or pray, even child-care centers. But by far, the U.S.O. was best known for their "camp shows," an idea that sprung up within months of the group's founding.

The camp show wing, founded in November 1941, was headed by Abe Lastfogel, who ran the massive William Morris Talent Agency. The idea of camp shows actually originated with Ed Sullivan. Best-known for his later *Ed Sullivan Show*, in the 1930s he was a famous gossip columnist in Los Angeles and New York. Sullivan began taking small groups of Broadway actors up and down the East Coast entertaining troops on weekends as early as 1939. The response was so great the Camp Shows, Inc., was formed.

Camp Shows was successful because it combined the efforts of anyone and everyone allied with William Morris. Talent agents, booking agents, theater owners, movie studios and performers were better-equipped to match the entertainment needs of the Army Camp Commanders with the supply of talent. A typical requisition sent to the Camp Show offices might read, "Immediately, five people, mixed, male and female, with star if possible. Accordionist essential. Tropical climate, three months." Camp Shows would match them up with an act or acts that were listed in their rosters and send the unit on its way.

By 1942 Camp Shows, Inc., was the largest booking agent in the world. In its first six months, 24 groups gave 3,791 performances to camp audiences of 2,217,968 men. There were four different types of tours. The Victory Tour was the biggest show with the most famous performers (sometimes including entire Broadway shows) mostly for large stateside bases. The Blue Tour was a vaudeville show, headlined by a famous comedian and offering three or four other acts to smaller stateside venues. While the Victory Tour got the most publicity, most U.S.O. performers were not famous movie stars. U.S.O. entertainers were paid, but far less than they would have earned normally, and most studios quietly discontinued their contract payments while they were volunteering.

Of the various circuits, the Foxhole Tours were the most arduous. These entertainers traveled to the battlefields, visiting troops literally often in foxholes. They were the most dangerous tours, but the most beneficial. The only tours that Carole would volunteer for were Foxhole Tours.

By 1945, Camp Shows artists would give 273,599 shows to a worldwide audience of 171,717,205. Through 1947 an almost unbelievable 428,521 shows were presented, during the height of the War at a rate of upwards of 700 shows going on *every day*! During the war, 28 entertainers lost their lives, usually in transport plane crashes. Hollywood's 5,500 "brave soldiers in greasepaint" were a favorite attraction, so the U.S.O. looked toward the Hollywood Victory Committee for volunteers at every turn.

Among the popular musical volunteers was Carole's first orchestra leader Carl Ravazza, whose orchestra had become very popular in the years since the 15-year-old singer fronted for him. During the war, Carl and his band made dozens of appearances at war bond rallies with Dinah Shore and Bing Crosby. The band's final appearance was at New York's La Martinique Café in 1945, after which Ravazza became the house conductor at New York's Roxy Theater.

The best known of the U.S.O. camp shows were the Bob Hope shows. Hope dedicated almost 50 years of his life to the cause, beginning with his first European tour in 1942. But Hope was not the first. Carole and her little band got to Europe first. While the U.S.O. was getting organized in 1942, Carole was flying to England. The troops had arrived there just six months before.

Carole's Victory Caravan was announced in March 1942, but it would take almost six months for the organization and coordination with the military to be finalized. Remember, this was the first-ever camp tour, and neither the military nor the entertainers had any idea what to expect or how to get ready. As she waited for her plane to leave for England, Carole busied herself volunteering at home, and was assigned two more forgettable B movies by Zanuck.

The performers were not allowed to tell anyone where they were going, or exactly when they were leaving. Most never actually knew where they were going or when until the last minute anyway. Carole said that she was told, "Just stand by. Be ready to leave any minute. We might call you in an hour or a day or in 36 hours, and be sure your luggage doesn't weigh more than 55 pounds."[32] This posed serious challenges for the actors and actresses, who were typically forced to juggle filming schedules and personal appearances (actually any personal time at all) anyway. The prohibition on releasing information was a logical precaution; celebrity entertainers would be logical choices for enemy attacks.

Actor Leslie Howard was killed when his commercial plane was shot down by Nazi aircraft off of Spain in June 1943. It was later learned that the Germans knew that Howard, an ardent supporter of his native England's wartime efforts, was aboard the British Overseas Airways flight. The U.S. government was very worried that such an accident could befall a large group of entertainers flying together; hence the secrecy.

In February Carole began work on *It Happened in Flatbush* with Lloyd Nolan. Originally entitled *Dem Lovely Bums*,[33] it was directed by Ray McCarey, who directed Carole in *Cadet Girl*, and was a B-movie ensemble piece. Also appearing were Sara Allgood, William Frawley, Robert Armstrong, Jane Darwell, Scotty Beckett and Joseph Allen. It is a seriously unbelievable love story between rich, young and beautiful society woman Kathryn Baker (Carole) who inherits the Dodgers, managed by a cliché in a baseball hat named Frank "Butterfingers" Maguire.

There is absolutely no chemistry between Carole and Nolan (nor would there be in their later film *Manila Calling*), and the movie is a litany of forced situations. Kathryn, of course, doesn't like baseball and wants to sell the team. Maguire is a former Brooklyn player whose error cost the team a pennant. He, of course, responds by courting her if only to persuade her not to sell the team. Neither sees through the obvious machinations of the other and the Dodgers inevitably win the pennant while Carole and Nolan seem to fall in friendship less than love. It's a strange relationship played out in a setting that is not believable, but Carole does her best to carry the film. She is the only pleasant part of the picture, which filmed until March 26; even she was not able to save such a poorly written work. The only people who liked this film were Brooklyn Dodgers fans.

Just as *Flatbush* was wrapping, Zanuck assigned Carole to perhaps the worst of all the bad films he threw her into, *Orchestra Wives. Wives* was less a movie than a semi-documentary about the lives of the musicians in the Glenn Miller Orchestra and their dancing cohorts Fayard and Harold Nicholas. Ann Rutherford starred as Connie Ward, a cute local girl who married trumpet player Bill Abbot (played by George Montgomery).

Unfortunately, after Connie marries Bill, she spends an hour or so learning the downside to life as an orchestra wife, dealing with the constant travel and the catty, jealous attacks of the other wives. When the band leaves the wives in Des Moines for a few days, all hell breaks loose. Natalie (Carole) tries to stir the pot by telling Connie that Jaynie (Bari) is after her new husband. Somehow Bill ends up in Jaynie's hotel room when Connie walks in, and all the wives end up fighting amongst themselves and their husbands, threatening the very life of the band before things are straightened out.

It is quite simply a terrible movie. It seems like everyone in the film was miscast. Rutherford can not seem to get her part at all. Carole comes off as an awful troublemaker; she doesn't seem to have it in her, even for the camera. Romero spends the entire movie as a comic peacemaker among the band.

The single redeeming part of the film was the music of Glenn Miller's Orchestra and the seemingly effortless dancing of the Nicholas Brothers. Harold Nicholas would later become a close friend to Carole when he married Dorothy Dandridge, one of her close pals.

Another of Carole's *Wives* co-stars was Virginia Gilmore, a relative newcomer at the Fox lot who also ran afoul of Zanuck, allegedly when she refused to have anything (sexual) to do with him. Gilmore was the daughter of a British Army officer who retired to California; she was educated in a convent. After she was hired by Zanuck, her career appeared to be on a fast track until she was suddenly relegated to lower-quality B's like *Wives*. Barney Oldfield confirmed that the story on the Fox lot was that Gilmore refused to even set foot in Zanuck's office after her first brief visit.[34] She left Fox shortly after *Wives* for the stage, and later became a successful and popular acting coach.

While Carole waited for the Camp Tour to be organized, she kept busy. On the personal front she was again in a whirlwind of dates. She had become somewhat of a regular "date" for Cary Grant, attending all manner of social and industry functions with the homosexual star, typically at studio request. Her dates with Grant came in flurries. If rumors of his true relationship with Randolph Scott became too obvious in the tabloids, his studio would send him on four or five dates with Carole or some other young starlet. Once those photographs and stories surfaced to replace the Scott stories, he could stop spending time with women and go back to Scott.

She spent a lot of time in early 1942 in the company of dancer Tony Martin and the two became very close friends. She also dated Greg Bautzer, radio commentator Robert Arden,[35] director Anatole Litvak and several wealthy young men. She dated A&P heir Huntington Hartford III and Woolworth's Five & Dime heir Woolworth "Wooly" Donahue.[36] The only serious dates seemed to be with Bautzer and Martin, but several other relationships both raised, and answered, questions.

It's doubtful that Carole believed her relationship with Bautzer would become very serious. He had a terrible reputation as a womanizer, and she had known him since her Busby Berkeley days. Any thoughts that theirs was a serious relationship were quashed when Jimmy Fidler noted in his column, "ATTENTION CAROLE LANDIS: Greg Bautzer has been telephoning Dorothy Lamour from Washington!"[37]

During the same period, Carole was seem with Rouben Mamoulian on any number of occasions. Sightings were not only at the typical studio photograph opportunities like the Trocadero or Mocambo or at premieres. They appeared to actually be a serious couple, which further supports the theory that Carole's dismissal from *Blood and Sand* had more to do with Zanuck than Mamoulian.

In March, Carole removed herself from the relationship with Mamoulian and began dating Gene Markey. Almost 25 years Carole's senior, Markey was a reasonably successful producer of films like Basil Rathbone's *The Adventures of Sherlock Holmes* (1939) and a writer of three dozen mostly B movies; he was better known for his wives than his work. When he began dating Carole in early 1942, he had been married and divorced by Joan Bennett and Hedy Lamarr (he would later marry and divorce Myrna Loy). The Markey–Landis relationship took most of Hollywood by surprise given the age difference and her beauty. By late March, rumors began circulating that Carole was going to marry Markey.

That was an interesting coincidence, since 18 months earlier both Markey and Carole were mentioned in the same newspaper story detailing three simultaneous "Hollywood divorces." The article described Carole's divorce from Willis Hunt, the John Barrymore–Elaine Barry split, and Markey's divorce from Lamarr.

The new rumors gained enough strength — with the help of planted stories from the Fox publicists — that newspaper stories described Carole leaving on March 31 to "Washington ... with the announcement that she will wed writer-producer Gene Markey, now a lieutenant commander in the Navy."[38] The publicists were behind the rumors, and behind planted photographs of the couple "confirming" that the couple had actually married. Some photograph-articles mentioned that "Carole Landis has made Gene Markey the happiest man in the world for the third time. It's also Carole's third marriage."[39]

The stories were obviously studio plants. Supposedly, the articles were wedding announcements, but all the photographs of Carole with the stories were of her wearing a bathing suit, and all began with, "It seems girls who look like this are always getting married." It's is unknown why the studio publicity people would allow this particular information (they knew to be false) to circulate so freely, but Carole did get tons of publicity from the cheesecake photographs attached to the false stories.

For her part, Carole was forced to deny everything when she arrived in Washington, telling reporters that she was "astounded"[40] at reports that she had flown from Los Angeles to marry Markey. But the couple dated on and off for over a year. When Carole returned to Los Angeles on April 3, she went to work on *Orchestra Wives*.

From the pre-war years, Carole was a favorite with the soldiers; first because of her beauty and later because of her personality. On April 3, she and Warren Hull, who played The Green Hornet in *The Green Hornet Strikes Again* (1941), appeared on a WBBM radio broadcast of the "Vox Pop" show at Fort Bliss, Texas. The show featured the two stars interviewing soldiers, filling in for regular host Parks Johnson. Carole gamely asked superfluous prepared questions like "What do you think about while you're on guard duty?," "Why is a second lieutenant called a 'shavetail?'" and "What is a corporal's guard?" The program was also broadcast to military bases around the world via short wave.[41]

On Friday, April 10 she was on the air again, appearing on the *CBS Playhouse*

Radio production of *I Wake Up Screaming*. For flying to New York to appear in a single episode, Carole was paid $1,500 (about $30,000 today). Because she had to miss a day of *Orchestra Wives* filming, Zanuck kept half of the payment.

Zanuck had other reasons to be angry with Carole in early April. For a month, Fox publicists had wanted to arrange a public "romance" between Carole and newcomer George Holmes to help his career. But Carole would not cooperate although several small items were planted with a few tabloid columnists.[42] Holmes was a handsome young actor who had appeared with Carole in *It Happened in Flatbush* and, for a short time in the early 1940s, Fox had big plans for him. But Carole knew that as long as she kept up appearances of a relationship with Markey, Zanuck would be unable to link her to anyone else since Markey was off serving his country.

Zanuck was furious that she held that power over him, and Fox was never able to use her to help Holmes' career.[43] After a few dozen mostly forgettable films, Holmes left the movies in the late 1940s. Carole must have been delighted to be able to tweak Zanuck after all he had done to her.

She also got some satisfaction reading that Rita Hayworth's costumes in her film *Tales of Manhattan* were old costumes that she (Carole) had worn in *Orchestra Wives* and *It Happened in Flatbush*. Walter Winchell noted in his "New York Heartbeat" column that Charles Boyer's *Tales of Manhattan* contract allowed him final approval of all of Hayworth's costumes and dresses. When he rejected everything originally made for her (he thought she was made too attractive, which would take attention from him), the studio made her wear Carole's old gowns.[44] It was interesting treatment for an actress whom Zanuck allegedly held in such esteem above Carole.

Near the end of *Orchestra Wives* filming, Carole was back in court. To literally millions of people she was Carole Landis, but she was still legally Frances Lillian Ridste Hunt. On April 24, 1942, she finalized the legal process of changing her name to Carole Landis. Sitting on a bench outside the courtroom just after the proceedings, looking glamourous in her suit and hat, she smoked a cigarette and sighed, "I'm certainly glad that's over."[45]

She probably was. She never *really* was small-town Frances Ridste. She was always Carole Landis. Legally someone else. Her fame would overtake her personal life so thoroughly that in later years the press usually called her mother Clara Landis. The date of this proceeding is sometimes offered as March 24, but court records confirm the April timing.

The first half of 1942 was a tiresome waiting game for Carole. She endured the ongoing torment from Zanuck's assignments and behind-the-scenes back-stabbing. One of his hobbies was announcing to the press that Carole had been given a lead in a film — a film he knew would not be produced. In early March he told writers that Carole would star with Cesar Romero in a remake of the film *Pieces of Silver*,[46] and later that month gave her the lead in *Lady in a Quandary*.[47] Neither film was ever made.

During the first few months of 1942 Carole worked almost full-time on her volunteering efforts. In January she flew to San Francisco for three days to visit and perform for sailors at the Alameda naval base. That same month, The *Los Angeles Times* described Carole's 16-hour weekend days volunteering for Bundles for Bluejackets and her weekly blood donations.[48]

On February 5, she hosted a fundraiser for Bundles for Bluejackets at Ciro's Restaurant. Two nights later she hosted a beach party in Long Beach for 1,500 children of sailors assigned to ships from the Long Beach Naval Air Station. She spent an entire day and night playing games with the kids, passing out food and gifts and singing. In March she volunteered as a hostess at the Convoy Cabaret (a restaurant near the docks in San Pedro) that was playing host to crews from the destroyers anchored nearby. She also made appearances at local military bases, usually unannounced, to simply sit in the base clubs and have a drink with the servicemen.

By the middle of April she was working almost full-time on volunteer projects. She visited the Los Angeles Victory House once a week and sold War Savings Bonds. On May 5 she helped host a party of 500 soldiers from the Carolinas and Texas organized by Harry Brand. On the 15th she and Betty Grable organized and ran a charity tea for the Bundles for Bluejackets committee.[49]

On May 21 she appeared with Bing Crosby on his popular *Kraft Music Hall* radio show, along with Virginia Weidler, Frank McHugh and Ruth Hussey. Crosby's weekly *Music Hall* program, which had been running since 1936, combined singing, skit comedy and the like. Carole appeared in several comedy skits and joined Bing in a song. For her appearance she was paid $1,000; again Zanuck retained half of the fee because she was away from the studio for a day, even though she was not working.

The radio was America's only other means of entertainment aside from the movies and sports. It was also important for the war effort. Edward M. Kirby was the director of Public Relations for the National Association of Radio Broadcasters when he was loaned to the War Department in December 1940 to head up the Armed Forces Radio Service. Kirby was responsible for developing programs for both government and soldiers. Almost immediately after the Japanese attack on Pearl Harbor, Kirby introduced *The Army Hour*, meant for listeners on the home front, and *Command Performance*, targeting those in uniform.

There were dozens of other programs but these two were the most popular. *The Army Hour* was Kirby's attempt to bring the reality of the war home to the American people, "supplied by the men who were doing the fighting." It was carried on NBC, the only network that agreed to carry the Army's new programs (and probably why the network still carries so much political clout). The program offered interviews with soldiers from high-ranking officers to lower-level combat veterans, as well as some of the most descriptive — and honest — battlefield reporting of the war. One early broadcast featured the terse translation of the last Morse code message from the besieged soldiers of Corregidor, about to surrender to Japan. The show's effect was powerful.

To balance the darkness of *The Army Hour*, Kirby asked Lou Cowan, who had developed the early radio classic *Quiz Kids*, to come up with something for the soldiers. He offered *Command Performance*, designed to entertain the troops overseas. It was broadcast via short wave to every wartime theater from Europe to Africa to the South Pacific. It was a simple concept: Soldiers at the front could ask for anything, and the show would try to provide it.

The requests ranged from the touching to the bizarre. A corporal who had never met his infant son reported that the "little guy is teething" and asked "to hear him

Carole, ca. 1942.

yowl." A group of soldiers from New York asked to hear the hubbub of Times Square on New Year's Eve. Yet another soldier just wanted to hear bacon sizzling in a pan!

Stars from Bob Hope and Bing Crosby to Judy Garland and Merle Oberon appeared gratis in response to some soldier's request. But the single most famous request involved Carole. Some writers attributed the request to a group of soldiers in New Guinea, but it actually came via letter written in May 1942 from H.F. Pennington, Jr., a sailor stationed at Pearl Harbor. He wrote, "Heard your broadcast of April 23 (1942) and ... send you my one request and desire. Now I admit I want

PLENTY but it won't take much of the program's time. Sooo, if you could have Miss Carole Landis just step up to the microphone and SIGH — that's all brother, just SIGH — I'll be happy."

Not talk, or sing. Just sigh. So she did. During a live show on Sunday evening, June 14, 1942, Master of Ceremonies Don Ameche announced, "Your wish is our command. Here she is, glamourous Carole Landis. For H.F.P., Jr. at Pearl Harbor, Carole Landis will now sigh." She marched across the soundstage in front of the large audience watching the taping, and sighed! Ameche followed, "That was it, fellows — the sigh heard round the world!" as Carole walked smiling off the stage.[50] The response from the soldiers across the globe was phenomenal. Carole's sigh became legendary across four continents and hundreds of battlefields. The program received thousands of requests over the following months to repeat the broadcast, which Kirby's people did on several occasions.*

Carole was available any time any branch of the service asked for help. She was regularly asked to escort visiting military personnel and dignitaries, which she did without complaint. If she was free, she went. She accompanied dozens of visiting R.A.F. wing commanders, generals and other dignitaries on arranged evenings out.

She also kept up her frenetic daily missions. On June 2 she spent the afternoon in the I. Magnins store selling bonds and war stamps.[51] From June 12 through the 15, she and her friend Dana Andrews traveled throughout the Midwest, from Kansas City to Indianapolis, selling War Bonds. The day she returned, she headed directly to the studio for *Manila Calling* filming.

On June 28 she escorted Navy Ensign Frances Pinter to a party at the Ambassador Hotel honoring 16 war heroes.[52] For the next month a photograph of Carole and Pinter appeared in newspapers around the country under the headline JOIN THE NAVY AND SEE THE LANDIS.[53] The photograph — featuring Carole in a sexy off-the-shoulder dress — ran in hundreds of papers, each time as if it had happened the evening prior.

At the same time, ex-husband Willis Hunt reappeared in Carole's life, still pestering her for a reconciliation. Hunt had even re-married — and divorced — since their marriage ended two years earlier.[54]

The first week of July, after she heard that Arthur Murray had offered free dance lessons to soldiers on leave in Los Angeles, Carole volunteered to be the first free dance instructor,[55] spending several free days dancing with the soldiers. On July 4th she escorted five visiting soldiers around Los Angeles, taking them dancing at the Trocadero. She was at the studio at 6 A.M. the next morning. Later in July she allowed the *Vox Pop* radio program to give a lucky soldier her home telephone number so he could call her any time he wished. She received hundreds of telephone calls from the winner and his fellow soldiers, chatting with everyone who called.[56]

On July 24 she left on a week-long Victory Tour, one of the Hollywood Victory Committee's visits to local Army camps. Rather than accompany a local group to bases

---

*Another interesting request occurred several weeks after Carole's visit, when a group of airmen "somewhere in England" asked Warner Bros. star Dolores Moran to appear in front of the mike for one minute "standing perfectly still, wearing a tight sweater." They didn't want her to talk — remember, this was radio — just stand there! Moran complied.

closer to home, she volunteered to go with the group traveling through Texas and Louisiana, the hottest and most uncomfortable of any of the domestic summer trips. As usual, she went without complaint.

Upon her return to California, Carole had a few more bits of film work to do before the Caravan left for Europe. The first was a passable B-movie that was written to mirror events already taking place in the Pacific theater, where Japan had invaded and taken over the Philippines. *Manila Calling* began filming in August, directed by Herbert Leeds. Carole starred with Lloyd Nolan, her *It Happened in Flatbush* co-star. This film suffered from the same lack of chemistry that had plagued their earlier pairing.

Originally, Carole's close friend Pat O'Brien was to play Nolan's part, but a scheduling conflict kept him out.[57] It would clearly have been a much better film with O'Brien and Landis versus Nolan and Landis. Other cast members included Cornel Wilde, James Gleason, Martin Koslcke and Ralph Byrd. The film was supposedly based on a true story of a group of soldiers that captures a Japanese radio station on the island of Luzon and uses it to counteract Japanese broadcasts.

Manila has the usual unreasonable plot challenges and contradictions inherent in Bs. Carole plays dance hall girl Edna Fraser, who had come to the Philippines to marry a wealthy man on whose plantation the Japanese had been operating a radio station. Lucky Matthews (Nolan) and two other radio engineers (Wilde and Gleason) capture the radio transmitter from the Japanese and spend the rest of the movie fighting off Japanese attacks even though they have no food or water and are surrounded by seemingly thousands of Japanese soldiers.

Wilde works to get the transmitter operational so they can escape and transmit a message of courage to the enslaved Filipinos nearby (assuming they had radios, another of those pesky plot challenges). At movie's end, two of the original crew manage to escape by plane, everyone else but Edna and Lucky having been picked off. But the two are (predictably) in love and decide to stay by the radio as the plane carrying their friends takes off. Nolan is dramatically shouting into the mike "Manila calling! Manila calling!" while bombs explode around them. We are left to assume that the heroic couple die while the credits are rolling.

For all of its plot challenges, *Manila Calling* was a very realistic war picture for the 1940s. Filming was often a little rough for the stars, particularly the women. Carole gamely put up with the exertion of diving and falling for days on end. One writer noted that he visited the *Manila* set and "saw Carole Landis, whose ends were nicely shaped by destiny, go through 10 rounds of calisthenics just dodging bombs... By day's end, if Miss Landis wasn't calling for the masseuse then she's a husky as well as a beautiful gal."[58]

Movie bombs were complicated affairs. The charge came from a small keg filled with powder, dust and ground cork that was placed near the actors, out of sight. Off to the side, grips placed a pipe-cannon (filled with more dust) that would be discharged using compressed air. Usually several other grips would either shovel or throw additional debris on top of the scene. The charge and the pipe-cannon were all wired to the same switch. The end result was a realistic-looking explosion, but they were notoriously unstable and injured many actors and actresses over the years.

During *Manila* filming, there were dozens of scenes with multiple explosions that would send Carole lunging under tables for cover. Carole got more and more worried about the numerous keg bombs igniting within eight or ten feet of her head. She finally told the director Leeds that, after the first explosion, she was staying under the table until they were done with each scene.

When *Manila* finished filming at the end of July, producer Charles Rogers arranged a loan-out from Fox so Carole could star in his film *The Powers Girl*. An incredibly lightweight musical starring George Murphy and Anne Shirley, it was perhaps best described in a period review that noted that the film "will enable [moviegoers] completely to forget the harsh realities of the world."[59]

The movie was based on the women working for a real-life top-of-the-line 1930s New York modeling agency. Actual Powers Girls alumni included Kim Novak, Jennifer Jones and Grace Kelly. A contrived, paper-thin plot and some of the most overhanded comedy routines make this a difficult movie to get through.

Carole was not thrilled about her role as a New York City waitress who becomes a Powers Girl, but her performance has been described as "luminous and believable." The *Powers Girls* role perhaps did more to enhance the Carole myth than any other of her films. Though Fox was clearly directing Carole *away* from significant roles in A pictures, her work in the Bs was making her famous.

Although she is third-billed behind George Murphy and Anne Shirley, she steals the movie. Once again, Carole turns a non-major character into the dominant female in the film. Once again, Carole outshines the actress who was supposed to be prettier and more talented. But it didn't seem to matter. Thankfully, she had her upcoming Victory Caravan to look forward to.

One unfortunate aspect of her travels was that she was forbidden by military secrecy regulations to tell anyone where she was going, or when. That was fine with Carole; she preferred doing that work privately anyway. But it caused problems on the set when Murphy became ill during filming and caused a delay that threatened to keep Carole from her Caravan trip. All she could do was wait quietly, not telling anyone about her concerns.

It was becoming more and more difficult for Carole to be taken seriously as an actor, particularly

During the filming of 1944's *Manila Calling*.

since Zanuck demoted her to lesser-quality films. She was worried that she was going to spend her life as just a pretty face and body in Hollywood, and felt she had more to offer.

Everywhere she turned, her body was all that was talked about. Walter Winchell called her "All Girl, all the time." It was becoming a heavy burden. There were only two options; you could break under the weight of it, or you could solve the cipher. Over the last few months, as she got farther and farther into her stateside war work, an idea slowly dawned on her. Her glamour was necessary. It was not her burden but her gift.

The war would change Carole; indeed, the pre–Caravan months had already done much to her. She would later characterize herself as an ambitious (she certainly was) and spoiled (she clearly wasn't) starlet before the war. Most of her volunteerism was not publicized. When it was, she made sure that whatever military person was close by got the press. She mentioned to a writer in March 1942 that the "chi chi and glitter" that had been so important to her didn't seem as important any more. Carole always wanted people to know her for something other than her looks, but during the war, that was the single most important thing she could offer the servicemen. So she did. With a smile. She even asked Fox to loan her out to a British studio so she could spend time there visiting the troops on her off-hours. Serious discussions were held, but by the time the summer rolled around the British studios had all been shut down because of labor shortages. In September it was finally confirmed that the Victory Caravan would depart in November.

As the summer of 1942 came to a close, the Caravan finally began to take shape. It was announced that Carole would headline a Victory Caravan heading to England. At about the same time, Al Jolson and Merle Oberon were scheduled to do the same thing.

As Carole quietly prepared to leave for a four- or five-month tour through the battle zones, the Hollywood Victory Committee came out with its camp tour plans. On August 4, the Committee announced "the greatest billing of famous screen players to make tours of Army camps to carry on the government's moral-building program since the outbreak of the war..." A list of 20 stars who volunteered to make camp trips was released, including George Burns & Gracie Allen, Joan Blondell, Eddie Cantor, Betty Grable, Rita Hayworth and a dozen others.

The Committee also named a group of Honor Members who had already begun visiting camps. That long list included Constance Bennett, Joe E. Brown, Bing Crosby, Oliver Hardy and several dozen other stars, including Carole. The interesting fact missing from the Committee's release was that *none* of the 40 or so stars had volunteered to visit any camps *outside* of the country except Carole and her three girlfriends.[60]

The same day the Committee was making its grand announcement, Carole and her neighbor at the beach, Johnny Meyer, quietly hosted several dozen soldiers from the Army's West Coast Training Center. After a day swimming and sunning at Carole's house, the men were taken by limousine to Andre's Restaurant for a surprise dinner. But Carole had arranged an even bigger surprise: When the soldiers arrived at the restaurant, they were met by a group of Carole's friends who joined them for dinner and dancing. Their dinner dates were a dozen stars like Linda Darnell, Marie McDonald, Martha O'Driscoll, June Storey, Mary Scott and Donna Reed.[61]

Carole's friends understood her dedication to the war effort. The day after her night out with the soldiers, Carole left for a week-long bond drive tour of the Midwest. When she returned, her neighbor Meyer picked her up at the airport and drove her home to a special surprise party. Guests who had gathered to honor Carole's efforts included most of the girlfriends who had served as Carole's soldier-dates, as well as other close friends Franchot Tone, Ben Cole, Charlie Morrisson and Cesar Romero.[62]

Bob Hope and Joe E. Brown headed for Alaska about a month later; besides Carole, Hope was the quickest to volunteer (also un-solicited) to entertain the troops. In fact, the week after Carole Lombard's tragic death dragged Hollywood even more directly into the fray, Hope began taping his radio program from military installations. She died on January 12, 1942; on February 3, Hope's show was taped at the Army Air Corps' March Field. On February 10 the show went on at Camp Callan near San Diego, then Camp Haan, Camp Roberts, Camp Cook, the Marine Base at San Diego, etc.

On September 10, 1942, "Leslie Townes Hope (known as Bob Hope)" affixed his thumb-print and signature to a request to the Alaska Travel Control for an "Application for Permit to Enter Alaska." But Hope's first official camp visit did not take place until December of 1943. Why he picked Alaska is not known. It was as far away from the war as one could go.

The day before Hope signed the paperwork, Carole attended a fundraising dinner and bond sale in Hollywood. She brought along six pairs of stockings, which at the time were among the most sought-after commodities in the U.S. Shortages of nylon made them literally impossible to find. Carole auctioned off her stockings to sell some bonds. She also auctioned off her 20-carat opal ring (reportedly given to her by Greg Bautzer) for $1,500 (about $30,000 today) and donated the money to the bond drive.[63]

Carole was a legend among servicemen long before the real war began. In October, visiting soldiers named Carole the "Most Popular Woman at the Stage Door Canteen." Not the Los Angeles Canteen. The New York Canteen. She appeared more often in the New York location (whenever she was near the East Coast she stopped in) than many of the actresses who lived there.

It was also reported around the studio in mid–October that Betty Grable received a letter from a soldier fighting on Guadalcanal in the South Pacific. As she proudly read the letter to the crew assembled for filming (she was working on *Coney Island* at the time), she was mortified to read that the soldier wanted to her "make sure to give Carole Landis a big kiss from all of us."[64] Grable spent the war visiting troops via photograph. That same evening, Carole spent the night working as a hostess at the Hollywood Canteen.

During the ensuing 18 months after Carole's group departed, 1,664 entertainers would be sent out by the committee to entertain soldiers, sailors and marines and to sell war bonds.[65] But Carole was first, and none of the others would make the trips, or take the risks, that she did.

The girls learned the second week of October that they would depart on October 30. They were still prohibited from telling anyone their departure date or where they were going, so Carole had to nervously await the completion of the filming of her loan-out *Powers Girl* with George Murphy. Just days before the scheduled departure, Murphy became ill, and shooting was delayed; it appeared that she might not be able to go at all. Fortunately, she received studio permission just hours before the group was to leave.

It was initially planned that Carole's group would visit soldiers in England only. Carole, Mitzi Mayfair, Martha Raye and Kay Francis left Los Angeles on October 22. They flew across the country on an Air Force B-17 that was on its way to England.[66] While in New York, Carole was honored for her work at the 21st Annual Naval Salute Awards, held at the New York Victory House.[67]

Carole, ca. 1943, about the time of the *Four Jills* tour of Europe.

On October 30, the women flew out of LaGuardia Airport bound for Bermuda. They would fly through Bermuda, the Azores, Ireland and Scotland, and then on to Britain. The first stop in Bermuda was supposed to have been a quick overnight refueling stop. They were also dropping off a group of entertainers who were touring that island (the Blossom Sisters, Eleanor French and Frankie Conville).

But when the Clipper landed in Bermuda, Customs officials informed the girls that they would have to stay on the island since their forms indicated they were visitors rather than transit visitors just flying through. They watched helplessly as their plane took off without them.

Near tears, thinking that they had missed their only chance to get to England, the women were approached by an American military officer who had been standing nearby. He offered his assistance, but then added, "You know, there are a lot of servicemen on the island. Don't you think you might like to do a show or two?"[68] When they were escorted to a launch that was waiting to take them to the Hamilton headquarters of the U.S. Navy on the island, it became apparent what had happened. The island's military commander and Washington officials had conspired with the British Customs people on the island to make sure that Carole and the other women stayed on the island for at least a few days.

They stayed at a U.S.O. lodge in Hamilton and gave daily performances for the American, Canadian and British soldiers that manned bases on Bermuda at the time. Primitive stages were set up at facilities all over Bermuda, from Castle Harbor to St. David's to Cooper's Island. So many servicemen wanted to see the women that they voluntarily added a second show every day.

The four were a perfect combination. Comedienne Raye had an effortless manner with the soldiers, almost as if she was one of them. Her favorite routine started by asking an officer in the crowd where the women were to eat. When the officer invariably responded, "You mess with the men," Raye answered, "I know that, but where do I eat?" The soldiers loved her.

Francis served as the mistress of ceremonies, more or less running the show and singing a few songs. Mayfair danced, and Carole was the finale. Her appearances always brought on the loudest cheers. She had a relaxed stage presence; she interacted well with the audiences and her beautiful voice added to the songs in the mix. And also, quite simply, she was breathtakingly beautiful as well as talented. By the end of the show, the audiences were exhausted from laughing and cheering.

After nine days of performances on Bermuda, a Clipper arrived from the States to take the girls to England. They first flew to the Azores, a chain of nine islands almost directly in the middle of the Atlantic Ocean. After a one-day refueling stop-over, they flew into Lisbon on November 10. It was an unsettling visit, since Portugal had not entered the war and was full of German troops, most on leave. Like a scene from the movie *Casablanca*, the girls sat in the bar in Lisbon's glamourous Hotel Aviz surrounded by tables full of Nazi officers also enjoying their evening out.[69]

They flew out of Lisbon late during the night of November 11. The skies over southwestern Europe and England were very dangerous, patrolled constantly by Luftwaffe fighters. The windows on the aircraft were all painted black so no light would shine out and expose the plane. From the moment the girls left Portugal, they were in a war zone, and in the line of fire. The night flight was to make it more difficult for their aircraft to be spotted by German planes out looking for easy prey.

They did not go directly to England but went first to Ireland, landing on November 11. The following day they flew into Bristol, where Carole got her first glimpse of the reality of the war.[70] Traveling to the station to catch the train that would take them to London, she saw bombed-out buildings, destroyed houses and huge craters in the streets. Carole said that she "felt sick" seeing the devastation.[71]

On November 12 the group finally arrived in London. Carole, long before she arrived, caused quite a stir. On October 25, before she left New York, she had a chance meeting at the Stork Club with an R.A.F. Wing Commander. They shared a few drinks and Carole promised a dinner when she arrived in London. When a *London Mirror* asked Carole about it some days later, embarrassed, she replied that she couldn't remember his name.

But as she was traveling through Ireland and England before her arrival in

November, newspapers were asking WHO IS CAROLE'S WING COMMANDER? and WILL SOMEONE FIND CAROLE'S COMMANDER? She received literally hundreds of telegrams asking the same question, "AM NOT YOUR WING COMMANDER. STOP. BUT WILL I DO? STOP?"[72] Eventually the phantom British airman — his name was O'Neal — arrived at Carole's hotel for their dinner.

During their first meeting in New York, Carole had been touched when O'Neal offered her the gift of a small blue book with an eagle on the cover inscribed "MY LIFE IN THE SERVICE." She dutifully kept that personal diary during her entire trip, often lying in her bunk writing by flashlight.

During the weeks that Carole was searching for O'Neal, the military press was inventing any number of other wing commanders for her (and their) use. Over a year later, *Stars and Stripes*, the primary newspaper for the armed forces, ran a photograph of Carole with one of their phantom wing commanders in a fall 1942 edition. Under the headline LONELY HEARTS, Carole was shown at a table with a "Lucky guy looking into the beautiful eyes of CAROLE LANDIS ... Wing Commander Bill McBrien, of the Royal Canadian Air Force. The *Stars and Stripes* found him for her after she forgot his name."[73] It mattered little that he was the wrong man.

Arriving in London, the girls checked into the Savoy Hotel. Early the next morning they were greeted by an Army Special Services officer who told them, "You are now under the rules and regulations of the U.S. Army. You will be given orders and you will obey them without question. You are not to know and you are not to ask questions as to where you are, or where you are going, or what time you are going to be there. This is for security reasons. We have worked out your itinerary for you and all you have to do is follow orders. We will give you one day to rest and one day to rehearse. You will then work six days a week and have one day off for rest." The girls understood and had no problem with the Army regimentation and concern for their safety. Sometimes they did one show a day, sometimes three, sometimes as many as five. It all depended on how big the camp or base was and how many men were there.

The girls awoke on November 13, their first full day in London, to a typical English fall day. Cold and fog. Fortunately, Carole had been warned by Cary Grant about the climate before she left: "For God's sake," he warned her, "listen to me and take the heaviest clothing you can find. You have no idea how bitter cold it can be over there. It's not like anything you've ever known ... it gets into your bones...." His advice led Carole to purchase all manner of woolen underwear, sweaters and coats, which she was often forced to lend to the other girls who were not as well-prepared.

The girls decided to spend their first day (an off day) just walking around. During their walk they ran into two U.S. Air Force officers, Joe Walling, a B-17 squadron leader, and Jim MacVeagh, a B-17 bomber pilot. Walling was just 25 and MacVeagh only 22. The airmen talked them into having a drink, telling them they were the first American women they had seen in a year. The two men and Carole and Mitzi were almost inseparable during the girls' time in England.

The next morning, the girls were driven by Jeep to their first performance. Bundled up with layers of clothing and extra gloves against the cold, they endured a three-hour ride through the English countryside to High Ercall, a tiny village northwest of London in the province of Shropshire. There they gave a performance in the auditorium of a small school that the Army was using as part of their airfield located there.

As the girls stood around a fire warming up, Carole was introduced to one of the pilots, Capt. Tom Wallace. She remembered the meeting: "Suddenly, everything went *boom, boom, crash*! and my knees felt weak ... I didn't even know what I was saying. I just couldn't function. 'Come on old girl,' I thought, 'better get hold of yourself.'"[74] For Carole, it was love at first sight with the dashing, blue-eyed fighter pilot. They arranged to meet later that evening for drinks, and after the girls were taken back to London, to have dinner the next evening.

Capt. Thomas C. Wallace was from Meadville, a small town an hour northeast of Pittsburgh, Pennsylvania. He attended Meadville High School and then went to work for a local machine shop. After his father died in the mid–1930s, he and his mother moved to Pasadena, California.

Wallace was one of the original American members of the legendary English Royal Air Force's American "Eagle Squadron," going to London among the first group of volunteers in 1940.[75] The legendary "Eagles" had somewhat controversial beginnings. In the summer of 1940, the war in Europe had been underway for over a year, but as Germany brought a fierce battle into the skies over England, the U.S. stayed neutral.

The R.A.F. was defending the country with 705 aircraft and 1,250 pilots at a time Winston Churchill described as "the British people [holding] the fort alone till those who had been half blind were half ready." Not all of America was "half blind."

During the worst days of the Battle of Britain—from July to September 1940—a handful of U.S. pilots came to England to fight alongside their British counterparts. Most simply crossed the American border into Canada and signed up with R.A.F. recruiters. The R.A.F. requirements for the Squadron— high school diploma, between 20 and 31 years of age, good eyesight and 300 hours of flying time — were less restrictive than the U.S. Air Force requirements. Most Eagles had no college education or prior military experience.

Almost every Eagle was there strictly for adventure. Upon arriving in England they had two weeks to learn to fly the Hurricanes and Spitfire V.B.s and learn whatever military tactics they could. They were then assigned to one of three squadrons, the 71st, the 121st or the 133rd Fighter Groups.

Since the U.S. Neutrality Act prohibited any U.S. citizen from participating, these men risked prison to fight off the German invasion of England. But fight they did. All that remains as testament to their work are notations in flight logs of names like "Donahue of 64," "Leckrone of 616" and, in some cases, listings that simply read "Tex" or "Uncle Sam." Like their British partners they flew the Hawker Hurricane and Spitfire fighters carrying the R.A.F. insignia.

The Eagles first flew out of an R.A.F. airfield at Martlesham Heath, on the northeast coast about 100 miles from London. They later moved to bases within 40 miles of London, at North Weald and Debden. The three Eagle squadrons were commanded by William Taylor, an experienced U.S. Navy pilot.

Nobody but they and their fellow pilots knew their true identities. The first U.S.

combatant to die in Europe was an Eagle, William Meade Linsley Fiske III, a wealthy Chicagoan who had attended Cambridge University in the pre-war years and married the former wife of the Earl of Warwick. The British pilots described him as "the best pilot [they had] ever known," but on August 17, 1940, his plane was shot down as it returned to his airfield and Fiske was killed. He and a dozen or so other pilots are buried in small church graveyards in places like West Sussex and Gravesend. They were the bravest of the brave and their efforts had a direct impact on the direction of the war.

Partly because of the U.S. pilots, the German Luftwaffe suffered serious setbacks in battles with the R.A.F. Hitler learned that Germany would have difficulty winning an air battle over the Channel. His proposed invasion of England, Operation Sea Lion ("the final conquest of England"), was postponed and later shelved completely because of the work of these pilots.[76] It was for them that Churchill uttered his celebrated, "*Never* in the field of human conflict was so much owed by so many to so few."

After the attack on Pearl Harbor had brought the U.S. into the war the Eagles became part of the 8th Air Force, but would not become fully operational for six months, flying their first sorties on July 4, 1942, out of Atcham and High Ercall. The 225 pilots were still flying the British Spitfire fighters, still alongside their British pals.

Tommy Wallace was one of the original members of the 71st Squadron, which was made up of 104 pilots. The 71st had been formed in September 1940, and by the time Wallace arrived was stationed at an airfield in Martlesham Heath, 90 miles northeast of London along the coast. The Squadron had bomber escort duty, flying alongside British and American bombers during runs deep into Europe, as well as air defense and ground attack missions. All were extremely dangerous; almost 40 pilots in the 71st would die in battle in less than two years. Wallace's best friend William Gieger was shot down over France in late 1941 and spent the war in a German P.O.W. camp. Tom Wallace was one of only 17 pilots in the 71st to record kills, shooting down two German Me-109 fighters during sorties over France in a P-47 Thunderbolt.

Carole and her dashing pilot hit it off from the moment they met. He must have seemed perfect to her — handsome, smart and adventuresome. Wallace was also very popular with his fellow fliers. Like seemingly every other man who got to know Carole, Wallace fell in love with her. On their second date, sitting in a tiny pub outside London, he asked her to marry him. Carole suggested they wait a little while to be sure, and told him she'd answer him some other time.

For the next week, Carole was in London. Every time they spoke, Wallace asked, "Are you sure yet?" At the end of the week the girls were loaded onto Army trucks and transported off into the English countryside. They spent the next two weeks visiting camps all over England, staying at tiny boarding houses or with local families. The accommodations were primitive, usually without heat and sometimes without indoor plumbing. Carole was not able to speak with Wallace during her travels due to Army restrictions on communication.

The shows were always entertaining for the servicemen and the girls enjoyed putting them on, but they were never very far from the realities of the war. While the girls were riding from base to base during the day, the airmen were flying dangerous missions over Europe. It was brought home to them often. Sharing a drink with a Commanding Officer during their first trip outside London, they asked why everyone was so down in the mouth. Pointing to a young-looking pilot at another table, he asked them, "You see that kid over there? He's Lt. Rader. He came in today with five dead men aboard ship. We lost quite of few planes and men we really loved. So you see, girls, we really need you here tonight, desperately."[77]

When the girls returned to London two weeks later, just before Thanksgiving, they were greeted by a lieutenant of the elite Grenadier Guards (one of the soldiers assigned to guard the Royal Family). He was there, he informed them, to go over the plans for the Command Performance. "What Command Performance?" they asked. They were told that Queen Elizabeth and her daughters Elizabeth and Margaret wished them to perform for the Royal Family at a hall in the Grenadier barracks at Windsor Palace. It was to take place on the evening of November 28.

Carole shared Thanksgiving dinner at her hotel with eight servicemen she had befriended during her few weeks in England. Among the group were airmen Walling and MacVeagh, who had been following them all over England, and their driver and aide Capt. Joe Penny. Walling, MacVeagh, Carole and Mitzi had become an unofficial foursome; nothing romantic was involved. Both of the airmen were married and Carole had Wallace in the wings.

Wallace was flying that day and could not come. But he did call Carole and yet again asked her to marry him. That evening Mayfair and Francis became ill, both fighting the flu and probably pneumonia. So that all four might be ready for the scheduled Command Performance just two days hence, Carole and Raye put on four shows over two days on their own.[78]

When Carole and Raye returned to London on Friday, they had three hours to prepare for the performance for the Royal Family. Against doctor's orders, Mayfair and Francis had checked themselves out of the hospital. Both were so weak they could barely stand, but they insisted on going on. Before the group left the hotel, a member of the Queen's staff met with them to instruct them on proper etiquette and decorum when meeting and conversing with the Royals.

The show took place in front of 2,500 soldiers, and including virtually every member of the extended Royal Family led by Queen Elizabeth and her teenage daughters Elizabeth and Margaret. King George had taken ill and was unable to attend. All four of the girls, each famous in their own right, were still star-struck in the presence of the Queen. Carole told the press she was "goggle-eyed" as she was presented to the Queen but like the others managed to perform wonderfully.

The show was much like a typical camp show with Francis as the emcee, Raye the comedienne, Mayfair the dancer and Carole the beautiful singer. When it came time for Carole to perform, Francis announced, "Here is the lovely Carole Landis," and the microphones all went dead. Undaunted, Carole almost shouted out "Deep in the Heart of Texas" so all 2,500 people in the hall could hear.

The audiences reacted with increasing enthusiasm to Carole's songs. With each song—she followed "Texas" with "Over There" and "White Christmas"—they seemed more and more excited. By the time she finished with "The White Cliffs of

Dover," the audience was as whipped up as a theater full of soldiers. The entire audience, including the normally staid princesses beneath their tiara crowns, joined in a rousing rendition of the final song. The show ended to a prolonged standing ovation that lasted over five minutes. Afterwards, the girls attended a reception where they were nervously introduced to the Queen and the Princesses.

That performance was an echo of things to come, and showed how dedicated and tough the women really were. They really were "troupers." Francis performed through severe laryngitis. In addition to her pneumonia, Mayfair had not fully healed from a severely sprained shoulder suffered during an overly physical jitterbug routine with an excited 225-pound soldier the week prior. Immediately after the performance, she went back into the hospital.

While Landis sang *sans* microphone, Francis stood in the wings holding a flashlight for a serviceman trying to fix the electricity.[79] But these problems paled in comparison to the hardships they would face in the coming months and coming tours.

The four were indeed troupers, but things were not always peaceful between the group. That is to be expected of any small group spending months cramped together. Of the four, Carole was the least likely to become angry over something. Kay Francis was most often upset with the other girls.

Kay, who through it all still thought of herself a true Hollywood star, was usually angry with one or all of the other girls. Although she was still pretty, at 40 or so she was the eldest, a fact she did not like to admit. She was jealous of the extra attention that (especially) Carole and Martha got from the servicemen and responded by picking fights with them. When Kay got into one of her moods, the other girls usually ignored her.

The Sunday after the Command Performance, Carole was able to spend the day with Wallace and, as usual, he tried to convince her to get married. She really wanted to wait, worried about the fuss the intrusive British press would make of the wedding. And there were the tabloids back home. Later that evening she left for Ireland by boat. They traveled at night because it was more difficult for the German U-Boats searching the waters off the English coast to locate ships at night. It was another reminder of the closeness of the war. Carole spent most of the trip in her cabin, suffering from acute stomach pains that she attributed to the flu.

During the visit to Ireland, which lasted from November 30 to December 6, Carole finally decided that she would marry Wallace. During her visit she was still tortured with serious stomach pain. The girls returned from Ireland aboard separate B-24 bombers. Carole spent most of her flight in the nose of the aircraft with a flight engineer. As the plane was cruising over Scotland, something caught fire in the cargo area below the planes deck. Just minutes away from having to crash-land, the pilot came across a small Scottish airfield where the plane put down. It had not even come to a complete stop when Carole tumbled out of the bomb bay followed by the rest of the crew.

When she returned from the Scottish airfield to London on December 10, Carole and Tommy Wallace celebrated their impending marriage over dinner at her hotel. Later that evening her stomach pains were so severe that she had to call a doctor. She was rushed from the hotel to a military hospital outside London. Once her condition had stabilized for a few days, she underwent an appendectomy on December 14. Her appendix had come perilously close to bursting, which could have killed her. If it had occurred during her trip to Ireland, she could easily have died.[80]

After the operation she was moved into a doctor's office that had been converted into the only single room in the hospital. As soon as she was conscious she thanked the doctors but said that she wanted to go back to the ward with her nurse friends. She spent the week there.

Carole spent over a week in the hospital ward reserved for injured nurses and was visited daily by the small legion of airmen friends she had taken to calling her "kids." Every morning the squadron's B-17s roared over the hospital on their dangerous bombing missions to Europe. Every night Carole counted the returning planes and made the nurses report on any injuries to the airmen.

One day she was handed a note from a wounded soldier in another part of the hospital. It was Bud Eilers, brother of actress Sally Eilers, one of Carole's friends. He was an infantryman who had been wounded in Europe. Bud and Carole traded notes back and forth for the rest of the week.[81]

On Monday, December 21, Carole asked to be moved back to London; she needed to start making plans for her wedding. The engagement was made public on the 22nd. Newspapers reported that the "blonde film star who came to Britain to entertain troops" had become engaged to Wallace, and that they expected to be married in Britain early in 1943.[82]

Carole tried to downplay the speed with which their relationship had developed. She would later say, "It was nowhere near as fast [as it was later made to appear in the film *Four Jills in a Jeep*]. I spent weeks getting ready to marry Tom. It took us more than two weeks just to find a pair of wedding rings."[83] In reality, she probably would have gotten married even sooner had not she been laid up recuperating from appendicitis.

Recuperating or not, Carole was determined to host a Christmas Eve party. She arranged for two rooms at her hotel to be decorated with holly and mistletoe and all the trimmings, and loaded

In her room at London's Savoy Hotel, Carole gets ready for her January 1943 wedding to "Tommy" Wallace.

the bar with whiskey, sandwiches and cake. Wallace had to carry her from the bed to the couch, where she sat covered with a blanket, beaming as several dozen of her closest airmen pals enjoyed Christmas Eve with her. All of Carole's friends were bomber crewmen and Wallace's buddies were all fighter pilots, so it made for an interesting evening of one-upsmanship.

During the party, Carole handed out presents to the airmen. At Carole's direction, her mother Clara Ridste bought over 70 presents and had each one wrapped and sent to a serviceman that Carole had befriended during her volunteering.[84] Among the gifts were presents for her bomber pals, the "kids" she called Joe, Mac, Kissy and Baby.

Kay, Mitzi and Martha also managed to make the party, returning from a week's worth of engagements in Scotland. Also attending was their State Department liaison Jim Wright, who would die soon after in a Lisbon plane crash. The group stayed up into the early morning hours singing Christmas carols and enjoying each other's company.

Wallace and Carole originally wanted to be married on New Year's Day but English law forbade that. She was just strong enough on Saturday, January 2, to apply for a marriage license which was picked up the next day. The couple planned to marry on Wednesday, January 6, at the Church of Our Lady of the Assumption in London.

Since Thanksgiving, Carole had been trying without success to get the Army to send the group to North Africa. The military thought the trip would be too dangerous since the African battle lines were so fluid. But out of nowhere, the girls were told on Saturday the 2nd (Carole had returned from the Caxton Hall Marriage License Bureau just minutes before) that they would be leaving for Africa the next day. The wedding was going to be postponed until the Africa departure was pushed back to Tuesday the 5th. Carole set about frantically to find a wedding gown.

Getting a wedding dress and shoes was next to impossible in wartime London. The only manner of currency were ration coupons that allowed for the purchase of items that were in chronic short supply. Anything clothing or leather-related (like shoes) was impossible to obtain without coupons. Carole of course had none. A pilot friend of Tom's gave Carole a king's ransom, his entire stash of 10 coupons (it might take six months to collect that number). Mitzi managed to scrounge up another six from nurse and troupe friends. Carole was able to get a bridal gown for nine of the precious coupons and a pair of shoes for seven more.

The wedding took place on Tuesday, January 5, at 2:00 P.M. at the lovely eighteenth century gothic Church of Our Lady of Assumption. Some of the windows were covered up with boards after having been damaged in bombing raids. The stained-glass window that had once filled the arched window above the front steps had been completely blown out. It was not the lovely English cathedral some might have expected. Carole was given away by Col. Schillinger, one of Tom's commanding officers. His best friend and fellow airman Major Richard Ellis served as the best man[85] and Mitzi Mayfair as the maid of honor. Dozens of Carole's bomber pals and Tom's fighter buddies filled the pews.

Carole was stunning in her fitted silk gown that covered her shoulders. A flowing

Carole and her airman husband leave the Church of Our Lady of the Assumption amidst a huge crowd of his flier friends and her fans.

veil and gown trailed behind her as she walked down the aisle carrying a bouquet of white carnations and lily of the valley. Around her neck was a simple strand of pearls. Barely visible above the pearls was the tiny gold cross given to Carole years before by her friend Mousie Lewis—the cross she never took off.

There were dozens of photographers inside and outside the church. They were even allowed to stand next to and behind the altar to take photographs of the couple kneeling in front of the priest, mid-ceremony. Afterwards, per British rules, a civil ceremony had to take place, so the couple returned to the hotel about 3:45. Carole had expected and was ready for a 4:00 departure for Africa. Again, fate intervened, and they were given a two-day reprieve due to weather. A reception of sorts was held at the couple's two-room suite at the Savoy.

Wallace behaved strangely that afternoon, a portent of things to come. As the reception was winding down, Carole wanted the last few stragglers to leave so she could be alone with her new husband. But he insisted that three or four of them join him and Carole for dinner. Later as the two chatted before bed, she said to him, "Gee, you're really my husband," and he responded, "Yes, gee, you're really my wife." She thought to herself that "for the first time since we met, we felt like strangers."[86]

When Carole was getting ready to leave for North Africa, Wallace begged off going to the train station with her, saying, "There'll be lots of people there saying goodbye, and in front of everybody it's no good. Let's say goodbye here and then I'll go back." The girls went by train to a military airfield near the English Channel at Southend-on-Sea to await their plane to North Africa.

Carole's travels were both a whirlwind and a long haul. Also, it was decidedly unglamourous. No five-star hotels or restaurants. They lived and ate with the soldiers, usually in tents. They traveled in military planes and convoys of Army trucks and Jeeps. In fact, traveling to and from their hotel in London for their command performance for the Queen, they were carted around London in a bus.

Jack Benny, whose volunteerism during the war was perhaps equal to Carole's, described the camp tours as being similar to his vaudeville experiences:

> It was so much like the days when Salisbury & Kubelsky worked the Western Vaudeville Circuit. There were the same one-night stands, split weeks, packing and unpacking, rushing for a bus or train or plane, grabbing a few hours of sleep when you could and plastering on a smile.[87]

The one thing Benny did remember as different than his vaudeville days were the audiences. He noted that they were as enthusiastic as any performer could ever have. A newspaper column in the form of a letter home from France, written by a female member of one of the traveling troupes, gives an accurate description of the hardships faced by Carole's group:

> [The girls] go out bartering every day... Soap, chocolates, and cigarettes were traded for eggs, fried rabbit, potatoes, etc. Eggs were all the style. For the eight months I've been in England I've had six. We fried them in our mess tins and eat outside — rain or shine. We do miss the news with no radio or newspapers, but the other night an RAF commandant let us listen to his radio. Suddenly on Tuesday our auxiliary officer arrived and we moved. I can't tell you where of course, but it was a little step closer to the front. Our trip took five or six hours to cover 30 miles. The roads are bad and the traffic appalling. We went through a small town, but instead of yellow rubble like Caen, it was pink. When we arrived at our field we put our tents up in a hurry, hungry and cold. As our show last night began, a torrential rain started. This outfit had only seen one show since D-Day, so the rain wouldn't stop us. We moved the instruments inside the chateau and the boys pulled trucks up and grabbed sheets and sat under them in the rain, clapping and honking horns like fury. They watched us through a huge doorway and two big windows on either side. The singers stood with the mike in the doorway.[88]

The young entertainer's tales are typical of the hardships that Carole faced and happily endured without complaint.

During Carole's London visit, a well-known anecdote was born. According to *New York Daily News* columnist Earl Wilson, Carole was dancing with an English soldier who indicated her low-cut gown and asked if the neckline represented "V for victory"? Carole allegedly replied, "Yes but the bundles aren't for Britain,"[89] referring to her breasts and the well-known British charity.

The story has been used for years as an example of Carole's personality, but in her later book *Four Jills in a Jeep* Carole attributes the remark to Lana Turner.[90] According to the book, the girls wanted to tell the story during their Command Performance and were worried that it might be too colorful for the Royal Family. This may have been a deflection though. The performance is thoroughly detailed in the book and they were given permission to use the story but did not. Also, it's doubtful that Lana Turner was sufficiently aware of the Bundles for Britain program to have come up with something so original and funny!

On January 15 the girls were readied to fly from the southeastern English coast to North Africa. They would make the trip on a B-17, flying through some of the most hostile airspace in the European theater. The Nazis were shooting down commercial airliners as well as military targets so there was no safe way to get there. At the airfield, the girls were given fur-lined flying jackets to cover the layers of warm clothing they already had. Over the flying suits they each wore a parachute as well.

The inside of a B-17 is remarkably cramped considering how big it looks from the outside. Underneath the cockpit is the nose-gunner; the only way into or out of the cockpit is through a small hatch on the lower left side of the nose. To get from the hatch area and nose position, one literally crawls up a narrow passageway between the pilot and co-pilot. Behind the flight deck is the bomb bay, 10 or 12 feet long with two racks running top to bottom on either side of a narrow gangplank. The bombs are stacked on the rack and simply slide down and out the bomb bay doors.

Above and beyond the bomb bay are guns above and below the fuselage; those gunners crawled into their spaces and stayed there. If anything happened, it was almost impossible for either ball-gunner to get out alive. Just past the bomb bay are several small spaces on either side of a narrow aisle, one for the navigator and one for the radio operator. Behind the tiny cubicles is the main area of the fuselage, with its cargo area and two waist gunners manning twin .50-caliber machine guns. B-17s are slow and very noisy and, contrary to the movies, it is almost impossible to be heard above the din of the engines and wind noise. Without fighter escort, they are very vulnerable to enemy fighter attack.

That was the method of travel from England to Africa. The four girls huddled together, stuffed into the radio compartment. They were originally scheduled to land in Gibraltar, but bad weather forced the pilot to detour to Casablanca and then back to Gibraltar. Approaching the island low on fuel, the B-17 was also flying blind since the fogged-in airport had lost its ability to transmit their locator signal. The pilot thought they were going to have to ditch the plane, and the girls were ready with flotation life vests. At the last moment, after the plane nearly slammed into Gibraltar's famous Rock, a break in the clouds made the airport visible and the plane landed, running out of fuel as it rolled to a stop.

The next day they boarded another B-17 and flew to Algiers. That was the most dangerous part of the trip. Every gunner on the ship made the flight at the ready, guns unlocked and loaded for firing. News reports from Morocco revealed that actor

Robert Taylor was with a group that had been arrested and held by Spanish authorities—who supported the Nazis—at the same time the girls were landing in Gibraltar.[91]

During an offensive that over ran the German consulate in Naples, Italy, American troops found a list prepared by the Nazi leadership of American actors that appeared in anti–Nazi films, or who were active in the camp tour arena. The most prominent name on the list was the first—Carole Landis. Others included Myrna Loy, James Stewart and Joe E. Brown. But even after Carole was informed of her position on the list, she never avoided harm's way.[92]

On January 16, Allied Headquarters in North Africa confirmed that Carole, Mitzi, Kay and Martha had arrived in Algiers to do a series of shows for Allied troops in North Africa. Raye made light of the men missing from their group, telling military reporters, "What soldier around here wants to look at a man anyway?"[93] The visit was scheduled to last two weeks and go as far east as Constantine and as far west as Oran and Casablanca.[94] They would cover the entire length of Tunis.

Typical of Carole, she never wanted to leave the soldiers she was visiting and convinced the group to stay longer. Photographs survive of the women in a North Africa chow line dated February 24[95] and they were probably there as late as the second week of March.

Carole's group was always close by the front, usually nearer than they should have been. But those were the soldiers she really wanted to visit. The first evening they were in Algiers, they were visiting the villa of the U.S. Commander in Algiers when a German bomber group attacked the ships in the harbor several miles away. Carole watched in amazement from the porch of the villa as the attack unfolded beneath her. Anti-aircraft guns popped, explosions wracked the harbor, all surrounded by the hum of the German planes. She watched several plunge flaming into the sea.

At the General's villa they were safe. But when they returned to their hotel, which was closer to the harbor, they learned that a stray bomb had flattened the hotel across the street. Even so, when the German bombers came back the next evening, Carole clambered up to the roof to watch the spectacle.

The detachment commander in Algiers had scheduled the girls to do nothing but evening shows at the Red Cross Club there, after which they would travel to Oran and Casablanca to the west. When Carole asked permission to visit the soldiers nearer the front, which was the other way, the commander forbade it as too dangerous. So Carole and Kay walked unannounced into the office of Gen. Dwight Eisenhower and complained that they were being prevented from visiting frontline troops.

Eisenhower allowed the visit but only if the girls flew there with a fighter escort. When the commander delayed making those arrangements, they again went over his head and approached Gen. Jimmy Doolittle. Doolittle told them, "By God, you'll fly and you'll have a fighter escort if I have to fly myself."[96]

The next morning the girls boarded a transport and flew east, escorted by a squadron of Spitfire fighter planes. When the transport rolled to a stop on the remote battlefield runway, the airmen and soldiers were thunderstruck when Carole and the girls exited the plane. That was the part of the travels that Carole most enjoyed.

Martha Raye signs an autograph for Major Glen Hubbard while Carole shakes his hand during visit to the 94th Fighter Group airfield, a P-38 squadron flying out of Biskra, North Africa. (Courtesy Noonie Fortin.)

They spent five or six days visiting the frontline positions, living in pup tents alongside the soldiers and putting on impromptu singing and dancing shows. There was no musical accompaniment and the makeshift stage was an aircraft trailer.

On January 26 or 27 the girls were chatting with a group of soldiers when they learned again firsthand just how dangerous their travels could be. When an air raid alarm sounded, they stood looking into the sky until one of the servicemen literally picked Carole up "caveman style" and dove into a crowded covered entrenchment with several others. The soldiers gave the women their helmets and covered the women with their bodies as they waited out the raid. The women sang "sentimental old American songs" for the men, sitting in three inches of mud in a trench in the desert while shells fell all around their camp.

Early the next morning their position was again targeted during a bombing raid by German and Italian bombers. As people scrambled for cover, an unperturbed Carole watched the explosions standing near her tent. Clad in her white negligee and bathrobe, she later told reporters that she thought "the lovely fireworks display" put on by the troop's anti-aircraft tracers was beautiful but paid no attention to the bombs.[97]

Flying back to Algiers, Carole's plane came under attack by three German JU-88 fighter bombers, who were driven off by their Spitfire escorts. Upon their return, the girls got together to survey their condition. They had been gone for three months. Of the four, the only healthy one was Martha Raye, who seemingly could survive anything thrown at her.

Kay Francis fought pneumonia during the entire tour and was nursing torn ligaments in her leg, injured when she fell while getting off a plane. Mitzi Mayfair suffered terribly with two months of tooth pain. A lack of antibiotics in England — and an Army doctor's misdiagnosis that she had a sinus infection — left her only option having teeth pulled. She told them that "no soldier wants to see me without teeth. I'll be fine." She also spent two weeks in the hospital with pneumonia.[98] Carole suffered a near-fatal bout with an e. coli infection and underwent an appendectomy. For the two months following, she was in almost-constant pain.

It was decided that the group would split up and end the tour. Francis and Mayfair would return to the U.S. immediately and Martha Raye would go on to Casablanca before her return. Carole wanted to get to England to see Tom Wallace before returning to the States. Francis and Mayfair arrived back in Los Angeles on February 5. Louella Parsons noted that "the first thing Kay Francis did when she landed ... was telephone Carole Landis' mother ... [to tell her that] Carole will remain in England with her bridegroom for several weeks longer."[99]

Several days after the other three girls departed, as Carole was in Algiers waiting for transport back to Gibraltar and then England, the harbor near her hotel came under German bomber attack. Hundreds of Nazi planes hammered the area for several hours. As Carole tried to secure the balcony doors in her hotel room, a bomb exploded next to the building, shattering her doors and windows and hurling her across the room onto the floor. Buildings all around the hotel were demolished.

The next morning she was able to secure a flight to Gibraltar and left Africa on February 6 or 7. Arriving in London, she spent two weeks with Wallace before returning to the U.S. She told London reporters that she would be back to Hollywood within a few weeks, and fully expected to "face the music" from her studio executives because of her decision to overstay the original leave.

They were originally expected to stay in England for six weeks, but due much to the urging of Carole they ended up visiting dozens of bases the length and breadth of the U.K., Ireland and North Africa. The traveled over 37,500 miles, living on a $10 daily per diem and staying with the troops for four and a half months.[100] For the entire length of the war, Carole wrote a letter to Wallace every day they were apart. Sadly, none of the letters survive.

Before leaving London, Carole agreed to one final request from the military. A Naval officer asked if she would visit the U.S. Navy facility located in Natal, Brazil, which had not yet had a camp visit from anyone. Carole detoured there on her way home, arriving on February 22[101] and staying a week before flying back to New York on March 4.

It's difficult to imagine the hardships that the women endured to support thousands of fighting men they did not know. They were the first (and only) all-female troupe to make a trip and theirs was the longest of any World War II U.S.O. trip. They never asked for special privileges and almost always turned down any extras. For over four months, they lived like the soldiers in tents through English winter cold and African heat. They ate military fare. They battled illness.

They were caught in air raids at least half a dozen times, came under direct enemy gun and artillery fire 12 times, were aboard aircraft that nearly crashed three times, and were aboard a flight attacked by German aircraft. And they earned the love and respect of thousands of U.S. servicemen. When Carole returned to the U.S., *Screen Guide* magazine featured an article and photograph of her under the title "A Heroine Comes Home."[102] The girls received the ultimate compliment when writer and G.I. favorite Ernie Pyle described them in a March 29 article as "FOUR GOOD SOLDIERS."[103]

Before Carole left, Zanuck had tried to send her to studio oblivion with terrible roles, but even he couldn't ignore all of the positive press that she received during and after her travels. While she was getting ready to leave England on her way to Brazil and home, Fox announced that the studio would produce a movie based upon the girls' exploits. The women's travels had become something of a domestic legend; stories had been in all the papers and magazines. Unknown to fans, dozens of the stories were written by Carole herself. The film would be entitled *Four Jills in a Jeep* and would star Carole and Martha (both of whom were under contract with the studio already), and Kay and Mitzi if they were available.[104]

★ Seven ★

The South Pacific

Carole was back in the U.S. on March 4 but would not return to Los Angeles until March 8. First she sat through dozens of photograph sessions and interviews with every branch of the military and commercial press. Pictures of Carole wearing the insignias of the Eagle Squadron, the French Foreign Legion, the Grenadier Guards and the Royal Air Force ran in papers throughout the country.[1] When she arrived at the airport in Burbank, she was met by a Jeep sent by a local Army detachment.[2]

She spent her first evening back relaxing at home with her mother and her sister's family. They all watched the 16mm movies taken of Carole's wedding to Tom Wallace.[3] But she only stayed in Los Angeles for a few days.

Screenland magazine ran an eight-page "war diary" detailing some of Carole's exploits.[4] Carole had written several magazine and newspaper stories and serials about her travels, and had penned dozens of articles for the AP and UPI wire services. On March 19 it was reported that Carole's writings would be turned into a book.[5] She was approached in late February by a division by Random House and agreed to the project. It was Fox publicity director Harry Brand who convinced Carole and the publisher to use the same title as their upcoming movie, *Four Jills in a Jeep*.

Although the book's content would be Carole's, Brand hired Edwin Seaver to help ghost-write the project. Seaver was a well-known writer and editor prominent in New York literary circles. Some historians and critics credit the entire work to Seaver but the text is similar to Carole's wartime correspondent writings and it comes off with so much of Carole's personality that it could not have come entirely from someone else. It would have been difficult for the erudite Seaver—who edited some of the most complex literary works of the 1940s and 1950s—to "fake" her personality and write it himself.

Broadway gossip columnist Earl Wilson, who befriended Carole when she lived in New York, spoke to her about the help she received from Seaver. When excerpts were first serialized in *The Saturday Evening Post*, the rumor that she hadn't actually written the book first arose. But she told Wilson, "The studio gave me two ghost writers but they stunk it all up. I finally decided to talk it to a steno typist. Naturally with some Scotch and soda under my belt. Yes, it was very droll. I'd go out to the kitchen and sneak a drink, and come back again with a lot of new inspirations. I had too many swear words, like hell, damn and Christ, in it. Edwin Seaver, the writer, whom I know, went over it, and he said, 'I think this part stinks' or 'that part stinks' ... and I cut a lot out. But I sweated it out and wrote it."[6]

Seaver did assist, a fact that was a secret until he testified before a Senate committee investigating Communist influence among studio writers in 1953. In the middle of his testimony he casually mentioned "I ghosted Carole Landis' *Four Jills in a Jeep*"[7] in response to a question from Committee lawyer Roy Cohn. He offered no other background or support, and by then Carole was not around to confirm or deny. It is more likely that he edited the text rather than ghost-wrote any of it.

The book would not be released until sometime in 1944, by which time the movie would also be released. But during the writing process the book made its first appearance (a four-month serialization) in *The Saturday Evening Post.*

She stayed in Los Angeles for about a week after her return. On March 20 she was back in New York to receive an award after being named the best-dressed screen star of 1942 by the Fashion Academy of New York. The Academy also presented Landis with a special award, naming her "the All-American girl who has done the most for the war effort."

In typical Carole fashion she downplayed the award and whether she actually deserved it, choosing instead to poke fun at herself. She told a laughing crowd that it was a good thing they didn't see her in Africa before they voted, wearing the long underwear through the freezing cold desert nights. Always self-effacing, she endeared herself to the audience saying, "I itched all the time, and when nobody was looking, I scratched and was a mess. It was like [wearing] a hair shirt."[8]

She returned to Los Angeles that same day. Earlier she had agreed to address a March 21 meeting of the Hollywood Victory Committee with Mitzi Mayfair in an effort to prod more actors and actresses to volunteer for camp tours.[9] Over 500 studio types heard their stories. The next night she attended the premiere of the film *Young Mr. Pitt* and hosted a reception, all of which benefited the Children's Convalescent Home. The U.S. Army asked that she attend a dinner and Hollywood Bowl event honoring Madame Chiang, wife of Chiang Kai-shek, head of China's ruling Nationalist Party, who was visiting on a diplomatic mission. She and Mme. Chiang visited during both evenings.[10]

Carole's escort to personal and social functions that week was Major Gregory Augustus Daymond. "Gus" Daymond was one of the most-decorated fliers during the Battle of Britain. He flew for the 71st Fighter Group of the Eagle Squadron along with Tom Wallace, and shot down seven German ME109 fighters between July 1941 and September 1942. He would later be promoted to command of the unit when the unit joined the U.S. Eighth Air Force.

Even after returning from the exhausting tour and to the studio, Carole continued volunteering. On weekends she organized visits to the military training camps located in remote, hot desert, hours from Los Angeles. She and Kay Kyser's Band made several such trips every month. She would eventually do more than 250 shows at military bases and camps coast to coast and also toured the country selling War Bonds.

While Carole was away, Clara Ridste went to work at the Douglas Aircraft plant in Long Beach. In early 1943 she moved over to the North American Aviation plant in the same area. She was working the swing (night) shift and enjoying the attention that came from being "Carole Landis' mother." Dozens of newspaper photographs showing her at work ran all over the country. One of her co-workers at North

American was Glen Anders, a Broadway actor and Tallulah Bankhead's former leading man. Too old for military service, he finished *Keeper of the Flame* (1942) with Spencer Tracy and Katharine Hepburn and then went to work building planes.

Clara wasn't working to support the war effort; she worked because she had to. Carole made it very clear that she would not completely support Clara. Although she often allowed Clara to live with her in her houses, Carole would not fund her mother's entire existence. Clara was still a hard worker; in 2+ years working at the factories, Clara only missed two days of work. She switched to the day shift after Carole returned from England.[11]

Carole often visited her mother at work, but after her return from England, managers at North American asked that Carole not visit except during lunch breaks. When she showed up during working hours, the entire production line would stop.[12]

Back at Fox, Zanuck assigned her to one of Sonja Henie's final ice-skating films, *Wintertime*. Henie won Olympic gold medals in 1928, 1932 and 1936, after which Zanuck hired her for a series of light comedies beginning with *One in a Million* (1936). Her movies were light on plot and heavy on skating and close-ups of the lovely Norwegian, but by *Wintertime* the public was growing weary after almost a dozen movies featuring ice skating. She would do a few more and then disappear into the ice show business.

Wintertime had an excellent cast including Jack Oakie, Cesar Romero, S.Z. Sakall and Cornel Wilde, plus the Woody Herman Orchestra for musical background. Nora (Henie) and her uncle (Sakall) end up in a hotel owned by Skip Hutton (Oakie) and Brad Barton (Romero). When Nora falls for Skip, she convinces her uncle to invest in the failing hotel. Carole's role is essentially unnecessary, playing a reporter who chases Romero around the hotel.

Henie and Carole enjoyed each other's company and spent time socially off the set along with Henie's then-husband, agent Dan Topping. Topping and Henie divorced in 1946 amidst the turmoil at the demise of her movie career.

Unless Zanuck was deluding himself into thinking that Henie's skating movies were still popular, *Wintertime* was essentially another lousy assignment for Carole. The highlights for Carole were the chance to work with her pal Romero again and a visit by some old friends from England: On May 10, the ten-man crew of the B-17 bomber "Jack the Ripper" visited the *Wintertime* set. Their bomber was part of the squadron in which her London flier friends flew. When the men arrived, Carole ran up and hugged them all. And called each one by his name. Writer Harrison Carroll noted the scene in his column, saying that was why "Carole Landis is so loved by servicemen."[13] Later that evening, she took the crewmen out to dinner at Ciro's.

That same week, Carole made the trip to the West Coast Training Center to visit some soldiers of the Sixth Armored Division. When one soldier mentioned that they didn't watch many movies because their projector was broken, she sent them her own as a gift.

On May 20, *Powers Girl* debuted at Grauman's Chinese Theater to mostly positive reviews. One reviewer noted that "no stress on the mentality"[14] was felt while watching the film, an apt description. The same day, Harrison Carroll had an

Carole makes scrapbooks at home in an obviously staged studio photograph.

interesting note in his Hollywood column. Carroll mentioned in passing to "make a bet that Carole Landis will be one of the first feminine stars to go to Australia, maybe after finishing *Four Jills in a Jeep*."[15]

During June, Carole made several radio appearances. Groucho Marx took his "Blue Ribbon Town" radio program to the Marine Corps base outside of San Diego and asked Carole if she would be his guest star on the evening on June 5. Even though she was scheduled to leave early the next morning for New York, she agreed to go along, much to the delight of the 2,500 Marines who came out for the show.[16] She joked with Groucho and sang several songs, and after signing autographs and posing for pictures for over an hour, returned to Los Angeles after midnight to prepare for her New York trip.

The next morning she boarded a train for New York for an appearance on the popular radio program "Duffy's Tavern." The show was the brainchild of Ed Gardner, a former New York promoter who wrote and produced a number of popular 1930s radio programs like *Ripley's Believe It or Not* and the weekly radio shows of Bing Crosby, Al Jolson, Rudy Vallee and George Burns and Gracie Allen; by 1940 he was one of the top radio producers in Hollywood. His weekly "Tavern" highlighted the travails and opinions of "Archie," a typical New York mug known for his fractured English.

The live program was first broadcast on CBS Radio on March 1, 1941, set in a mythical Brooklyn tavern run by Archie the bartender. It was a World War II–era *Cheers* with Archie as Sam Malone. Regulars were Archie's daughter Miss Duffy, her friend Vera, Eddie the waiter (played by Eddie Green, who would become famous as Stonewall the Lawyer on *Amos 'n' Andy*) and Clifton Finnegan (played by ex-vaudevillian Charlie Cantor). The show was performed twice every Tuesday night at 9:00 and 9:30, first for the East Coast listeners and later in the evening for those on the West Coast.

The show was essentially a comedy and most of its movie-star guests appeared for exposure or to promote a new film. Carole would not talk about her films; she agreed to appear only in support of the war-time work efforts, and so the script for her visit highlighted the importance of women in the wartime workplace. Carole received $1,000 (about $20,000 today); unlike other episodes, her appearance was also broadcast throughout the Armed Forces Radio Network.

In the script, Carole is appointed Archie's new boss by bar owner Duffy. The jokes and Archie's ill-conceived comments were designed to show that women workers could do anything men could. To howls from the live audience, Archie describes Carole for Duffy during a telephone conversation as a "curvaceous cookie from Hollywood, a beautiful dame who's got ... yeah ... yeah ... that too ... and also a very high forehead ... with calves like hers, nobody's gonna order the pigs feet."

Speaking to Carole in his typical style, Archie asks her to "just stand there in all your glorious comfortude ... never before has such radiant lassitude ever desecrated our portholes ... clean that barstool, just sit down and wiggle a little...." When Carole says, "I'm here to talk about a very serious problem," Archie asks, "What's that stuff about women taking jobs? Dames like you, a frail gossamer who should be placed high on a pedestal...."

After Carole informs Archie that a woman's place is *not* in the home, he retorts that "tomatoes should cling to the vine ... in our own home with a couple of ivy-covered kids...." As Archie continues to downplay the ability of women to do men's work, Carole gets her message across. Through it all, she also shows perfect comedic timing sparring with Gardner. The episode was a huge hit.

In addition to public forums like "Duffy's Tavern," Carole also continued her personal, private efforts on behalf of the soldiers. From New York she traveled to Camp Van Dorn, Mississippi, to visit soldiers of the 99th Artillery Division getting ready to head to Europe. A Clearfield, Pennsylvania, newspaper reported the effects of a Landis visit with a story about one of their local teenagers who attended her visit.

> Earl Guelich, son of Mr. and Mrs. Earl F. Geulich of Turnpike Ave., Clearfield, still has a high fever from that big kiss he got from Carole Landis after his jitterbug dance with her. He hasn't calmed down sufficiently yet to play those drums of his in the dance orchestra.[17]

Carole was deeply affected by the experiences of her European travels. Even before the trip, she took her responsibility to support the war effort seriously. But, even so, her wartime travels had a profound effect on her. During the trip she told a writer friend that it was impossible to think about her career after seeing the devastation of war. After seeing bombed-out villages, hastily dug cemeteries, thousands of dead and wounded soldiers. After her own dangerous battlefield experiences that included crouching in muddy foxholes with mortar shells exploding over her head. After everything she saw, movies seemed unimportant.[18]

Many of the stars who took part in the trips only had a vague notion of the benefits they were bringing. At least until they arrived and saw the unmitigated joy from the G.I.s for the simplest things. Simply seeing an American woman was a big deal. One soldier told this writer that during his entire 18-month European tour, "the closest I came to seeing American girls in Europe was a couple of Red Cross gals handing out coffee and donuts, and this was months after the war ended."[19] Hearing a live band instead of sitting in a sweltering tent listening to what they called the "Mosquito Network" was a thrill. Movies were a treasured favorite.

In his diary of life at a base on Bougainville in the remote Solomon Islands, Stanley Frankel noted, "We go to the picture show this Wednesday night. It begins at 7:30 and the moon is starting to come out full again. Good. We don't need to lug our flashlights and precious batteries with us. There are five hundred soldiers altogether at the show, half our own battalion and the other half a black port outfit." Over 500 G.I.s battled the elements just to watch a movie starring Fred MacMurray being shown on a sheet strung between two poles on an island in the Pacific.[20] The simplest things were appreciated.

Jack Benny said, "We found out they also get a kick from civilian clothes. Larry [Adler] and I wore our loudest neck-ties and I got the biggest howl when I held mine up so they could get a good look. Some of the fellows just wanted to feel it, and one kid told me, 'Jack, the best part of the show was that tie.'"[21]

At the end of June, Carole spent a week traveling up the West Coast visiting military camps and attending bond rallies. She went through the coastal bases to San Francisco and then on to Seattle, where she performed at the Air and Navy bases on June 27.[22]

That same month, Carole notified her friends at the California military bases that her house at the beach could be visited any time by soldiers on leave. She actually had it classified by the military as a recreation center. There was hardly an evening during the summer of 1943 that a soldier, sailor or airman on leave didn't occupy one of the guestrooms at 703 Ocean Front. During the weekends, the house was packed with visitors.

Everyone, it seemed, wanted to know about Carole's pilot husband. The initial coverage was less than flattering. *Life* magazine's story describing their wedding featured the headline "PING GIRL WEDS EAGLE."[23] Subsequent articles were a bit more complimentary. Her rebuttal to the *Life* piece was a self-written article in *Screen Guide* saying "I'm Glad I'm a Fighting Man's Sweetheart."[24]

She described "My Wartime Honeymoon" to writer Adele Fletcher for a June issue of *Photoplay* magazine. The *Movie-Radio Guide* featured Carole as a "Fighting War Bride."

In a June 1943 *Look* magazine article entitled "Movie Star Finds Happiness in War Marriage," Carole described her life as waiting for her husband's next letter. The article noted that "she had traveled more miles to entertain soldiers than any girl in the movies."[25] But she hadn't seen her husband in four months. In an *Women's Home Companion* interview, Carole told the writer that she "wanted to go back to England so I can be with my husband."[26]

Just after Carole's return from her East Coast and southern travels, she received a cable from Tom Wallace. The four-word cable "put Carole in the seventh heaven of happiness" according to Harrison Carroll. All it said was "ARRIVING MIDSUMMER. VERY EXCITED."[27] It would be the first time Wallace had set foot back on American soil since he left to join the Eagle Squadron four years earlier.

During that time, he flew two and one-half years with the R.A.F. and another one and one-half with the U.S. Air Force. He saw extensive action during the Battle of Britain, took part in sorties over France and Norway and flew convoy protection duty as well. He had also just been promoted from captain to major.

Since their marriage the couple had barely spent a total of two weeks alone together. They had a two-day honeymoon before Carole left London for Africa after their wedding, and they had ten days together on her way back to the States a month after that. They would surely be able to put on a perfect face for the cameras, but Carole was no doubt worried how they would get along. There had been those ominous signs during their brief time together in London.

On July 15 she emceed a bond rally — and personally greeted — a large number of the 40,000 employees arriving at or leaving the California Shipbuilding plant in San Pedro. She stayed through all three shifts, arriving at 10 A.M. and staying until 4 the next morning. She gave pep talks to groups of employees exiting the shipyard at 8 P.M., 4 A.M. and 12 noon.[28] In between she visited with the workers in the lunch rooms. The highlight of the long day's festivities: christening the yard's latest ship, the S.S. *Vernon Kellogg*.[29]

A few days later she left for New York to await Tom Wallace's arrival from England. Military leave and travel times were notoriously unreliable, so there was no telling exactly when he would arrive. Louella Parsons announced on July 23 that she was in New York.[30] She would spend her wait time visiting friends, traveling to nearby military installations and making numerous radio appearances. She usually

During a day-long visit to the California Shipbuilding plant at San Pedro harbor on July 15, 1943, Carole launched the Victory Ship S.S. *Vernon Kellogg* in front of 10,000 sailors and workers.

accepted the radio invitations because she knew how popular they were with the servicemen. She made her first appearance the night she arrived in New York.

On July 23 she starred on the Philip Morris Radio program version of "Too Many Husbands" on WABC. On the 24th she went to the Sheepshead Bay Training Center in Brooklyn to appear on WABC's Military Maritime Service Show. She never accepted any honorariums for her military appearances; if they offered to pay, she either declined or donated the money to that group's charity. While she was offered $1,500 for the Phillip Morris production ($40,000 today), she made the Maritime Service appearance gratis.

On July 27 she appeared on Frank Sinatra's "Broadway Band Box" with Eileen Farrell and Cab Calloway.[31] On the 29th she appeared on "Stage Door Canteen" with Monty Wooley, "Slapsie" Maxie Rosenbloom and the singing Andrews Sisters. Still waiting for Tom on August 20, she and Jerry Lester appeared on KNX radio for a performance of "Love Crazy."[32]

On the 24th it was confirmed that Tom Wallace would arrive sometime during the first week of September. Carole kept working as she waited for him. When she agreed to appear at a bond drive and sale on August 27 outside the Polo Grounds, the line began forming in the early morning hours and by the time she arrived it stretched over ten city blocks.[33] She later gave a rousing speech to over 5,000 people who had waited for her. The next night she was back on Armed Forces Radio, appearing on the Army Service Forces radio program.

On September 2 she again appeared on "Stage Door Canteen" with Bert Lytell and Paul Robeson. Three days later she was a guest on Jerry Lester's program.

Wallace arrived from England on September 8. But Carole kept her commitment to appear as a guest speaker at a New York War Finance Committee Rally to help sell $4,000,000 in war bonds, and the next evening appeared at a small rally at a New Jersey theater.

After his arrival in New York the distance between the two was still evident to Carole, though they were out somewhere almost every night. Maybe that was evidence of their strange relationship. It was almost as if they didn't like to be alone together. Or maybe they *were* alone together.

They were photographed almost everywhere they went, she in her glamourous gowns and he resplendent in his uniform. They were almost nightly visitors to the popular New York cafés like The Stork and The Rainbow Room. But his behavior continued to baffle. On September 10 Carole performed before 20,000 people at the New York Harvest Moon Ball; Wallace stayed at their hotel room and slept.[34]

The next day, Fox wired Carole and told her that they could not wait any longer to begin production of *Four Jills in a Jeep*. She was being called back to Los Angeles.[35]

Even though she'd only had a few days with Wallace and another week or so left, she fulfilled her remaining commitments. On the 16th she appeared at one final Bond drive (called Third War Loan Drive) with two-year-old baby Owen Murphy, who had become famous for a war bond photograph taken of him.

The next night, *Wintertime* was released. Just earlier, Carole signed an endorsement contract with Stetson hats to appear in their advertisements. As usual, the ads would also include a descriptor of whatever film she was appearing in. Fox would reap more than Carole from the ads that read "These Stetson hats are worn by Carole Landis, favorite 'Pin-Up' Girl now appearing in the 20th Century–Fox picture *Wintertime* in Technicolor."[36]

Between September 15 and 22 Carole performed at sold-out shows at the Roxy

Visiting New York's Stork Club during a fall 1943 visit with husband Tommy Wallace, Carole already knew the marriage was a mistake.

Theater. The shows benefited a number of military charities, and half of the audience was made up of servicemen. She got fabulous reviews, New York critics saying that she "knocked 'em dead" during her performances.[37] The show had a military theme, from the opening when she was driven on-stage in a Jeep to the encore, where she invited soldiers to come up and dance a lightning-fast jitterbug with her. In between she sang for them and danced with the Roxyettes dance line. The soldiers loved the show.

After her final appearance, Carole gave a benefit performance at the Brooklyn Federation of Jewish Charities fund-raising rally at the Hotel Commodore.[38]

Wallace was still awaiting his final stateside assignment. He and Carole assumed that she would have to depart (for the *Jills* assignment) before he did. She asked her mother to come to New York to meet her new son-in-law and keep him company after Carole's expected departure.[39]

The military ordered Wallace to California for his final stateside posting. He left for California on the 26th and arrived on the 27th. Both he and Carole assumed he would be assigned to a West Coast air base.

Carole left for California on October 1 and was reunited with Wallace on October 2. They moved into her Santa Monica beach house.

Just a few days later, the military again interrupted the couple's reunion by assigning Wallace *back* to New York and a posting at Mitchell Field on Long Island. He would stay in Los Angeles for two weeks and then return to New York as she turned her attention to the *Four Jills* movie.

At first Carole was excited that her overseas travels would be publicized but it soon became apparent that the movie would be more fiction than fact. The girls were all upset about that. They all wanted an honest portrayal of the difficulties of their travels, the wonderful men they met and the realities of war.

Francis, Mayfair, Raye and Carole would be the "Four Jills" in the William A. Seiter–directed film with the screenplay written by Robert Ellis. It also featured Phil Silvers and Dick Haymes (in his film debut) and guest appearances by Alice Faye, Betty Grable, Carmen Miranda and Jimmy Dorsey and His Orchestra. For five years in the mid–1930s, Haymes worked as an extra and driver for character actor Chick Chandler, who paid him $2 a week.[40] But he later became a popular radio singer and one of Carole's closest friends, even though almost nobody else had much nice to say about him.

Jills comes off as just another wartime musical. Fox's sanitized version of the women's travels offered almost none of the deprivation and certainly almost none of the real danger the girls faced.*

In the film, the girls spend more time singing and finding romance than entertaining or bonding with the troops. Francis goes after Lester Matthews, Raye after Phil Silvers, Mayfair after Haymes and Carole after John Harvey. Carole's in-movie marriage was the only romance that mirrored the actual story. Minor characters are featured more than the girls, especially comic Phil Silvers as their amusing Army sergeant escort. The girls are almost secondary. They were required to film events that never happened. For three days they rode camels around the set.

Filming had begun before Carole returned from New York. So had the censors' problems with the film. On September 23, within days of the start of filming, censors

---

Between 1915 and 1930, screenwriter Robert Ellis acted in over 100 silent films and directed another 30 before turning to writing. When he was assigned Jills he had written about 30 films, the most memorable being several minor Charlie Chan movies of the late 1930s. During the 1940s he wrote musicals for Alice Faye (Sun Valley Serenade in 1941) and Betty Grable (Song of the Islands and Footlight Serenade in 1942). War films were not Ellis' specialty at all.

announced that sweaters would not be allowed in the film. Carole explained to the studio that the women — especially she — wore sweaters all the time, both to keep warm and to please the boys.[41] But the censors would not allow sweaters. She told a reporter, "That's what we wore all the time in England and Africa. It was freezing cold." But she still played the game, mentioning "with a sly smile, 'Wait till you see the dresses I'm wearing. I don't think people will miss the sweaters. It's a 'whistle dress!'"[42] Those final comments were probably the creation of Fox publicity men; Carole was furious about the removal of the sweaters and numerous other issues during filming.

Originally, Carole and her three friends were announced as "collaborators" on the screenplay. They were told they would be consulted on decisions affecting the film. Unfortunately, the studio decided to produce a feel-good musical, a genre inappropriate for almost all of their real-life adventures. Carole told a reporter, "Now, every time we make a suggestion someone tells us to go sit in the corner. When the boys we entertained in Africa see the picture, I hope they know the meaning of dramatic license."[43] One writer quoted the girls "If the four jills have their way, the picture *Four Jills in a Jeep* will be released with an introduction reading: 'Any resemblance between this picture and trip to Africa is purely co-incidental.'"[44]

While Carole, Frances, Mayfair and Raye thought the movie was funny and went along with the studio publicity mandates, none thought the movie did their real work justice. The movie almost made the trip seem vacation-like. In the film they fly commercial planes with cushions and back-rests versus the bombers they usually flew. In several scenes they arrive at camps in evening gowns and formal hats instead of sweaters and camp wear.

During a scene in which their camp is bombed, the women casually clamber into a nearby foxhole. Carole described the reality as far different and far more terrifying, saying, "We didn't get into those foxholes gracefully. We ran, scared to death."[45] Illness was totally absent from the film. Nobody even caught a cold. The pneumonia that almost killed Mitzi and Carole, as was Carole's near-fatal bout with e-coli and appendicitis and Francis' knee injuries, was all ignored. About the only instance when the film mirrored life was Carole's character getting married to an American flyer in England (Harvey).

The movie was released in March and April 1944 to mixed reviews. *Film Daily* described it accurately as a "union of comedy, music and romance." Supporting Carole's opinion, the writer also noted that it would "probably not live up to what one may have expected of it ... and was nothing to get excited about."[46]

Another critic probably explained Zanuck's strategy with *Jills*, describing the film as "taking the lighter side of the actual experiences of [the women] on their recent overseas trip.... [It] is a good tonic for the war-weary movie goers who have been up to their ears in Nazi leers and Jap teeth."[47]

Strangely, some critics, knowing that the movie was based on Carole's war-time diaries, attacked her personally, saying the film was "self-praise." That was certainly not true. She never looked for "self-praise," particularly from her military work. If anything, she avoided accepting praise for her work.

On October 25, she participated in a War Chest rally held at the Rose Bowl. With

25,000 people attending, it featured over ten military bands playing dozens of rousing patriotic songs. The evening climaxed with 64 well-known "pin-up" girls marching into the stadium and forming a huge "V" for "victory." Carole led the group.

Writing about Carole, "The amazing resurgence of Carole Landis ... can be credited to her own good judgment in managing her publicity. She's never too busy to co-operate with the newspaper boys and girls."[48] With Carole, it was not a phony co-operation just to get into print. She genuinely liked most of the reporters she dealt with and treated them like friends.[49]

Several *Jills* cast members appeared on the NBC Radio Thanksgiving Program. The show was a reunion of the two most popular Camp Tour groups, those headlined by Jack Benny and Bob Hope. Benny appeared with Carole, Francis and Mayfair. Hope was joined by his co-stars Francis Langford and Merle Oberon. Carole's good friend Pat O'Brien also made an appearance.[50]

Every year just before Christmas, the Hollywood Women's Press Club awarded their "Golden Apples," given to the three stars most cooperative in interviews. On December 20, 1943, Carole was honored along with Ann Sheridan and Lucille Ball. On the male side, the nicest were Bob Hope, Humphrey Bogart and George Murphy. They also "hurled lemons" at the worst: Joan Fontaine, Greer Garson, Ginger Rogers, Errol Flynn, Charles Boyer and the thoroughly unlikable Bing Crosby.[51]

The U.S.O. ran regular full-page advertisements in local newspapers listing all of the businesses and people in town who donated to the charity. These ads were a quiet reminder of Carole's popularity among the soldiers. Even though some far bigger stars appeared at some of these shows—stars like Benny, Hope, Langford, Joe E. Brown and Carmen Miranda—Carole was featured in most of these ads.

Under the headline YOU GAVE THEM HOPE was a picture of Bob Hope and Carole on stage behind microphones. The ads mentioned "One of the biggest jobs the U.S.O. did last year was to carry a slice of home to our boys overseas. Traveling shows that gave to those fighting men the best talent and entertainment this country had to offer ... Bob Hope ... Carole Landis ... Joe E. Brown ... Kay Francis ... the top names of radio and Hollywood. Singers, dancers, magicians, swing bands."[52] From among the 5,400-plus entertainers from every field who visited camps, Carole was a clear favorite everywhere she went.

Just after Thanksgiving, Carole gave up her Santa Monica beach house and moved into the luxurious Sunset Towers Apartments on Sunset Plaza Drive. The Towers were a popular movie-star abode. Her neighbors included bandleader Tommy Dorsey, studio executive Harry Cohn and actors Victor Moore and Paul Lukas. Another neighbor was her ex-husband Willis Hunt.

As early as December 1943, rumors began circulating that Carole's marriage was heading toward divorce. She was also seen at several clubs with other men, like Mickey Rooney and George Jessel. But she denied the rumors.

Even so, as 1943 came to an end Carole was probably coming to grips with the fact that her marriage was doomed to failure. She liked living at 703 Ocean Front as "Tom Wallace's war bride," entertaining troops and enjoying the beach. But she couldn't live there as simply "Carole Landis." Hunt first suggested she move into the Towers, which she did, on December 1. She hired her close friend, innovative (some said garish) decorator and clothes designer Don Loper, to decorate the apartment for her.

Carole spent much of the 1943 holidays promoting *Jills* and volunteering. On December 16 she appeared with her friend Dick Haymes on Bob Burns' radio program. The couple did several scenes from the movie and spoke of her travels to the far-flung bases during her European and African trip.[53]

She did spend the holidays with Wallace in New York, arriving there on December 21. As usual, even though they had very little time, they spent it with other people, in public rather than alone. They spent their evenings at the clubs. Christmas Eve was spent at the Stork Club.[54] *Screen Guide Magazine* featured the couple in an article and photographs under the heading "Reunion in New York."[55] It's not likely that the reunion was as romantic as the photographs.

At the same time, the serialization of Carole's own *Four Jills* writing appeared in the weekly *Saturday Evening Post*. For four weeks, from December 14 through January 15, 1944, readers learned from Carole what the war was really like.

On the 26th she appeared on the Jerry Lester radio program in a taped "We the People" interview segment. Other stars who appeared that evening included Carole's acting hero Bette Davis and John Garfield. On December 29 she guested on the radio program "Star for a Night," and instead of talking about her films spent her half-hour telling stories about the soldiers she had met during her trip.

On the radio, Carole carried herself well and had a great radio voice. In early January 1944, CBS Radio approached Carole to potentially host a live radio program. CBS would negotiate with Fox for almost four months trying to get Carole signed, and she really wanted the job.

She coveted the job not so much for the money or prestige, but for the ability to stay connected to the servicemen she thought were her friends. But no matter how much CBS offered, Zanuck kept asking for more. In April, CBS reluctantly pulled out of the negotiations. Zanuck had again blocked a career opportunity for Carole, and humiliated her at the same time.

Carole got another movie offer from old friend Pat O'Brien.* He had formed a production company with his close friend, Phil Ryan, named Terneen Productions after O'Brien's daughters Terry and Mavourneen. It was a tribute to their Irish roots, as was the shamrock trademark logo of the production company.[56] O'Brien and Ryan wanted Carole to co-star in a WWII–themed film originally entitled *Pilebuck*, which they were to film in early 1944 for Columbia Studios. The film was about a group of pile drivers working in a Naval shipyard building Victory ships. Pile drivers were called "pilebucks," and were known as the roughest and toughest men working on the waterfront. O'Brien was to play an F.B.I. agent working as a pilebuck to investigate sabotage and Ruth Warrick would co-star as O'Brien's old girlfriend.

O'Brien badly wanted Carole to play an F.B.I. agent posing as his wife. On January 2, she signed to play in the film. She would be paid $2,500 per week, with a

---

O'Brien was playing on Broadway when Howard Hughes brought him to Hollywood to star in The Front Page *in 1931. By the 1940s he was an established star with films like* Bombshell *(1933),* China Clipper *(1936) and* The Fighting 69th *(1940). Carole had tiny roles in several earlier O'Brien films, including* Women are Like That *and* Boy Meets Girl *(both 1938), and he remembered her from those days.*

minimum guarantee of $20,000. That was an impressive contract (worth probably $400,000 today) for a month's work. Production would start on January 17.

On January 2, after signing the *Pilebuck* contract, Carole accepted a last-minute invitation to join George Raft on a short visit to England to visit the troops. The trip would last just a few days. Even so, she also agreed to appear at a bond rally the morning of their departure for England, January 5.

Former New York Governor Al Smith asked Carole to come help him recruit 20,000 war bond salesmen during a short street rally. January 5 dawned bitter cold. Freezing rain pelted down and the temperature was in the twenties when Carole arrived with a group of WACs in one of six Jeeps.[57] In spite of the weather, she spent two hours at the rally.

At the request of someone in the crowd she sang an impromptu version of "Oh, What a Beautiful Morning" to the crowd gathered in the Wall Street neighborhood. About 1,000 people braved the weather to see her. Carole stepped up to a microphone and said to the crowd, "You can't stop a war for the weather. The boys over there don't. If every person in Manhattan could spend one hour at the scene of actual fighting, Al Smith would have 20,000 bond salesmen applying every hour."[58]

She then walked through the crowd personally handing out pledge cards before leaving for the airport. She went directly to LaGuardia Airport to fly to London, arriving with Raft on the 6th. They joined a group that was already touring England and spent the weekend visiting a dozen camps within an hour's drive of London and several military hospitals in London.[59]

Carole returned from England on January 8 and spent the next week visiting with her husband in New York. On the 9th the couple was back at the Stork Club and back in front of photographers.[60] Carole announced that she and Wallace would stay together for another week, but she left New York just four days later.

On the 14th she was back in Los Angeles. She probably knew then that her marriage to Wallace was not to last, although she still denied the rumors. The night after her return, she was seen at the Mocambo Café having dinner with Willis Hunt.[61] By then Hunt had no doubt given up any hope of reconciling with Carole, but the two apparently had developed a close friendship in the years since their hasty marriage and quick divorce.

Three days later, on January 17, Carole arrived at the Columbia lot to do *Pilebuck*. Director Eddie Sutherland liked Carole from the moment she arrived. Sutherland asked Carole and Pat O'Brien if they had ever worked together, and Carole answered, "Sure, we played in a picture together ... called *Women Are Like That*. What's more, I remember my whole part. Shall we do it for him, Pat?" O'Brien agreed, made an imaginary entrance and asked, "Where's my wife?" Carole answered, "She went that way," and then went silent.

Sutherland softly asked her if she had forgotten the rest of her lines. Laughing at herself, she told him, "No, that was my entire part!"[62]

Pilebuck was based on the *Saturday Evening Post* story "The Saboteurs" by John and Ward Hawkins. O'Brien is an undercover F.B.I. agent who returns to his hometown with a fake wife (Carole) to root out Nazi saboteurs in the local shipyard. Standard B-movie complications serve to do little more than confuse the viewers; the shipyard foreman (Chester Morris) is O'Brien's brother, still angry that O'Brien left his family and fiancée (Warrick) to work with the F.B.I. Morris is in love with Warrick, O'Brien is falling in love with Carole, and everyone suspects everyone else of being Nazi sympathizers.

What could have and, given the timing, should have been a pretty good film was dragged down by uninspired directing by Sutherland and awful special effects. The studio also determined that the term "pilebuck" would confuse or amuse viewers, so the film was released as *Secret Command* on July 30, 1944. Barton MacLane, who played the lead in several 1930s *Torchy* films in which Carole had bit roles, had a supporting role in this film.

Until January, the Wallaces' marriage difficulties had remained a private matter. But by late January the rift went public. On January 26, *The Hollywood Reporter* confirmed that Carole and Wallace were having problems and would likely divorce. Even so, Carole continued to deny the rumors.[63] Just by chance, at the same time an article appeared in *Movies* magazine (with Carole on the cover) entitled "Love Would Come First! Carole Landis on Marriage and Career."[64]

In early February, as rumors of marriage troubles intensified, Wallace was assigned temporarily to the West Coast Air Force Training Center at March Field. Photographers and reporters were invited to not only their airport reunion on February 20 but to Carole's new Sunset Towers apartment to join the couple for breakfast. Over the next two months, Carole would continue to deny the obvious problems with the marriage, calling the stories nothing more than "malicious gossip." The two lived at the Sunset Plaza apartment for about a month until Wallace was sent back to his base in New York.

That same day, February 20th, Carole was the guest of honor at a Trocadero Restaurant party hosted by her manager Glenn Billingsley. Dozens of film stars including Pat O'Brien and Patsy Kelly and a hundred invited soldiers turned out to honor Carole for her work on behalf of the war effort. Wallace was not at the party.

The following evening, Carole was one of the hosts of a premiere and dinner benefiting the Naval Women's Auxiliary. The movie was *The Sullivans*, based on the true story of five Iowa farm brothers—Joseph, Francis, Albert, Madison and George Sullivan—who served together aboard the Navy light cruiser U.S.S. *Juneau*.

On November 13, 1942, during the sea battle off Guadalcanal the *Juneau* was struck by a Japanese torpedo and sank. All five Sullivans died, either in the initial explosion or in the waters off Guadalcanal in the ensuing days. In one of the great tragedies of World War II, rather than risk further submarine attacks, the ships in the *Juneau*'s task force did not stay to check for survivors. Unbeknownst to the men on those ships, over 115 of the *Juneau*'s crew survived the explosion. By the time the ships returned eight days later, exposure, exhaustion and shark attacks had killed all but ten men. The movie was one of the great propaganda efforts of World War II, although it completely ignored the awful fate that befell most of the sailors.

Again, Wallace did not attend, but that was not the oddest thing about the evening. What was most interesting about *The Sullivans'* premiere was that Zanuck had ordered Carole to assist the Chairwoman of the benefit evening. The Chairwoman? Zanuck's wife, Virginia. Likely the loudest voice heard among the "wives" and their vendetta against Carole. The Zanucks seemingly haunted Carole; the next week, Zanuck put an end to the CBS radio efforts to give Carole her own radio program.

The next evening, Carole hosted lunch for a dozen soldiers at the Trocadero Restaurant and then invited them back to the studio for the afternoon. Again, Wallace was not in attendance.[65]

How much time Wallace and Carole spent together during his brief few weeks in Los Angeles is hard to decipher from available records. But between her normal studio work and volunteering at the Canteen and camp visits, there wasn't much time left for her marriage and Wallace. Especially if he kept avoiding her appearances as he obviously did.

Perhaps he was just shy, and disliked the constant photographers. Whatever the reason, they were not together much, and it was apparent that after the two were reunited in the U.S., Wallace quickly became disillusioned with marriage to a movie star. To make matters worse, whenever he *did* go out with Carole, reporters invariably asked if their marriage was in trouble.

It would be an over-simplification to imply that the marriage to Wallace dissolved amid simple jealousy of Carole's celebrity. But it has to be said that it was one thing to be a flyer in England whose movie star wife was traveling on U.S.O. tours. It was another thing entirely to be living with her in a Hollywood apartment and watch her leave the house every day on one of her myriad commitments, no matter how patriotic. To see her popularity first-hand, to see how much people loved her, must have been disconcerting. Wallace was apparently not strong enough to handle it.

On March 2, the industry held the annual Academy Awards ceremony. Carole was thrilled when she was selected to serve as a presenter. She awarded the Oscar for Art Direction to James Basevi, William S. Darling and Thomas Little for their work in the classic *The Song of Bernadette*, a Fox production. It was quite an improvement from her previous Academy Award appearance, when her slip fell down to her ankles as she walked down the stairs into the hall.

At about the same time, Carole announced that she was going to fly to New York to see Wallace on the 15th. But she stayed in Los Angeles, and the evening of the 15th appeared on Eddie Cantor's radio program on WEAF. The tabloids speculated that she had cancelled the trip because the marriage was faltering. When Wallace flew to Los Angeles for an unscheduled visit two days later, the *Los Angeles Times* ran the headline CAROLE LANDIS GREETS MATE AND DENIES RIFT.[66] The night he arrived, Carole left to appear on Groucho Marx's radio show.

Seemingly every time a marriage rumor hit the tabloids, a matching story about their happy marriage ran somewhere else. In March 1944, it was an *American Magazine* article entitled "War Wife, Hollywood Style."[67] Also, seemingly to quiet the critics, on March 24 she and Wallace appeared in public at the premiere of *Follow the Boys*, a Universal propaganda film version of a camp tour film.

Their next public appearance was on April 2, when Carole bid Wallace goodbye as he left to return to his New York assignment. It's easy to speculate, but impossible to know, why Carole held onto the obviously doomed marriage for so long. Surely she would not want a third marriage to fail. Not just to keep the "wives" quiet, but for her own peace of mind. But her unwavering support of the servicemen she so admired probably added enormous pressure to stay together for appearance sake.

After Wallace's departure, Carole was back to her pre–Wallace visit schedule of four nights a week volunteering at the Canteen and semi-weekly radio appearances. On April 11 Carole appeared in another episode of "Duffy's Tavern" on April 26 she guested on "Orson Welles' Almanac."

The last week of April, Zanuck loaned Carole out to RKO Pictures for the Eddie Sutherland–directed comedy *Having Wonderful Crime*. The movie — strictly a B film — featured Carole alongside her buddy Pat O'Brien and George Murphy with supporting actors like George Zucco, Richard Martin, Josephine Whittell and Wee Willie Davis.

Carole, in 1944 just after filming *Having Wonderful Crime*, in one of her many fashion shoots, this one featuring clothing designed by Edward Stevenson at RKO Pictures.

The film fails for any number of reasons, not the least of which that "screwball comedies" like this one had gone out of favor several years earlier. Also, like every B picture, *Crime* features an unrealistic plot, ridiculous situations and a too-convenient ending. And some of the weakest dialogue put on paper. A typical exchange:

> CAROLE: Not so fast, my skirt's too tight....
> GEORGE: Oh, I told you you didn't know how to dress for a murder.

Carole and Murphy play wisecracking newlyweds who team up with O'Brien, a gruff Chicago lawyer. After they stumble upon a magician called the Great Movel, they get involved in a confusing series of events involving Movel's assistants, a missing $50,000 check and Movel, who turns up dead at a hotel where everyone is coincidently staying.

During productions, Carole usually spent her evenings visiting the Hollywood

Canteen. On Thursday, May 18, she left the studio and traveled to Camp Hunter Liggett, some two hours into the desert, to perform for a group of soldiers at an enlisted men's club. She supposedly caught a cold and was very sick but still traveled all day Friday by train to the remote Del Monte filming site. Working on the 20th, she reportedly collapsed on the set and had to be rushed to the hospital with pneumonia.

This incident has become known as one of Carole's alleged suicide attempts. There seems evidence in both directions. Those who believe it was indeed a suicide attempt point to her crumbling marriage to Wallace as the primary motivator. Those who don't believe that this was a suicide attempt point to Carole's multiple divorces as evidence that one single divorce would not drive her to suicide. Perhaps a *third* would, though.

It is believable that the pressures building up on and inside Carole could easily have led to a suicide attempt. Her marriage was failing and Zanuck was continuing his torment, forcing Carole to work with Mrs. Zanuck on the *Sullivans* premiere benefit, preventing her from doing her own radio show and assigning her more bad films.

The biggest factor weighing *against* this being a suicide attempt was her upcoming Camp Tour with Jack Benny. It had already been announced that Carole would spend the summer on another camp tour, this time to the South Pacific. It is hard to believe that she would have killed herself just before this trip, knowing how much she loved seeing the servicemen. The truth of the 1944 collapse is another Landis mystery.

When *Crime* was released in April 1945, critics described the story as "fair" and the comedy as "silly." But everyone seemingly talked about Carole. They commented on her acting — she had just turned 26 and had developed a maturity (maybe from her wartime travels) that allowed her to handle the comedy expertly — and her beauty, which was by 1944 fully developed as well.

Crime might have been Carole's best film performance. It is clear that she knows that she is beautiful but her on-camera persona in *Crime* shows a vulnerability that hadn't been visible before. It was as if she had finally grown "into Carole Landis."

During *Crime* shooting, columnist Erskine Johnson noted that Carole would be wearing a mink-trimmed nightgown in one scene. He mentioned that the view "should be better than bank night."[68] RKO marketed the film to concentrate on Carole's beauty and figure in the advertising campaigns, featuring the tag-line "When a Body Meets a Body ... in a trunk!"[69]

The Wallace marriage rumors continued to fill the tabloids. Dorothy Manners predicted divorce in a late April column. Carole is allegedly quoted describing the incredible loneliness with her husband gone, living for his letters.[70] To counteract the rumors, Carole would later agree to pay a movie magazine $25,000 if she and Wallace separated before a story of their happy marriage ran somewhere else.[71] All of the silliness was part of the game that movie stars had to play with the press.

On May 4, Carole was again re-united with Francis, Raye and Mayfair at the Los Angeles premiere of *Four Jills in a Jeep* at Grauman's Chinese Theater. After the movie Carole went over to the Hollywood Canteen and drank with the servicemen.

In June, *Life* magazine ran a story about Carole and Florence Wasson, her longtime stand-in and best friend. He was entitled "Movie Stand-Ins: They do the tedious, monotonous work for Hollywood's most glamorous stars," and in it Flo described working for her pal Carole. The story and accompanying photographs evidenced their obvious close friendship, unlike the other actor–stand-ins featured in the story.[72]

The 1942 death of Carole Lombard in a plane crash as she returned from the very first Hollywood Victory Committee Bond Tour devastated Jack Benny. He and his wife Mary Livingston were returning home late in the evening on Friday, January 16, when he saw the headline in Saturday's paper announcing the death. Benny's grief was almost beyond description; he tried to get to the crash site, knowing that it would make no difference. He decided that for as long as the war lasted he would record his program from military camps and bases whenever possible. During the next three years he and his star guests performed the show at such unglamourous locations as Mather Field in San Francisco, the Army Replacement Center in Santa Anna, Fort Devins in Massachusetts, Quantico Marine Base in Virginia and the Marine Corps air base in the middle of the Mojave Desert.

The format of the shows was decidedly different, with the characters playing much more to the audience than in the regular shows. Initial locations were close enough to Los Angeles to enable the cast to be close to home to intersperse camp and regular shows. But as the war extended, he began traveling farther and farther from California.

Benny made his first camp tour from July to September 1943 with Larry Adler, singer Wini Shaw and actress Anna Lee. The group toured several bases in Brazil and British Guiana and then flew to Africa, stopping in (what were then known as) Sudan, Khartoum, Eritrea, Aden, Nigeria and Egypt. The group finished in Israel and Iran after 32,000 miles and 168 performances.

In early 1944, Benny organized a second trip, this one to bases in the South Pacific. Carole had told him that she would come along any time he wanted her. He requested that she join him as his co-star. With Benny and Carole were world-famous harmonica player and 1930's movie star Larry Adler, singer Martha Tilton and pianist-singer June Bruner. During the tour, First Lt. Lanny Ross, known to millions in the 1930s as the "Idol of the Airwaves" before he enlisted, was assigned to travel and appear with the group since he was stationed in the area in 1944. He would hook up with the group in New Guinea, where he was stationed. Newspapers reported the proposed trip in early April.[73]

The performers knew that this would be the most strenuous tour of the entire war. It would involve traversing an incredible 70,000 miles of islands, tiny atolls and jungle camps and would involve the harshest of conditions. They would often be hundreds, sometimes thousands of miles from the nearest hotel. Often from the nearest running water.

The tour would cover the South Pacific, from Hawaii to New Guinea, Australia, the Solomon Islands, the Marianas Islands, the Gilbert Islands, Kwajalein — literally anywhere there were U.S. troops. Carole didn't hesitate when asked if she wanted to come along. The 1944 trip would be almost three times the length of her European tour, and cross the entire South Pacific battle theater.

The South Pacific was the most grueling of all of Carole's war-time travels. Unlike her earlier trips through the European theater, there would be no opportunity to avail herself — even for a day — of cities and even marginally comfortable surroundings. During the 1944 trip she went where the "real" troops were, seeing the men she really wanted to visit. The men doing the fighting.

Before she left, Carole made one final effort to save her marriage. Tom Wallace was originally supposed to be in Los Angeles for

Jack Benny's South Pacific Troupe 278: Benny, pianist June Bruner, Carole, singer Martha Tilton and harmonica player Larry Adler.

over a week before her departure, but military transportation delays and administrative conflicts kept him in New York. At the last minute, the only travel arrangements he could get was a flight to the Alameda Air Station east of San Francisco. He would arrive on July 4. She flew up to San Francisco to meet him.

What was discussed or agreed during those few days in San Francisco is not known. But he was originally scheduled to return to Los Angeles with Carole.[74] Ominously, when she joined up with Benny on the 7th in Los Angeles, Wallace was nowhere to be seen.

Benny's Troupe 278 first went to Pearl Harbor and several bases on the Hawaiian Islands. From there they traveled 10,000 miles to New Guinea for two weeks, and then spent three weeks visiting bases throughout Australia. Then it was six weeks traveling to hundreds of far-flung encampments in the Solomon Islands, the Marianas Islands, the Marshall Islands, the Gilbert Islands and Kwajelein Atoll. The islands that the group visited had been only recently been re-taken from the Japanese during 18 months of fierce battles from late 1942 through mid–1944. The pilots and crews stationed in these areas were all young, most in their teens or early twenties. Very few crew members were older than 25. Their living conditions were difficult. In the early months, they lived in tents stretched under the wings of their planes. The bases were chronically under-manned. Writing to the newspaper in his tiny Illinois hometown of Dixon in August 1944, Sgt. Albert Bieschke described the places Carole would encounter:

This is a strange, no-good land, no place for a white man. All jungles and swamps ... terrible heat with lots of rain and mud. It is the monsoon season, so it rains continuously.... It is also winter time now, but one wouldn't know it for the heat. All travel must be done by air, or on foot, as the only roads are what we build and that is slow work in the mud and jungle ... we get paid in Australian money, but have no place to spend it and the same food day after day ... C ration and dehydrated potatoes....

Carole and her troop lived just like the men they visited. But she and the others never complained about the harsh conditions that often bordered on horrifying. They never asked for anything the soldiers didn't have. Bieschke went on to write, "Carole Landis and Jack Benny flew in and gave us a show the other night, but the rain nearly washed them out." But they put on the show anyway, in a monsoon rainstorm at a front-line battlefield position somewhere in New Guinea.[75]

Troupe 278 performed two shows almost every day, and three most weekend days. The pace was grueling; they rarely got more than four or five hours of sleep a night, which left them all susceptible to various illnesses. None, though, were affected worse than Carole, because she never declined an invitation to visit with the soldiers, leaving her even less time for sleep. In their off hours they visited hospitals.

Benny opened each show with a comedy monologue, always starting with the same joke about his World War I service: "In those days, they used to place you according to what you did in civilian life. If you were a mailman, you were put in the infantry, if you were a cowboy, you went into the cavalry; and if you were a mechanic, you became an engineer. How I ended up on a *ferry* boat, I'll never know."[76] For the black soldiers in the audience, he always included several jokes about his radio and movie sidekick, Eddie "Rochester" Anderson.

Bruner normally performed next, followed by Tilton and then either Ross or Adler. Carole was usually last, since she was the most-awaited member of the group. Benny—and the soldiers—truly enjoyed the make-believe love scenes that he would enact with her. Her songs routinely earned standing ovations that began during the music and continued long after the songs were completed. A big part of Carole's performance was her banter with the audience, and she almost always invited several audience members to join her on stage for a jitterbug, a song and, always, a final kiss. That usually drew the loudest cheers.

Between mid–June and mid–July, Troop 278 visited close to 50 bases scattered among the islands, including nearly three weeks traveling 10,000 miles across Australia. On July 14, they flew by military transport to Port Moresby, New Guinea, where they were met by Ross.[77] They flew into a tiny airfield in the jungle behind Port Moresby called Kila Drome or "3-Mile Field" (for the distance from the town). The two runways in the jungle next to Bootless Bay were in the middle of nowhere.

New Guinea is a 1200-mile-long jungle island. Today the eastern half is known as Papua and the western half—Irian Jaya—is considered part of Indonesia. Port Moresby is located in the southern end of Papua, New Guinea. The group spent the second half of July and most of August traveling the length of New Guinea visiting bases large and small, some in cities but most deep in the jungle.

From the 14th through the end of July the group visited Army and Air Corps

The visiting entertainers often performed in converted mess halls, like this one in Helton Hall in Australia.

bases throughout Papua. They visited camps in remote jungle and seacoast locations like Daru, Bulolo and Morobe. On July 24, they visited a camp in the town of Lae along the eastern coast.

Photographs from a private collection, taken during the performance in Lae, are interesting for several reasons. First, a note on the back of one of the photographs indicates that it was the last show given at the base. Lae was 100 miles north of Port Moresby and very difficult to get to; apparently the other U.S.O. troops that followed 278 did not want to risk the trip.

Second, photographs of the audience show an interesting contradiction. One of the secrets of the World War II camp tours is that the audiences at most of the shows—like the rest of the military—were segregated. Often the black soldiers were not even treated to shows. But in the photographs of the audience for Carole's show at Lae, blacks and whites are seated together, unsegregated.[78] Carole would not allow segregated audiences during her visits to any of the bases, and made it clear to the officers in charge as soon as she arrived at a camp if she got wind of such arrangements.

Visits by the U.S.O. troupes and the movie beauties were very important events for men, many of whom had been away from home facing death for over a year. When the Marines and Army personnel on the Marshall Islands learned that Carole was going to perform, hundreds of the GIs moved their cots into the makeshift theater they had cleared out of the jungle. They braved the snakes and the night-time bugs to insure front row seats.[79]

Left: With Jack Benny on an outdoor stage at the remote airfield at Lae, New Guinea, July 1944. *Right:* Carole during her performance at the Lae airfield, wearing her favorite beaded blue dress. She carried it with her through her wartime travels, and would be buried in it.

In a letter to a hometown friend in Reno, Nevada, from "somewhere in the South Pacific," a pilot described the visit by Carole and the Benny troupe.

> Jack Benny and his gang had flown in that afternoon and the big show scheduled for that night. Naturally we had to get in on this event. He had Carole Landis, Martha Tilton and three or four others in his troupe, and golly, what a show they put on... [T]he show was held in the great out-of-doors and it was a beautiful night, with a full moon coming through the coconut trees, for all the fun and festivity. They were using a home-made stage the Seabees threw up... [W]ith that moon and a grand breeze whistling through the trees, it was some evening for all hands. Carole got the hand of the evening, when she put on a jitterbug contest with about 7 enlisted men out of the crowd, and then gave all the jive experts a resounding kiss at the completion of the fun. Two of the men were from our outfit and they aren't over the experience yet. She and Martha both appeared in long evening dresses and this alone was enough for our money. Gee but they looked wonderful and really broke the monotony of having to look at your fellow man for 24 hours a day and month-on-end.[80]

All of the stars deserve kudos for their wartime efforts, but some obviously were more dedicated to their visits than others. Carole spent months near front-line

Opposite: Carole visits with pilots of the 38th Bomber Group, New Guinea, 1945. (Courtesy Pam Johnson.)

CAROLE LANDIS

battlefield positions and genuinely enjoyed spending time with the lowliest of the enlisted men. She was not there to impress the officers or for publicity. She really liked the men, and they truly loved her.

Many of the U.S.O. volunteers were uncomfortable visiting the actual hospital wards, seeing firsthand the devastation of war. Many of the more squeamish refused to visit. So often, the wounded soldiers missed out on the benefits of the camp shows. Carole made a point of searching out the hospitals during her travels. In November 1944, a Navy nurse forwarded this letter from her brother, stationed in New Guinea, to *Photoplay Magazine*:

> Several days ago, Jack Benny, Martha Tilton and Carole Landis paid our patients a visit... Carole Landis was the one, though. A regular trouper and a wonderful person. She spent all of her time with the wounded speaking to each patient individually. Not just saying hello and passing on but stopping and sitting on the edge of each patient's bed and chatting for some time. That was on a Saturday afternoon and ... she promised she would be back "tomorrow afternoon." Sure enough, Sunday noon she came ... alone ... and stayed until six o'clock, doing all that she could, which was a great deal, to cheer up the blind, the limbless and the sick. To come overseas to entertain the soldiers is doing a lot. To do what Miss Landis did is doing infinitely more.

Benny himself marveled at Carole's dedication to the wounded, and her incredible bedside manner, noting in his autobiography:

> Carole Landis was especially sympathetic with the patients. She had a way of sitting on the edge of a patient's bed and holding his hand and just getting into a friendly conversation. You soon forgot she was Carole Landis, the Sex Symbol, the Hollywood star, the sweater girl, because she was a real human being and had a warm heart that spilled over with kindness.[81]

Even Louella Parsons, Hollywood's acid-tongued gossip queen, paid Carole homage for her efforts. As the war was ending, she noted that "Carole was getting in very solid with the Los Angeles Army Air Field, entertaining as she does so often."[82]

Carole picked up a little habit from Benny: She carried a little notebook during her hospital visits, and jotted down notes about the men she spoke with. When she was back in the U.S., she often called the families of the injured soldiers to tell them stories that she had written in her book during her visits. She also wrote hundreds of letters to other families.[83]

The soldiers responded, often remarkably so, to Carole's efforts. During the first week of August, she became ill, collapsing on stage just after a performance at the Milne Bay Army Base on the southern shore of Papua, New Guinea. She was stricken with a severe case of pneumonia brought on by her exhausting schedule. For two weeks she was confined to a primitive hospital near Port Moresby and on several occasions came near death.

The soldiers were affected when they learned how seriously ill she was. There was a steady stream of worried soldiers visiting her bedside, and she probably could

Happily signing autographs at a New Guinea airbase, 1944. (Courtesy Don Esmond.)

have recovered sooner had she not allowed unlimited visitor access for soldiers who wished to speak with her. In the end, she wound up comforting *them* from her own sick bed!

On August 7, word of her condition reached the Milne base, 18 miles from Port Moresby. The soldiers and airmen who had watched the show did not know how sick

During their visits to the forward SWPA (South West Pacific Area) bases, Troup 278 often entertained at improvised stages built into the South Pacific jungles, like this one in New Guinea.

Carole was when she performed. A corporal stationed at Milne hacked through the steaming jungle surrounding the camp until he found enough tropical wildflowers to make a bouquet. He arranged the exotic red, hibiscus-like blooms in a corsage, dug up some wax paper to wrap his flowers and wrote a personal note to Carole. He then walked the 18 miles from Milne to Port Moresby deliver it in person. Carole burst into tears when she learned of the soldier's efforts.[84]

Her condition worsened, and she was airlifted to a bigger hospital in Australia on August 8. She returned less than a week later, however, joining the group as it headed westward to visit bases located in the western portion of New Guinea. The group traveled west toward the provincial capital (and Gen. George MacArthur's headquarters) of Hollandia (now called Jayapura). From there they went as far as the island of Biak, located 400 miles farther northwest, off the coast.

Hollandia had been controlled by the Japanese army since early 1942, and was only re-taken by U.S. Marines the previous April 1944. The nearby island of Biak was re-taken in July 1944. Carole and Troop 278 arrived to visit the soldiers and airmen at Hollandia and Biak within just a few months of those battles, which cost the lives of over 15,000 soldiers and airmen.

Among the Air Corps groups that Carole visited was the 90th Bombardment Group, renowned among the rest of the Air Corps as "The Jolly Rogers." She and Troupe 278 visited them in August at their New Guinea airfield near Hollandia. The Rogers also flew out of Biak Island, and were well-known for their battlefield exploits. They are the stuff of the movies.

The 90th was among the first bomber groups to arrive in the Pacific battle theater, flying into Queensland, Australia in November 1942 with 48 brand new B-24D Liberator fighter bombers with names like "Pride of the Yanks," "Emma," "Hellzapoppin'," "Big Emma" and "Eight Ball." The B-17s are better-known for their World War II exploits, but it was actually the B-24s that flew the most missions and suffered the highest losses. When the 90th arrived in the South Pacific in 1942, their B-24s had never before been flown in combat situations.

The Jolly Rogers were commanded by Atwell W. Somerville, a handsome officer who was given command of the group in September 1942. "Slim" Somerville would command the 90th through the war. From their island bases they flew extremely dangerous missions attacking Japanese positions throughout the region. As the Marines re-took the Solomons and then New Guinea

Carole and Col. Atwell "Slim" Somerville, commander of the legendary "Jolly Rogers" Bombardment Group, New Guinea, August 1944. (Courtesy Loyde Adams.)

moving toward the Philippines, the Rogers took over the airfields within days of their recapture. They flew out of Guadalcanal and bases in New Guinea, from Port Moresby in the south to Biak Island in the north.

Their distinctive tail markings distinguished Jolly Roger aircraft from any other bomber group. The planes of the 90th were adorned with a large white version of the pirate "skull and crossbones" insignia on a black background. The crossbones were made up of two crossed bombs. One of the Rogers bomber groups, the 400th, painted shark's teeth around the nose of their aircraft, calling themselves the "Moby Dicks."

Carole visited with the 90th at their jungle base near Nadzab, in north-eastern New Guinea, in early August 1944. The men of the 90th were a popular target for U.S.O. visits; Bob Hope visited another 90th base just a few weeks after Carole. When Carole's group visited, the Rogers re-named one of their new planes—B-24J, #44-40340—"Buck Benny Rides Again" in honor of Jack Benny. ("Buck Benny" was a character on Benny's radio program.)

Carole visited with the men for several days, and the group gave a performance on an outdoor stage on the evening of August 1. As the group was preparing to leave the 90th, the airmen gave Carole a pilot's jacket for a picture taken beneath the famous Jolly Rogers insignia on the tail of the "Buck Benny" aircraft.[85]

In late August, the group visited the Solomon Islands, to the east of New Guinea, as they headed back toward North America. The Solomons are a group of dozens of small islands like Florida Island and a number of larger ones including San Cristobal, Guadalcanal and Bougainville. Some of World War II's fiercest fighting took place in the Solomons, particularly on Guadalcanal and Bougainville. During August, Carole and the group visited the Guadalcanal headquarters of the 44th Fighter Squadron.

The 44th was formed at Wheeler Field near Pearl Harbor in early 1941. Known as the "Vampire Squadron," their pilots were among the first to attempt to attack the invading Japanese aircraft. Two Vampire pilots were strafed and killed as they attempted to take off and a third pilot was shot down just as he was airborne. Before other pilots could get in the air, the attack ended. Their efforts were re-enacted in the 2003 film *Pearl Harbor*.

Vampire pilots were among the bravest in the Air Corps. Between 1941 and 1944, the Vampires flew from New Caledonia, Efate and the Espirito Santos islands in the Solomons. They flew dangerous combat missions during the battles for Guadalcanal, Munda, Bougainville and Rabaul, as well as western New Guinea, Morotai and the Philippines. From there they flew eight to ten-hour missions to hit remote and heavily fortified targets on Borneo, Formosa and the China Coast. Vampire Squadron pilots were among the best-known in the South Pacific.

Aside from their dangerous missions, they fought constant battles with the weather, insects, malaria and shortages of food, planes, pilots and equipment. When the war ended in August 1945, the 44th had become the most successful fighter squadron in the 13th Air Force with 169 enemy planes shot down. But their victories came with a high cost—the lives of 42 pilots.

According to former Vampire pilot Bill Starke, one of the airmen had gone to high school with Martha Tilton so, when the group visited Guadalcanal, the pilots arranged for a big party in the squadron area. The pilots were ecstatic when Martha got out of her Jeep with Carole and a group of Navy nurses. Starke, thrilled to have his picture

With an unidentified 90th flier during her visit to the 90th. (Courtesy Loyde Adams.)

snapped with Carole, was taken by her charm and beauty. "She was a very exciting young lady, and treated us like friends."[86]

Carole further endeared herself to the pilots and mechanics at the end of the first afternoon of their visit. Officers had arranged for a more formal dinner for the entertainers at the Regimental Officers Mess. It would be as formal as their situation allowed, meaning it would have meant a nice dinner with good food, served hot, and indoors. The officers were all disappointed — and according to Starke pretty angry — when Carole ignored the invitation and spent the evening hanging around the tents smoking and drinking with the pilots, mechanics and enlisted men.

Carole's war-time travels totaled over 125,000 miles visiting and entertaining troops and civilians in Algeria, Australia, Bermuda, Brazil, Scotland, England, Wales, Guam, Ireland, New Guinea, New Zealand, Australia, dozens of Pacific Island groups, Tenerife Island and the United States. But the 1944 South Pacific trip cost her immeasurably more than time.

Carole, beautiful in this candid photograph though beginning to show the effects of malaria, during her visit to the 90th.

Toward the end of the trip, a severe case of malaria that she had quietly battled for a month forced her again into a camp hospital. Like her bout with pneumonia, the malaria and painful amoebic dysentery that resulted from it almost killed her. The last infection ulcerated her stomach, which tortured her for the rest of her life.

The last month of the trip was extremely difficult for Carole. She lost 20-plus pounds from her 125-pound frame; photographs show an almost emaciated Carole, obviously suffering from the ill effects but still with a smile. These photographs clearly show the immense physical toll the trip took on her.

One of the last visits in the South Pacific before heading home was an Air Corps base on the Island of New Caledonia, located east of Australia between the continent and the islands of Fiji. During their August 29 visit to the base, Benny and Carole did a radio program that was broadcast throughout the South Pacific over military radio. It was also sent back to the U.S. A few days later, Troop 278 headed toward Hawaii.[87]

Hawaii was initially to have been a few days rest and relaxation. But Benny and

Wearing the gift from her flier friends in front of one of the 90th Bombardment Group's B-24s, emblazoned with their legendary skull and crossbones insignia.

Carole insisted on visiting with troops stationed there and the group gave a show for almost 20,000 servicemen. *Tarzan* creator and writer Edgar Rice Burroughs, in a letter to his daughter-in-law Jane, described their visit:

> When Jack Benny was here this week I had him and Larry Adler at lunch at the Outrigger Canoe Club with some of my friends. The next day we all went as Jack's

At the beach in Santa Monica, ca. 1944.

guests to see his show at one of the [military] recreation centers here. We had staff cars and a motorcycle escort of MPs. I rode to and from with Carole Landis. She is very lovely and very sweet [oh, to be seventy again!]....[88]

After the war, she would transfer her energies to the American Cancer Society, chairing benefits and fundraising. Her volunteerism was almost frenetic in its devotion; in a March 6, 1945, handwritten postcard from actor Robert Cummings to a Naval officer who mentioned his surprise that Carole had taken the time to respond to one of his letters, Cummings wrote

> I would look up Carole and get together with her in person if my constitution could stand a prolonged high voltage, after all she's not the type one relaxes with — Heh!....
> Bob

Many other entertainers offered their support to the servicemen stationed around the globe. But the South Pacific trips were the longest, the most difficult and the most dangerous. Only a small number of stars made that trip. Aside from Carole, perhaps Bob Hope worked the hardest and visited the greatest number of servicemen. (Hope and Frances Langford traveled much of the same route through the South Pacific that Carole did, barely a month after she went through the area.)

Aside from Benny and Hope, few others ventured as far as the islands. Comic Joe E. Brown also visited Australia and New Guinea in 1943. Brown became active in the camp tours after his son, an Air Force pilot, died in a California plane crash as he learned to fly a new P-38; he was killed when another plane accidentally landed on top of his plane as he readied for a take-off.[89] But Brown's group did not get onto any of the smaller islands, most still under Japanese control. In November 1943, Gary Cooper and Phyllis Brooks visited one of the Jolly Rogers' bases in Doba Dura, New Guinea, and several bases in Australia. During one performance, Cooper sang with the women in his group.

Troupe 278 headed out of the Solomons on August 30. On August 29, the group broadcast an impromptu show via short-wave to the battlefields that they were not able to get to. Benny, Carole, Adler and Bruner did the show in a cramped Air Force radio shed at a New Caledonia airfield. The broadcast was also picked up across the U.S.

The Benny troupe returned to Los Angeles on September 15. Carole stopped by the Sunset Towers apartment to drop off her luggage and her collection of souvenirs (she had literally hundreds of small tokens given to her by the servicemen, including unit emblems, chevrons, photographs, etc.). She also had an island named after her by a group of Marines, which was reported by columnist Harry Crocker.[90] On September 23, she left for a two-week schedule of stateside camp and hospital shows.

During the war, the studios were not alone taking advantage of the publicity offered by their stars' war-time work. Carole's face was featured in advertisements for dozens of products, from beauty soap and hand lotion to cigarettes and soda. A full-page ad for Chesterfield Cigarettes that ran in dozens of magazines offered Carole in the military uniform of a W.A.C. Above a facsimile autograph was the notation

With airman pal Bill Starke during her stop in Guadalcanal, August 1944. (Courtesy Bill Starke.)

Traveling with Martha Tilton in Guadalcanal. (Courtesy Bill Starke.)

"What your boy wants most ... Letters from Home & Cigarettes that satisfy." The ad also notes, "Back from the war zone, Carole says, 'I saw thousands of cartons of cigarettes given to our boys overseas and can say without reservation that Chesterfield is always a favorite.'"[91]

Royal Crown Cola paired Carole with Bob Hope in full-page newspaper ads themed "Hollywood Stars Back the Attack" that ran for two years through 1944. Beneath the bold headline HOLLYWOOD STARS — A global message from BOB HOPE just back from overseas, Hope and Carole tout Royal Crown Cola while endorsing the purchase of war bonds.[92] Cross-selling like this was common in World War II–era advertisements.

During her trip she wrote an article for a military publication, *MAST*, that appeared in November 1944. Entitled "United We Stand," Carole rallied support for the war effort.

> Hitler wasn't guessing when he incorporated into his psychological warfare the strategy of "divide and conquer." It worked in Norway and it worked in France, and because there is no immunity to Fascism, it's trying hard right here in the United States. There is one antidote. We've got to remember that we're all in this together. British, Russians, Chinese. And French-Polish-Yugoslav-Jewish-Irish-Mexican-English or what-have-you-Americans. Indians, whites and Negroes. Soldiers, Sailors, Marines, Coast Guardsmen, boys in the AAF or Merchant Marine. And civilians. Yes, civilians.
>
> All the names from Pearl Harbor onwards are written on our memories and on our hearts and in your steel and your blood and your courage. The exploits at home aren't of this kind. But believe me, boys, they do exist.

In two and a half short years, the country has rolled up its sleeves, and our production record can be heard in the planes that roar over Germany; our War Bond record is built into every tank and destroyer, and the blood banks of the Red Cross are only one of the "musts" on the daily lists of the men and women on the home front.

None of us here can give as much as you. We all know it. That's why there is such a determination to give all we

Right: Getting some needed R&R on an Australian beach, fall of 1944. (Courtesy Don Esmond.) *Below:* Carole signs the *Miss Beverly II* with a member of the 25th Liaison Squadron during her visit to the Lae airfields. Their small Stinson L-5s were originally used for observation only, but the 25th pilots — some of the bravest in the Air Corps — were soon attacking enemy positions without any fighter escorts, often throwing hand grenades out the windows at Japanese positions! They also flew search and rescue missions, saving dozens of downed Allied pilots in the jungles of the South Pacific.

can, in time, spirit, money, work. We believe in you. We know you're good. But you've got to believe in us, too, because the home front is also a fighting front. And because this belief, this unity, brings the day of Victory right up there in plain sight. Unity is the one thing Hitler and his cohorts cannot cope with.[93]

Carole wrote the letter herself; it was not produced by a studio publicity person. It an example of the kind of open-mindedness that she learned growing up in the San Bernardino melting pot she did. She had no prejudice in her at all, no intolerance. It just was not present, whether it was standing up for black soldiers by forcing commanders to allow blacks to see her show or by visiting black nightclubs or openly befriending black studio workers, she lived it every day.

★ Eight ★

Coming Home, but to What?

Carole returned from her domestic camp tour on September 30. (Tom Wallace had been re-assigned from his New York airfield to a field in San Antonio, Texas, where he was a pilot advisor at the Aviation Cadet center.) She packed her bags and headed for New York the next day.

Before leaving, she finally confirmed the rumors that she and Wallace had separated. She told Louella Parsons that their marriage, entered into in the throes of war, had been a mistake. Though she had been a faithful, busy war wife, the couple simply never had enough time to get to know each other. For his part, Wallace simply said, "I've had enough of being the guy Carole Landis married."

Carole would never criticize Wallace, to anyone. But mother Clara blamed the divorce on Tom's inability to cope with life after the war. She said, "We all knew when we met Tom Wallace why Carole had fallen in love with him. He was so sweet, so sensitive — but so shaken ... had had too much war to come back to the old life without tension... Now he came back to a strange life. He didn't feel at home in the Hollywood life ... came back with war nerves ... it was just too much of an adjustment for two war-sick young people to make."[1]

On October 1, 1944, the *Los Angeles Times* headline read "CAROLE LANDIS BREAK WITH MATE DISCLOSED."[2] Carole gave an interview that ran in the January 1945 edition of *Photoplay* entitled "Don't Marry a Stranger."[3] They *were* strangers; they had spent a total of a month together during over two years of marriage.

As soon as the Wallace separation was announced, the press began linking Carole with every available man she met in New York. On October 12, Walter Winchell reported that "the humidity felt over the weekend can be traced to Carole Landis and Lt. Topping." Topping would later marry Lana Turner, and coincidentally, would rent Carole's house in Brentwood while she did some filming in England.[4]

Staying in a luxurious furnished apartment at 755 Park Avenue, Carole jumped into the social whirl — normal for her after a breakup. She dated wealth Five & Dime Store heir Woolworth Donohue, and would see him on and off for a year. Winchell dutifully reported that "if Woolworth Donohue keeps spending that much time in Carole Landis' dressing room, he'll have to join [Actor's] Equity!"[5] She also spent time with George Jessel, dating him occasionally for years.

During October and November, Carole made several dozen personal and radio appearances. On October 2 she received a special award from the Treasury Department for her work selling war bonds. She received a standing ovation from the crowd filling Ebbets Field during a fund-raising baseball game between the Brooklyn Tigers and the Service All-Stars, a group of baseball players serving in the military.

She appeared on a number of radio programs, including the "Hollywood Canteen" program on the 6th and the Armstrong Theater radio program on the 10th. On the 14th she appeared on "The Palmolive Party Show" with Barry Wood and Patsy Kelly. On the 27th she led a long list of stars on a radio program celebrating the New York Newspaper Guild Canteen Anniversary program. She shared the stage with Gertrude Niesen, Burl Ives and Dan Murphy. On the 29th she was a guest speaker at a fundraising dinner for the Greek War Relief Association and a number of other Greek charities.

Carole at home after the war, 1945.

When she wasn't making personal appearances or with one of her many male admirers, Carole shared the company of a large group of female friends in New York. She spent most evenings with her pals Ann Sheridan, Jinx Falkenburg and Dorothy Kilgallen.

At the same time she was approached by Broadway impresario J.J. Shubert to appear in a play. She asked the studio for a temporary release from her contract so she could do the play and Zanuck agreed, since he had nothing for her. The release would run from October 23 to May 1, 1945.

The post-war Broadway era was a busy one for movie actresses. Shubert hired Carole to appear in the play *A Lady Says Yes*, scheduled to debut at the Broadhurst Theater on West 44th Street on January 10th. Carole went into rehearsals on December 15.*

The play, described as "thirty lovely ladies of fashion and passion," also starred

---

*The year 1945 began on a funny note with a mention in Bob Hope's syndicated column "It Says Here" (January 28, 1945). Hope noted, "I was reading a very interesting article about the new 1946 automobiles now being displayed in the nation's showrooms. It had a picture of Carole Landis posing on the hood of one of the new models. I repeat, it was a VERY interesting article. If all the new cars had radiator caps like that, we'd have a lot less trouble with traffic cops."

Jack Albertson, Bobby Morris and Sue Ryan. The music was composed by Fred Spielman and Arthur Gershwin, younger (by two years) brother of George. Carole was one of the leads. Another was a beautiful young actress and writer named Jacqueline Susann.

The play was an expensive and lavish production that the New York critics savaged. One said it "couldn't possibly live up to its checkbook." The Post's critic labeled it "an undistinguished musical." Walter Winchell noted, "[T]he only good lines in it are those that Mother Nature gave Carole Landis."[6]

Like their movie critic brethren, theater critics liked Carole much better than her material. Walter Winchell wrote in *The New York Sun* that "Carole Landis of the films and darling of GI's makes her Broadway debut in *A Lady Says Yes* and comes through surprisingly well."[7] Nothing could save the play. After 87 performances, it closed in March.

Carole appeared six days a week, with Sundays off. Most stage actors value their days, since their work hours last from late afternoon until late evening. Carole usually arrived at the theater by four in the afternoon for makeup and wardrobe. But she often gave up her days during the play's run for appearances.

On January 26, she traveled to the Brooklyn Armed Guard Center for a March of Dimes Rally. During the war, the Center served as a way station for soldiers and

Left: Singing for patients and sailors at the Brooklyn Armed Guard Center for a March of Dimes rally, January 1945. *Right:* At almost every performance, Carole offered to dance with the servicemen. Here she jitterbugs at the Brooklyn Armed Guard Center. (Courtesy Clarence "Korky" Korker.)

sailors en route to the European theatre. Most of the men only stayed there a few days. But those were the men that she cared most about — men either in battle or on their way to battle. So she convinced Guy Kibbee to come along, and the two made a visit announced just the day prior. The sailors were obviously much more interested in Carole, a fact Kibbee gamely endured.

The Center's band set up on a small stage and Carole sang songs for the boys and danced with them. Gunners Mate 2nd Class Tom Bowerman, awaiting orders to transfer to a new ship, remembered the visit. "Carole [visited] two times ... she was very spontaneous and came into the audience when we started calling out to her. She had a hard time getting back on the stage ... a sailor picked her up and set her on the stage."[8]

Bowerman would later spend several weeks in a South Pacific hospital for frostbite after spending hours in the freezing waters of the northern Pacific Ocean after his ship had been sunk. As he lay in his remote South Pacific hospital bed, who should come up but Carole. Bowerman remembered Carole "visited every bed and chatted" with every soldier in the hospital.

Carole made literally hundreds of such visits. Often unannounced, almost always unpublicized. A few days later she was honored by the men she so admired, one of the guests of honor at the Town Hall War Bond Benefit at the Waldorf Astoria on January 31.

During her run in *Lady*, Carole entered into the strangest of all of her romantic entanglements. According to Jacqueline Susann biographer Barbara Seaman and most of her contemporaries, Carole "fell in love with Jackie and was not reticent about showing it."[9]

When Carole met Susann during the *Lady* rehearsals, Susann was a wannabe stage actress and singer who was married to agent and public relations guru Irving Mansfield. Theirs was an odd union. Married since 1939, their relationship was marked by two things: their fights and their affairs. Most of hers were with women.

Mansfield's money allowed Susann to live the lifestyle of a star, even though she was a terrible actress. They shared a luxury suite in a ritzy hotel on Central Park South. They reportedly did not share sex, but Mansfield helped her by keeping her name in the newspapers. Susann did whatever she wanted to do. She traveled extensively, usually without him, and dabbled in theater.

She engaged in innumerable affairs with members of both sexes. Her men included J.J. Shubert (producer of *Lady*), Eddie Cantor, George Jessel (who also pursued Carole incessantly) and Joe E. Louis. Susann evidently fell in love with Louis, but when she told him she was leaving Mansfield to marry him, he applied for a U.S.O. tour and left for the South Pacific the next month. Her female lovers included a variety of women like actresses Margalo Gillmore and Helen Harris, fashion designer Coco Chanel (during one of her Mansfield-financed vacations to Europe) and Ethel Merman.

Carole and Susann spent almost every evening together, either out at restaurants or at Carole's Park Avenue apartment. Their relationship was an open secret in New York theater circles. Carole openly pursued Susann, sending her flowers and buying expensive gifts of jewelry like $1,000 pearl drop earrings and a mink coat.

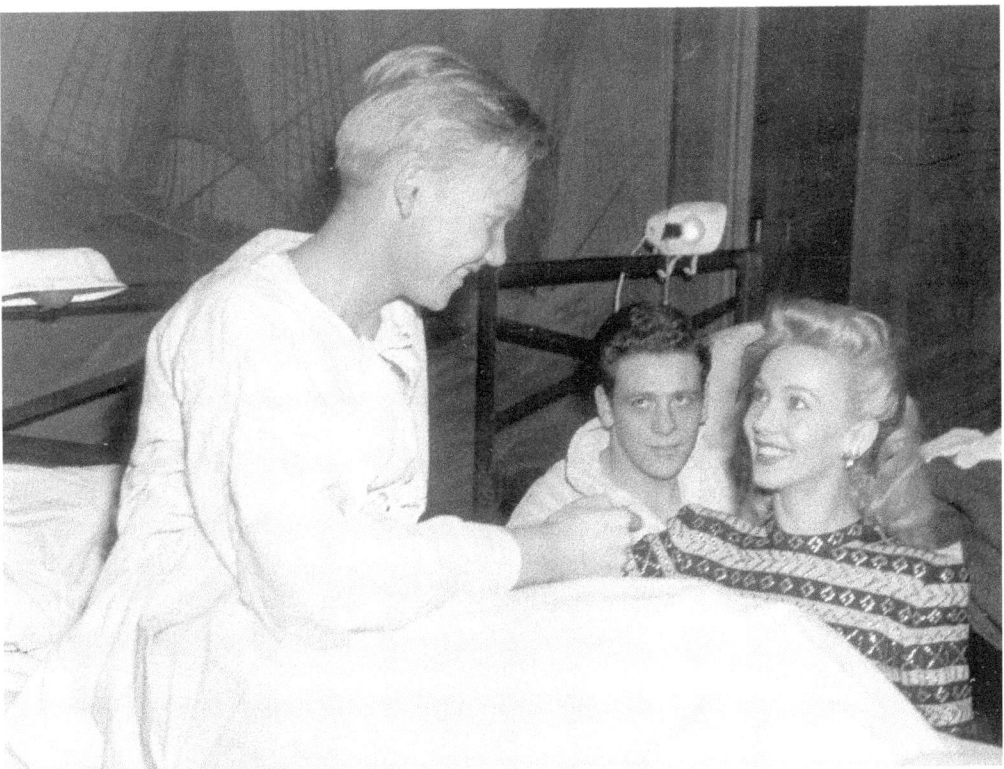

Visiting with an injured serviceman at the Brooklyn Armed Guard Center hospital, January 1945. (Courtesy Clarence "Korky" Korker.)

Susann described their sensual lovemaking to her friends and again later in her 1966 book *Valley of the Dolls*, the story of three friends who become victims of Hollywood. She based the blonde sexpot character Jennifer North on Carole, sympathetically describing a lesbian relationship between North and a Spanish woman she met at a boarding school. It is widely regarded as a description of the relationship between her and Carole.

The character of Maria is a "glacial Spanish beauty" and obvious lesbian that Jennifer meets in Swiss boarding school. It is Maria who controls the relationship and the exploration of lesbianism. Susann writes that Maria knows just what to say to remove "any taint of abnormality. We like one another. I want to make you know about sex, to feel thrilling climaxes— not let you learn about it by being mauled by some brutal man. We are doing nothing wrong. We are not Lesbians like those awful freaks who cut their hair and wear mannish clothes. We are two women who adore one another and who know about being gentle and affectionate."[10]

The relationship was more than a fling for both women. Seaman described the affair with Carole as "one of the most intense relationships of [Susann's] life." It also affected her later writing, according to Seaman: "The depth of Jackie's feeling for Carole, and the nature of their physical relationship, can be surmised from the tender lesbian affair described in *Valley of the Dolls*. Jennifer North, the blonde beauty based at least in part on Landis, has the only truly satisfying love of her life with a woman — a brunette like Jackie. It is echoed in the affair between Judith and Karla in [Susann's later work] *Once Is Not Enough* and in the posthumously published interplanetary fantasy *Yargo*."

It's hard to decipher the importance of the Susann affair on Carole. She was obviously a willing and interested participant and, given her proclivity for falling in love with almost everyone who showed her affection, she probably *did* believe she loved Susann. It would be like to Carole to accept an experiment in homosexuality without caution or regret. To her, any love was good love.

When the relationship ended, as with all of her other failed relationships, she seemed to move on without any apparent ill effect. No mourning or adjustment periods seemed necessary. The only obvious side effect of her breakups was the absence of her normal dating frenzy in the months after the end of a relationship. This is the only time that didn't happen, but she had a man waiting.

After *Lady* ended its run in March, Susann left to do a revival of Philip Barry's *The Animal Kingdom* in Toronto, while Carole remained in New York. But before Susann left, she introduced Carole to her friend, sometime Broadway producer W. Horace Schmidlapp. Schmidlapp described himself as a Broadway "producer" but that was a generous description. Originally from Cincinnati, since the early 1940s he had been living in New York City financed by his family fortune.

Schmidlapp was an heir to a huge fortune built by his grandfather, a turn-of-the-century Cincinnati industrialist. Jacob G. Schmidlapp, the son of German immigrants, was born in southern Ohio in 1849. He and his brother Charles founded several successful breweries, first the Live Oak Distillery in Memphis, Tennessee, and then the Mellwood Distillery in Louisville, Kentucky, before returning to Cincinnati in 1876. They stayed in the liquor business, founding the Export Storage Company, the largest malt producer and distributor in the Midwest.

Jacob was soon one of the best-known businessmen in Cincinnati. Just after his return he founded the Union Savings Bank, which later merged with Fifth Third Bank shortly before his 1919 death. The surviving entity was the precursor to the huge Fifth Third Bank empire. He was a visionary in both business and social issues. He established one of the country's first housing developments for low-income people. In 1911 he founded the Model Homes Company and developed Washington Terrace, 325 small row houses built specifically for low-income African-American workers. Terrace residents were required to become involved in "community clubs" as a prerequisite to living there. He would build over 100 more. He served on the boards of a dozen large companies, including the Equitable Life Insurance Company in New York; endowed or built hundreds of free libraries all over Ohio and the Midwest; and funded dozens of professorships and scholarships.

He quietly became one of the wealthiest men in the country, a friend to business leaders like the Rockefellers and confidante to several presidents. His regular meetings with President Taft and Attorney General Wickersham were called by the three their "Coffee Trust."

The Schmidlapp estate was one of the largest in Ohio. The "Kirchheim" manor house stood amid 50 clifftop acres overlooking the Ohio River just off Grandin Road near the old-line Cincinnati Country Club. Built in the style of a Rhineland castle, the mansion boasted almost 40 rooms.

But amid his business success, Jacob was beset by family tragedy. After a son died shortly after birth, his wife Emelie and young daughter Emma were killed in a railroad accident in California. Another daughter, Charlotte, had already died (in 1907) at the age of 19 in an automobile accident while the family vacationed in France. A heartbroken Jacob spent his remaining years involved in philanthropic endeavors dedicated to their memories. He endowed literally hundreds of charities for tens of millions of dollars. He funded the Charlotte R. Schmidlapp Trust in 1911, and it is still the largest charitable foundation in the United States dedicated to women's charities. Well into its 90th year, the trust gives away over $1,500,000 annually.

Jacob's sons would also become successful. His eldest son Louis (also a successful Cincinnati businessman) had a son Heinrich, known by his Americanized name H. William Schmidlapp. William moved west in 1903 to pursue mining interests with the Silver King Consolidated Mining Company in Park City, Utah, and was an early partner of Charles W. Schwab, one of the first great mining entrepreneurs, managing his operations in Nevada and California before moving to Montana in 1908.

By 1915 he was managing the Montana Power Company, and living with his wife and daughter Jean in Lewiston. In an odd coincidence, his huge mansion and estate was just a short distance from the site of Carole's childhood home in Fergus County.[11] It is quite possible that Carole's family knew of the wealthy Schmidlapp family nearby. William's daughter Jean was later briefly engaged to William Ringling North, of the circus family, in 1952.[12] William Schmidlapp stayed in Fergus County until his death in 1977.

Jacob's other son W. Horace (born 1883) attended Cornell University, returned to Cincinnati and in 1907 became President of the Monitor Stove & Range Company, a successor to one of the oldest and largest companies in Cincinnati, the William Resor Company. He married Jean Maxwell, the daughter of a wealthy attorney, and had four sons: Lawrence Maxwell, Jacob G. (known as "Jack") and Carl, born in 1907, 1910 and 1913, respectively, and W. Horace, Jr., born on April 22, 1916.

Horace's family lived on a lavish estate adjacent to the Kirchheim grounds, just south of the Cincinnati Country Club at 2235 Grandin Road. Their lavish lifestyle included a half dozen live-in servants, memberships in the Cincinnati Golf Club and Cincinnati Country Club and private social clubs like the Couvier Press Club and the Queen City Club. Horace grew up a child of privilege. After his father's death in the mid–1920s, the boys and their mother continued living at the estate well into the 1940s, though they were down to two live-in servants.

Like his three brothers before him, Horace attended Princeton University, graduating in 1938 (all four brothers graduated between 1932 and 1938). But he never took a real job, and by the early 1940s was living in New York playing the role of Broadway impresario. He shared his 524 Park Avenue apartment with his mother, who lived there half the year. Though he is known as a "Broadway producer" still today, he was involved in only five plays during his "career." And he wasn't the producer on the longest running of the five, but an assistant, and the play never made it to New York.

His first production was *Return Engagement* at the John Golden Theater. It ran for only had eight performances (November 17, 1940). Next he was an associate producer on the musical *Let's Face It*, which starred Danny Kaye and Eve Arden, and ran for 547 performances at the Imperial Theater between 1941 and 1943.

Count Me In was produced by a group of six led by J.J. and Lee Shubert, with Schmidlapp the last name listed. It is likely that his input was restricted to cash. The play starred Charles Butterworth and Jean Arthur and lasted 61 performances at the Ethel Barrymore Theater (October 8–November 22, 1943). As a production supervisor on *South Pacific* the following December, Schmidlapp fared even worse. It ran for five performances at the Cort Theater between December 29, 1943, and January 1, 1944.

His final play was *Polonaise* which ran for 113 performances at the Alvin Theater and later at the Adelphi Theater (later the George Abbott Theater). He was obviously not much of a producer as much as a financial backer. He was best-known for his financial backing of the popular Broadway play *Oklahoma*.

He really was a non-celebrity in Broadway circles but he was nonetheless offered a judge's spot in the 1943 Miss America pageant. He joined other semi-celebrities like the editor of the Pittsburgh Press, a commercial artist, someone described as a "noted magazine artist, the creator of the cartoon strip *Flash Gordon*," and Prunella Wood, a New York fashion stylist.

To everyone else Horace and Carole made an odd couple but he probably seemed perfect to her. He was bright and secure, wealthy and independent, and he didn't need Carole. It is doubtful that the relationship was truly passionate; friends have described the two as "friends" and the relationship "collegial."

Carole enjoyed her social life in New York. She and her group of friends had lunches at the 21 Club and spent evenings at the popular clubs. Her favorite evening haunt was the El Morocco Club, though she often stopped in to the Zanzibar, where Cab Calloway's Orchestra played. She loved her evenings out.

She also befriended veteran *New York Post* writer Earl Wilson. "Midnight Earl" covered the Broadway gossip scene and was famous for wisecracks like "Always remember, money isn't everything, but also remember to make a lot of it before talking such fool nonsense" and "Success is a matter of luck—ask any failure." He described an evening with Carole in his memoirs: "One night I pub-crawled for about six hours with Carole Landis who, I'd read, had the prettiest legs and the champion chest of Hollywood."[13]

As spring bloomed in New York, Carole got the itch to go back to Hollywood, this even though she was considered and offered numerous roles on the New York stage as well as the movies. In January it was noted in the tabloids that she would return to Hollywood to appear in the George Jessel–produced *Naked Genius*,[14] but in February it was announced she would appear in the Broadway production of the Louis Jean Heydt play *It Never Rains*.[15]

On March 20, Carole was one of 12 women in different fields chosen by the Fashion Academy in New York as the Best Dressed in their chosen fields. Hers was for Best Dressed stage star. She would not normally be very interested in an award like this, but this particular award was given to the best dressed women in her field *who were most active in the war effort.* It was one of the few honors that she was proud of.

They even mentioned her favorite silver blue evening dress, one that she wore to Hollywood functions and took with her to the South Pacific. Jack Benny's wife Mary Livingston earned the radio version, and Ann Sheridan for film. Other winners came from fields like business, society and journalism.[16]

At the end of March, Carole wired the studio to announce that she would be returning to Hollywood on May 7. Part of her reason for returning was no doubt so she could finally divorce Wallace, but after the New York experiment — both with the stage and with women — Carole wanted to get back to something she knew. Some place comfortable. She liked New York, but she loved Hollywood.

An unlikely couple, Carole and Horace Schmidlapp having dinner at the Stork Club in New York during 1945.

Newspaper ads with photographs of Carole in a two-piece bathing suit top and her smile trumpeted "CAROLE'S BACK!" with a short note: "Screen star Carole Landis is back, boys! She'll soon be seen in *Doll Face*, her first picture after two years' absence from the screen."

Zanuck knew what Carole's wartime work had done for her popularity, and (perhaps grudgingly) announced that he was assigning her to *Doll Face*. The movie was an A assignment; her co-stars were going to be Dennis O'Keefe, Perry Como, Carmen Miranda and Martha Stewart. Carole was to play the lead, named Doll Face Carroll, a dancer who can't find work on Broadway because she is uncultured. With the help of her manager and sometime boyfriend (O'Keefe) she phonies an autobiography written by someone else (Como), but falls in love with her ghost writer.

Doll Face would be a break-out film for Carole. It was a perfect role for her, and would have allowed her to showcase her beauty, her acting, her dancing and her singing. The movie featured a variety of different musical numbers, all of which would have suited her well. Filming was to start in June or July.

At the same time, Carole was offered $15,000 ($300,000 today) a week to make a ten-week personal appearance tour in South America.[17] As late as August 28 she was said to be still "mulling over" the extended trip.[18] Even though Carole was concerned about being gone for that long, it's hard to believe that she would turn down that kind of money.

But she did have other things on her mind. She needed to divorce Wallace, and she had Horace. Perhaps she thought Horace was worth more than what the trip would pay. Harry Crocker confirmed the offer, describing it as "one of the highest fees ever paid a screen star for personal appearances."[19]

Carole finally returned to Hollywood on May 4, and just two days later on the Fox lot told reporters she would be seeking a divorce from Wallace when her schedule permitted her to leave for Nevada. (At the time, Nevada law made it mandatory for one party to any divorce to stay six weeks in the state.) The timing, she said, would depend on when she started shooting her next picture; she was "considering several roles."

The reporters knew that she had arrived from New York three days earlier, accompanied on the same plane by Schmidlapp. It was an open secret that they had been seen together almost constantly during her New York stay — her relationship with Susann was a well-kept secret, so remarkable that nobody would have believed it anyway — so she was asked if her divorce plans were a prelude to another marriage. She told them that she and Horace were "dear friends" and had been "going together" but had no plans to marry.

The newspapers reported LANDIS WANTS DIVORCE without mentioning Schmidlapp. Only basic details were mentioned, indicating that she would file soon, that Wallace was back at his at San Antonio, Texas, and that he was not expected to contest the filing. It was noted that they had been separated since the previous September.[20]

The divorce announced, Carole could now take Horace public. So the next evening she and Schmidlapp were photographed having dinner and drinks at the Joe E. Brown show at Ciro's. Almost every gossip writer mentioned their date; the first was Sidney Skolsky.[21]

She also continued her volunteering. On May 12 she traveled via train to help sell war bonds at a City of San Francisco rally and fundraiser. The Seventh War Loan Rally was held at the Bay Meadows Race Track. Carole and Mrs. (Admiral) Chester W. Nimitz auctioned souvenirs collected by Adm. Nimitz especially for the event. Hundreds of reproductions of Joseph Rosenthal's already world-famous Iwo Jima picture flag-raising picture were also sold. Rosenthal was a photographer for the *San Francisco Chronicle* before the war.

When Carole to Los Angeles, Zanuck and the studio assumed that she would be ready to work on *Doll Face* beginning in the middle of June. At the same time, it was announced the she had been given the lead role in the murder mystery *The Spider*, with Richard Conte and Kurt Krueger. It was to commence on June 4th.[22] It seemed that Fox had finally recognized Carole's abilities and was offering her the meatier roles she deserved. So it was a shock to everyone when Carole made her next announcement.

Eight * Coming Home, but to What?

Carole ca. 1947.

On May 26, she told reporters that she would be moving to Reno, Nevada, within two weeks to begin the formal divorce proceedings against Tom Wallace. Wallace, at his airfield in Texas, signed a consent decree without complaint.[23] Carole would have to stay in Nevada for over a month to satisfy the residency requirements for obtaining a divorce there. The same day *The Hollywood Reporter* announced that

Carole had earned the lead in *The Spider*, they announced that she was heading for Reno to get a divorce.[24] Zanuck, maybe for the first time in his relationship with Carole, was rightly furious.

He flew into a rage when she left the studio. He threatened to sue her and to cancel her contract; when Carole repeatedly tried to telephone him to explain and apologize, he refused to take her calls. She left for Nevada not knowing if she would have a job when she returned.

The Nevada trip was one of those self-destructive situations that Carole put herself in. She had to know that it was the worst possible time to leave the studio for almost two months. She had finally been assigned major films—*Doll Face* and *The Spider*—both of which would showcase her talent and make her an even bigger star. She had forced Zanuck to recognize her beauty and talent.

In effect, she had beaten Zanuck. He could no longer throw her into lousy roles in bad movies. The public adoration for Carole forced him to cave in, and he did, no doubt bitterly. She had also beaten the "wives," who could no longer assert that Carole slept her way into roles, could no longer ignore the public praise.

But even so, Carole decided to walk away from the *Doll Face* role. It was given to last-minute replacement Vivian Blaine, who could not handle the role that would have been easy for Carole. And she walked away from *The Spider*. That role was given to Faye Marlowe. She walked away from the two roles that would have given her everything she wanted from Zanuck, from Fox, from the movie business, and from Hollywood. She gave it away. It's impossible to even guess at the reasons behind her self-defeating motives and behavior.

But leave she did, on Tuesday, June 4. She asked her maid to come with her and drove to Reno, where they settled into a cabin at the Washoe Pines dude ranch in the hills above the city. But a few days later she decided to move to Las Vegas, telling friends that the altitude was bothering her. She sent her maid back to Los Angeles and moved to Vegas, flying there aboard a private plane chartered for her by the El Rancho Vegas Hotel. She flew into Vegas on the 8th.[25]

It would be almost six weeks before she could get a hearing. During that time, Carole made almost daily visits to the nearby Las Vegas Army Air Field to visit with the fliers. She gave impromptu performances at the officers' and enlisted men's clubs and just hung around with the airmen. On Thursday, July 19, she was finally granted her hearing. Newspapers noted simply that "film star Carole Landis obtained her third divorce ... granted a decree yesterday against Maj. Thomas C. Wallace, Army Air Force pilot of Pasadena, California, after a brief hearing before Judge Charles Lee Horsey. She was represented by Assistant District Attorney Oscar A. Bryan, and Judge Horsey granted her divorce in a matter of minutes. She charged extreme mental cruelty."[26] The matter over, she got back in her car and drove alone back to Los Angeles. She returned to her apartment on the 20th.

She was single, again. She had failed at love yet again. It is difficult to determine if she would have been terribly disappointed, a little unhappy, or thrilled to be free to take up with Horace. That part of Carole is impossible to decipher. Most likely, she would simply turn her back, move on and pretend it never happened. It was a new day, and she had a new beau. But she still had a very angry Zanuck back at Fox.

For months the press had speculated about her relationship with Schmidlapp, wondering if she would divorce her airman to marry the producer. As soon as she returned from her Las Vegas divorce exile, United Press took the story public. "The divorce cleared the way for the actress to marry New York producer Horace Schmidlapp, who has been her constant escort in recent months."[27]

A few days later, Landis confirmed the story to gossip giant Louella Parsons. "I arrive in New York August 4 and as soon as I catch my breath Horace and I will be married."[28] (Carole knew better than to announce to her impending wedding to anyone but Louella or Hedda Hopper and she hated Hopper.) She was to marry the man she called "Poppie"; he was only 30 years old, but looked much older.

Though the press was given the story on July 23, announcing CAROLE LANDIS WILL WED FOURTH TIME,[29] Carole and Horace did not appear to be in a hurry to even set a date during the summer. Gossip columns noted that the two were "a nightly New York twosome ... [but] neither making any comments about wedding plans."[30]

Carole was excited about the prospect of marrying Schmidlapp. She told her friends that she had never been happier in her life. It looked like she honestly thought that this time would be different. In a July *Silver Screen* interview she said, "This time it's for keeps."

When Carole returned to the studio, Zanuck would not see her. After years of command performances in his office and hundreds of private meetings, he would not even allow her in to try to explain herself. There really was no explanation; it is not likely that Zanuck would let her off the hook because of love. She did not have a leg to stand on, and there was nothing she could do except grimly accept whatever punishment Zanuck dealt out. She knew she would have no assignments waiting, which is what allowed her to commit to meeting Horace in New York a week later.

But Zanuck didn't want her trip to be a vacation. He forced her to travel there along with a press junket as part of a series of premieres of Rodgers and Hammerstein's *State Fair*. Her pal Dick Haymes was also on the tour — he co-starred in the film — as was George Jessel. But the trip was far from the glamour of Hollywood. On the 2nd she was in Des Moines, Iowa, photographed receiving the gift of a baby pig from Governor Robert Blue at the Iowa State Fair.

Jessel would later write that he had a long-time on- and off-again affair with Carole, and that during this trip it was renewed. It's hard to confirm, but the two were romantic at different times during Carole's life. She arrived in New York on August 7 and settled into her 775 Park Avenue apartment, surely assuming that she was in for a long siege with Zanuck.

She kept busy. The day after she arrived, *Esquire* magazine shot an extensive fashion spread of Carole at her apartment. On August 14 the war in the Pacific was over. The atomic bombs at Hiroshima and Nagasaki had finally forced Japan to its knees, and V-J Day was celebrated around the world. Strangely though, it had the opposite affect on Carole.

On the 14th Carole called her ex-lover Susann, depressed. With the war over, Carole was concerned that she had no real "role" in life. Carole's insecurities ran so deep, and so much of her personal identity was tied up in what other people thought about her, that she was petrified *not* to have a role. During the war, her role as a tireless supporter of the military was never in doubt. But with no war, what would her role be now? She worried about movie roles also, complaining to Susann about her assignments. Susann tried to re-assure her that she was indeed loved, and that she didn't need camp visits to carve out an identity. She was a beautiful, talented actress that people liked anyway.

Susann's pep talk did little to persuade Carole that she was worth something. Later that same day, she felt the need to accompany flying ace Eddie Rickenbacker to a new Ford plant in Edgewater, New Jersey. The two of them — a World War I flier and Carole — were photographed in the front seat of a new car.[31]

Carole no doubt expected Zanuck to write her off immediately, and began relaxing in New York with Schmidlapp. Zanuck not only began returning her calls but he assigned Carole a better role in a movie scheduled for the fall. The feud seemed to be ending with a Zanuck capitulation. (Louella Parsons would dutifully report the end of the fight a month or so later, noting, "[T]he tiff she had with her company — 20th — is patched up. They had the proverbial pouting spell when she walked off a picture to go to Reno for a divorce."[32])

It was a pretty substantial lead role in a police thriller tentatively entitled *Precinct 33*.[33] She would co-star with William Gargan in the film, which by the time it reached theaters had been re-named *Behind Green Lights*. It was scheduled to begin filming in mid–September. At the same time, Zanuck arranged to loan Carole out to producer Arnold Pressburger at United Artists to play the second female lead (to Signe Hasso) in Douglas Sirk's *Thieves' Holiday*. It would be filmed at General Services Studios and would be entitled *A Scandal in Paris* when it made the theaters. She would start filming on *Holiday* as soon as *Precinct 33* wrapped, probably some time in October.

Even Carole's seemingly self-destructive behavior had not yet ruined her career at Fox. Now if she could only safely navigate through her movie assignments and her relationship with Schmidlapp, everything would be fine.

During the summer and fall of 1945, their engagement was in and out of the gossip columns. Strangely, it was reportedly much more "off" than "on." As soon as the engagement was announced, there were literally dozens of notes in various gossip columns indicating that the relationship was on shaky ground from the start.

It was rumored that Schmidlapp's wealthy family in Cincinnati was not pleased with the prospects of their wealthy son marrying a thrice-divorced movie actress. Jimmy Fidler reported in his column that "according to inside rumors, Horace Schmidlapp's family won't welcome Carole Landis as an in-law unless she agrees to give up her acting career and be 'just a housewife.'"[34]

The relationship changed every day. In July, Carole was quoted as saying they would marry by mid–August, but as early as August 3 Carole was denying reports of "a rift between her and Schmidlapp."[35] On August 4, Walter Winchell reported that "the Horace Schmidlapp–Carole Landis merger (due next month) is expected to be mutually cancelled."[36]

Later that month, well-respected film writer Dorothy Kilgallen mentioned a competitor for Horace's affections: "Courtney Kane, the young Buffalo moneybags, has made the Carole Landis–Horace Schmidlapp wedding look less of a sure thing."[37] Kane was a wealthy Buffalo socialite who had dated Horace.

Carole and Schmidlapp broke off their engagement on numerous occasions, the first time within a few days of Carole finding out about Courtney Kane. Some of the break-ups were publicized, some were not. During one of the formally announced break-ups, Carole told Dorothy Manners that she had ended the engagement because "he wanted me to give up my work and stay in New York. I wouldn't ask him to give up his career to come to Hollywood and just sit around while I make pictures."[38]

Even the writers had a hard time keeping up with the status. On August 24, Kilgallen wrote, "Carole Landis and Horace Schmidlapp, who are no longer engaged to each other, were looking very engaged to each other at the Latin Quarter Restaurant."[39] Parsons was told that the engagement was off and noted that same week, "It may be all off between Carole Landis and Horace Schmidlapp ... as love flew out the window her interest in her career revived and now the curvaceous belle is heading back to Hollywood for the top role in George Jessel's musical *Girl on the Moon*."[40]

Carole at her glamourous best, but showing the sadness that invaded her life in the late 1940s.

Carole returned to Los Angeles in the middle of August to go back to work. First, she wanted to find a new home. She gave "make a clean start" a new meaning with the efficiency with which she moved back to Los Angeles. She stopped off at the Sunset Towers apartment only long enough to have her clothes and personal stuff packed up for moving. Then she called the prestigious Los Angeles auction company Hart & Newman and told them to pick up everything else in the house. They loaded a moving van with every stick of furniture, lamp, knife, fork and spoon. Her belongings were sold during a quickly arranged sale that took place September 3–6.

She spent two weeks looking for a new house before settling on a lovely Spanish-stucco mansion in the "Flats" of Beverly Hills between Sunset and Santa Monica Boulevards. On September 15 she rented a ten-room house at 621 Hillcrest Road from concert violinist Jan Rubin and moved that same day in what little she had. She then called her old fried Don Loper and asked him to fill and decorate her new home.

The street was decidedly "movie star," like the rest of the Flats. Her pal James

Cagney had once lived in 621, and Darryl Zanuck himself had lived at 510. Director Howard Hawks was at 502 and Buddy Rogers at 520; Ted Healy had lived at 623 before his 1937 murder. Other neighbors included cameraman Harold Rosson, Preston Sturges and Jose Iturbi.

Within two weeks of her return to Hollywood, all evidence of Carole's marriage to Tom Wallace was gone. She was living in a new house with new furniture. She had a new beau and new roles. The first one—*Precinct 33 (Behind Green Lights)*—began filming on September 13. *Thieves Holiday (A Scandal in Paris)* would start immediately after.

Precinct 33/Green Lights was directed by Otto Brower, who tried to produce a film noir piece but came up short because of his lack of technical expertise. The entire film takes place during a single night in an unnamed city. All we know about the locale is that there are stockyards. Beneath the green globes outside a police station, a car drives by and dumps the murdered body of a private detective onto the empty sidewalk.

The murder victim was a blackmailer who apparently had been demanding money from Janet Bradley's (Carole) father, who was running for mayor. The police and the press want to pin the crime on Bradley, but honest police Lt. Sam Carson (Gargan) stops the sleazy newspaperman (Don Beddoe) from helping dishonest policemen railroad Bradley.

Aside from Brower's misdirected efforts, a second problem was the casting of Gargan, who is almost completely devoid of charisma in what should have been a great role. Carole has a hard time responding to both Gargan and the script, and for the first time in a feature role is not able to rise above bad material or direction.

She comes off like Gargan, with no real passion. A director would almost have to *work* to get that kind of performance out of Carole, but that's what is on screen. She didn't like the script the first time she read it, which certainly couldn't have helped. During an interview done in the middle of filming, she is most certainly referring to the film when she speaks of half-heartedly playing a role she did not want to take. The title of the story was "Do You Think I Was Wrong?"[41]

Meanwhile, off the set, the Landis–Schmidlapp watch continued. The first week in October, Carole was linked with Joseph "Jay" Gould, a publicist and writer.[42] On October 14 she hosted a housewarming party at the Hillcrest house for her friends. She refused to tell the invited writers who gave her the very expensive orchids she was wearing, other than to say that they didn't come from Horace and had been flown in "by Clipper from Hawaii."[43] But on October 25, when a reporter told Carole that Horace had just flown into Los Angeles, she said she "wasn't interested."[44]

On Friday, October 20, Carole hosted a nineteenth birthday party for young actress Patrizia Cobb, who had only recently been signed by Fox, and was to star in their upcoming *Anna and the King of Siam*. She would play the wife of the king, who was played by British actor Rex Harrison. "Buff" Cobb was an unusual choice; she had never done a film before. But given Zanuck's typical casting process, it could be speculated why he gave her the role. She was indeed beautiful, and had just ended a six-month marriage to lawyer Greg Bautzer.

To impress the movie star guests at the party, Cobb wore a two-foot-tall hat covered with black netting made especially for her by Carole's friend and costumer Don Loper. During the party she walked too close to some candles and the netting burst into flames. Victor Mature and Cobb's fiancé, actor William Eythe, grabbed ice buckets and water pitchers and doused the unfortunate actress.[45]

Anna and the King of Siam was Buff Cobb's only film. She hosted an early television show, *All Around the Town*, in 1951, and was a panelist on the 1952-53 program *Masquerade Party*, but then disappeared from the movies.

Thieves' Holiday (A Scandal in Paris) began production on October 8 under the direction of Douglas Sirk. Unlike most of Carole's other Fox assignments, *Scandal* boasted a top-level cast and crew. The camera work was by Eugene Shuftan and the music by Hanns Eisler. The cast is a Who's Who of 1940s character players including stars George Sanders and Signe Hasso, and supporting actors Akim Tamiroff, Vladimir Sokoloff, Alma Kruger, Gene Lockhart and Alan Napier.

Sirk was a renowned German theater director in the 1920s and moved to film in the 1930s, but fled the Nazis for France in 1937. He ended up in Hollywood in 1939 working for Columbia and Universal. Sirk is a renowned director best known for elaborate, almost baroque melodramas. Among his better known films are *Magnificent Obsession* (1954), *All That Heaven Allows* (1955), *The Tarnished Angels* (1958) and *Imitation of Life* (1959). He was an erudite director who always got the most out of his scripts. At first he seemed an unusual choice for *Scandal*, a strange mix of drama, comedy and farce about a French thief.

The film is the story of sophisticated eighteenth century French criminal François Eugène Vidocq (Sanders), from his birth in a French jail in 1775 to his appointment as chief of police of Paris, where he intends to rob the city bank. After escaping from jail with Emile (Akim Tamiroff), he poses as a policeman to rob Loretta showgirl (Carole), of her ruby garter, and steals the jewels of a wealthy sponsor in whose home he is a guest. But the marquise's granddaughter (Signe Hasso) falls in love with him, and it becomes a battle between the girl and the bank.

Sirk produces a richly colored and textured film that is usually ranked among his best work. Jean-Loup Bourget called *Scandal* "a masterpiece of ironical cinema."

Carole knew her role would be a sexy portrayal before she began filming and not from the script. Before shooting began, she wired producer Pressburger to ask about the costumes she would wear. He wired her, "COSTUMES FRENCH PERIOD. STOP. SKETCHES IN MAIL." Her sense of humor showed through in her wire response to Pressburger, "HAVE JUST SEEN SKETCHES. STOP. CORRECTION. STOP. COSTUMES FRENCH EXCLAMATION POINT."[46] She told a reporter that in *Scandal*, "I go around practically stripped to the waist."[47]

Censors worked overtime trying to de-sexualize Carole and the film. She and Gene Lockhart, who play man and wife in the film, occupy twin beds in a period almost 100 years before the concept was even thought of.[48] Lockhart would go on to play the husband of another gorgeous actress, playing opposite Hedy Lamarr in *The Strange Woman* (1946).

Many Landis critics think that *Scandal* was Carole's finest work. It was certainly her sexiest work, due in no small part to Sirk's direction. He first introduces viewers to Carole's character in a nightclub. Carole is performing "Flame Song," the film's

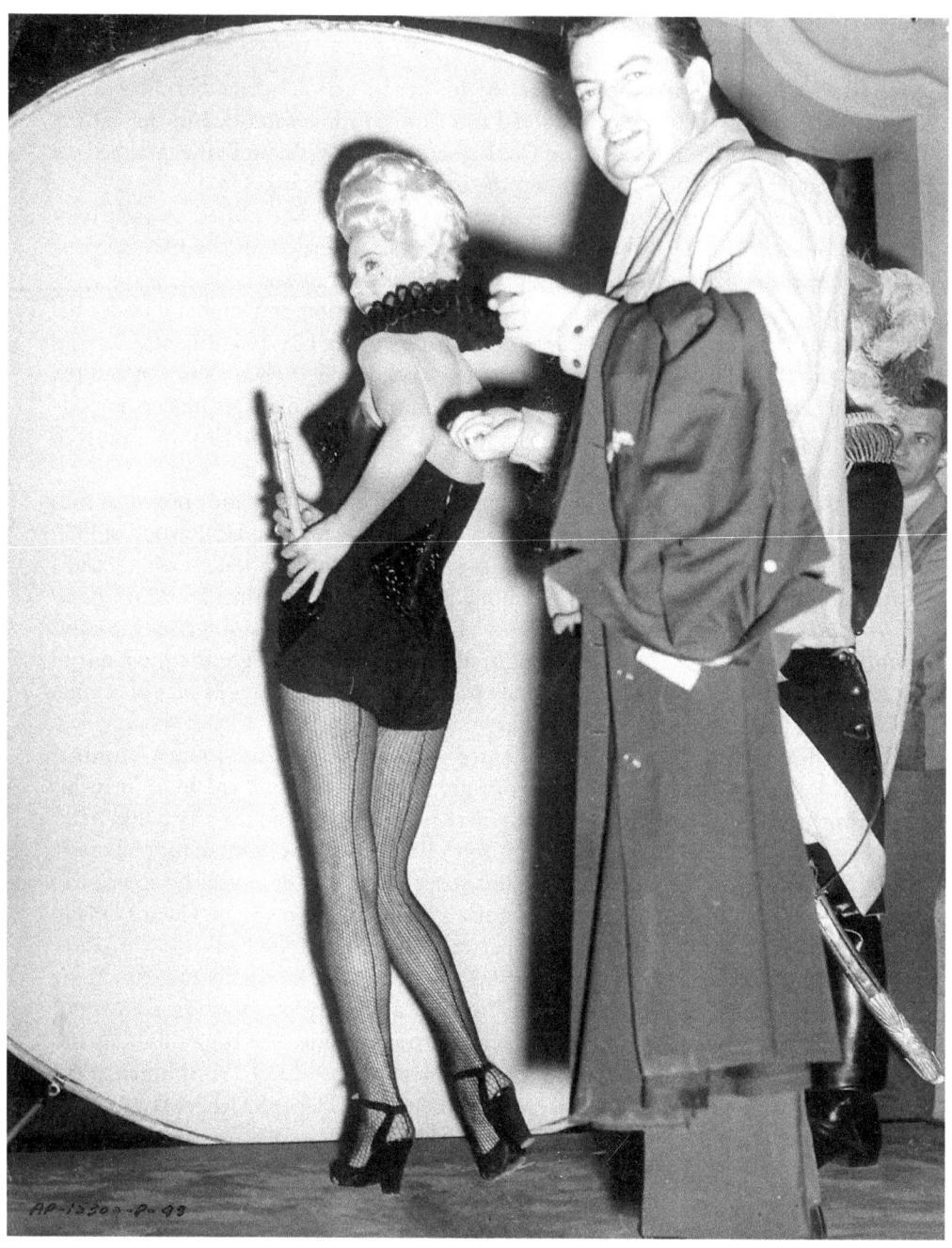

Carole gets ready to shoot the famous backlit "Flame Song" scene — in which she appears to undress in silhouette behind the screen — during *A Scandal in Paris* filming.

only musical number. She is first seen in silhouette behind a large round, white screen, which she sets on fire. Stepping through the flames, she tantalizes the men in the club, including of course Vidocq, who steals her ruby garter.

During rehearsals for that scene, several members of the Johnston Office (the censors group) appeared on the set to watch filming. When she stood in profile behind the screen, she appeared to be naked. The censors were predictably appalled and wanted the scene removed from the film. Producer Pressburger almost begged them, saying, "I'm telling you, she's not naked. She's wearing a form-fitting costume and black tights on her legs."[49] The censors allowed the scene, but only if a scene was added showing Carole getting *dressed* before she takes the stage.

Vidocq arranges a fake jewel theft from a rich patron so that he will be named chief of police, replacing (in one of the film's more Machiavellian concoctions) Carole's husband, chief Richet (Gene Lockhart). Vidocq must avoid discovery by the cuckolded Richet, maintain his plan to rob the bank, deal with one woman who loves him and another he loves, all the while dealing with his partner Emile's constant suggestions to follow the path of evil. The film's climax is a murderous confrontation between the two.

Sanders was known for an aloof and standoffish attitude toward almost everyone on his sets, in stark contrast to Carole's warm and friendly attitude. In an arranged prank that drove Sanders to fury, Carole flirtatiously dropped a handkerchief. When Sanders bent over to pick it up, a crew member nearby ripped a large piece of cloth. Everyone but Sanders roared with laughter.

This is indeed one of Carole's finest performances, and showed what she could do with a good story, good direction and even a passably exciting co-star. Her time on camera was limited but, as always, she stole the scenes she had. One critic wrote, "Sanders portrays a thief but Carole Landis steals every scene."

Carole always enjoyed her loan-outs more than the work at her home studio. It was a vacation. And like almost every loan-out she was given, she worked with better casts and crew. But her relaxing reprieve from the Zanuck lot for the *Scandal* filming was marred by a bizarre incident with yet another stalker. This time the stalker got closer than her mailbox; he got into her dressing room.

On November 14, after a long day of filming, Carole was relaxing in her dressing room getting ready to get out of that day's costume, which happened to be a very sexy spangled black bustier and tights combination. According to Carole, a man entered her dressing room and said, quite amiably, "I'm Grauman the attorney. I met you two weeks ago."

She was so shocked she couldn't really respond as he sat down beside her on the sofa, threw his arm around her, grabbed the zipper on her black skin tights and, according to Carole, "became unduly familiar."[50]

Carole began yelling, which caught the attention of her co-star Sanders, who had the dressing room next to hers. He and two gatemen dragged the intruder out of Carole's dressing room, but he broke free and ran from the set.[51] At a tiny apartment two blocks away from General Studios, police arrested a former attorney from Marietta, Ohio, 31-year-old Charles Gramlich. Gramlich had graduated with Phi Beta Kappa honors from Marietta College and from the Ohio State University School of Law, and had a reputation as a brilliant attorney early in his career. However, during the early 1940s he began to suffer mental problems of an undetermined origin.

He had come to Hollywood three months earlier, and apparently had been following Carole since his arrival. It is not known how he was able to gain entrance into the studio. He was originally charged with attempted rape, telling police over

A post-war studio photograph, ca. 1946.

and over, "I deny it, I deny it," as he was booked. But police also investigated Gramlich for similar attempts to "annoy actresses Greer Garson and Claudette Colbert" by a man of identical description.[52]

The publicity department would not waste this opportunity for free press. Numerous arranged photographs were taken of Carole, the first allegedly showing

Carole just "moments after the attack," seated on a bench. Still wearing the same bustier and stocking set, "consoled by actor George Sanders after eviction of man who entered her dressing room ... and sought to molest her." The headlines read MOLESTER EVICTED.[53] Carole is shown nervously wiping the hair from her face as Sanders softly rubs her arm.

The next day, surrounded by a phalanx of photographers, Carole arrived at the Hollywood police station to formally identify Gramlich. As flashbulbs popped she pointed a finger at a forlorn-looking man in a long coat handcuffed to a bench in a long hallway and said, "That's him." Gramlich had to be placed into a hospital psychiatric ward when he became violent in his cell, and it was soon discovered that he was a former mental patient who had been committed to the Athens (Ohio) State Mental Hospital in 1941 after spending time at several other institutions.

Just a few months earlier, on July 10, he had been released on a trial visit to his mother's home. But he quickly disappeared, surfacing in Hollywood in August or September.[54] On December 5, Gramlich was committed to the state mental hospital at Norwalk.[55]

Even though she was fourth-billed, Carole's performance obviously dominated *Scandal*. Studio publicists used her character as the basis for their marketing. At the end of the first week's production, the studio held a party for writers, hosted by Carole. She wore her costume from the famous fire dance scene. Almost 100 men showed up.[56]

A few weeks later, perfumed garters—reproductions of the one that Carole has stolen off of her leg during the film—were sent to hundreds of movie reporters and critics. Attached was a note signed by Carole: "This is your pass to our movie set and I hope you'll come by and let me put it on."[57] It was estimated that somewhere around 200 columnists mentioned the garter in their columns around the U.S. On January 7, *Life* magazine ran a story on the movie, with a photograph layout of Carole's flame dance and her costume. The article described the lucky writers putting the garters on Carole's gorgeous legs.[58]

After *Scandal* wrapped, she reported back to Fox the last week of November. She received a telegram at home on November 23 instructing her to report for wardrobe fittings for the film *Somewhere in the Night*. *Night* was a film noir crime drama that would be directed by Joseph Mankiewicz. It had a strong cast as well (John Hodiak, Nancy Guild and Lloyd Nolan). But Carole was to be seventh-billed—yet another lackluster Zanuck assignment into an insignificant role.

After thinking about it for a few days, Carole informed Zanuck on November 26 that she was turning down the role "because it would be detrimental to my career." The forgettable role went to Margo Woode.

Again, Zanuck seemed to be almost baiting Carole with a few good roles, and then a lousy role. Making it seem like she was on her way, and then a roadblock. It was extremely frustrating for her, but was probably done purposefully by Zanuck. On the 29th, just after turning down the *Night* role, Carole left Los Angeles for New York. Zanuck immediately suspended her from the Fox payroll.

If Carole was serious about her relationship with Horace during the October–November *Scandal* filming, it didn't show up anywhere. She wouldn't talk to reporters about him and led as active a social life during those months as she ever had. Even so, by the first week of December writers were mentioning that fans should "watch for a revival of the Carole Landis–Horace Schmidlapp romance...."[59]

Carole arrived in New York on December 3 to visit her "Poppie" at his luxurious Carlton House apartment at 22 East 47th Street. They shocked almost everybody when, on Saturday, December 8, they were married there. Reporters mentioned incorrectly that the apartment belonged to his mother; the rest of the Schmidlapp family lived in Cincinnati, Ohio. She probably had purchased the apartment but Horace lived there.

Newspaper photographs running the next day show a mismatched couple, both holding champagne glasses and smiling for the cameras. On the right a radiantly beautiful blonde with a beautiful smile and a flower pinned to the plunging neckline of her flowered dress. And on the left a bookish-looking, not particularly handsome man, unassuming in a white shirt and striped tie, with a nose that dominates a rather plain face. His smile is almost a sneer, trying to effect some sort of "cool." He looks out of place; more like an accountant than a sometime theatrical producer. And now the husband of one of the most beautiful woman in Hollywood.[60]

The couple left the next day for a Cuban honeymoon. The Cuba of 1945 was a distant version of the poverty-stricken island of the 2000s. In 1945, the jet-set vacationed on a beautiful island with five-star hotels, European-style casinos and some of the most beautiful beaches in the world. Fronting the ocean in Havana was a glittering esplanade called El Malecon, lined with expensive shops and bistros. Ernest Hemingway wrote of it as a "Garden of Eden." When the couple honeymooned there, a young Fidel Castro was a student at the University of Havana.

Carole and Poppie flew from Havana to Cincinnati to meet Horace's mother, Mrs. Jean Maxwell Schmidlapp Sturgis. She lived at the Schmidlapp family's 100-acre "Ca Sole Estate" outside Cincinnati. After visiting for a few days, the couple returned to New York on January 2, 1946.

I believe that Horace wanted to marry the movie star, and just wore her down. After breaking up with him so many times, she simply gave in. A hint of that can be found in a Louella Parsons column written the day after Carole left for New York to marry Schmidlapp: "The reason Carole Landis took off for New York in such a hurry is Horace Schmidlapp telephoned her the night before and she hurried east. She said goodbye to no one, not even her good friend, Colonel Kimberly."[61] (He was an Air Force officer whom Carole had been dating during the most recent break-up with Horace.)

Schmidlapp made no secret that he wanted to become an independent film producer as well as producing plays, telling reporters that he wanted Carole wanted to star in them if she could get out of her 20th Century–Fox contract.[62] In fact, just a few months later he invested $500,000 ($5,000,000 today) into the building of a movie and television studio at Central and Tuckahoe Avenues in the Westchester County (New York) city of Yonkers. The facility would house his newly formed production company, Associated Filmmakers, Inc., which would be run by Stanley Neal. Neal began with Mutual and Vitagraph in the silent era before returning to his native England to produce films there. Horace's studio was scheduled to open on July 1, 1946.[63]

Even Carole seemed to sense that Horace's plans for her could present a problem for other studios, telling a writer that while she was pleased with Horace's plans to get into films, that he would have to deal with her agent directly and it would be her agent's decision regarding the desirability of a particular role. Horace could not have been pleased when that story appeared in the newspapers.[64]

It was also well-known in stage circles that Schmidlapp wanted to star Carole in plays that he produced. Perhaps he saw her as a meal ticket as well as a glamourous wife. Before the wedding, Carole told Broadway writer Jack Lait that she would wed Horace, "sure that he's got everything." But Lait voiced the opinion of many Broadway folks by adding, "He has everything, but he's going to back a new musical and he may lose a lot of it. Anyway, I don't think this will end up as a duet." Addressing rumors that Schmidlapp wanted to star Carole in a remake of *Li'l Abner*, Lait continued, "No more do I think he'll present her as Daisy Mae in *Li'l Abner*. She's as much Daisy Mae as Fred Astaire is Abner...."[65]

After their early January return to New York, Carole was negotiating with Zanuck to come off of suspension and return to work at the studio. On January 7, she wired Zanuck asking to be allowed to live in New York and return to Hollywood to work. The studio countered by offering her a six-month leave. Carole responded by wiring back the she was "Ready, willing, and able to render my services to you. Carole." It had been accepted that she would take another suspension and stay in New York, but she told reporters that she wished to "go on with my career,"[66] and returned to Los Angeles on the 13th.

Zanuck's wedding gift to Carole was an assignment to possibly the worst film she ever did. It was perhaps the worst film Fox ever made. On the 14th she dutifully reported for her costume fittings for the aptly titled *It Shouldn't Happen to a Dog*.

Zanuck must have been trying to put a final nail into Carole's career coffin when he assigned her to *It Shouldn't Happen to a Dog*. Brower's *Behind Green Lights* was a bad movie, but the Herbert Leeds–directed *Dog* was worse. It was obvious that Zanuck and Fox were through with Carole. There was no pretense left after such an awful assignment. It was Carole's final movie for Darryl Zanuck; it just couldn't get any worse.

The film would rightly be called a "dog," and everyone but Zanuck knew it even before filming began. Writer Bob Thomas, meeting with Carole during filming, noted in his column, "Carole ... is appearing in something called *It Shouldn't Happen to a Dog* (the guy who puts up the marquee sign will probably think the same thing)."[67] Jimmy Fidler described the film as "a far-fetched story that shouldn't happen to an audience."[68] And these were printed even before filming was completed.

Carole starred with Allyn Joslyn, Margo Woode, Jean Wallace and Harry Morgan (then known as Henry Morgan). The movie was a farce. Joslyn's character was a crime reporter before going off to war; he comes back to find that his old job was given to Wallace. The only reporter job left is as the Science Editor. Joslyn is hanging out in a Brooklyn bar when policewoman Carole walks in with a large, well-trained Doberman Pinscher and with the dog's aid seems to rob the place. Though he wants to report the robbery, Joslyn and Carole are soon on the trail of black market crooks. The best role in the film was the Doberman's.

During the Thomas interview, Carole also discussed her unorthodox marriage to Schmidlapp. Bi-coastal unions are not uncommon today, but in the mid-1940s it was very unusual for a husband and wife to live on opposite coasts. Asked if it was disconcerting to work while Horace was in New York, she downplayed the issue, telling Thomas, "I may grab a plane any minute, studio or no studio." Laughing, she added that she planned to make New York her home, but "I'll be working out here [Hollywood] a few months a year. Maybe I should rent a stratoliner[69] and use it for an apartment."[70]

Filming ended in early February and Carole, probably sensing that the end was near with Fox, moved out of the 621 Hillcrest Road house and moved back to New York with Schmidlapp on February 18. Actor Richard Greene rented the house after Carole moved out.

But Carole, it seemed, could not fully abandon Los Angeles. Before going to New York, she rented yet another house, even though she intended to live in New York almost full-time. It was as if she needed something to help her hold onto Hollywood. She rented a lovely home at 232 South Mapleton Drive in Bel Air, just south of Sunset Boulevard. Like the Hillcrest house, the Mapleton house was even more of a movie star neighborhood. Sonja Henie lived on the corner at 120 in a mansion that Lana Turner would later purchase, director Hunt Stromberg lived at 144 (now 130), Jesse Lasky was at 133 and Jane Withers was at 292. It was a neighborhood that Humphrey Bogart described as "where all the creeps lived, all the millionaires."[71] Even so, in 1952 Bogart and Lauren Bacall would purchase 232 themselves.

The mansion was a 14-room brick French Colonial with white-shuttered windows hidden among huge trees and standing atop an acre of manicured lawn. The house was perpendicular to the long driveway, making it difficult to see. It had a marble veranda, two tennis courts, a pool and a four-car garage. An oak-paneled family room overlooked the backyard grounds. The walls were covered with shelves for all of Carole's books, and there was a bar and a huge fireplace. It had a massive living and dining rooms, five bedrooms and servants' quarters.

A wartime glamour pose; her stunning beauty easily attracted a philandering Rex Harrison.

The Mapleton house seemed, quite frankly, fit for a star of much higher standing than Carole. And she wasn't even living in Los Angeles. She intended on using the house during her visits, and would only infrequently visit the lovely estate during 1946–47.

Even after all of the torment heaped upon her by Zanuck and his wife's pals, Carole never had an unkind word for the studio. But she knew when she left for New York that, even though she had ten months left on her contract, her time with Fox was over. She hated Zanuck, but she loved hundreds of the studio employees. And they loved her.

She spent the spring of 1946 relaxing and enjoying her friends and life in Manhattan. She was back into her large circle of New York pals headed by Dorothy Kilgallen and including Barry Wood, Phyllis Brooks and Billie Burke. Her closest friends all saw Carole for what she was: unaffected and normal, an unpretentious, friendly person and a loyal friend.

At a glamourous party attended by wealthy friends of financier William Gottlieb, the guests included members of the Broadway stage elite, movie stars and members of some of New York's wealthiest families. Carole fit in perfectly with the wealthy and the café society, at the same time enthusiastically participating in a lively game of musical chairs. Wearing her favorite blue beaded gown and high heels. She won. Second place went to heiress Hattie Carnegie.

If anything, Carole's "round-table" friends were intelligent and talented to a fault, and she fit right in. She spent the spring of 1946 doing some radio appearances, like "The Continental Celebrity Club Show" on March 16 and "The Jack Smith Show" on March 20. Although her Smith visit coincided with the premiere of *It Shouldn't Happen to a Dog*, she was asked by Fox to plug the Dick Haymes–Maureen O'Hara film *Do You Love Me?*[72] Probably out of loyalty to her friend Haymes, Carole agreed to do so. She was still receiving weekly invitations to appear on radio, and was paid between $1,000 and $1,500 an appearance (upwards of $20,000 today).

She made some volunteer visits but those were becoming fewer and farther between. With the military volunteering becoming less important, she turned her attention to a new pet charity, cancer research. On April 2 she appeared at a large street festival to raise funds, and on the 19th performed at an All-Star Show at Carnegie Hall for the same charity.

She spent her days with her friends, going to lunch, shopping, doing volunteer work or taking short trips to visit friends in Philadelphia, Horace's family in Cincinnati and, once a month or so, back to California. In April she spent a week in Los Angeles with old friends, visiting with Ann Sheridan on the set of *Nora Prentiss*. She seemed to enjoy being married to Schmidlapp although they spent very little time together.

For his part, Schmidlapp just didn't seem to care about spending time with her. It was as if he was content having *married* her, and now that she was his, he didn't have a need to be seen with her. It was a very strange relationship. It wasn't contentious; they almost never fought. They just didn't seem to care about each other. Friends described the two as almost "collegial." There was plenty of mutual respect; there just wasn't any romantic love or passion in the marriage. But Carole didn't appear ready to divorce a fourth time. Not yet anyway.

It Shouldn't Happen to a Dog opened on June 29. The film was so bad that even on the premiere bill, it was most often offered second-billed to another film. The same week, another Fox film opened, *Anna and the King of Siam*. The film starred newcomer Buff Cobb (who caught fire at Carole's house) and Englishmen Rex Harrison.

On June 29 *A Scandal in Paris* opened at Grauman's Chinese Theater and most of the other large theaters in Los Angeles. It would open nationwide on July 19. The movie and Carole indeed created a press scandal. Everyone loved the film. It was featured in every major (and minor) movie magazine. *Silver Screen* offered "19th Century Siren Carole Landis"[73] and *Screenland* "Carole in and out of Character in Scandal."[74]

In an interview with Gladys Hall that ran the same time as the *Scandal* articles, Carole spoke glowingly of her marriage to Horace. The article oozed domestic bliss, an obvious fabrication. But Carole was still playing the game, telling Hall that she was "happier than I've ever been in my life... I send him off to the office in the morning and I'm there to greet him when he comes home at night... He surprises me with little gifts ... for the first time, I feel like a woman instead of a man."[75] She re-affirmed her love for Horace in an article in an issue of *Silver Screen* two months later, saying, "Now it's for keeps ... I'm sure I have the right husband at last."[76]

The rumors that dogged Carole from her first days in Hollywood began with her relationship with Busby Berkeley. He probably initiated her on the Hollywood casting couch, but he also arranged for her first studio contract with Warners and made sure she worked more than any other contract actress during her first year in Hollywood.

Their personal relationship ended when his domineering mother (actress Gertrude Berkeley) put an end to his plans for marrying Carole. The relationship quickly eroded and died. At the same time, so too was public interest in his musical numbers ebbing and they were both dropped from Warners in the spring of 1938. While Carole was able to take her career to a higher level, Berkeley's was effectively over. From that time to the mid–1940s he was only able to find choreography work in minor films, usually charitable assignments offered by old friends trying to keep him solvent. Between 1940 and 1943 he worked on just six films; from 1943 to 1946 he did not find any work at all.

His 25-room mansion on West Adams had been replaced with a tiny apartment at 1583 Altivo Way, a distinctly blue collar neighborhood near Elysian Park. He spent his time drinking in the dusty neighborhood taverns. He was charged with public intoxication and brandishing a gun on November 27, 1945, the judge fined him only $10 because he was told that was all the money Berkeley had.[77]

His older brother, once an accomplished athlete and businessman, was found dead of a drug overdose on a New York City park bench in the early 1940s. When his overbearing mother died suddenly in June 1946 — she ran his life to the day she died — Berkeley tried to kill himself. On July 17, police were called to the apartment by his houseboy, who found Berkeley on the bathroom floor. He had slit his wrists and his throat and almost bled to death. He was rushed to the Georgia Street Receiving Hospital nearby and barely survived. He spent most of 1946 institutionalized.

From a career perspective, 1946 was a lost year for Carole. She was still technically working for Fox, although they would assign her to no films. She was waiting for the October renewal date of her contract. Assuming that Fox would not renew, she would then be able to take some of the offers she was getting. She was not allowed to do any other films, but she still did radio and earned money doing personal appearances. In August she spent from the 16th to the 23rd in Philadelphia making appearances, for which she was paid $5,000.

On October 22, Carole was admitted to St. Johns Hospital in Santa Monica for what her doctor W.L. Marxer called "an acute abdominal condition,"[78] supposedly a relapse of the intestinal problems that began in the Pacific. Doctors reported that it was very serious, but probably not critical. It was supposedly a recurrence of the ulcers that had resulted from her severe dysentery. She was hospitalized for 11 days, and it made the newspapers right away. Sheilah Graham was among the gossip writers who confirmed the story, "Carole Landis was all set to resume her film-acting career when she was rushed to the hospital. She'll make pictures again when she is better."[79]

Many Carole researchers blame this hospital stay on an overdose of sleeping pills—an attempted suicide. There is circumstantial evidence that this may indeed have been one of the three or four attempts allegedly made by Carole to kill herself. There are indications that this would be a likely time for Carole to do this. First, an 11-day hospital stay for a recurrence of her stomach ailments would seem long, even to an outsider obviously unfamiliar with medicine. Another bit of telling evidence was that, on October 26, just four days into the stay, Dr. Marxer wrote her a prescription for 50 Seconal sleeping pills. This little bottle of pills would later figure largely into Carole's death. It was a surprisingly large prescription for anyone, let alone someone hospitalized with stomach ailments.

Perhaps this stay *was* due to stomach problems. Additional confusion may be from another supposed suicide attempt which reportedly took place at about the same time, an attempt reported only after her death. This particular story was propagated by the mother of actor Dick Haymes, a close friend of Carole's.

According to the story passed among friends of Carole and Dick, she had planned to kill herself by driving her car off a cliff along the Pacific Coast Highway, but at the last minute was distracted when a kitten walked in front of the car. She grabbed the kitten and drove to Dick's house, where he lived with his mother. According to Haymes' mother, while Carole held the kitten in her lap, the two women were able to talk out Carole's problems, whatever they were.[80] The story has several obvious holes but is also impossible to discount.

But it's hard to believe Haymes' mother, who gave Carole singing lessons and first introduced her to her son. Dick Haymes was an interesting choice in friends for Carole, who normally had very strong reads on people. She was not good at picking husbands, but she was usually pretty good at picking friends. Most of her closest friends—like Cesar Romero, Pat O'Brien and Florence Wasson—were un-Hollywood, family-oriented types. But Haymes was a mess. He was paranoid and an awful person.

The Argentinean-born singer earned fame fronting for the likes of Tommy Dorsey, Harry James and Benny Goodman in the Big Band Era of the 1940s. He made a fortune on movies and records—some say as much as $5,000,000 during the '40s alone—but would end up blowing all of it. By the late 1940s his money was all gone, and his reputation in Hollywood was in shambles. He was known as a deadbeat and a loser who doggedly pursued Rita Hayworth in the early 1950s so he could marry her and pay off his debts. One of his ex-wives was Nora Eddington Flynn, one of Errol Flynn's child brides.[81]

But just two days before she ended up in the hospital, Carole received the news that she probably expected but perhaps dreaded. Fox would not renew her contract. Officially, at least, she was out of work. The studio wired the news to her on October 24.

Carole might have been relieved to finally be out from under Zanuck, literally and figuratively. She now had control of her own movie life. She had to know that roles would be offered and that she would survive professionally. It's hard to believe that she would have tried to kill herself over this. But her insecurities had caused her to do so many self-destructive things during her life that it's not far from the realm of the possible that on a Saturday night in October, just a few days after being fired, Carole tried to kill herself. We'll never know.

By mid–November she was back in circulation. On November 12 she performed at a United Jewish Appeal "Night of the Stars" benefit concert at Madison Square Garden before 14,000 fans. She appeared healthy, although she had clearly lost quite a bit of weight. For much of that fall she also worked on the committee running the Southern Conference on Human Welfare's dinner honoring Joe Louis, which was held on the 16th.

Carole spent the Christmas holidays with Horace in New York. The day after Christmas, gossip columnist Dorothy Kilgallen described her as "a dreamboat in a white velvet dress, looking like a grownup boy's notion of a white Christmas, as she glides into Toots Shor's Restaurant...."[82] Sometimes she was out with Horace but more often she was alone or with other escorts.

For the first Christmas in five years, Carole chose a non–military-themed Christmas card. In previous years her holiday cards were either U.S.O. of Naval Auxiliary Association cards in the red, white and blue. But for 1946 she chose a white card with a picture of Santa, smiling and smoking a pipe.

✶ Nine ✶

Rex

Heading into 1947, Carole's press was mixed, as usual. The Landis-Schmidlapp watch continued without break. And Jimmy Fidler, who never seemed to miss an opportunity to take a swipe at her, mentioned in his annual New Year's predictions that she would be among the actresses who would probably "lose ground" in 1947. At least she had some famous company; the others who would also suffer during 1947 were Deanna Durbin, Alice Faye, Bette Davis and Rosalind Russell.[1]

On a more amusing note, Joan Smith, the most prolific swimsuit and underwear model in the U.S. in the 1940s — she posed for over 5,000 ads in 1946 alone — offered her annual "Top 5 Best Undressed" list as a response to the annual Best-Dressed lists. Smith's list was similar to the present-day Blackwell list, half serious and half tongue-in-cheek, offered with the advice, "With all this competition out there today a girl has to look her best in undress."[2] Marie MacDonald and Chili Williams were "most beautiful in bathing suits," Lana Turner was "prettiest in a slip," Rita Hayworth "most languorous in a negligee" and Carole "loveliest in a nightgown."

Tongue-in-cheek or not, by 1947 Carole knew she would probably never escape her image as just a beautiful body. It must have been disappointing to think that everything she had done during the war wasn't enough to change people's attitudes. She must have known that she was probably not going to change anything. But the shots kept coming, for some reason.

Just a few days after the Smith award, Bennett Cerf wrote in his column that she "puts fresh meaning into the word 'curvaceous.'" A movie critic, taking a swipe at Katharine Hepburn, managed to hit Carole with shrapnel when he wrote, "Katharine Hepburn doesn't have enough of what Carole Landis has too much of."[3] Sidney Skolsky said to her when they met walking the studio lot, "Honey, you look like a million dollars and you sure have got the money invested in the right places." The usually friendly Carole just turned and walked away.[4] Skolsky would later attribute the remark to Groucho Marx.

What was sad was that Carole was so unlike her image. In New York for the New Year's holiday, she shared lunch with writer pal Dorothy Kilgallen and several others, chatting about everything from how to make coffee to their husbands and their favorite movies (Carole's was the little-known *Halfway to Heaven*). The real Carole showed through when she was with her friends.

She laughed outrageously as she told her friends of a visit to Don Loper's clothing salon in Los Angeles before she left for New York. Loper suggested she purchase a "pair of lounging pajamas topped by a beaded ermine bolero." But Loper warned her that it was "*just* for sitting on the floor ... if you sit on a chair, the entire effect is ruined."[5] Her friends understood that Carole would find the outfit preposterous, but the public would probably believe just the opposite.

She was also much smarter than people ever gave her credit for. In fact, although her secretary answered most of her voluminous fan mail, letters requesting more individual response were set aside for Carole's attention. Rather than try to dictate responses to one of her secretaries, Carole answered all of those letters herself. She felt that she expressed herself better typing than trying to dictate her thoughts and was a faster typist than any of her assistants.[6]

Kilgallen was one of Carole's closest friends. In a column during that early January visit she noted that "the 'new' Carole Landis—whose toned-down beauty and brown hair is on the soignée rather than the spectacular side—seems to be winning her one-woman war against being typed as Another Luscious Hollywood Blonde. She's superstitious about announcing it in advance, but she flew to Hollywood on the spur of the moment Monday to screen test for a part that is one of the most coveted of the year ... half of the actresses in Hollywood have been mentioned for it...."[7] The film was probably *Joan of Arc* (the role went to Ingrid Bergman), but was also rumored to have been *Johnny Belinda* (eventually played by Jane Wyman).

Carole returned to the west coast on January 14, 1947, Horace a week later (the 22nd). Meeting with her agent Arthur Lyon, she learned that any number of studios were interested in hiring her for all types of films even though she hadn't worked since the disastrous *It Shouldn't Happen to a Dog* almost a year earlier. There is a persistent rumor that Carole's career was flat and that her prospects were dim. That just isn't supported by the facts; she had multiple offers, all of them lucrative.

Universal Studios producer Mark Hellinger wanted Carole to fill out a foursome of gorgeous actresses to star alongside Burt Lancaster in *Brute Force*,[8] a prison movie starring Burt Lancaster as a wronged prisoner and Hume Cronyn as a brutal guard. Hellinger had known Carole for years. A one-time New York writer, Hellinger counted among his friends some of the most vicious mobsters in America.

Ostensibly to "research" his crime scripts, his inner circle included Al Capone, Lucky Luciano and Ben "Bugsy" Siegel. Dutch Schultz left Hellinger a white, armor-plated Rolls Royce in his will. When Siegel was arrested for bookmaking in Los Angeles in 1944, Hellinger appeared in court—in what the press described as his every-day uniform, "a dark blue shirt and white necktie"—to testify that his pal was "a man of good moral character."[9]

In an interesting coincidence, when Siegel was arrested at his apartment on the bookmaking charge, George Raft was there celebrating his return from a U.S.O. tour in which Carole participated. Raft's friends included people like Siegel, Meyer Lansky, Charlie Fischetti and Lucky Luciano.[10] It was likely that Hellinger introduced Carole to Pat DiCicco, a mob lawyer turned agent, whom she dated in the early 1940s.

Hellinger wanted Carole as a female lead in *Brute Force* and Carole probably would have taken the role, but Lyons negotiated a richer contract with Eagle-Lion, the U.S. distribution arm of the English studio British-Lion. She would make two pictures a year for $7,500 per picture (the equivalent of about $250,000 today). Her first film would be Leigh Jason's *Out of the Blue* which would begin filming in February. George Brent and Virginia Mayo were set to co-star.

In Britain, American films were more popular than their British counterparts, and American actors and actresses added marquee value to British films. By hiring American actors, the British studios helped blunt the popularity of American films. The British studios also paid well. Carole, always the groundbreaker, was the first American star to take advantage of this opportunity. During the next five years, there would be a virtual exodus from Hollywood to London.

But Eagle-Lion also wanted Carole for her popularity among the British citizenry. Unlike their

Carole Landis

June 1946

Dear Elsa:

Thanks so much for the sweet letter and the darling pictures. They're very pretty and it was sweet of you to send them. I don't know which I like best- they're both excellent.

Am still away and having a fine time but may be back on the coast pretty soon for a new picture. I don't know yet just what it will be though- may have news next time I write.

Thanks again, and all the best,

Carole

Carole personally typed many of her own letters to fans, including this 1946 note. It was the same personalized stationery upon which she would scrawl her suicide note to her mother.

American counterparts, Brits thought Carole a true heroine. Perhaps several hundred thousand had met her in person during her 1943-44 camp tour. One writer later described Carole as "royalty without a crown, a Princess Diana of the war years." Eagle-Lion executives were thrilled when Carole agreed to their contract.

In early February, Carole and Horace spent a week vacationing in Palm Springs, amid rumors that the marriage was again crumbling. Sheilah Graham wrote, "Carole Landis, also at Palm Springs, was billing and cooing … with husband Horace Schmidlapp. And the day before I had been told that they were on the verge of splitting up. If they are, they're hiding it very well."[11]

Back on the coast, Carole showed an interest in several hobbies, some old and some new. She got back into the cockpit, flying again for the first time since the middle of World War II when domestic flight restrictions made flying difficult. She also bought a partial ownership in an Offenhauser ("Offie") Midget car racing team.

In the 1940s and '50s, Ferraris and Maseratis dominated racing with drivers like Alberto Ascari and Juan Manuel Fangio. In those years before American racing teams were backed by manufacturers, drivers like Billy Vukovich were financed by private money from race fans. In early 1947, Carole purchased a half-interest in a car driven by young driver Billy Oakes.

Oakes drove for Gilmore Racing, a company that sponsored racing aircraft like the powerful Wedel Williams 44s popular in the 1930s and '40s. Carole paid for half of the car that Gilmore owned along with their planes. She loved the speed of the cars, and spent most weekends during the spring of 1947 at the Gilmore race track watching the cars run. Over Labor Day weekend she and Horace flew to Indianapolis to attend the Indianapolis 500 auto race from the pits. She would later award the Borg Warner Trophy to the winner, Mauri Rose.

Walter Winchell was the first columnist to mention that Carole and Horace might divorce, announcing on February 12 that "those nasty old gossips are saying that, despite denials, the H. Schmidlapps (Carole Landis) have phoooffft."[12] For her part, Carole continued to deny that there were problems. On her own (she wasn't connected to a studio that would have cared anyway), Carole sent a telegram to Winchell, who noted in his column a few days later that "Carole Landis wires the gossips are wrong again — that distance is the only thing keeping them temporarily apart."[13]

To further confuse her pursuers, Carole let a rumor slip to writer Jimmy Fidler that she and Horace were planning to adopt a baby from an East Coast orphanage. It was patently untrue but he dutifully inserted in into his April 12 column. The relationship with Horace was only getting worse, with less and less contact and more and more avoidance.

Carole did not renew her lease on the Mapleton house and instead went house-hunting. At the end of February she found a lovely New England colonial–style mansion near the border of Brentwood and Pacific Palisades in the Riviera Country Club neighborhood. The mansion at 1465 Capri Drive was on a lovely tree-covered knoll and had 13 lavishly appointed rooms and a landscaped yard with a pool. Horace has always been given credit for giving Carole $100,000 to buy the house, but if he gave her anything it was at most the $35,000 used as a down payment on the note. The mortgage was in Carole's name. She immediately set about decorating the house.

After moving into the house during the final days of February, Carole began filming her last American-made film, *Out of the Blue*, for Eagle-Lion. The movie is an ensemble comedy set in a Greenwich Village apartment building and is best-remembered for having every star play against type. Carole plays beautiful-but-domineering Mae Earthleigh, with George Brent as her henpecked husband Arthur. Turhan Bey plays Bohemian artist David Gelleo and Virginia Mayo his model Deborah. Ann Dvorak plays brandy-guzzling and always-drunk neighbor Olive Jensen, whose motto is "love and let love."

When Olive passes out in the Earthleigh apartment while Mae is out, Arthur — believing her dead — deposits her on Gelleo's porch. Gelleo then tries to blackmail Arthur. Everyone is funny in the comedy, but Dvorak steals the show.

Carole's press continued to be mixed. Sidney Skolsky visited the set and opined, "Carole is what is known as a good sport on a set, always good company and very friendly. I have never found her otherwise. Carole has taken off plenty of weight, looks fine, and it might be difficult for you to recognize her if it were not for a couple of things that haven't changed."[14]

But the July issue of *Liberty* magazine offered a better description of Carole in an update article for all of her servicemen friends. The piece was written by Elizabeth Wilson and entitled "Carole Landis Without the Leopard Skins," a reference to her role in *One Million B.C.* Wilson mentions some of the physical changes in Carole that were evident during *Out of the Blue*. The story details her weight loss and her new hair color, and mentions that "curvaceous, vivacious Carole ... always sold to the public strictly on her sex appeal, decided to change her personality."[15]

Describing Carole accurately as "tireless and intelligent" and not able to "stand phonies," the final part of the article was a plea from Carole: "A very honest person, Carole is the first to tell you that publicity is responsible for her popularity. And she has no intention of biting the hand that has fed her so well for seven years. But, just for a change of pace, she would like some good pictures. It isn't asking too much, she thinks."

During the filming of *Out of the Blue*, probably during March or April, Carole met Rex Harrison. How they met is lost to history. But within days of their meeting, they were sleeping together and Carole was on a downward spiral toward death.

Harrison is often described as having become an overnight star after *Anna and the King of Siam* (1946). It was his first successful movie but he had actually worked for years in British film and stage before that role made him famous. Harrison was born in 1908 in Lancashire, England, as Reginald Carey, but changed him name to Rex. He picked the name because it was the Latin word for "king." King Rex was blind in one eye due to a childhood illness.

At 26 he began doing plays in London and by 1930 was appearing in small roles in British movies. He debuted in a bit part in 1930's *A School for Scandal* and did a number of forgettable films like *Leave It to Blanche* (1934) and *All at Sea* (1935). However, by 1936 he was getting better roles in bigger films like *Men Are Not Gods* (1936) with Miriam Hopkins and *Storm in a Teacup* (1937) with Vivien Leigh. His first lead was in *School for Husbands* (1937) but it was still a dozen more British films before Zanuck gave him the lead in *Anna and the King* in 1946 opposite Irene Dunne and "Buff" Cobb. After *The Ghost and Mrs. Muir* with Gene Tierney, Harrison arrived as the "overnight" star.

His early Hollywood work after those two break-out roles was not spectacular, however. *The Foxes of Harrow* (1947) was a mediocre film directed by John Stahl. Critics savaged Harrison, describing his acting as a "stampede of a white elephant."[16] But Harrison was totally indifferent to the critics—and, really, to anyone. He hated films and felt they were beneath his stage sensibilities. The only thing he liked about Hollywood was the money. Zanuck paid him over $250,000 a year. The only thing he liked better was women. During *Harrow* filming, he met Carole.

By early 1947 he had been married twice. As a young actor he had wed young French teacher Collette Thomas in 1934. Like Carole, she was feisty and held her own with men. Friends described her as almost "roguish."[17] The couple had a son in 1935 but spent the next five years fighting, drinking and cheating on each other. In 1941 he met young German-born actress Lilli-Maria Peiser, who called herself Lilli Palmer.

Palmer was terribly insecure but kept it well-hidden behind a wall of poise and acting ability. Their affair led to his divorce from Collette and a January 1943 marriage to Palmer. Harrison was chronically unfaithful to Palmer. It's difficult to even estimate the sheer volume of his dalliances. In the spring of 1947, Palmer was working on *Body and Soul* with John Garfield while Harrison shot *The Foxes of Harrow*.

It is not difficult to imagine Carole having an affair, given the nature of the relationship with Horace. But, as with many decisions in her life concerning men, the decision to have an affair with Harrison was a bad one. Harrison was a chronic liar and womanizer widely disliked in Hollywood. The gossip columnists routinely attacked Harrison because of his vocal anti–U.S. and anti–Hollywood comments. The press hated Harrison, and they obviously would take his girlfriend with him. Much like her other good friend Dick Haymes, nobody seemed to like him. Except Carole.

It's not difficult to see why Harrison was attracted to Carole. Like his first wife Collette, Carole was feisty and independent. She was a guy's woman, and enjoyed the repartee with men. They both also hated Fox and Zanuck, which probably made them feel like allies as well as lovers. Biographer Anthony Havelock-Allan said that Carole "was courageous and ahead of her time in the way she was prepared to risk scandal by doing her own thing. I suspect it was this daring side of her that attracted Rex."

Harrison was probably feeling a bit insecure about his prospects in Hollywood. Despite his success in *Anna and the King*, he was not doing as well as his wife. While he was filming the awful *Harrow*, she was in the lead in a wonderful Robert Rosen–Abraham Polonsky boxing expose. He needed a diversion, and in walked Carole. The problem was, she needed love, not a dalliance.

Carole and Harrison began spending almost every afternoon together. With Horace in New York and probably not caring, and Lilli Palmer filming *Body and Soul*, their trysts were easy. They often borrowed the mansions of Harrison's friends Cary Grant and Tyrone Power (in the same neighborhood as Carole's Capri house), or they rented a secluded bungalow at the Bel Air or Beverly Hills Hotels. They spent afternoons at Carole's beloved beach too. At that time, it was easy to drive up along the Malibu coast and find the privacy of miles of empty beach.

Harrison arranged a phony "first" meeting between the two in early July at the Palm Springs Racquet Club, which was owned by his friend, former actor Charlie Farrell. The two arranged to be there the same weekend; while Farrell, Harrison and Lucille Ball had dinner, Carole walked up to the table to "meet" Harrison.

Harrison described the meeting in his memoirs, saying that as soon as they were introduced, "soon we were swapping funny stories and limericks, sitting up late in the electric desert air." The two then began appearing in public as a couple, attending parties semi-together, playing doubles on the courts at their friend's houses, or having drinks at the Trocadero or Mocambo.

By June 1947, Carole Landis and Rex Harrison were an open Hollywood secret. Every studio executive, actor and gossip columnist knew. Pretty soon, so would everyone else.

Palmer's later thoughts on that period in her life were an amusing example of denial (but she also denied most of the details of the Carole-Harrison relationship). Palmer wrote in her memoirs that after their meeting, "Things took their inevitable

A post-war glamour shot, probably about the time Carole became involved with Rex Harrison.

course. Rex spent a lot of time away from home, but his explanations were always plausible." It is an interesting comment; she must have known that the inevitability came from Harrison's proclivities more than Carole's. Palmer went so far as to say that she and Harrison "didn't take *The Hollywood Reporter*" or she might have found out sooner, and she blamed friends who "didn't let on."

Harrison's position at Fox—or rather, the money that Zanuck had invested in Harrison—served to protect the two from at least some of the writers. But the scribes still did everything they could to savage the actor they considered an uppity Englishman who hated Hollywood but still took the money. And Carole was standing near the target.

After Carole's work in *Out of the Blue*, Eagle-Lion asked her to star in two movies being made back-to-back in England, *The Silk Noose* and *The Brass Monkey*. The filming would begin in September and would take approximately six months. The movies would be made by the company's Edward Dryhurst Productions and Diadem Films groups. Carole looked forward to getting back to England, where she still had many friends. She was to leave on the liner SS *America* on August 20.

Horace flew to Los Angeles during the first week of August; the evening of his August 1 arrival, Carole appeared on an A.A.F. Anniversary Radio Program with Tyrone Power and Dinah Shore. The next afternoon she hosted a backyard pool party for several dozen friends at the Capri Drive house. In addition to her guests (they included the Tyrone Powers and Cary Grant), a *Screen Guide* magazine photographer arrived with a set of Christmas decorations.

Photographs were taken of the guests lounging around the swimming pool, appointed with a faux Christmas tree and presents, and a table covered with food. The pictures ran in the December 1947 edition under the heading "CHRISTMAS AT CAROLE'S."[18] That same week, Carole rented the house to agent Henry J. ("Bob") Topping. Topping was looking for a house for him and his girlfriend Lana Turner, who was going through an ugly divorce from actor Lex Barker. They were to be wed that fall and only needed a house for three or four months while they had another house re-done. Coincidently, Lana had been living at 120 South Mapleton, just up the block from Carole's former home.

On August 4 Carole flew east, landing in Baltimore. She stayed there making personal appearances until the 11th, making $5,000. She then went to Boston, earning another $2,500. She was initially scheduled to depart for London on the 20th but the *America* was delayed by a strike. She would not depart until the 25th and land in London on September 1 or 2.

When Carole's arrangements were finalized with Eagle-Lion for her London filming, Harrison was frantic. The normally unflappable, unperturbed philanderer— who could have had almost any woman in Hollywood—*had* to have Carole. The moment he heard that she would be leaving, he began pressuring Zanuck to let him go to England to film something. *Anything*. After initially refusing Harrison, Zanuck gave in because of a political fluke.

The British government had been threatening to impose a strict levy on imported American films to help their own studios edge out of their post-war depression. When the major Hollywood studios agreed to invest in British films, the levy idea was shelved. Harrison's film—appropriately entitled *Escape*—was the first film made under the new agreement.

Harrison confirmed his plans so quickly that he was able to arrive in England *before* Carole. With wife Lilli and their three-year-old son Carey in tow, he steamed into the Southampton docks on August 21. Carole did not arrive for another ten days.

Harrison started filming *Escape* during the first week of September in London and Dartmoor. Carole worked on *The Silk Noose* in London. While she and Rex were reuniting in London, an article written earlier appeared in September offering glimpses into the confusion that defined her life, in and out of love.

The piece in *Silver Screen* seems to have been written by Carole versus ghost-written or taken from an interview done during the later filming of *Behind Green Lights* entitled "Do You Think I Was Wrong?" She still publicly glowed about her "year and a half of a happy marriage," but beneath the veneer, there appears much more self-awareness than might have been assumed. She described herself as "too nice" and wrote that on too many occasions in her personal and professional life she let other people dictate her direction.

Ironically, the same issue of *Silver Screen* included an article about "Rex and Lilli's New Home." The couple was photographed at their 1928 Mandeville Canyon Drive home which Harrison had rented for them. It was just 1.8 miles from Carole's Capri Drive house.

The Silk Noose was filmed between September 15 and November 24, entirely on location at the London British-Lion Studios. *Noose* was what was referred to in post-war England as a "Spiv" movie. Spivs were among a group of films based upon the 1930s U.S. gangster films but, instead of bootlegging, the profiteers were working the post-war rationed black markets.

Noose was directed by Edmond T. Gréville and co-starred Joseph Calleia, Derek Farr and Stanley Holloway. Gréville was a well-known French director who began as an actor and starred with Albert Préjean in *Under the Roofs of Paris* (1930), the first major French sound film. He also wrote a dozen others.

Carole plays fashion reporter Linda Medbury, who overhears a conversation about the murder of a black marketeer's mistress in the ladies room. Carole exposes the gangster Sugiani (Calleia) in her newspaper, putting her and her ex-commando boyfriend Jumbo Hoyle (Farr) on the trail of his gang of post-war black marketeers. (The Sugiani role was based on a real-life post-war London criminal.) Hoyle and Farr team up with comical local "Spiv" Bar Gorman (Nigel Patrick) to trap the profiteers. The film is an entertaining bit of film history, and is faithful to the portrayal of the problems caused by England's post-war black markets. *Noose* became one of the most popular British post-war movies.

Carole dominates the screen, perhaps because her charm is so visible against the almost thuggish backdrop of this often-dark film. The fights between the various good and bad guys are filmed in almost documentary-style. In the post-war British cinema, when a bad guy gets beat up, he gets *beat up*. The film was just an average role for Carole, akin to a B-movie in Hollywood.

During the *Noose* shoot, Schmidlapp found his way to London, arriving during the second week of October. He was in London traveling with Katherine Dunham, a New York Broadway friend. Educated at the University of Chicago, Dunham was a dancer, choreographer, composer and songwriter who made world tours as a dancer and director of her own dance company. Dunham was one of the most influential African-American artists of the 1940s and 1950s. Her troupe was appearing in London.

Schmidlapp was in the middle of the three-month European vacation that would take him from London to Paris, to St. Moritz and to Rome and then back through London. During his entire trip, the only time he saw Carole was during those first few days when he was with the Dunham show.[19] As they had done since the earliest days of their marriage, they ignored each other. But this time, when she called him, he didn't call back.

Carole had plenty of other social opportunities. During her off hours, if she wasn't with Harrison, she re-visited dozens of the places and hundreds of the people she had gotten to know during her wartime travels. She loved those visits, writing to her mother, "The people are wonderful, too. They like me for myself."

On November 25 she was invited to participate in a special Command Performance of *The Bishop's Wife* for King George VI and Queen Elizabeth I and their daughters (a benefit for England's film industry). Carole joined a group of actors who had arrived from the U.S. that morning. Led by Bob Hope, the group included Robert Montgomery, Loretta Young, Alexis Smith, her husband Craig Stevens and David Niven. Carole took one of the two starring roles, spending nearly an hour on stage.

Afterwards, the group drove in a motorcade through a crowd of Londoners (estimated at over 5,000) to a private reception at the Savoy Hotel, where they watched a half-hour film of the recent wedding of Princess Elizabeth to Prince Phillip (now the King and the Queen). Harrison and Lilli were staying at the Savoy.

Harrison and Carole saw each other regularly, more than Harrison perhaps saw Lilli, who also visited with family and friends during his shoot. When Carole and Rex were in town, they escaped to secluded hotels or to the homes of Harrison's London theater friends. But when Harrison was moved out to Dartmoor, some hours from London, it was more difficult. They decided to meet in the middle, and began spending their weekends near the beach at Plymouth.

Carole was scheduled to start Thornton Freeland's* *The Brass Monkey* on December 1. Co-starring Carroll Lewis, Herbert Lom, Avril Angers and Ernest Thesiger, *Monkey* is a spy movie set among entertainers in a music hall. Freeman's direction makes for what can only be described as a bleak, even desolate film. Although there are several musical scenes, Carole does not sing a complete song, just bits of songs. For the first time, Carole looks physically older, tired, almost wan.

Just before Christmas, Carole flew to Paris after an invitation from her close friend Dorothy Dandridge. Carole's friendship with Dandridge went back to their meeting in the 1937 comedy *A Day at the Races*. Carole had a bit part, as did Dandridge, then a gangly but extremely talented teenager.

White stars were routinely warned against becoming too involved with black friends or establishments. Carole would have none of that. When she was first beginning to move up the studio ladder, long before she was an established star, she was a regular visitor at L.A.'s black clubs like the 333 Club and the Club Alabam. According to Geri Branton, close friend and confidante to Dandridge, "Every once in a while, people like Tyrone Power and of course Carole Landis ... and a few daring whites would mingle with us [blacks]."[20]

Freeland had been on the stage since he was a child, and began working for Vitagraph Studios in 1918. He was a cameraman before turning to directing, usually romantic comedies or musicals.

In late 1947, Dandridge and her best friend Branton joined their husbands, the dancing Nicholas Brothers, Harold and Fayard, on a European tour. During the tour, Dandridge and Carole visited in London and Carole later joined the group in Paris in December.

Egypt's King Farouk happened to be in Paris at the time and ran into the Dandridge-Landis group at a restaurant. Farouk, who knew Carole from her days visiting Allied troops in Egypt, invited the entourage to fly back to Egypt with him for a vacation. They spent two weeks, including the Christmas holidays, at the palace being treated like royalty.

In her column, Hedda Hopper later criticized Carole, and may have been referring to the trip to Egypt as the cause. On April 28, she noted, "Don Hearn, who is with Special Services in the European sector, stopped by to ask me to help line up stars to entertain our troops abroad. Rita Hayworth, who went over last year, entertained 20,000 troops in eight days ... Carole Landis disappointed them twice and will never be forgiven."[21]

First, it must be remembered that Hopper never had anything good to say about Carole; the two disliked each other tremendously. Hopper went out of her way to criticize Carole during most of her career, and Carole never gave her any interviews or information, which further fueled Hopper's criticisms. Secondly, it is obviously incorrect to assert that the military Carole would "never be forgiven" by the military given all of the work that she did.

It is possible that Carole's spur-of-the-moment trip to Egypt may have resulted in the cancellation of a proposed camp visit. It's hard to imagine Carole disappointing her troops like that, but perhaps the relationship with Harrison was turning her head even from that. But Harrison would not have been able to go with her — his wife Lilli Palmer was with him in London at the time — so I tend to believe that Hopper was overstating the case.

Harrison wanted to see Carole all the time. Some of his efforts were so obvious, it's a wonder Lilli didn't follow him. One afternoon Joseph Mankiewicz, who was directing *Escape* and staying in the Savoy with Harrison, spotted his star strolling down through the lobby carrying a set of golf clubs. He had obviously told Lilli that he was going to play golf, which is what he told Mankiewicz. Mankiewicz of course knew that he was heading over to Carole's nearby hotel and casually mentioned to Harrison, "Have you looked out the window?" It was pouring buckets. A disappointed Harrison thanked Mankiewicz and skulked back to Lilli.

Their affair continued until the Harrison family left London on January 18, 1948. They traveled to Southampton and boarded the *Queen Mary* for the five-day trip to New York, and arrived at Burbank Airport back in Los Angeles on the 29th.[22] When Harrison arrived at his New York hotel on the 23rd, he found his next script had been expressed to him there. The title? *Unfaithfully Yours.*

At this point in the relationship, it had to be clear to Harrison that Carole was in love with him. All of his affairs were conquests, and sexually driven. Nobody knows what his real feelings were for Carole. But he had to know that for Carole it was not just a fling, not just sexual. She loved Harrison. For whatever reason, from whatever he said, she was convinced that he loved her too and they would be married. Harrison biographer Alexander Walker wrote that "Rex tragically underestimated how seriously Carole took the affair."[23] That's a mischaracterization based in trying to shield Harrison from blame. He didn't underestimate anything. He just didn't care. He was aware that her living room was decorated with almost a dozen photographs of the two of them.

Everyone knew that Carole loved Harrison, and planned on marrying him. Their friends also knew that it was Harrison pursuing Carole as much or more than the other way around. After all, who chased who to England? Carole was already going there when Harrison forced Zanuck to send him so he could be with her. For the pursuer to feign ignorance of the prey's feelings is the height of shamelessness.

Walker gets so caught up in his defense of Harrison that he attempts to portray Carole as the aggressor, somehow trying to use Harrison to further her career. Walker also conveniently ignores almost all of Harrison's countless affairs going back to his first marriage and tries to do the same "blame shift" on first wife Collette, second wife Palmer and later Rachel Roberts. Nothing could have been further from the truth. For Walker to blame the victim and then title his biography *Fatal Charm* says something as well.

When Carole returned from London, she tried to work on a play with Ross Hunter, then an actor but destined for greatness as a movie producer. Hunter had a small but popular tent theater that drew big-name talent. She was to play the lead in Elmer Rice's *Dream Girl*, but Hunter recognized right away that she couldn't do a play at that time. She was too distracted by something else. What was it? According to Hunter, "She was absolutely head-over-heels in love with [Harrison]."[24]

In a February wire to Louella Parsons, Carole mentioned that she would be back in London later in the summer to do more films.[25] Carole had meetings with the British-Lion executives before departing, and was told that they wanted to do more movies with her. Her agent Arthur Lyon began working on those arrangements. When she arrived at her Capri Drive house, waiting for her was a cablegram from the English studio. The film company wanted her back in England as soon as possible.

Her next wire to Louella was to let Parsons know that she was divorcing Horace Schmidlapp. Carole told her that even thought Horace refused to return any of her calls, she still hoped for reconciliation. It was all part of the dance. The star always had to say they "hoped for reconciliation." Than when the inevitable occurred, there was no blame.

Carole filed her divorce petition during her first week back, on the grounds of cruelty. Movie divorces had to be choreographed like a party. First a rumor was planted with Parsons or Hopper (Carole preferred Parsons over her enemy Hopper). Then an announcement that there might be a divorce in the works, although one or both "hoped for reconciliation." Then the expected, formal announcement. The Landis-Schmidlapp marriage fiasco was pretty public already and almost everyone knew they had been separated since the previous year, but they went through the Hollywood formalities nonetheless.

Carole herself planted a story with her friend Dorothy Kilgallen during the Christmas holidays. Kilgallen mentioned in a December 13 column that "intimates wouldn't be startled if Horace Schmidlapp and Carole Landis made the fatal announcement in January."²⁶ Friends knew the divorce was a *fait accompli*, knowing how close Carole and Dorothy were. They knew this tidbit came directly from Carole.

On March 11, Carole communicated to the press through Arthur Lyon that she might hold a press conference in the days or weeks ahead to announce that she had engaged an attorney and would divorce Horace "if reconciliation appears impossible."²⁷ It was obvious that the divorce was imminent, but the announcements were purposely hopeful for the sake of the fans. This was Carole's formal notification to Horace that they were to divorce.

It became formal on March 22, when her attorneys Greg Bautzer and Bernard Silbert filed the divorce papers against Schmidlapp in Santa Monica Superior Court. She charged Horace with extreme mental cruelty, requested a division of the couple's community property (which she estimated to be "of great value") and asked the court for alimony. In her filing she also mentioned Horace's three-month trip to Europe while she was in London — the trip where he only visited her for three days: "I couldn't even get him by telephone. You can't have a good marriage and be parted as we have since our wedding."²⁸

Some writers couldn't pass up the chance to have some fun at Carole's expense, even at such a difficult time. Just after the divorce announcement, New York columnist Earl Wilson noted that his friend Stan Arnold warned, "Carole should know better than to change Horaces in midstream."²⁹

Once Carole filed for divorce, the press was freer to actively pursue the couple (she and Harrison) and print their rumors. Perhaps due to the ongoing dislike of the egocentric and amoral Englishman, their affair began making the papers as soon as they were both back in Los Angeles in March.

Edith Gwinn Wilkerson's *Hollywood Reporter* column had almost monthly updates on "the carryings-on of the English star whose name begins with 'H' and the local glamour girl whose name begins with 'L.'"³⁰ Another offered, "Which actors with initials beginning with 'H' and 'L' are co-starring in their own productions?"³¹ It's impossible to believe that Lilli Palmer was still clueless about the affair. Somebody had to say something to her, even if she didn't read the papers.

There were obvious problems in the Harrison marriage after everyone returned from London. In March, Rex moved out and took guest quarters at his friend Roland Culver's house at 750 Napoli Drive. It was even more convenient to Carole's than the Mandeville house; it was only a mile away.

When the story broke, it was a bombshell. Walter Winchell blew up the last vestige of camouflage by noting "Carole Landis' next and fifth husband, when she becomes available, will be Rex Harrison." The jig was up. There could be no hiding now. There were more sniggers from the studio wives, but Carole didn't care. Surely now he would leave Lilli and marry her. That's what he had been telling her.

Reporters and photographers camped out at the Capri house, the Harrison estate on Mandeville Canyon and at the sets of Palmer's *No More Vices* and Harrison's *Unfaithfully Yours*. Even the newspapers were having fun at the coincidental titles of Mr. & Mrs. Harrison's movies.

Zanuck was apoplectic. He had millions invested in Harrison and his movies.

He called Harrison into his office and threatened, yelled, cajoled and warned. Harrison could be fired for breaking the "moral turpitude" clause in his contract. If the public boycotted his films, he would be liable for cost overruns. Zanuck also cautioned him that he must be careful. In a situation like this, where Harrison sought out a married woman, Schmidlapp could conceivably have grounds for a claim for "love theft" similar to the situation between Carole, her first husband and Busby Berkeley.

When Harrison asked Zanuck and the Fox lawyers what to do, the response was a unified, "Deny everything!"[32] So they did. Everyone involved. There was no affair. There was no adultery. There was no nothing. Harrison quietly moved back home from Culver's house.

Incredibly, even as late as early April, Harrison was still denying everything to his wife! How, why or if she believed him is not known. He would not tell her the truth until late May. In her memoirs, she indicated that after he finally came clean, "I did the best thing one can do in such a situation; I withdrew myself from the battlefield and flew to New York." If she did go to New York, she didn't stay long. She was back in Los Angeles in July and August.

Horace's life didn't change much after the divorce filing. He had always taken the marriage for what it was, a formal friendship more than a romantic adventure. When both grew tired of the arrangement — she because she fell in love with Harrison and he because he didn't really care — it was not difficult to allow the divorce to happen. And Horace was never at a loss for women.

Broadway producers, even ones who looked like Horace, attract beautiful young women. A week after Carole filed, Dorothy Kilgallen reported that "showgirl Gene Courtney has been consoling Horace Schmidlapp since the breakup of his marriage."[33] One wonders if this young woman was the Courtney Kane who pursued Horace before his marriage to Carole. On April 8, Erskine Johnson mentioned that "wealthy Horace Schmidlapp will marry Rusty Reagan, an actress, immediately following his divorce from Carole Landis."[34]

Louella Parsons got into the act in May: "The expected fireworks in the Carole Landis–Horace Schmidlapp divorce may flicker out. I hear tell he's very interested in Nan Wynn these New York evenings and, goodness knows, Carole, who used to be a night club girl, has been very quiet in Hollywood."[35] Parsons reported a few weeks later that "the way Horace Schmidlapp is concentrating on Doris Lilly in New York doesn't sound like reconciliation with Carole Landis to these cynical ears."[36] Harrison had little to fear of a "love suit" from Horace.

The denials seemed to quiet the media frenzy a few decibels, but it wasn't over yet. Now that Carole had filed, she fully expected Harrison to do so as well. She lay pretty low during in the weeks after she filed, waiting for Harrison to follow suit.

She made some public appearances, and she was negotiating with British-Lion on a longer, more lucrative film contract. On May 13, Edmund Gréville, the director who worked with her in *The Silk Noose*, arrived in Hollywood to meet with Carole about her next three projects for the studio.[37] She had not yet formally signed the contract that Arthur Lyon had been working out, and British-Lion sent Gréville as a personal emissary to help convince her to sign.

Later that month, Carole's pal Dorothy Kilgallen decided to give Harrison a little "shot" when she penned that Carole was "in the process of divorcing Horace Schmidlapp, and having fun trying to decide between Turhan Bey and a British movie actor."[38]

Carole kept a few social engagements during April and May. On April 30 she threw out the first pitch at the Western States Girls Softball League, a professional softball league.

On May 4 Carole presided over a U.S. Loan Drive Bond Sale benefit gala in Los Angeles. Also in May, Carole offered to become "the financial angel" behind Joey Preston.[39] In 1948 Preston was an eight-year-old drumming prodigy who had appeared with several Big Bands—including Benny Goodman's—by the age of six. He had also recorded a six-record set for Hollywood's Modern Records called "America's Youngest Drumming Sensation: Joey Preston's Sextette." Rumors that Carole was having financial difficulties were apparently incorrect.

In mid–May Parsons reported that all Carole wanted from Schmidlapp was $10,000 and the Brentwood house.[40] Writer Walter Winchell added his own opinion-postscript; "Nh'nh!"[41] But a few weeks later he also told his readers not to be surprised if "Carole Landis and her groom reconcile."[42] Winchell was usually either really right or really wrong.

Parsons reported on May 17 that Carole had inked a deal with British-Lion for two more pictures instead of the three that they had requested. She was reportedly to be paid $10,000 each. Arthur Lyon never confirmed that the final contract was formalized, but it was indeed offered.

During April and May, Carole's only real concern was when Harrison was going to tell his wife that he was leaving her so they could be married. She had done her part; she was discarding *her* husband. Now all Harrison had to do was discard his wife. Almost unbelievably, amidst all of the media frenzy and turmoil caused by the discovery of their affair, Harrison never stopped seeing Carole. Not even for a few days.

At the same time he was continuing to lead Carole on—even after he had been caught—he was telling friends, "Lilli and I fought it together so we were able to deny the rumors and stop a complete shambles. I must say she has been magnificent."[43] Carole obviously expected him to do what he had promised, to divorce Lilli. It was clear that he had told her he would.

He had gone through the equations *ad nauseam* with his friends, knowing that he was going to have to decide one way or the other. Carole or Lilli. He hated Hollywood though Lilli liked it there. Carole would have gone back to England with him in a second. But he did not want to go through another divorce, to change what he referred to as "his background," his family. He knew that he would have more excitement with Carole, and admitted to a friend that if he stayed with Lilli, he'd have to make do with "the odd eroticism on the side."[44] He also admitted that he loved Carole.

But as much as he told his friends that he loved Carole, he also knew that he could not face up to divorcing Lilli. But he would not tell Carole. She told the same mutual friend that Harrison mentioned that perhaps Lilli would divorce *him* quietly. "It's impossible to know whether she will or she won't," Carole told friends, adding,

"We hope."⁴⁵ As deluded as it sounds in retrospect, Harrison's assurances can almost be *heard* in the things that Carole said.

As May turned to June, Harrison was making no headway toward a decision. It had to be getting clearer to Carole by the day that Harrison was leading her on, that as much as she loved him, he was not willing to make the sacrifice necessary to be with her. It was shattering.

A final fly in the ointment arrived in late June when Harrison was offered a lead role (King Henry VIII) in a Maxwell Anderson Broadway production *Anne of a Thousand Days*. He wanted the role, and told Carole so. He even had her read the play during one of his nightly visits to Capri Drive, hoping that she would see what a great opportunity the play represented. Having her read the script was like forcing a condemned man to read his own death warrant, the height of insensitivity.

Carole probably understood the opportunity that the play would give Harrison. But she also knew what it *really* represented. Harrison was leaving. He was escaping to the stage. He would not have to make the dreaded decision between her and Lilli. Well, he would not verbalize it. It was obviously already made. The play was his excuse not to have to deal with Carole's feelings. He would go to New York and their relationship would die a natural death. She was crushed.

★ TEN ★

July 4, 1948, Independence Day

By the Fourth of July holiday, Carole had had about two weeks to digest what Harrison was doing — or not doing — and what was going to happen between the two of them. It had probably become clear that Harrison was using her, and deep inside her tortured psyche, it was yet another example of what almost every other man she had known had done to her. Somehow.

On Friday, June 2, Carole drove herself into Hollywood for two appointments. The first was a lunch interview with Crawford Dixon, a writer for *Movieland Magazine*. The interview would not run until the following October. By then she would not be around to clarify Dixon's analysis of their interview so it's difficult to decipher truth from opinion. While much of Dixon's article is obviously his own fiction, some of Dixon's take on Carole is right on the money. And it is clear that the bitterness that was the product of Harrison's actions was being vocalized.

Dixon describes Carole as a "playgirl ... who seemed to consider men a bunch of little boys she could amuse and entertain without too much effort." He also mentioned that "she had seen through the illusion of life. She was jaded. She knew all there was to know about men."

Carole had indeed seen through much of the illusion of life during her fruitless searches for love. She *was* probably jaded. If she wasn't before June and July and Harrison, she certainly was on July 2. She was in love with Harrison but knew it was hopeless. And she most certainly did not know how to control men, and in fact probably *really* knew almost nothing about them.

After lunch with Dixon, she drove to Hollywood Star Records on Sunset Boulevard to record a "talking picture" for her fans. Done for publicity purposes in the days before videos and CDs, these promotions were usually little more than a movie star "chatting up" a new film project. The star's photograph graced both sides of the cover sleeve and the record itself.

The recording Carole made that afternoon (2½ minutes) was a story about some party games played with friends at her home. She sounds in good humor throughout, starting with a cheery "Hello! May I say that I'm very pleased to be talking to you right in your home. It's so much warmer and nicer than merely knowing you by letter, which has been the custom for the past year. I'm certain that you have read all about the lavish and sophisticated parties that are now being given here in Hollywood, and many people are of the impression that this is the manner in which Hollywood stars always entertain. Well, it isn't true. A great many of us still enjoy the type of games we did in our own home town before becoming residents of filmland. When I gather my friends at my home, we invariably play two of my favorites...." She then describes how she and her friends play two parlor games. She concludes by saying, "Oh dear, time's up, but invite me again, soon, and I'll have some more games for you. Bye now."

It's impossible to deduce someone's mood by listening to a recording, but she doesn't offer any hint of a low mood. In fact, she sounds almost jovial. George O'Brien, the owner of Hollywood Star Records, offered that she gave no hint of depression, saying, "In the studio, she was full of fun and cheer — and even promised she would come back to make a second recording 'within a month.'"[1] After leaving the shop, she drove to the retail district near Wilshire Boulevard and Rodeo Drive and did some shopping.

She had plenty of money from her English work and personal appearances. And she was also said to have received a $7,500 advance from British-Lion against the two upcoming pictures. She seemed in fine spirits to everyone who came across her that day.

Sunday, July 4, was a hot California summer day. Had Carole and Willis Hunt managed to stay married, she would have been celebrating her eighth wedding anniversary. Instead, Carole hosted a pool party in her backyard for about a dozen friends, including Harrison, who stopped by after his own barbecue broke up late in the afternoon. Guests enjoyed the pool and relaxed in the beautiful setting, and Carole seemed to everyone there to be in fine spirits. The guests had been informed that it was strictly an afternoon affair, and that everyone would be gone by five o'clock.

Her close friends knew why. They knew that she had planned a private dinner with Harrison, and many probably assumed that it would involve an ultimatum. Fannie Mae remembered the menu: a salad, a cold chicken plate and a chilled lemon chiffon pie that Carole had made herself. Sometime after the guests left, she changed from her afternoon pool clothes into a frilly white blouse, a blue-and-white checked dirndl skirt and a pair of gold lamé pump sandals.

Around her neck she wore her ever-present oversized St. Christopher medal and the tiny cross from "Mousie" Lewis, and on her arm a gold wristwatch engraved on the verso "C.L."[2] When Harrison arrived for dinner, "Warm Kiss, Cold Heart" was appropriately playing on the phonograph. He also noticed that, oddly, for the first time that he could remember, Carole wasn't wearing her four gold wedding bands.[3]

By the next morning, Carole was dead. What happened during and after dinner and the next morning is only conjecture. But Harrison was at the center of all of it.

Harrison's version of his activities from Sunday night to Monday afternoon is filled with self-serving inconsistencies. He told investigators that he was alone for the holiday weekend because wife Lilli was in New York visiting her sister. We now know that she was *not* in New York, but over at the Mandeville house.

He told police that he called his agent Leland Hayward on the 4th and arranged for the two of them to meet Monday with playwright Maxwell Anderson. Why would Harrison be making business arrangements on the holiday afternoon? And why would Hayward be around to make them?

Harrison said that dinner with Carole was uneventful and that he left about nine, driving to his friend Roland Culver's nearby house on Napoli to chat about the play. He told investigators that he and Carole had "talked pleasantly" until he left. Harrison alleged that he spoke with Culver about the play until about 2 A.M., when he drove the short distance home. He told police that he returned to Capri Drive the next afternoon when he couldn't raise Carole on the telephone.

Clearly, during dinner Harrison and Carole did more than talk "pleasantly." More likely, Carole confronted Harrison with an ultimatum. Was he staying with Lilli or divorcing her? Was he going to marry her as he had promised? The answer was obvious, the results a *fait accompli* to everyone but Carole. Whether she held onto the hope that Harrison was truly in love with her and would leave Lilli, or that Lilli might divorce him, is not known. But she would obviously be crushed by the most devastating abandonment in her life. And crush her Harrison did, no doubt telling her that he could or would not leave Lilli. They would never be married. Then he left.

Harrison told intimates that he told her that the affair was over. For the rest of his life he swore to friends that it was never more than that, and that Carole knew it, which was a blatant lie. He also said that he told her that he would do whatever he could to help her financially and professionally.[4]

I don't think Carole had a plan to kill herself before that evening. It is doubtful that she had decided that she would have a last meal with Harrison and then kill herself. She had not made any arrangements that would indicate that she had actually *prepared* for that night, other than making a lemon chiffon pie.

Aside from the strain of waiting for Harrison to make a decision on their relationship — and she still held out hope that he would leave Lilli, or vice versa — her activities and attitude were cheerful and positive in the days leading up to July 4. Whether he specifically told her at dinner or she figured out from the conversation, the raging insecurity, the inner hopelessness that had been bred during a lifetime of male abandonment finally overcame whatever strength she had held onto for so long. That's when she acted out the final tragic chapter of a tragic life. She decided to kill herself during dinner.

After Harrison left the house, Carole had four or five drinks as she sorted through her large collection of photographs, albums, newspaper clippings, letters and career memorabilia; she carefully separated them into piles strewn about the living room. When she was done, two medium-sized travel cases were carefully filled with the most personal of the materials. On one of the suitcases was attached a note to Harrison. The other she carried out to her car.

She may have been a little bit drunk but was likely well in control of herself. Some time after midnight she drove the mile down Capri and across Sunset to Roland Culver's house. She didn't knock. She took the case full of papers and left it, along with another note, next to the Culver mailbox. Harrison's red convertible was supposedly parked in the driveway. Nan Culver would find the suitcase the next morning.

Leaving Culver's house, she drove back to Capri Drive in the early morning hours of July 5.

According to some historians, when she got home Carole wrote two notes. One was left in the kitchen for maid Fannie Mae Bolden, saying simply, "The cat has a sore paw. She must go to the vet. Thanks." The other, written to her mother on the light blue stationery that read "Carole Landis" across the top, was almost pleading:

> Dearest Mommie—
> I'm sorry, really sorry
> to put you through this
> but there is no way to avoid it—
> I love you darling you
> have been the most wonderful
> Mom ever
> And that applies to all
> our family. I love each
> and every one of them
> dearly—
> Everything goes to you—
> Look in the files and there
> is a will which decrees everything—
> Good by, my angel—
> Pray for me— Your Baby

This note was propped up against a row of ornate cologne bottles on the dressing table in her bedroom.

Some time soon after, she swallowed between 30 and 50 Seconal tablets, known in 1940s movie circles as "red devils." Seconal is a barbiturate, a family of drugs (also called "downers") that were originally developed to treat sleeplessness, anxiety, tension and convulsions. Seconal is a trade name versus a medical term, and is a slightly bitter-tasting white powder. It is extremely fast-acting, even in small doses.

Short-term effects of normal use include a slowing down of the central nervous system, a "calming" feeling, which is why people take it. Large doses produce blurred vision, slurred speech, impaired reflexes and perception of time and space, slowed breathing and sometimes a reduced sensitivity to pain. An overdose will produce a quick and profound impairment followed by unconsciousness, coma and death.

It is often used by suicides— Lupe Velez and Judy Garland both died of Seconal overdoses—but it was routinely prescribed in the 1940s as a sleep aid, which was why Carole obtained this original prescription. Contrary to the comments from some historians, Carole was not a chronic user of Seconal, or any drug. She was not even a heavy drinker. The prescription date on the empty bottle was October 26, 1946.[5]

After she took the pills, she tried to telephone Dick Haymes' mother in New York, leaving a message with a maid who answered the phone. But Mrs. Haymes was out celebrating the 4th and when she returned later that evening she thought it too late to call anyone back. Some time not long after making the call, Carole collapsed in a heap on the floor. Before doing so, she laid on the bed for a short time; the next morning, the indentation on top of the covers was still there.

It may have been her third, fourth or fifth suicide attempt, depending upon whom you believe. Or it may have been her first. Though circumstantial evidence points to perhaps three previous attempts, none can be conclusively proven. But her friends' accounts in each case followed a pattern that was well-known. After taking the pills, she would telephone a friend and would be eventually rescued. If this was yet another cry for help, the rescue never came because Mrs. Haymes wasn't around to take her call. But I think this try was more serious.

When Fannie Mae Bolden arrived the morning of July 5, the house was quiet. But that was not unusual; Carole often slept late. Bolden took one phone call that morning from millionaire Atwater Kent, who wanted to invite Carole to a party.

Harrison's contacts with Bolden and the Capri house are in dispute but, according to him, at about 11 A.M. he made his first phone call to the house, and Bolden told him that Carole was not yet awake. He supposedly called again a few minutes later before heading to Malibu for his lunch meeting with Hayward and Maxwell Anderson. It was not shocking that Carole wasn't up yet, but it was a bit surprising; unless she had a very late night she rarely slept past 9:30 in the morning.

After lunch, Harrison purportedly called again, and Bolden told him she *still* hadn't seen Carole. He knew then that something was wrong. The next thing Bolden knew, Harrison was standing in the back doorway into the kitchen. When she told him that Carole was still upstairs, he said quietly, almost as if he was speaking to himself, "Well, I think she's dead."[6] From this point, Harrison's actions are not in doubt. Perhaps his motives, but not his actions.

The two went upstairs and found Carole on the bathroom floor. According to Bolden, as Harrison bent down to listen for a heartbeat, he said, "Oh, no, my darling [or "honey" in a later account], why did you do it?" Even though he said in a later deposition that he thought he felt a faint pulse,[7] everything he did from that moment on is consistent with finding a dead body.

He later described in a deposition for the coroner that — even though he said he felt a pulse — he went looking for Carole's address book so he could call her own doctor. "By looking from A to Z," he said, "I hoped to find a name I could identify as a doctor."[8] Bolden was astonished as Harrison, without a word, then bolted out the back door and roared off in his red convertible. He would later tell police that he sped to his own house so he could call his own doctor. He didn't explain why he simply didn't call him from Carole's house. He was trying to run.

Harrison probably called Harry Brand, Fox Studios publicity director and the chief Fox "fixer." Knowing that the press would find out from Bolden that Harrison was at the house, Brand or perhaps Zanuck probably told Harrison to return there. They would have also told him to call for an ambulance and then the police, in that order, which Harrison did when he returned to the house an hour later.

He also called for his friend Roland Culver, who was at Riviera Country Club playing golf, and spoke to Culver's wife Nan. Nan also told him to get back to the house at once and call the police, then left to meet him there. When her husband returned from golfing — he simply walked from the course up a hill into his own backyard above the eighteenth fairway — he saw his neighbor (and landlord) Gladys Cooper in her adjacent backyard and happily asked, "Where's my tea?" Cooper told him, "There's been a terrible accident. Carole Landis is dead. She killed herself." Harrison's best friend simply snarled, "Selfish bitch."[9]

Harrison returned and first called St. John's Hospital in Santa Monica. According to him, it was the hospital that first put the idea into his head that he should call police. He later said, "The thought hadn't entered my head before ... so I called them." He refused to give his name, telling the police he was "calling for the maid."[10] His call to police was logged in at 4:10 P.M., at least an hour (and probably up to three hours) after he found Carole dead. A neighbor alerted by Bolde had already called.

As was usually the case in situations like this, when police arrived at about 4:20 P.M. the house was crowded with studio people and reporters. People from Fox and others from Lilli Palmer's Warners studio were there. Harrison was flanked by Nan Culver and her best friend, actress Judith Fellows. Florence Wasson, Carole's stand-in and best friend, was also present, most likely called by Bolden. Softly crying, she was the only one who appeared genuinely saddened by Carole's death. The group stayed at the house speaking with police for several hours. Outside the house, the driveway and nearby street were already lined with dozens of reporters and photographers. The police were unable to enter the driveway when they first arrived.

Harrison told Jones and his investigators a much less personal story than the truth. He said that he had a luncheon appointment with Carole that Monday and called the house at 11 A.M. The couple was to discuss a "business matter," a movie they were to make in England. He also told them that she had been ill for the previous week with a recurrence of the intestinal infection she incurred during her South Pacific travels.[11] Strangely, he was the only person to mention such an illness. Carole's friends and doctors reported no such medical problems that week.

He told police that when he came over, he and Bolden discovered Carole dead. He mentioned nothing about their relationship, nothing of the dinner the evening before, and nothing of the dinners they had shared each of the previous seven nights that maid Bolden described.

When Detective Capt. Emmett Jones and Detectives John Layman and Herbert W. Brittingham entered the master bedroom, they found nothing amiss. The brown and red bedcovers on the large bed were neat and unwrinkled, except for the indentation from someone lying on the bed some time earlier. There was nothing scattered about; certainly not like the living room, filled as it was with piles of photographs and papers. There was an empty prescription bottle on a dressing table next to the bed and the carefully folded note.

Near the bathroom door was a pair of red slippers—described as "boudoir slippers" in the police reports—and hanging on the bathroom door was a sheer peignoir—described as a "dressing gown."[12]

Beneath the open bathroom door, in front of an open vanity, Carole's body lay as if she were getting ready to stand up. Other than slight discoloration on the exposed right lower leg, there was little else to suggest that she was dead. Curled almost into a fetal position on her left side, her head rested on a small brown leather jewelry box (sometimes described as velvet, it was in fact leather). She was wearing the same clothes—white blouse, dirndl skirt and gold lame pumps—that she had put on as she

Ten ★ July 4, 1948, Independence Day

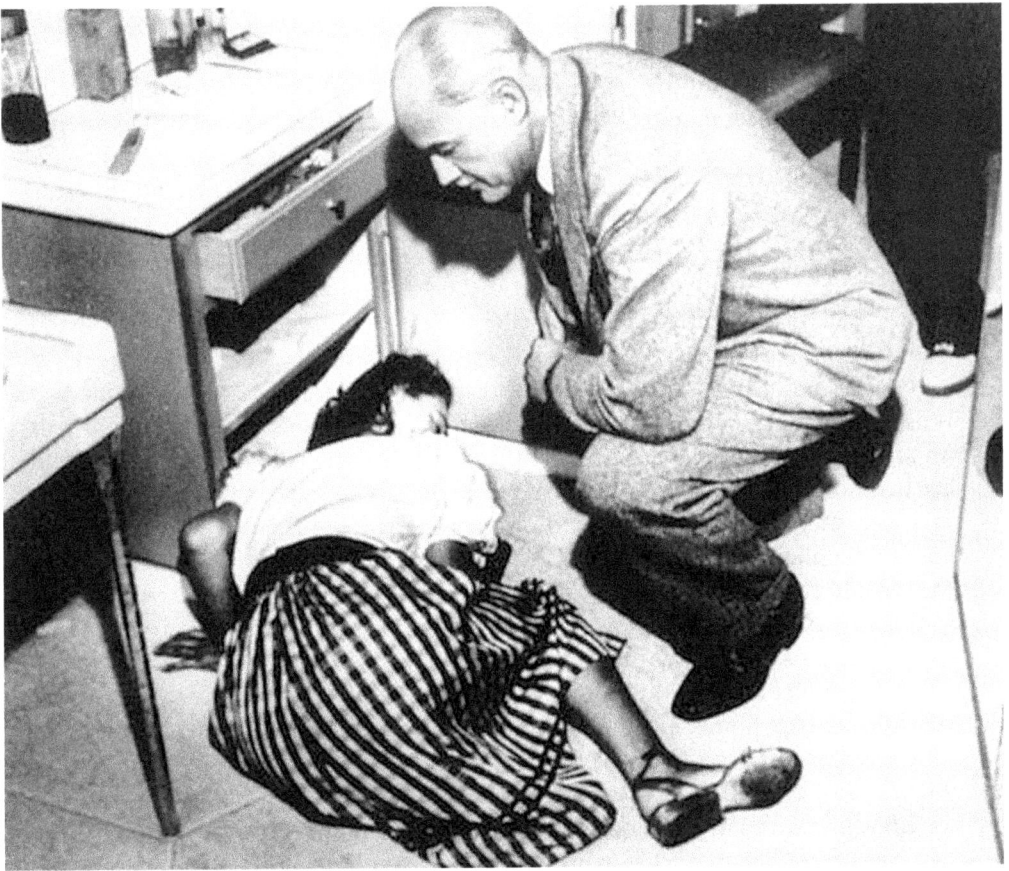

Carole lay in death curled on the bathroom floor while police and photographers filled the house. Here, L.A. police Detective Emmett Jones has his photograph taken with the body.

waited for Harrison to arrive for dinner. Her arms were at her sides but, interestingly, both bent with her weight on her hands. It appears almost as if she were trying to lift herself off the floor when she died.

Initial newspaper reports mentioned that "the willowy actress, a faint smile on her face, was found at 3 P.M. by actor Rex Harrison."[13] Many newspaper reports also included the passé comment that she looked "almost peaceful," and one that "her long hair fell casually to the round neckline of her white lace blouse."[14]

In her clenched left hand were a satin ribbon-style bookmark imprinted with *The Lord's Prayer* in gold lettering and a white envelope holding a single white pill. Written on the envelope were doctor's notes regarding a prescription: "Red — quick — two hours. Yellow about 5 — can take two. Use for severe pain."[15]

Detective Jones told reporters that the death was "definitely a suicide. There were four bottles of sleeping pills in Miss Landis' bathroom [and] an empty bottle was found near the body."[16] There was also a half-filled water glass, rimmed in red lipstick, on the washstand above the body.

Rigor mortis had set in, so it appeared that she had been dead for at least 12 hours, putting the time of death some time in the early morning hours—perhaps two or three A.M. It also puts into question Harrison's claim of finding a pulse.

Carole's sister Dorothy (Ross, living in Long Beach) was called and sped to the house, arriving several hours after the first policemen. Clara was not brought to the house until after 7 P.M. The newspapers (still) called her "Mrs. Clara Landis" and erroneously listing her residence as Seminole Hot Springs, California, but she (still) did not correct them.[17] She arrived almost inconsolable and had to be helped into the house. She sobbed, "Oh, my baby, I want to see my baby. Why didn't somebody call me?"[18] She then collapsed in a heap as she was led in the front door by Dorothy and was kept downstairs for some time.[19]

In the early evening a hearse from Boggs & Mashmeyer's Funeral Home arrived for Carole's body and took it for the short drive to their Santa Monica location on Wilshire Boulevard. Her funeral was scheduled for the following Saturday, July 10. An autopsy would be performed early the next morning, Tuesday, July 6, by Coroner Ben Brown. His report would be released on July 7.

Just before the hearse arrived, Harrison drove down the driveway leaving the house. He obligingly rolled down his window and stopped the car so that photographers could get a picture of him leaving.[20] He also told reporters gathered at the end of the driveway, "Miss Landis was a great friend of mine and a great friend of my wife."[21] He also said he was "astonished" at her suicide.[22]

If he thought it would be easier at 1928 Mandeville Canyon, he was mistaken. When he arrived home, an equal number of press had camped out in front of his white-shuttered manse. Police were guarding the gate. Some neighbors were startled the next day when smoke was seen rising from the chimney at 1928. Rex and Lilli were meeting with lawyers from Fox and Warners. And burning things.

They were burning what sympathetic Harrison biographer Alexander Walker described as a "reproachful bundle" of photos—everything that Carole had left in the valise at the Culver house the night of her death. Culver gave the package to Leland Hayward, who gave it to Harrison, who had begun burning items the evening before.[23] While all of this was going on at the Harrison house, their four-year-old son Carey was staying with the Culvers.

Horace Schmidlapp was informed as he visited with his mother in Cincinnati and left the next morning for Los Angeles, making stops in Memphis, Chicago and Salt Lake City before arriving in L.A. late in the evening. At every stop, the scholarly-looking bald man in the glasses who somehow married Carole Landis was besieged by reporters and photographers. All he would tell them in response to their shouted questions was that he was "shocked."[24]

Reporters were able to track down Alfred Ridste, then living in Richmond, California, a blue-color town north of Oakland on the San Francisco Bay. Now a machinist for a railroad, he had been told by neighbors of the death. Even though he only saw her once during the last decade of her life, was probably not her father, and had abandoned her before birth, he often proudly told neighbors of his famous daughter.

He said that he could scarcely believe that his daughter had committed suicide, saying he had received a "perfectly normal letter" from Carole in March. He had last seen her in 1942 when he visited her at the Santa Monica beach house. With a clarity that comes from a combination of lack of empathy and almost total denial, Ridste said, "I don't know what could have caused her to die, but I don't believe she would ever commit suicide. She may have been worrying about her four marriages. She wrote rather often, but she didn't seem depressed."[25] For some reason Carole apparently had never stopped trying to rekindle *some* kind of relationship with the first man to abandon her during her lifetime.

Carole's death dominated the Tuesday morning newspaper headlines. The front pages were topped with versions of the same awful truth, from the bland CAROLE LANDIS COMMITS SUICIDE — REX HARRISON FINDS BODY,[26] to the vague MYSTERY CLOUDS DEATH OF FILM STAR,[27] to the impersonal CAROLE LANDIS FOUND DEAD IN BATHROOM OF HER HOME.[28]

Even in death, Carole could not escape undeserved barbs from people who knew nothing about her. Along with a perfunctory — and error-filled — biography and a list of some films, the obituary in *Time* magazine described Carole as "a torso, not an actress."[29] It's difficult to imagine what would motivate someone to be so mean-spirited, but for some reason Carole brought that out in some people.

At the same time that her private life was becoming very public, Carole endured a final indignity as the coroner's photograph of her body began appearing everywhere. Often the image was underneath the biting headline CAROLE LANDIS ENDS HER CAREER. That photograph of Carole's body was featured more than photographs of Carole herself. Sometimes the papers ran a photograph of Detective Smith standing over her body; others just the body. The pathetic image of the beautiful actress curled up on the floor, dead, somehow made her death seem that much more pitiful.

Along with the minute details of Carole's death and the controversy regarding how and when her body was discovered, reporters rehashed some of the rumors that had been appearing in the months and weeks prior — the same rumors that likely drove Harrison to end the affair, or at least the promise of marriage. "A few months ago the gossip columns reported that Harrison and Miss Palmer had separated, and that the actor was dating Miss Landis. Later the Harrisons denied separation rumors. The actor telephoned the news to Miss Palmer in New York. She was to fly to the cinema capital today."[30] That was the first of dozens of lies that the Harrisons would tell about that weekend.

Newspapers reported that although Harrison was "married to actress Lilli Palmer" and "said he knew no reason for her death ... Miss Landis had been swimming, dining and lunching daily with Harrison the past weeks [and] had him over to dinner Sunday night."[31] Another article mentioned that their dinner Sunday was "their last rendezvous in weeks of lunches, swims, and dinners while Harrison's wife was away."[32] Yet still another, "[M]arried to Lilli Palmer ... the suave British actor and Miss Landis had dated constantly the past few weeks."[33]

The first interview given by Harrison and Lilli took place on the patio at Mandeville on the 6th shortly after they and their lawyers had burned the Culver package. Again Harrison denied noticing any unhappiness in Carole during their "business dinner" and repeated that he had offered to help her find work in England because "I knew some producers there."[34] The reporters, knowing that she was already under contract to a British studio and already very popular there, responded with obvious skepticism, asking, "Is that all you talked about, for two hours?" and "Was Carole in love with you?" Harrison lost his temper and tried to stalk back inside, but stopped at his lawyer's urging. He denied that Carole and he were in love. Lilli than mentioned that they planned on going to New York the next day and perhaps then to England.[35]

It was when police began comparing Harrison's version of events with Bolden's version that red flags began appearing. Harrison's assertion that Carole was asleep when he called at 11:00 and 11:15 A.M. Monday would have been unusual. (Carole was a midmorning riser). Harrison then said that he "was detained, and I rang her again at three. The maid said she still was sleeping and I thought that was very strange so I decided to come over. I went to her home, which is near mine, and the maid and I knocked on her door. We entered and found her."[36] He did not mention the alleged lunch meeting with Hayward and Anderson. Maybe because there was no meeting.

His story was at odds with Bolden's from the start. She had already described her surprise at seeing Harrison standing just outside the entryway to the kitchen. He had entered the house through the back door and according to Bolden looked awkward and stiff, not like his usual self. She told police that she knew something was wrong; his voice was dry and he didn't address her with the typical sharp bark with which he ordinarily spoke to the staff (he was habitually rude with servants).

She described finding the body and the way he left the house and returned some time later. When he returned, he was met by Nan Culver and Judith Fellows. Florence Wasson arrived a few minutes later. The police began taking a harder look at the relationship between Carole and Harrison, and at his activities that day.

The autopsy report was released Wednesday morning. Brown studied Carole's internal organs, including her heart and lungs, stomach, intestines and digestive tract, kidneys and brain. There was no sign of the digestive problems Harrison told police had plagued Carole in the last weeks of her life.

The autopsy indicated that Carole had a blood alcohol level of only .12 percent. She was barely drunk (the legal limit in California at the time was .15 percent[37] though it's .08 today) and certainly knew exactly what she was doing. Death was caused by "barbiturate poisoning" due to "ingestion of overdose of Seconal."[38] Brown later told reporters that the amount of Seconal in her system was five times the amount needed to cause death.

She probably became severely impaired within just a few minutes of taking the pills and, after staggering around her bedroom for a few minutes, simply passed out on the bathroom floor, where she may or may not have been trying to pick herself up when she lapsed into unconsciousness and died.

Brown's autopsy results were included on Carole's death certificate. At first glance, a death certificate seems an impersonal, almost cold document. But a death certificate is a life story. It's a very personal history and tells a very personal story.

The death certificate for Carole Landis Schmidlapp was L.A. County Registrar's no. 11686, signed and filed on July 13, 1948. She died at 1465 N. Capri Drive in Pacific Palisades, and she was 29 years, 6 months and 4 days old. Her Social Security Number was 565-14-5742. Married to 33-year-old Horace Schmidlapp, her occupation was "actress" and her industry or business "cinema." Wisconsin-born, she had lived "in this community 13 years" and in "California, 27." The "informant" was Mrs.

Clara Ridste—a rare occurrence of her name in the press as "Mrs. Clara Ridste" instead of "Mrs. Clara Landis"—who lived at 1506 E. 64th Street in Long Beach.

One thing not mentioned in the death certificate: Discovered during the autopsy was the fact that Carole was unable to have children due to endometriosis.

Beyond the medical cause of her death were the rumors swirling around Hollywood. Some were true, some false and absurd. But they seemingly all whirled around the head of Rex Harrison. Newspapers also mentioned what much of the movie colony already knew: "widespread unconfirmed rumors that Carole left Harrison a personal note."[39]

In a highly unusual occurrence, Walter Winchell didn't conceal the nature of the note, or Harrison. In his July 12 column from New York, Winchell wrote, "I see [people in Los Angeles] feel as we do—that poor Carole Landis left a farewell message to Rex Harrison that night. Since he was first to discover her suicide, he could have destroyed any note, even as you or I would... [I]n one of his films, *The Notorious Gentleman,* one of his women destroys herself after he makes a decision."[40]

According to Harrison biographer Alexander Walker, a long-retired Los Angeles policeman told him that he had indeed seen the second note, and that it contained a three-line "lover's farewell" to Harrison. The unnamed policeman told Walker he had no idea what happened to it.[41] Coincidently, Lilli Palmer's memoirs refer to a Los Angeles policeman offering to sell her the note for $500, which she declined to pay but implied that her lawyers did. She described that note as the note about the cat.[42] Perhaps she was confusing the two. The existence of the note has never been proven.

Florence Wasson admitted that she had seen the note. She initially suggested that it said to "take care of Landis' cat" but did not mention from where the note came. She said that someone handed her the note when she was at the house and she handed it back. She did not know who took it from the house.[43] The stories came to the attention of Coroner Brown.

Wednesday, July 7, began on a bizarre note when unemployed actor and set designer Robert Love leapt to his death from a Hollywood office building after telling a friend he admired Carole for "her courage" in committing suicide. Actor-friend Daniel Harris said Love was especially upset by her suicide. Both men knew her slightly at Fox and were deeply touched by her kindness. The two men visited a fifth-floor doctor's office. Love ran to a window, shouted, "Here I go," and leapt out.[44]

Speculation and innuendo immediately turned toward Harrison, whose every move from Sunday to Monday was now under a microscope. His demeanor during the entire day of the discovery of Carole's body raised collective eyebrows. Dorothy Manners all but identified him in her column the day after Carole's body was found when she noted, "They say the shocking suicide of beautiful blonde Carole Landis was induced by malaria ... but knowing the gay laughing girl well ... I believe she died of a broken heart and loneliness ... she had been deeply in love with a man who was forced to tell her that nothing would ever come of their romance."[45]

As headlines noted sadly SPECULATION CONTINUES ON REASON FOR UNHAPPY END FOR CAROLE LANDIS,[46] Carole's body was being prepared at Boggs & Mashmyer's and the funeral home inundated with floral arrangements from the famous and not-famous around the world. At the same time, Coroner Brown made an interesting decision *not* to convene a formal inquest into the death. A coroner's inquest was a typical formality for any high-profile suicide, but Brown told the press, "Miss Landis' suicide was unquestioned. There will be no formal inquest,"[47] even though he knew of the purported note to Harrison and that Harrison had not mentioned anything of the sort to police.

He did, however, order that Harrison appear before him, telling reporters that it "would be a sort of informal hearing ... [with] our intent in calling Mr. Harrison ... to leave nothing undone to clear up completely any unexplained points in Miss Landis' death."[48] Informal or not, headlines yelled ACTOR REX HARRISON FACES QUESTIONING IN ACTRESS' SUICIDE. It was suggested that Lilli Palmer's innocuous comment to *Examiner* reporters that they were heading to New York and possibly England and out of his legal reach allegedly compelled Brown to order Harrison to his office.

Publicly, Brown was hoping to find some motive for the death, since he was still telling the press that friends were insisting that Carole killed herself over a blighted love life and faltering career. Privately, Brown wanted to speak with Harrison about the note.

Thursday afternoon, the 8th, Harrison arrived at Brown's office inside the Hall of Justice an hour after the 2:30 P.M. time set by Brown. He was pale, sweating profusely and wetting his lips nervously. He wore a checked suit, white shirt, and a black print tie. He was accompanied by his attorney Judd Downing and a second man.

Not a single photograph was taken by the dozens of photographers surrounding the hallways leading to Brown's office. Not a single question was fired at any of the three from the 100 reporters who were there. Nobody even spoke, so shocked were they to see that the second man was Darryl Zanuck.

Zanuck's power—indeed the power of any studio head in 1948 Hollywood—would be difficult to overstate. He wielded so much power over the press that when the "word" was put out that no pictures were to be taken and his name was not to appear in any newspaper stories about this day, that is what ensued. In fact, the only Los Angeles reporter to even *mention* the 20th Century–Fox Studio—not Zanuck, but the studio itself—in relation to Harrison's appearance was long-time Los Angeles *Herald Examiner* reporter Harry Lang. Lang was the most ardent Harrison-basher during the week of Carole's death. But even he simply described the third man as "a publicity man from 20th Century–Fox Studios."[49]

Harrison, Downing and Zanuck marched directly to Coroner Brown's office, where Downing told a baffled Brown that Harrison would give his testimony in the form of a deposition to be read into the record. Brown was told that another lawyer, Richard C. Sieg, had taken the deposition "under oath" at Downing's Beverly Hills offices. When Brown told the group, "Taking that deposition yourself wasn't my idea," he was brushed off by Downing, who dismissively said, "No, it was mine."

Brown let Downing and Zanuck do whatever they wanted. He first had to delay the meeting yet another hour because the 20th Century–Fox group had neglected to even *bring* the prepared deposition with them. Brown was incredulous as he was told, "It's being typed now, and is on its way over." This was no doubt in case Brown had decided to stand up to them and cross-examine Harrison aggressively regarding the facts in the deposition. He went so far as to tell the press, "It's only fair, I suppose. Mr. Harrison and his lawyer are being so cooperative. If there is anything they have overlooked, Mr. Harrison has agreed to answer under oath, here."

Interestingly, Brown also said the hearing would have no bearing on his verdict, since "there is no question but that Miss Landis' death was suicide." When the deposition arrived, Deputy Coroner Ira Nance read it into the record. Afterwards, Brown asked Harrison perhaps six questions, none of which involved the note or anything outside of his deposition.

Harrison, dressed in a Prince of Wales checked suit and black tie, fidgeted nervously as he denied he received any note and insisted that he had no idea why Carole might kill herself. According to Harrison, their meeting on Sunday night and the scheduled meeting Monday morning were to talk "about scripts of a new play I had and the possibilities of her playing in it. We also discussed her project of returning to England. I told her I might be able to help." He also volunteered that Carole was having "financial embarrassments" but he did not think this depressed her and again mentioned her allegedly suffering from an amoebic infection. He noted that the illness did not seem to depress her, either.

Volunteering that he didn't "believe she was entirely happy with her career," he repeated his original story, conveniently leaving out the period when he fled the scene. He ended his testimony with, "I'm sorry, but I can't give you any explanation for it at all."[50]

When Brown excused him, Harrison literally jumped up from his seat and, with Downing and Zanuck, quickly walked out. Reporters joked amongst themselves how amusing they looked walking out lock-step in a tight formation. Zanuck had managed to keep the studio name out of the papers yet again, and for a final time he kept the Harrison-Landis relationship out of the headlines.

Brown and Nance called Fannie Mae Bolden and Detective Jones. Strangely, Wasson did not repeat her earlier assertion that the well-known second note contained a reference to Carole's "cut" in something. She would only affirm that it mentioned something about the cat, but with all the confusion in the house could remember nothing else about it.

Perhaps the growing turmoil surrounding her friend's death was stressful for Florence and her husband. When she left the building, all she said to reporters was, "You're going to get me a quick divorce from my husband if you don't go away."[51] Lou Wasson, head golf professional at Culver's Riviera Country Club, may have been feeling some pressure to be quiet as well.

Each of the other witnesses testified briefly. No new ground was covered, and the inquest into the death of Carole Landis was over. The *Los Angeles Daily News* described the hearing as "pretty much a frost."[52] Nance adjourned the hearing without making any findings. Chief Autopsy Surgeon Frederick Newbarr added, "This is just a garden variety suicide."

A few minutes after the Harrison contingent left the building, Brown appeared before reporters and noted, "I've gone as far as I can. I have gone to the limits of my authority. The testimony itself had revealed no criminal action, and I cannot go further."[53]

There was public clamoring for the District Attorney to re-open the case, chattering that went on for quite some time. Dorothy Kilgallen wrote, "Hollywood is wagering that the Carole Landis case will be re-opened. Heavy local pressure on the district attorney's [sic] office is demanding to know how the case could be dropped so quietly after it was established at the inquest that a second note had been found and destroyed. The cries of obstructing justice are getting louder."[54]

But as a matter of law, the coroner was correct. Brown went as far as he could. The responsibility of the coroner's office is only to establish the cause of death, not to question facts that are not pertinent to the cause of death. Those questions, and answers, are the responsibility of the police department or the district attorney.

The D.A.'s office dutifully took a copy of the coroner's transcript but, as expected, Chief Deputy District Atty. S. Ernest Roll soon confirmed that their offices would be taking no action. There would be no complaints brought, no grand jury hearings, and no indictments. The Carole Landis case was "dead." Whether or not she left a second note had little to do with the fact that Carole had indeed killed herself. Harrison might be a jerk, but that is not criminal in this instance. As one writer mentioned sadly, now all that was left was to bury the girl.

Doubtless Zanuck was behind the entire fiasco at Brown's office, and likely guaranteeing that the case was never seriously reviewed by the District Attorney's office. He probably had a hand in the arrangement that Harrison could give his formal testimony to Brown privately, in an "informal" setting. It was pre-arranged that Harrison's bogus "under oath" deposition could be read into the record rather than have Harrison questioned directly. The final result was a foregone conclusion. All of this would be highly unusual given the high-profile nature of the death, and the persistence of the rumors.

This is not to say the Carole did not commit suicide or that there was a grand conspiracy to cover up her death. But what is not arguable is that Harrison had much more to do with her death than he reported, and knew more about that final night. But he would never be forced to reveal his secrets.

When Harrison met with the press after his deposition with Brown, Lilli Palmer—who was said to have just arrived back in Los Angeles from New York—was at his side. As photographers snapped photos of the couple arm and arm,[55] he told reporters, "Miss Landis and I were just friends. Miss Landis was not in love with me. She never, never told me that she loved me." Both he and Lilli denied that they were "estranged or ever had been." For her part, Lilli piped up, "I love Rex and we are happy."[56]

What the press didn't know was that Lilli Palmer was *not* in New York the day Carole died. Her being in New York lent at least a casual air of legitimacy to Harrison's multiple visits to Carole's house that weekend. Lilli was actually two miles away in Mandeville Canyon. Before he attended his quiet dinner with Carole, Rex and Lilli hosted a barbecue of their own. One of the guests was Esther Williams, then a big star at MGM.

After the barbecue, most of the guests left the house, but Williams stayed to visit with her close friend Lilli. For most of the evening, the two chatted in the family room waiting for Rex to return from Carole's. According to Williams, Palmer knew where he was that night, knew about the affair, but also knew that he would not leave her for Carole. It was not the first time Lilli had suffered through one of Harrison's affairs.

According to Williams, Lilli's "official alibi" was orchestrated by the studio. The studio fixers arranged for a phalanx of studio employees to "vouch" for every minute of Harrison's and Palmer's time that weekend. The 20 or so people who had been at the Harrison-Palmer barbecue on Monday all vouched that Palmer was in New York that weekend.

Palmer claimed to have returned to Los Angeles at 6:30 A.M. on Tuesday morning to be picked up by agent Leland Hayward. But no flight records existed to confirm she was ever on a plane, nor were there any photographers at the airport waiting for her arrival. There is no way that Palmer would have been able to return by plane to Los Angeles the day after Carole's body was found without a single photographer being present. There would have been dozens.

In her memoirs, Palmer attributes a quote to herself allegedly made to the waiting photographers. Unfortunately, she repeated a quote that she actually later gave to waiting reporters after the coroner's inquest. Williams characterized Palmer as "holding her head high during the maelstrom that followed" Carole's death. She also described her as giving "one of her finest performances" when she stood next to Harrison at the courthouse.[57]

The couple left the courthouse, returned to their Mandeville Canyon house and burned the rest of Carole's photo albums and letters that she had left for him at Culver's house. *The Hollywood Reporter* spoke for all of Landis' friends when Edith Gwinn Wilkerson wrote that "we don't remember an actor, foreign or domestic, who has breached so many rules of good taste ... the wonder of the whole thing is that he hasn't had his face smashed by now."[58]

As Harrison was bolting out of the Courthouse at 3:30 P.M., visitation for Carole was beginning at Boggs & Mashmeyer's. In her will, which she had signed on June 22, 1944, Carole limited her funeral expenditures to a maximum of $2,500,[59] a reasonably large sum, but the event was not as lavish as it could have been. The wake was scheduled to last just one day, but the massive crowds made it apparent that more time would be needed, and Friday the 9th was added. The funeral would be held Saturday the 10th.

Clara desperately wanted Carole to have a Catholic funeral, but the local parish priest refused to provide a Roman Catholic service.[60] The Church has a long-standing tradition of refusing church-sanctioned funeral services to those who kill themselves. Although there is much more flexibility today, at the time of Carole's death it was almost impossible unless the victim was extremely powerful politically or financially. Carole was not powerful enough.

The service, to be conducted by Bishop Fred L. Pyman of the Evangelical Orthodox Church of Santa Monica, was scheduled for 12:30 at Forest Lawn Memorial Park in Glendale. The funeral service would be held at Forest Lawn's Church of the Recessional, a beautiful stone church on the side of a hill, followed by burial in a roadside plot at the top of a hill deep inside the Park.

Pallbearers would be her good friends Dick Haymes, Cesar Romero, Pat O'Brien,

Florence Wasson's husband Lou, Carole's long-time makeup man Ben Nye and actor pal Willard Parker. When Haymes was delayed by weather and could not get out of Chicago for the funeral, director Eddie Sutherland stepped in for him.

Carole was to be waked during Thursday and Friday but by Wednesday the front room at Boggs & Mashmeyer's was filled to over-capacity with over 250 floral arrangements as a long line of friends, co-workers, fans and movie stars visited. Landis looked as lovely in death as she had in life. Ben Nye, who had done her makeup since she arrived in Hollywood, did it one last time.

Florence Wasson chose Carole's turquoise blue dress with blue and white sequins and beads. It was Carole's favorite dress; she wore it to the more important Hollywood functions and took with her to the South Pacific. She lay in a mahogany casket lined with peach-colored silk cushions.[61] Although she had requested gardenias in her will, a blue orchid was pinned to each shoulder of her dress. In her right hand was another orchid, and a rosary was inter-twined through her fingers. Around her neck she wore "Mousie" Lewis' little cross.

Clara was inconsolable; sister Dorothy did most of the greeting of mourners. For every movie star paying their respects, there were dozens of grips, cameramen, commissary waitresses and regular studio folk slowly passing by the casket, most in tears.

On the day of the funeral, Carole's adoring fans began arriving at the cemetery before the huge wrought-iron gates were opened at 9 A.M., three and a half hours before services were to begin. The streets outside the huge cemetery were jammed with cars, buses, taxicabs, streetcars and, amazingly, hundreds of people walking toward the gate from all directions. They walked, seemingly as one, toward the tiny, beautiful stone church on the side of the hill surrounded by hundred-foot trees. A steady line of people literally streamed up the winding road. In less than an hour, there were probably 2,000 people surrounding the church. Flowers were still arriving, carted into the church by the carload. A cross of white gardenias was placed behind the coffin. A huge bouquet of roses, from Mr. and Mrs. Darryl Zanuck, sat at its foot.

As the noon hour approached, fans began pressing even closer to the church, awaiting the arrival of Carole's famous friends. It was stiflingly hot and there was not a hint of a breeze. The city that spread out beneath the cemetery was shrouded in a thin fog.

Wearing a pink sun-dress, a young woman who had driven to Hollywood in her dusty car from Texas stood tiptoe on a running board peering through binoculars. She squealed when she spotted Cesar Romero walking toward the church. Pat O'Brien hurried into the church, his eyes wet with tears. None of the stars obliged the hundreds of vulgar requests for autographs from within a sea of waving books and pencils.

The red carpet that led from the street to the main entrance of the church was jammed with a thousand people. There was barely enough room to squeeze through the crowd, even with dozens of policemen trying to keep the path clear. Amidst the noise and swell of bodies, hundreds of flashbulbs popped, and then fell and shattered on the sidewalk.

In a small vestibule to the side of the main sanctuary, the pallbearers gathered. Willard Parker and Ben Nye had arrived an hour earlier, joined by Cesar Romero. Romero was having a problem staying composed, repeatedly breaking into loud sobs. Pat O'Brien walked in with Eddie Sutherland.

At 12:15, Landis' family arrived, avoiding the red carpet and heading for a side door. Leading the group was Carole's sister Dorothy Ross, walking hand-in-hand with her nine-year-old daughter, Diane Carol Ross. Clara Ridste walked beside them, almost catatonic, and Alfred Ridste walked in behind Clara. Carole's brother Lawrence walked together with her best friend Florence Wasson and her pallbearer husband Lou, both following slowly behind the main family group.

Halfway to the church, Clara suddenly crumpled, weeping. She reached out her hand and grabbed little Diane's shoulder to hold herself up. As the family entered the church, several hundred fans surged forward against the restraining ropes, broke them down and swelled as one toward the doors and windows of the small church.

A few minutes before 12:30, Horace Schmidlapp stepped from a car with actor Lee Bowman beside him. A moment later, Rex Harrison and Lilli Palmer and Roland and Nan Culver (along with two bodyguards hired by Zanuck and Fox) arrived in a studio limousine. Like Landis' family, the Harrisons avoided the gauntlet of the red carpet. Palmer and Harrison walked in arm in arm, Palmer wearing a navy blue dress that she had borrowed from Mary Fairbanks, who had told her, "One doesn't wear black to the funeral of one's husband's mistress."[62] The group were recognized and mounted police had to surround them to offer them safe passage into the church. Following the Harrisons—and also requiring a police escort through the throng of onlookers—was leading man Van Johnson.[63]

Carole's family and friends—and the Harrisons—walked across the bier where Carole lay in her coffin under a blue spotlight. Fresh orchids had been pinned to each shoulder. Her right hand had originally held another orchid, but just before the service a tiny nosegay of roses was put in its place. The flowers were sent by one of her childhood Bryant Street friends. Together, O'Brien and Johnson knelt at the head of the bier, crossed themselves and prayed for several minutes. O'Brien began to cry. Romero was still weeping, tears streaming down his cheeks. When Harrison walked quickly past the body, he barely stopped and would not look directly at Carole.

At 12:30, cemetery attendants opened the front doors and allowed the public to fill the remaining seats. Newspapers had mentioned that the public would be able to view the body in the church at 11. Because of the size of the crowd, that plan was scrapped, leaving over a thousand people in the sweltering heat for an hour and a half after they thought they would be let in.

It was no surprise then that the surge toward the door literally knocked the doormen off their feet and back into the church; they were dragged to the side by other attendants, barely escaping injury. For five or ten minutes, there literally were so many people crammed into the doorway that nobody could move forward.

After about a half-hour of jostling, elbowing and fighting for space and seats, the 350 or 400 remaining seats were filled. They were also people lined six to eight deep in all of the sides and back of the church. But it wasn't morbidity or celebrity watching that swept the people in; if there is such a thing as a solemn mob, that was what it was. These people just seemed to want to be with Carole.

Nonetheless, when the church was filled, the doors were forced shut, and over 1,000 people were left outside in the heat. As soon as the door closed, Irma Reed played *The Lord's Prayer* and Schubert's *Ave Maria*, and then the services began. Bishop Pyman's seven-minute eulogy praised Carole's spirit and love for others, and cleverly compared the way she lived her life with her acting.

Above Clara's loud sobbing, Bishop Pyman noted, "All the world's a stage, and all the men and women in it players. People in show business have a peculiar philosophy, whether they be Catholics, Protestants or Jews, but Shakespeare was correct in writing these lines. Some of us make our entrances best. Some make our exits best. Some overplay, flub their lines. But this beloved star made her entrances perfectly. She did not overplay. Fellow troupers, you don't have to call a second time for people like our beloved friend. Whenever there was a call, she always came; witness her U.S.O. experiences entertaining troops in Europe and Africa and the Pacific." Then, perhaps understanding the Catholic Church's stance on the fate of suicides, "From the doors of Hell, deliver her soul. May she rest in peace."[64]

When Pyman finished, tenor soloist Fred L. Scott sang "The Lord's Prayer" and "In the Garden," Carole's favorite song. The moment that the main ceremony ended, Harrison left the church. Different newspapers reported that "the suave Englishmen, surrounded by Miss Palmer and a corps of press agents," either "rushed" or "dashed" from the church and "leapt into his limousine." However described, he fled within moments. Bishop Pyman had not yet left the altar, nor had the coffin even been closed.

Harrison would not be at the burial. The next day, the Harrisons and the Culvers were ensconced at the Del Monte Lodge on the Monterey Peninsula playing golf at Pebble Beach. Roland Culver said he felt that "the change did them good."[65]

As Harrison took flight, Bishop Pyman signaled for the opening of the doors so the people standing outside could enter. Over 1,250 heads were counted as they slowly walked past the casket, which was tipped slightly forward so passing mourners could view Carole without having to lean and peer inside.

After viewing the body, mourners were led directly out of the church; almost all of them filed quietly further up the hill, deeper into the cemetery, to her gravesite. Once the church was empty of everyone but close friends and family, Clara Ridste walked to the casket with son Lawrence and daughter Dorothy. Along with young Diane Carol Ross, they all knelt and prayed. Clara stared quietly at Carole.

As she said to Carole, "Oh my baby, I'll pray for you, every day," Clara keeled over onto the floor. She lay unconscious for seven minutes before Bishop Pyman and Lawrence were able to revive her so she could endure the rest of the ordeal. Once Clara was conscious, the pallbearers carried Carole's casket through the side door to the hearse. Slowly making its way up the hill to the top of the Hillside of Everlasting Love, it stopped next to Plot 814, a lovely spot next to Cathedral Drive. The plot is on the side of a hill just past and just below an area called the Cathedral Slope. The site boasts sweeping views of Los Angeles and the San Fernando Valley.

Surrounding the gravesite on all sides were over 1,000 mourners. Plot 814 had already been blanketed by flowers for 25 feet in every direction. The gravesite right next to Carole's was still scarred dirt instead of grass. Long-time Broadway and sometime movie actor Robert J. Montgomery had died just seven months earlier and was interred in the plot to the side of Carole. No grass had yet regrown on his plot.

The crowd was more boisterous and less respectful at the gravesite for some reason. Sightseers perched on top of the lid of the concrete vault until they were removed by police. Romero and O'Brien wrapped their arms around Clara to protect her from the pushing and shoving.

Schmidlapp was not able to get near the chair reserved for him next to the gravesite. After four attempts to get to his spot, each time shoved backwards by the crowd, he gave up, listening from about 50 feet away as Bishop Pyman performed the graveside service. The sound of loud sobbing could be heard throughout the large crowd, many shirtless and hatless in the sweltering heat as the coffin was lowered.[66]

As the family was quietly led to waiting limousines, the crowd surged toward the grave. The mob rushed to the floral pieces and literally tore them to shreds, leaving leaves and torn flowers strewn for 100 feet in every direction. Men, women and children were yelling and running wildly among the ruined floral arrangements. Bishop Pyman described it as "the most revolting thing I've ever seen." The gravediggers and attendants had to form a cordon around the casket area to make sure that was not damaged.

After her coffin was lowered into the crypt and the rest of the dirt shoveled into the grave, the last of the looters took the last of the flowers. When they were done, there were no flowers left, just a pile of torn stems. These were unceremoniously heaped on top of the dirt. Some time later, a marker was placed above the grave that said simply;

> CAROLE LANDIS
> 1919 — 1948
> To our beloved Carole
> whose love, graciousness
> and kindness touched
> us all — who will always be
> with us in the beauties
> of this earth until we
> meet again.

In death as in life, Carole had different effects on different people. Some newspaper headlines simply said TEARS GREET LANDIS RITES.[67] Other editorials noted that SUCCESS MEANT FAILURE FOR LANDIS.

Predictably, almost before Carole's gravesite was covered with flowers the studios began using her tragic death to sell tickets. In the newspaper advertisements for the movies then playing, Carole's name went from small print to larger than the movie's titles. Zanuck and Fox also shamelessly re-released *Four Jills in a Jeep* with a special ad campaign. Newspaper ads read:

> NOW SHOWING
> A picture based on the well known book by Carole Landis,

bringing back to you the experiences she had while
entertaining at camp shows during World War II
CAROLE LANDIS
Four Jills in a Jeep
-with-
Alice Faye
Martha Raye
Kay Francis
Jimmy Dorsey and his Orchestra, Phil Silvers, and other great stars!
This is a special Booking in tribute to the late
Carole Landis

Carole's picture was prominent and her name was mentioned three times in the ads; in other ads, five times. Her name was printed in text twice the size of the movie title. The ads began running in papers around the country on July 8, two days before her funeral.[68] Implicit in this campaign is that it usually took at least two days to arrange for delivery of the film and the design and contract of the advertising. Studio publicity people began this process on Tuesday, July 5 — the day Carole's body was discovered — for the movie to be in place around the country by that Friday, July 9.

Carole's family met at Jerry Giesler's Wilshire Boulevard offices on Tuesday morning, July 12, for the reading of her will. The will was executed by Carole on June 22, 1944,[69] replacing an earlier 1941 will.[70] A friend, Bo Roos, was appointed executor. The cryptic note left for her mother was probably intended to ensure that no problems arose from either the Schmidlapp divorce or the fact that the will hadn't been updated. Giesler, who was also representing her in the divorce proceedings against Schmidlapp, read Carole's will.

Signed during her marriage to Tom Wallace, it had not been updated in the interim. Wallace was to have received whatever residual value remained after setting up a $50,000 trust fund for Clara, her sister Dorothy and Dorothy's children. Clara was also to receive her household and personal belongings. Giesler indicated that her divorce from Wallace would exclude him from receiving anything, ensuring Clara would get everything.

The will was filed on July 14, probate number 284436, and was admitted to probate on the 20th. Since the Capri Drive house was in the process of being sold to B.M. and Laura Stewart, Giesler had Carole's belongings moved from the house to the Redman Storage Company in Santa Monica for a later appraisal.

When a full appraisal was done in late 1948, Clara's "everything" turned out to be significantly less than what might have been expected. Carole was successful but, like most actresses of the era, was not wealthy. Maintaining the appearance of movie success was an expensive proposition, and Carole's lifestyle was no exception.

The Capri house was in escrow to the Stewarts for $67,000, which would leave $44,000 after paying off the mortgage. (The house was worth the equivalent of perhaps $800,000.) Carole had very little cash — just a single bank account listed in the estate appraisal, at the Bank of America in Beverly Hills. The balance was $412.12. For a "movie star," her personal property was equally unimpressive. The estate appraisal listed 34 pieces of jewelry, the most expensive pieces being two dinner rings, one set with a star ruby and baguette diamonds and another with a star sapphire and diamonds. Each was worth $500; all of Carole's jewelry was worth $7,147 (perhaps $100,000 today). She owned a dozen furs worth about $4,800, and there was $750 worth of clothes, bedding, wardrobe trunks and miscellaneous household furniture stored in the Santa Monica warehouse.

The total value of the estate appraisal was $81,455.12. After paying off the mortgage on the house, Carole left $58,455.12 before expenses. Contrary to claims that Carole had serious debt problems, the only claims against the estate were an $85.46 charge for the appraiser, $485.36 for her personal assistant and secretary Jan Lowry's work during June and July, and $493.92 from Boggs & Mashmeyer's Funeral Home. After Giesler's legal bills, Carole left just over $50,000. Perhaps $750,000 today, it was a tidy sum but far below what movie fans may have expected.

Another significant asset that was to have been part of Carole's estate was a $30,000 payment that Schmidlapp had agreed to make as a condition of the divorce settlement. Carole was to have signed the agreement that Tuesday, July 5, at Giesler's office.[71] At the time of the reading of the will, he indicated that he would still make the payment.[72]

But within a week of the reading of the will, Schmidlapp threw the entire estate issue into disarray. With Carole dead, he felt that he shouldn't have to pay the $30,000 portion of the divorce settlement, since it would go to her estate rather than to her. In a letter sent to Giesler and to the Bank of America Escrow Department on July 19, Schmidlapp also informed the family that he considered the entire pre-divorce property settlement to be null and void as well.[73]

Schmidlapp contended that, since Carole had not actually signed the agreement prior to taking her life — she was supposed to have done so on that Tuesday — the agreement was voided. Giesler responded by arguing that Carole had agreed orally to the settlement and that Schmidlapp had agreed (also orally) to proceed with the $30,000 payment even with Carole dead.

It is obvious that Schmidlapp was lying when he told the family — and the press — that he intended to honor his commitment to make the promised $30,000 payment. Coincidentally, as the couple was going through their separation and divorce the previous April, he told a columnist that the only thing he wanted out of the marriage was "$30,000 he invested in their Hollywood home."[74] Referring to money he put into the Capri Drive house as she left to film in England, he also complained that he was "hurt because she allowed him to put the money into it after she went to Europe and their marriage (*although he didn't know it*) [italics added] was over." He most certainly knew it was over in April; he purchased the house to facilitate the divorce.

Schmidlapp also sought to legally stop the pending sale of the Capri house and asked that he be reimbursed for other house-related expenses.[75] Giesler asked the courts to appoint an executor, which was scheduled to occur later in July (on the 30th), and asked to have Schmidlapp's claim thrown out. After those proceedings, the sale of the house was finalized that November.

The personal items that Clara and Dorothy did not want were auctioned. The auction of Carole's clothes, jewelry, personal and household items began the evening of March 21, 1949.[76] There were 800 items auctioned during the three-day event, beginning with her clothes on Wednesday, her furniture on Thursday and personal items on Friday. Carole's furs, included a full-length mink, a white mink cape, a white Russian ermine jacket and a Russian broadmill suit with white ermine trim. Thousands of people came to the viewing and auction but it generated less than $20,000.

The previous January 29, British-Lion sold the rights to her final films for television.[77]

Walter Winchell wrote a touching note about Carole in the days after her death, noting that he "can't get that photo of Carole Landis crumpled up on the floor out of my mind. She was so full of pep, laughing, yelling 'Hi!' and being All Girl All the Time. All the time, that is, except when the heart can't stand the pain, anymore."[78]

But just two days later, Winchell would be the first to dredge up the rumored 1946 suicide attempt and subsequent visit with Dick Haymes' mother. No longer pained with the memory of the photograph of her body, he was by then compelled to report that "when she appeared in *A Lady Says Yes* (a Broadway flop), a well-known doctor described Carole as "one of the most sexicological women in and out of show biz...."[79] The doctor's name was never released, nor was the definition of "sexicological." Even in death, Carole was still trapped.

Reporters and editorial writers speculated in dozens of articles as to why Carole killed herself. An obviously recurring theme was clearly outlined on a small-town New Hampshire newspaper's editorial page:

> Carole Landis—young, beautiful, at the top of her fame as a screen actress—a career which had brought her wealth and public acclaim, has taken her own life... From a humble beginning she had battled her way to the top, only to find that she could not adjust her life to a fame which at most was synthetic and visionary because it was based upon those values which make life pleasant and secure ... death appeared the only means of escape... A woman's beauty is a lovely asset, provided she has the emotional balance to live normally like other women.[80]

Carole was obviously ill-equipped emotionally to achieve that type of balance in her life. Still another editorial appeared the day of her funeral under the title DUSTY ANSWERS FOR CAROLE:

> Sweet and pretty girls in every part of the land ... are eating their hearts out with longing for a career in motion pictures. One wonders whether these girls have been impressed at all with the tragic story of Carole Landis. One wonders whether they have learned, from reading that story, the dusty answer that so many sweet and pretty girls get when they go to Hollywood.
>
> Carole was an unhappy girl, more unhappy than the innocent ones who think all they want in the world is a chance to appear in the movies, with their names in lights. Carole Landis won that. She won fame. She formed friendships, or least acquaintances, all over the world. She had a huge income. But, in the end, she gained nothing or believed, at least, that she had won nothing. And so she took her own life. Why she did so is not wholly clear.
>
> There were her vain attempts to find happiness in love and marriage... Four husbands are not the answer, but they reflect the restless turning here and there, the ceaseless quest of this one unhappy girl for joy in family life....
>
> Any one, or a combination of all of these things, may have led the unhappy girl to end her life. She, young, pretty, successful, widely known, vibrant with sheer

exuberance of living, found the answer to her needs so disappointing that she could not find the courage to carry on.

It is the story of many of them who have gone to Hollywood. The city, the movies, have their fascination. But the world in an unreal world, and it calls for high character, determination of the sternest type, an ability to face reality in its starkest form, if one is to make a name in Hollywood, and making that name, avoid the dangers, the pitfalls, the dusty answers that its false and glistening façade so well conceal.[81]

These types of writings typically gloss over important details unknown to the writer who is attempting to generalize an event larger than themselves. No suicide is that simple. But there are interesting accuracies included. Carole was an unhappy girl. And she had more acquaintances than true friends. Her attempts to find happiness in marriage were indeed in vain. She *seemed* to have everything. But in the end, she believed she had nothing.

An article written just after the June 1969 death of Judy Garland, which may or may not have been a suicide, described the perils of Hollywood under the title HOLLYWOOD NOT AS GLAMOROUS AS IT MIGHT APPEAR TO OUTSIDERS. It referred to Carole, Lupe Velez and several other tragic figures who paid the ultimate price for fame in Hollywood.

Paying particular attention to the problems faced by stars that began as child actors, the writer described the numerous relationship issues faced by the likes of Garland, Shirley Temple and Jackie Cooper. Psychologist Dr. Mason Rose described Garland as typical, "suffering from a chronic state of unhappiness because many things she should have done as a teenager she was never permitted to do. They all missed out on a normal childhood."[82] He could have been speaking directly to poor Carole, who never had anything remotely resembling a normal childhood.

On August 9, 1948, actor Cesar Romero, one of Carole's closest friends, responded to a request from the president of Carole's fan club for a letter describing how Hollywood *really* felt about Carole. Romero, who sobbed uncontrollably throughout Carole's funeral, personally wrote a quite moving and heartfelt tribute and paid to run it in the trade papers *Variety* and *The Hollywood Reporter*:

> My dear Carole,
>
> I have been asked by some of your fans to write something about you in the way of a tribute so that it may be published in the club journal. I confess this is a job I have never had to do before and I don't know just how to start, so don't be too angry if I don't do you justice.
>
> You left the stage of life way too soon my dear and your friends and fans miss you very much. Personally I am very happy and proud to have been one of your friends and to have had the honor of working with you in four pictures. There was never a dull day on the set with you. Your lovely face, the warmth of your personality, your vitality and delightful sense of humor were something I always looked forward to and which made the average working day truly a pleasure.
>
> I remember the fun we had when we made *Dance Hall* together and what a wonderful sport you were on the nights that we had to work until five o'clock in the morning. You never complained about a thing, but took it in your stride as part of your job and loved every minute of it. I'm afraid that couldn't be said about all our fair ladies of the screen.

> You were a good actress Carole and you owe it only to yourself. You worked hard, studied and learned a great deal in a very short time. What is more important, you were a good daughter, sister and aunt. You loved your family and never shirked your duty toward them. You helped them in every way possible and brought them much happiness. Of that you can be extremely proud.
>
> I think that I can say in all honesty that you did more than your share in life. Your record during the war will always stand as a monument to your memory. The boys that you entertained over-seas will never forget and neither will their families. You brought them cheer and a touch of home when they really needed it most. That was a tough job, as I know only too well, but as usual you sailed through it with flying colors — a trooper if there ever was one. You were a fine girl Carole, and you made every moment of your life count. I only wish that life had treated you as kindly as you treated it. As I said before, I'm proud to have been your friend.
>
> Sleep well my dear.
> Cesar Romero

Romero's words echoed the feelings rumbling inside all of her friends: Wonderment, shock and, most of all, heartbreak. People who knew little or nothing about Carole but did the most criticizing — her critics among the studio wives and other actresses — accepted her suicide as almost pre-destined; "that's what *they* do," they probably thought amongst themselves. But the people who knew the real Carole, the sensitive, caring, thoughtful Carole who just wanted to be loved, could not accept her death. They *knew* it was a mistake, a tragic miscalculation of a woman who had no idea how much she was loved. How important she really was. What a wonderful person she was.

Like her friend Romero, we look for answers. With any unexpected death, once the proverbial dust settles people try to make sense of the situation. With so many friends and fans who loved her, it is hard to imagine that someone like Carole could be so lonely. But she was. She was lonely and probably not able to love. She wanted to love. She just never learned from Clara how.

After her funeral, everyone had an opinion. Evelyn Ross, who was married to Carole's sister's husband's brother, spoke to the press allegedly for the family, saying, "What Carole wanted more than anything else in life was home life and a family of her own. And this was denied her. We in the family knew what Carole's heart trouble was. That's why she married four times."[83] It's doubtful that Evelyn ever even met Carole, but she was correct about Carole's "heart trouble."

Initial press reports indicated that Carole "left no clues to indicate why she had taken her life." They also mentioned that unnamed "friends said that the glamorous star, in the middle of her fourth divorce, had seemed restless and dis-satisfied."[84] These comments contradicted everything said by the people who had seen her during the last week of her life, all of whom were emphatic that she was in good spirits.

Film magazines also weighed in. The first was the British tabloid *Picturegoer* magazine with the "True Story of the Landis-Harrison Tragedy."[85] *American Weekly* told of the "Hollywood Heartbreak: The Story of Carole Landis."[86] Writer Florabelle Muir tried to explain "What's Behind the Carole Landis Tragedy?" in *Motion Picture* magazine.[87] During the month of October alone, no fewer than a dozen magazines analyzed Carole's death, including *True Story, Modern Screen, Movieland* and *Photoplay*.

Defining a suicide is at best tricky work. It is probably impossible to ever explain precisely why someone kills themselves. It appears that it's always a combination of factors, but in this case there is a primary cause. Harrison. But where there other factors at work? Was the rumor mill accurate to some extent? Was she depressed? Was her career foundering? Was she facing financial ruin? Had she tried a half-dozen times before? The answer to "why?" is perhaps a combination of everything but all roads lead to Harrison.

Carole's mood in the weeks before her death was excellent, according to everyone who knew her well enough to have an informed opinion. Fannie Mae Bolden was with Carole every day during the last three weeks of her life. She had just been hired. Like everyone else, she spoke well of her new boss, saying, "Carole was always nice to me. A very sweet person, more like a friend. She seemed very happy-go-lucky all the time."

At the same time, she hated Harrison. "I think he was kind of snooty. There were a lot of people who didn't like him. I hated him because he would come in demanding things; he would want to know where his towel was, where this was and who had been using that...." And she didn't like the way Harrison acted around Carole: "She would get so mad because he would be eating his food and she would just sit there watching him. And he would be eating just like a dog."

Horace Schmidlapp said that he had spoken to her by telephone just the Friday previous and she seemed normal and cheerful.[88] When he was asked if the couple had spoken of reconciling, he declined to answer.[89]

If she was not in a depressed state during the last days or weeks of her life, than it is doubtful that the suicide was pre-planned. That is, it doesn't appear that Carole intended to kill herself until the hours just before she did it. Whatever drove her to suicide pushed her past the line that night. Harrison.

It appears that Carole's suicide was a last-minute decision versus a pre-planned event. Cancer-ravaged director Woodridge "Woody" Van Dyke spent the last month of his life having celebratory dinners with his closest friends before he killed himself. Love-ravaged Lupe Velez planned an ornate suicide in a house full of candles, including a lavish final meal. Not Carole.

She didn't load up on drugs to use. In fact, contrary to early police assertions that there were "prescription drug bottles all over the bedroom,"[90] there was in fact no great quantity in the house. Even the Seconal tablets were not recently purchased. They were from an almost two-year-old prescription given her during her 1946 hospitalization. If it were well-planned, Carole would have gotten newer drugs rather than rely upon two-year-old sleeping pills. Her physician, Dr. Maynard D. Brandsma, told police that he did not prescribe any Seconal, indeed no sleeping pills at all, for her.[91] She seemingly grabbed whatever she had, in this case a bottle of pills from 1946.

Just the Friday before, on July 1, Carole signed up to play the lead in Ross Hunter's production of *The Play's the Thing* at his North Hollywood tent theater. When she first returned from England, Hunter had hired her for *Dream Girl* but her Harrison distractions prevented her from concentrating on a play and she left the show. But now she was ready to return to the stage. Coincidently, in a column written the week before but published the day Carole's body was found, Sidney Skolsky announced, "Carole Landis will play the lead in *The Play's the Thing* when Ross Hunter presents it in his Tent Theater."[92]

Whether Carole had tried to kill herself before is a question that is easy to speculate upon but impossible to confirm. There is plenty of anecdotal evidence to support that assertion, but nothing concrete. As early as July 10th the *Los Angeles Examiner* reported that police sources were aware of at least two previous suicide attempts, one in Hollywood and another in New York. No specifics were ever offered.

On July 7 the *Examiner* reported that Carole was supposed to have said to an unnamed "friend" after Lupe Velez's December 1944 suicide. "I know just how Lupe felt. You go just so far, and then what have you got to face…? There's always the fear of being washed up… You begin to worry. You get bitter and disillusioned. You fear the future because there's only one way to go and that is down."[93] Another "friend" allegedly overheard Carole talking about committing suicide in a conversation she supposedly had *with* Lupe Velez. Since Carole and Lupe were not friends, it's hard to believe that suggestion. One previous attempt supposedly occurred during the 1944 filming of *Having Wonderful Crime*.

Than there was the alleged attempt in October 1946, which I believe to be the only likely earlier try. Her friend Dick Haymes and his show-business mother propagated this story for years after Carole's death, but not before. According to Haymes, she had planned to drive her car off a cliff but at the last minute was distracted by a kitten, grabbed the kitten and drove to Dick's house, where he lived with his mother. According to Haymes' mother, while Carole held the kitten in her lap, the two women were able to talk out Carole's problems, whatever they were.[94]

A recurring theme in the attempted suicide scenarios was that she invariably got someone involved so that she would be rescued at the last minute, and saved from herself. In her memoirs *Change Lobsters and Dance*, Harrison's wife Palmer refers to several previous attempts in which Carole took pills and then called a friend who would come and rescue her by having her stomach pumped.

Florabelle Muir wrote an article in the October 1948 edition of *Motion Picture* magazine entitled "What's Behind the Carole Landis Tragedy?" Muir, again citing some of Carole's many "unnamed friends," alleged that there was evidence "that Carole had attempted to do away with herself at least three times before." She also wondered in print if perhaps Harrison had been involved in any of these earlier attempts and perhaps had helped rescue her earlier.

The "come and save me" scenario is not totally far-fetched in Carole's case. She was indeed known to call her friends late at night if she was feeling down. More often, though, she called her pals when she got drunk. She was actually something of a notorious late-night caller, to the point that some inside jokes made the gossip columns. One scribe noted, "So git on, Star, with a yippee-e-e and a shrdly etaoin. It that's Carole Landis on the phone again, tell her we don't want any."[95] She took the jab in good humor, and her friends were all sympathetic to Carole's late-night interruptions.

On the night of her death, Carole did indeed call up Mrs. Haymes but was not able to get in touch with her. If the 1946 story—or some version of it—is true, it would be logical for her to call the woman who had saved her once before.

The package that she left at Culver's house could also have been a vague attempt to get someone to come back to the house. Probably Harrison, though. She and the Culvers were not close friends. They socialized because Harrison and Roland Culver were best pals. She did not leave the package at the Culvers for the Culvers. She left it there for Harrison and left it right next to the mailbox where he might easily see it. Right next to his Jaguar convertible parked in the driveway.

Remembering that Harrison left her house heading to the Culvers, Carole probably took the letters there and left them near his car, which she knew would have been parked in the driveway next to the mailbox. Harrison told police and the coroner that he stopped by the Culvers to visit about his proposed play. But remembering also that he had been *living there* for several months during a separation from Lilli, he was probably still living there that night.

Police were told that Lilli was in New York, but we know that to be a lie. She was in Mandeville Canyon. Perhaps Harrison was still living at the Culvers, and not back home, as Culver told biographers. No matter. Carole knew that the suitcase would quickly find its way to Harrison. Maybe she hoped that he would find it that night, if indeed he would have to go to his car to drive home.

A slightly more far-fetched variation has been offered, that she left the package by the mailbox so that Nan Culver would find it in the morning when she got her mail. If indeed Harrison had felt a pulse when he bent over Carole's body, maybe she waited until the next day, hoping that the mail would lead someone to the suitcase and back to Capri Drive. The flaw in that plan was that no mail was delivered on Monday, July 5.

There is no real need to be certain that Carole tried to kill herself before. When all is said and done, she killed herself on July 5, 1948. She was successful that time. Proving that she had tried before does little more than indicate the propensity *for* suicide, which she obviously had, at least that evening. But just for the sake of the record, it does appear to me that she made at least one earlier attempt. I believe that the 1946 incident was more than likely a suicide attempt. But that being said, again, it doesn't mean much. We're still trying to reason why.

Carole's finances might be one of the most overrated reasons offered for her suicide. The only two people to cite financial problems were Harrison and Clara. Harrison mentioned in his self-serving quasi-testimony before the Coroner that he thought that "she was in financial difficulties." Newspapers headlines read FINANCIAL INSTABILITY SEEN FACTOR IN SUICIDE DEATH OF CAROLE LANDIS but offered no real proof other than comments from "movie sources" who alleged that "she had bought lavishly in recent years and that many of her accounts were long overdue. She had started a retrenchment of expenses in the last few weeks and among other things released her press agent."[96]

Most of that is false. She always paid her bills on time, and if she had died with accounts "long overdue" there would have been claims against the estate. No claims were made. She did release her press agent, but that was at the recommendation of agent Arthur Lyons. She was heading for England and would use the studio press people there.

Clara said, "Carole was deep in financial trouble. She had sold her house, her car — but things still piled up. She told me not long ago with bitterness, 'Marry a rich man and support yourself.'"[97] It is not likely that Clara knew the extent of Carole's financial situation. We know that Carole had long been tired of financially supporting her mother — and was the reason she moved her to the Long Beach bungalow, *away* from Beverly Hills. It is unlikely that Carole confided much to her in this regard.

Carole did indeed sell the Capri house, but not because she needed money. She was divorcing the man with whom she had purchased the house and had no desire to live there. Friends knew that she wanted to move back down closer to the beach, but she was also planning on living in England for six of the next nine months. And the sale of the house would net her $30,000 (about $450,000 today).

Even her departing press agent Ed Ettinger said that he didn't think she was unhappy about her career, certainly not unhappy enough to kill herself. His opinion was that although her financial situation was somewhat strained, she was far from destitute and did not have money problems.[98]

On Tuesday the 5th she had an appointment with her attorney Giesler to sign the paperwork that would entitle her to another $30,000 from Schmidlapp in their divorce settlement. Not only is it a financial reason to live, it adds to the evidence that the event was un-premeditated.

She probably earned $25,000 in personal appearance fees during the last year of her life in addition to the money from British-Lion. With the new contract, that was about $40,000. Between the two that represented about $700,000 today. Her Lion contract was paying her $1,200–$1,500 weekly, far more than her studio contract would have paid her.

Carole was also in demand for endorsements, and now free of having to share the fees with Zanuck and Fox. During the spring of 1948, Carole signed a contract for her pictures to appear in full-page newspaper advertisements for Levitz Jewelry, a national chain. Appearing with Carole in the ads were fellow stars Sylvia Sydney and Dinah Shore.

She had just received an initial payment from British-Lion — her new English studio — of $15,000 — and had happily embarked on a Beverly Hills shopping trip just two days prior. She was also assured of a comfortable divorce settlement from Schmidlapp and in fact could have kept the house had she wanted to do so. Yes, she was independent, but she was also in great demand. British-Lion was not the only studio after her.

Schmidlapp himself told the press upon arriving for her funeral that he could see no reason for her to take her own life, and volunteered that she was "all right" financially.[99]

Jerry Giesler, who was representing her in the divorce, said, "I don't think this divorce had anything to do with her suicide."[100] While divorce can obviously be traumatic, Carole had been through three, and had an almost cavalier attitude towards the procedure. Her relationship with Schmidlapp had been friendly more than romantic for several years, and they were still friends. Remember too that she regularly wore her four wedding rings together, gleefully telling friends it was a reminder not to marry again. Certainly she must have been disappointed in the outcome of the marriage but clearly not enough to kill herself over.

It all leads to an inescapable conclusion, that she simply killed herself over a man — Rex Harrison. Carole was absolutely totally in love with him. Harrison told her that he loved her, and that they would marry, and Carole believed him until the night she killed herself.

But Carole's biggest problem was probably that she more than likely didn't really know *how* to love anyone, let alone someone as disagreeable and amoral as Harrison. Her entire life was a litany of failed relationships, failed love. With every conceivable kind of man.

It's impossible to find a serious relationship that Carole chose that made any sense at all. It's unfortunate that she didn't have — and we don't have — the power of hindsight to see the men that she let get away. The men that she *should* have chosen and didn't, for whatever reason.

The reason is probably pretty simple. Carole just didn't know *how* to love someone. Anyone. She was emotionally unable to understand love though she wanted to be in love more than anything in her life. She spoke the words repeatedly, but I don't think she knew the difference between infatuation, lust and love. To her it was all the same. To her, even attention was perceived as love. Her upbringing — her mother — left her totally ill-prepared for any mature relationship.

She only showed real sadness after the end of two relationships. When she killed herself after Harrison walked away. And when her dog Donner died.

★ Epilogue ★

Ghosts

Rex Harrison paid dearly for his role in Carole's death. Columnists began attacks on Harrison the week of Carole's death and kept them up for years. The month after Carole died Dorothy Kilgallen hinted that "police, who never stopped investigating the sleeping pill death of actress Carole Landis, now have a 'clue' which may put the case back on the front pages."[1] She was referring to the rumors that Harrison lied during his dealings with the police and the coroner.

After Carole's death, he was effectively blacklisted from U.S. films. He was only offered five small roles during the next 12 years, forgettable films like *The Long Dark Hall* (1951) and *The Constant Husband* (1955). His personal life suffered equally. Incredibly, or perhaps inevitably, his affairs continued. Even so, it was almost ten more years before Lilli Palmer divorced him.

Harrison began an affair with actress Kay Kendall during the 1954 filming of *The Constant Husband*. He learned from her doctor that she was terminally ill with leukemia and agreed with the doctor not to tell Kendall the real nature of her illness. He divorced the long-suffering Palmer to marry Kendall in 1957, and actually planned to remarry Palmer after Kendall died! But Palmer wouldn't return and Harrison lost both women (Kendall died in 1957). Harrison said that the death affected him greatly, but it isn't known which death — Kendall's passing or his marriage to Palmer.

If a potential role in the U.S. arose, one of the Hollywood writers would pick up the flag. As late as 1955, Louella Parsons spoke of Dorothy Dandridge, describing her as "very wise in the was [she had] handled her career, and she's continuing to avoid mistakes. She's been offered a revival of *Salome* on Broadway but before she accepts she'll talk to Darryl Zanuck. The reason for the huddle is that on the same bill might be Rex Harrison and Lilli Palmer in *Amphytrion 38*. Darryl has never forgotten, and neither have many other people, the articles Rex Harrison wrote against Hollywood right after the suicide of Carole Landis."[2]

The lack of movie work continued into the 1960s so Harrison took a stage role as Prof. Henry Higgins in the stage production *My Fair Lady*. A Tony award led to the movie version in the same role that earned him a 1964 Oscar. It had been two decades since Carole's death but Harrison was then welcomed back to Hollywood. He did 16 more films and died in 1990 from pancreatic cancer.

He would marry three more times. In 1962 he wed actress Rachel Roberts, divorcing in 1971 to marry another mistress, Elizabeth Harris. In 1975 that marriage ended and he picked up a sixth wife, Mercia Tinker, in 1978 — then rekindled an affair with ex-wife Roberts soon after. In an eerie replay of Carole's death, after a year of promises to divorce Tinker and marry her, Harrison told her they would not marry. On November 26, 1980, she took a mouthful of pills and a bottle of lye and died on her kitchen floor. Like Carole, Roberts was beautiful, bright and spoke her mind, but was not strong enough to live through an affair with Harrison.

In her journal (published after her death), Roberts wrote of Harrison, "Rex cannot be pleased. Servants have gotten slapped with his tongue or hand. Eventually, his servants and wives leave him. Rex is one of those who thinks living well is the best revenge. It may be, but the revenge is taken out on his nearest and dearest."[3]

Lilli Palmer fared little better than Harrison. Ignoring Harrison's pleas to wait for him and for Kay Kendall to die, Lilli married Argentinean actor Carlos Thompson. She was tarred with the same brush that painted Harrison after Carole's death, and found it very difficult to find U.S. film work. In the early 1950s she returned to her native Germany, where she appeared in almost 50 films. She came back to the U.S. in the early 1970s.

Palmer was a gifted writer. Her autobiography *Change Lobsters and Dance* is fascinating although it completely glossed over Harrison's involvement in Carole's death and supported the invention that she was in New York that weekend. Her only other book was published in 1976. The well-written *The Red Raven* is a novel about a love triangle.

Palmer appeared in three or four television series in the 1970s before suffering a heart attack on January 27, 1986. At the time she was battling cervical cancer. She is buried near the Great Mausoleum at Forest Lawn, just a short distance from Carole's gravesite.

Carole's mother Clara stayed in Southern California after her daughter's death. She moved out to San Bernardino where she died on August 9, 1976, at age 82. Alfred Ridste, who may or may not have been Carole's real father, died in Santa Rosa, California. Like Clara, he was 82 when he died in on March 4, 1973. Ridste married three more times after his marriage to Clara ended just before Carole's birth, and he worked for the railroads for his entire life. He is buried in Memorial Gardens in Santa Rosa next to his last wife, Evadna Clifton Stone.

Charles Fenner, who was most likely Carole's biological father, rarely left Montana during his lifetime. He died in July 1971 in the tiny northern Montana town of Cut Bank, on the edge of the huge Blackfoot Indian Reservation just 25 miles from the Canadian border. He probably worked for the railroads, since Cut Bank is the site of a huge railroad switching yard. He was 85 at the time of his death.

Horace Schmidlapp had no real success on Broadway before Carole's death, and none after. In 1952, Earl Wilson reported that Horace had "returned to Cincinnati to get financing for his return to show business,"[4] but little was heard from Schmidlapp in the years after Carole's death. He had other girlfriends long before the divorce proceedings were started, but after her death his romances somehow seemed more interesting. Schmidlapp's romantic escapades were of interest only because of his relationship with Carole, but it kept him in the gossip columns literally for years.

Less than three weeks after Carole died, Louella Parsons mentioned that "Horace

Schmidlapp has a new interest, and ironically her name is Carol—full name, Carol Lynne, the ice-skater who headlines an ice show at the Roxy Theater."[5] During 1949 he was linked to a succession of beautiful women that included Lady Ellen Barton,[6] Gay Poling,[7] Pat Dane (ex-wife of bandleader Tommy Dorsey)[8] and actress Pat Smart.[9]

His early 1950s girlfriends included Pert Dixon,[10] Vera Scott,[11] Lorraine Cugat,[12] Sheree North[13] and Lana Turner.[14] He reportedly almost married several times, each supposed engagement to a young—and very wealthy—heiress. His first reported engagement was to socialite Jo Kuhlmann[15] in early 1953. In October of that year, Walter Winchell wrote that Lorraine Manville, whom he described as "a 'walking Fort Knox,' has ... Horace Schmidlapp breathless waiting for her nod to his proposal."[16]

When the Manville engagement fizzled, he took up with Georgette Cushing,[17] Cami Wilson[18] and water-skier Jann Holden. In 1955, he became engaged to yet another wealthy debutante, Patricia McClintock. Earl Wilson reported that Schmidlapp and McClintock were "waiting for her Arkansas divorce decree from an Oklahoma 'oilionaire,'" after which they would wed.[19]

Schmidlapp and Pat McClintock were married on February 27, 1958, in Palm Beach, after which they split their time between the Schmidlapps' New York City apartment and Cincinnati estate, several lake properties in the Midwest and their Florida home. By the late 1960s they were living full-time in Florida, where they were prominent fixtures in Palm Beach social circles. Horace Schmidlapp died on August 12, 1987, in Palm Beach at the age of 71.

According to Mrs. Schmidlapp, Horace never once mentioned Carole to her during their 30-plus years together. "He was a very quiet person anyway, but particularly quiet about her. He *never* discussed, or even mentioned Carole Landis. He just didn't want to talk about it ... [I] knew enough not to ask."[20] Patricia Schmidlapp still lives quietly in Florida.

Four Jills in a Jeep was the career high watermark for two of the other three "Jills," Kay Francis and Mitzi Mayfair. Francis only made two more films before retiring in 1945. She died of cancer in 1968 in New York, leaving most of her $1,000,000 estate to train dogs at Seeing Eye, Inc. *Jills* was the last film for Mitzi Mayfair, who was more of a dancer than an actress. She married Fox Studio executive Charles Henderson in 1944. She died in quiet retirement in Arizona in 1976.

Martha Raye, the last of the *Jills,* did half a dozen movies in the 1940s before turning to television in the 1950s. She continued making U.S.O. visits through the Vietnam conflict in the 1970s, making her a legend with servicemen.

But her personal life was a mess. Going back to the 1940s her desperate fear of flying forced her to get drunk before flying anywhere. Her drinking and conduct on flights over the years left her banned from almost every major airline by the 1970s. She married six times, the last time in 1991. She was 74 and her bisexual husband Mark Harris was 42. When she died in 1994, Harris had her body taken from the hospital within ten minutes of her death and had her cremated.

Raye had so little formal schooling that she never knew how to read; her scripts had to be read to her. But she was awarded the Presidential Medal of Freedom in November 1993 by President Bill Clinton, was awarded the Jean Hersholt Humanitarian Award in 1969 for her work with charities and for entertaining U.S. troops, and was named the first female honorary member of the Friar's Club.

She was also an honorary Green Beret. During her (usually unpublicized) visits to U.S. Army Special Forces camps in Vietnam, the registered nurse and lieutenant colonel often helped out in the hospitals when things got busy. Her Green Beret friends affectionately nicknamed her "Colonel Maggie." When she died, she was given an almost complete military funeral at Fort Bragg, North Carolina. Her funeral was attended by hundreds of members of the Special Forces, the 82nd Airborne, the Special Forces Association and other military personnel.

One-time Carole lover Jacqueline Susann turned from a non-career in acting to writing in the 1960s. Husband Irving Mansfield first urged her to collect her stories, telling her to write down whatever she and her friends talked about at lunch. The result was *Valley of the Dolls*, about the lives of three friends ground up in the Hollywood dream machine. Susann based the character of Jennifer North on Carole.

It would be turned into a film of the same name in 1968. The character of Helen Lawson was based on Susann's lesbian lover Ethel Merman. Carole's Jennifer North character was played by Sharon Tate, who was murdered by the Manson family in Beverly Hills in August 1969. Susann and Mansfield stayed together for almost 30 turbulent years full of affairs before she died of cancer in 1974.

* * * *

It's difficult to measure Carole's career impact in Hollywood. She appeared in almost 50 films, none of them blockbusters or classics, but she still has a star on the Hollywood Walk of Fame. It's located at 777 Vine Street, between one-time boyfriend George Jessel and director William Beaudine.

She's better-known for her death than for the accomplishments during her short life. On December 27, 1948, gossip writer Bob Thomas' "In Hollywood" column featured his annual "Best" and "Biggest" in Hollywood. The "Best Picture" was *Hamlet*. "Biggest Social Event" was the "Lana Turner–Bob Topping wedding." "Biggest Female Discovery" was Betsy Drake. The "Biggest Shock" was "the Carole Landis suicide."[21]

It's surprising that anyone would think Carole's suicide was shocking. Knowing what we now know about her upbringing, her parents and the family history, her treatment by the men in her life and her inability to understand love, it isn't shocking at all. The tendency is to label a suicide, since we have so much trouble accepting them. There must be a reason. One writer said Carole "just couldn't face life."[22] She could face life, but she couldn't face Rex Harrison.

In her final film, *The Brass Monkey*, Carole sings a lovely song by Ross Porter called "I Know Myself Too Well." Its poignancy is obvious.

Unfortunately, Carole's tragedy will be forever linked with the allure, the glamour and, ultimately, the power of Hollywood. And she will be forever linked with other actors who could not survive Hollywood. Peg Entwhistle, who jumped to her death from the top of the "H" in the "Hollywoodland" sign in 1932. Karl Dane, who shot himself in the head after going from silent screen star to selling hot dogs outside studio gates when sound arrived. John Bowers, one-time silent star who sailed out toward a Pacific Ocean sunset and drowned himself when his career ended. Lupe Velez. George "Superman" Reeves. Marilyn Monroe.

Eight years after Carole's death, Jimmy Fidler reminisced, "Even today, it is difficult to imagine that she was haunted by despair. The girl who was admired by millions vainly searched for the love of one man."[23] Instead of remembering all of the wonderful things she did, her immense talent, and her once-indomitable spirit, sad to say, all we remember is a photograph of the beautiful girl on the bathroom floor.

Appendix A: Filmography

1937

A Star Is Born
Produced by Selznick International Pictures and United Artists, 111 minutes
Production: 11/1/36–12/28/36; *Release Date:* 1/25/37
Director: William Wellman
(Carole's role uncredited as "girl in beret seated at Santa Anita bar")
Cast: Janet Gaynor, Fredric March, Adolphe Menjou, May Robson, Andy Devine, Lionel Stander, Owen Moore, Peggy Wood

A Day at the Races
Produced by MGM, 111 minutes
Production: 9/1/36 and 12/21/36–4/2/37; *Release Date:* 6/11/37
Director: Sam Wood
(Carole's role uncredited, unconfirmed in final film)
Cast: Groucho Marx, Chico Marx, Harpo Marx, Allan Jones, Maureen O'Sullivan, Margaret Dumont, Leonard Ceeley

Broadway Melody of 1938
Produced by MGM, 110 minutes
Production: 2/25/37–7/20/37; *Release Date:* 8/20/37
Director: Roy Del Ruth
(Carole's role uncredited, appears to be seated on couch in hotel lobby)
Cast: Robert Taylor, Eleanor Powell, George Murphy, Binnie Barnes, Buddy Ebsen, Sophie Tucker, Judy Garland

The King and the Chorus Girl
Produced by Warner Bros., 90 minutes
Production dates unknown; assumed to be late 1936–early 1937; *Release Date:* 3/27/37
Directed by Mervyn LeRoy
(Carole's role uncredited, supposedly in Follies Bergere chorus)
Cast: Fernand Gravey, Joan Blondell, Edward Everett Horton, Alan Mowbray, Mary Nash, Jane Wyman, Luis Alberni

The Emperor's Candlesticks
Produced by MGM, 89 minutes
Production: 3/11/37–4/22/37; *Release Date:* 7/2/37
Director: George Fitzmaurice
(Carole's role uncredited, unconfirmed in final film)
Cast: William Powell, Luise Rainer, Robert Young, Maureen O'Sullivan, Frank Morgan, Henry Stephenson

Varsity Show
Produced by Warner Bros., 120 minutes
Production: 5/37–7/37; *Release Date:* 9/4/37
Directors: William Keighley and Busby Berkeley
(Carole's role uncredited)
Cast: Dick Powell, Fred Waring and His Pennsylvanians, Ted Healy, Rosemary Lane, Priscilla Lane

Alcatraz Island
Produced by Cosmopolitan Pictures and First National Pictures and Warner Bros., 63 minutes
Production: 5/24/37–6/14/37; *Release Date:* 11/6/37
Director: William McCann

(Carole's role uncredited, perhaps extra in courtroom scenes)
Cast: John Litel, Ann Sheridan, Mary Maguire, Gordon Oliver, Dick Purcell, Ben Welden, Addison Richards

Fly-Away Baby
Produced by Warner Bros., 60 minutes
Production: 6/19/37; *Release Date:* 6/9/37
Director: Frank McDonald
(Carole's role uncredited, "blonde at airport")
Cast: Glenda Farrell, Barton MacLane, Gordon Oliver, Hugh O'Connell, Marcia Ralston, Tom Kennedy

Adventurous Blonde
Produced by First National Pictures and Warner Bros.
Production: 6/25/37–8/1/37; *Release Date:* 11/13/37
Also released as *Torchy Blane and the Adventurous Blonde*
Director: Frank McDonald
(Carole's role uncredited, unconfirmed in final film)
Cast: Glenda Farrell, Barton MacLane, Anne Nagel, Tom Kennedy, George E. Stone, Natalie Moorhead, William Hopper

1938

The Invisible Menace
Produced by Warner Bros., 54–59 minutes
Production dates unknown, likely 10/11/37; *Release Date:* 1/22/38
Director: John Farrow
(Carole's role uncredited, "woman wanting to go with her Johnnie")
Cast: Boris Karloff, Marie Wilson, Eddie Craven, Regis Toomey, Henry Kolker, Cy Kendall, Charles Trowbridge, Eddie Acuff
Released in U.K. as *Without Warning*

Over the Wall
Produced by Warner Bros., 66 or 72 minutes
Production: circa 7/29/37; *Release Date:* 4/2/38
Director: Frank McDonald
(Carole's role uncredited, "Peggy, Scanlon's girlfriend, or moll at the beach and the apartment")
Cast: Dick Foran, June Travis, John Litel, Eddy Chandler, Dick Purcell, Veda Ann Borg, Alan Davis, George E. Stone

Hollywood Hotel
Produced by Warner Bros., 100, 103 or 109 minutes
Production: 8/1/37–11/1/37; *Release Date:* 1/15/38
Busby Berkeley
(Carole appeared as "hat-check girl")
Cast: Dick Powell, Rosemary Lane, Lola Lane, Benny Goodman, Raymond Paige, Hugh Herbert, Ted Healy, Glenda Farrell, Johnnie Davis

The Patient in Room 18
Produced by Warner Bros., 58 or 60 minutes
Production: 8/29/37–10/1/37; *Release Date:* 1/8/38
Directors: Bobby Connolly and Crane Wilbur
(Carole's role uncredited, unconfirmed in final film)
Cast: Patric Knowles, Ann Sheridan, Eric Stanley, John Ridgely, Rosella Towne, Jean Benedict, Charles Trowbridge, Cliff Clark, Harland Tucker, Edward Raquello

Blondes at Work
Produced by Warner Bros. and First National Pictures, 63 minutes
Production: 10/1/37–11/1/37; *Release Date:* 2/5/38
Director: Frank McDonald
(Carole appeared as "Carol," or "Miss Hilden, salesgirl," or "department store model")
Cast: Glenda Farrell, Barton MacLane, Tom Kennedy, Rosella Towne, Donald Briggs, John Ridgely, Betty Compson, Thomas E. Jackson, Frank Shannon, Jean Benedict

Love, Honor and Behave
Produced by Warner Bros., 71 minutes
Production: 11/21/37–12/31/37; *Release Date:* 3/12/38
Director: Stanley Logan
(Carole appeared as "wheel-watcher at party")
Cast: Wayne Morris, Priscilla Lane, Dick Foran, Thomas Mitchell, John Litel, Mona Barrie, Dickie Moore, Audrey Leonard, Minor Watson, Donald Briggs, Margaret Irving, Gregory Gaye, Crauford Kent

Women Are Like That
Produced by Warner Bros., 75 or 78 minutes
Production: 8/29/37–10/1/37; *Release Date:* 4/23/38
Director: Stanley Logan
(Carole appeared in party scene)
Cast: Kay Francis, Pat O'Brien, Ralph Forbes, Melville Cooper, Thurston Hall, Grant Mitchell, Gordon Oliver, John Eldredge, Herbert Rawlinson, Hugh O'Connell, Georgia Caine, Joyce Compton, Sarah Edwards

A Slight Case of Murder
Produced by Warner Bros., 85 minutes
Production: 10/15/37–11/25/37; *Release Date:* 3/5/38
Director: Lloyd Bacon
(Carole's role uncredited, appeared in party scene over Edward G. Robinson's shoulder, wearing polka-dotted dress)
Cast: Edward G. Robinson, Jane Bryan, Allen Jenkins, Ruth Donnelly, Willard Parker, John Litel, Edward Brophy, Harold Huber, Eric Stanley, Paul Harvey, Bobby Jordan, Joe Downing, Margaret Hamilton, George E. Stone, Bert Hanlon

He Couldn't Say No
Produced by Warner Bros., 57 or 61 minutes
Production dates unknown, assumed to be late 1937; *Release Date:* 3/19/38
Director: Lewis Seiler
(Carole's role uncredited, unconfirmed in final film)
Cast: Frank McHugh, Jane Wyman, Cora Witherspoon, Diana Lewis, Berton Churchill, Ferris Taylor, William Haade, Tom Kennedy, Raymond Hatton, John Ridgely, Chester Clute, Rita Gould

Men Are Such Fools
Produced by Warner Bros., 66 or 70 minutes
Production: 12/15/37–1/15/38; *Release Date:* 7/16/38
Director: Busby Berkeley
(Carole appeared at train station as "June Cooper, girl with Jimmy's school chums")
Cast: Wayne Morris, Priscilla Lane, Humphrey Bogart, Hugh Herbert, Johnnie Davis, Penny Singleton, Mona Barrie, Marcia Ralston, Gene Lockhart, Kathleen Lockhart, Donald Briggs

Penrod's Double Trouble
Produced by Warner Bros., 60, 61 or 65 minutes
Production: 12/15/37–1/15/38; *Release Date:* 7/23/38
Director: Lewis Seiler
(Carole's role uncredited, appeared in party scene in coat with fur collar, said, "Give him the 25 cents, you skinflint")
Cast: Billy Mauch, Bobby Mauch, Dick Purcell, Gene Lockhart, Kathleen Lockhart, Hugh O'Connell, Charles Halton, Bernice Pilot, Jackie Morrow, Philip Hurlic

Gold Diggers in Paris
Produced by Warner Bros., 95, 97 or 100 minutes
Production: 1/15/38–3/5/38; *Release Date:* 6/11/38
Director: Ray Enright
Released in U.K. as *The Gay Imposters*
(Carole appeared as first gold-digger)
Cast: Rudy Vallee, Rosemary Lane, Hugh Herbert, Allen Jenkins, Gloria Dickson, Melville Cooper, Mabel Todd, Fritz Feld, Curt Bois, Edward Brophy, Victor Kilian, Georges Renavent, Armand Kaliz

Four's a Crowd
Produced by Warner Bros., 85 or 91 minutes
Production: 2/1/38–3/25/38; *Release Date:* 9/3/38
Director: Michael Curtiz
Also released as *All Rights Reserved*
(Carole appeared as "Lansford's second secretary")
Cast: Errol Flynn, Olivia de Havilland, Rosalind Russell, Patric Knowles, Walter Connolly, Hugh Herbert, Melville Cooper, Franklin Pangborn, Herman Bing, Margaret Hamilton, Joseph Crehan, Joe Cunningham, Dennie Moore, Gloria Blondell

When Were You Born?
Produced by First National Pictures and Warner Bros., 65 minutes
Production: 2/15/38–3/15/38; *Release Date:* 6/18/38
Director: William McGann
(Carole's role uncredited as ship passenger, prominent about nine minutes into the film)
Cast: Margaret Lindsay, Anna May Wong, Lola Lane, Anthony Averill, Charles C. Wilson, Jeffrey Lynn, Eric Stanley, James Stephen-

son, Leonard Mudie, Olin Howlin, Maurice Cass, Clayton Moore

Boy Meets Girl
Produced by First National Pictures and Warner Bros., 86 minutes
Production: 3/5/38–4/5/38; *Release Date:* 8/27/38
Director: Lloyd Bacon
(Carole uncredited as Commissary Cashier)
Cast: James Cagney, Pat O'Brien, Marie Wilson, Ralph Bellamy, Frank McHugh, Dick Foran, Bruce Lester, Ronald Reagan, Paul Clark, Penny Singleton, Dennie Moore, Harry Seymour, Bert Hanlon

Girls on Probation
Produced by First National Pictures and Warner Bros., 60 or 63 minutes
Production: 5/2/38–6/5/38; *Release Date:* 10/22/38
Director: William McGann
(Carole unconfirmed)
Cast: Jane Bryan, Ronald Reagan, Anthony Averill, Sheila Bromley, Henry O'Neill, Elisabeth Risdon, Sig Ruman, Dorothy Peterson, Esther Dale, Susan Hayward, Larry Williams, Arthur Hoyt, Peggy Shannon, Lenita Lane

1939

Three Texas Steers
Produced by Republic Pictures Corporation, 56 minutes
Production: 3/17/39–4/5/39; *Release Date:* 5/12/39
Director: George Sherman
Released in the U.K. as *Danger Rides the Range*
(Carole appeared as "Nancy Evans," female lead)
Cast: John Wayne, Ray Corrigan, Max Terhune, Ralph Graves, Roscoe Ates, Collette Lyons, Billy Curtis, Ted Adams, Stanley Blystone, David Sharpe, Ethan Laidlaw, Lew Kelly

Reno
Produced by RKO Radio Pictures, 73 minutes
Production: 8/25/38–9/25/38; *Release Date:* 12/1/39
Director: John Farrow
(Carole's role uncredited as "Mrs. Humphrey," in scenes with lawyer)
Cast: Richard Dix, Gail Patrick, Anita Louise, Paul Cavanaugh, Laure Hope Crewes, Louis Jean Heydt, Hobart Cavanaugh, Charles Halton, Astrid Allwyn, Joyce Compton, Frank Faylen, William Haade

The Cowboys from Texas
Produced by Republic Pictures Corporation, 57 minutes
Production: 10/10/39–10/18/39; *Release Date:* 11/29/39
Director: George Sherman
(Carole appeared as "June Jones," female lead)
Cast: Robert Livingston, Raymond Hatton, Duncan Renaldo, Ivan Miller, Charles Middleton, Betty Compson, Ethan Laidlaw, Yakima Canutt, Walter Wills, Ed Cassidy

Daredevils of the Red Circle
(12 chapter Serial)
Produced by Republic Pictures
Production: 4/15/39–5/1/39; *Release Date:* 6/10/39
Directors: William Witney and John English
(Carole appeared as "Blanche Granville," female lead)
Cast: Charles Quigley, Bruce Bennett, David Sharpe, Miles Mander, Charles Middleton, C. Montague Shaw, Ben Taggart, William Pagan, Corbet Morris, Raymond Bailey, Fred "Snowflake" Toones, George Chesebro, Ray Miller

1940

Topper Returns
Produced by Hal Roach Studios, 95 minutes
Production: 11/1/40–12/20/40; *Release Date:* 3/21/40
Director: Roy Del Ruth
(Carole appeared as "Ann Carrington," second female lead)
Cast: Roland Young, Joan Blondell, Eddie "Rochester" Anderson, Dennis O'Keefe, H.B. Warner, Patsy Kelly, Billie Burke, George Zucco, Donald MacBride, Rafaela Ottiano, Trevor Bardette
Notes: Academy Award nominations for Best Sound Recording and Best Special Effects

One Million B.C.
Produced by Hal Roach Studios, 80 minutes
Production: 11/15/39–unknown completion date; *Release Date:* 4/5/40
Directors: Hal Roach, Sr., Hal Roach, Jr., D.W. Griffith (assisted in casting, unknown how much directing he might have done)
Released in the U.K. as *Man and His Mate*, re-released in 1952 domestically as *Cave Man*
(Carole appeared as "Loana," female lead)
Cast: Victor Mature, Lon Chaney, Jr., Mamo Clark, John Hubbard, Nigel De Brulier, Inez Palange, Edgar Edwards, Jacqueline Dalya, Mary Gale Fisher, Norman Budd, Harry Wilson, John Northpole, Lorraine Rivero
Notes: Academy Award nominations for Best Musical Score and Best Special Effects

Turnabout
Produced by Hal Roach Studios, 83 minutes
Production: circa 2/19/40; *Release Date:* 5/17/40
Director: Hal Roach, Sr.
(Carole appeared as "Sally Willows," female lead)
Cast: Adolphe Menjou, John Hubbard, William Gargan, Verree Teasdale, Mary Astor, Donald Meek, Joyce Compton, Inez Courtney, Franklin Pangborn, Marjorie Main, Berton Churchill, Margaret Roach

Mystery Sea Raider
Produced by Paramount Pictures, 76 minutes
Production: circa 5/5/40; *Release Date:* 8/9/40
Director: Edward Dmytryk
(Carole appeared as "June McCarthy," female lead)
Cast: Henry Wilcoxon, Onslow Stevens, Kathleen Howard, Wally Rairden, Sven Hugo Borg, Henry Victor, Roland Varno, Louis Adlon, Willy Kaufman, Monte Blue, Matthew Boulton, Gohr Van Vleck, Jean Del Val

1941

Hedda Hopper's Hollywood No. 2
Produced by Paramount Pictures, 10 minutes
Production: dates unknown; *Release Date:* 12/5/41
Director: Herbert Moulton
Carole appeared as herself, attending premiere
Cast: Joe E. Brown, Jinx Falkenburg, William Farnum, William Hopper, Arline Judge, Evelyn Keyes, Kent Rogers, Anne Shirley, Jane Withers

Meet the Stars: Hollywood Visits the Navy
Produced by Republic Pictures
Production: dates unknown; *Release Date:* 4/24/41
Director: Harriet Parsons
Carole appeared as herself, with a number of other stars touring a Naval installation.

Road Show
Produced by Hal Roach Studios, 85 minutes
Production: circa 7/1/40; *Release Date:* 2/18/41
Directors: Hal Roach and Gordon Douglas
(Carole appeared as "Penguin Moore," female lead)
Cast: Adolphe Menjou, John Hubbard, Charles Butterworth, Patsy Kelly, George E. Stone, Margaret Roach, Polly Ann Young, Edward Norris, Marjorie Woodworth, Florence Bates, Willie Best, Ira Williams, William B. Williams

Moon Over Miami
Working title: Miami
Produced by 20th Century–Fox Film Corporation, 92 minutes
Production: 3/3/41–4/25/41; *Release Date:* 7/4/41
Director: Walter Lang
Locations: Cypress Gardens in Winter Haven, Florida, Silver Springs, Florida, Rainbow Springs in Ocala, Florida, studio
(Carole appeared as "Barbara Latimer" and "Miss Sears," second female lead)
Cast: Betty Grable, Charlotte Greenwood, Don Ameche, Robert Cummings, Jack Haley, Cobina Wright, Jr., The Condos Brothers, George Lessey, Fortunio Bonanova, Robert Conway, Robert Greig, Minor Watson, Lynne Roberts, Jack Cole and Co., George Humbert

Dance Hall
Previous working titles: The Bouncer and the Lady, The Giant Swing
Produced by 20th Century–Fox Film Corporation, 73 minutes

Production: 4/21/41–5/25/41; *Release Date:* 7/18/41
Director: Irving Pichel
(Carole appeared as "Lily Brown" and "Venus," lead female)
Locations: Elysian Park, Hollywood for outdoor scenes.
Cast: Cesar Romero, William Henry, June Storey, J. Edward Bromberg, Charles Halton, Shimen Ruskin, Willian Haade, Trudi Marsdon, Russ Clark, Frank Fanning

Cadet Girl
Produced 20th Century–Fox Film Corporation, 69 minutes
Production: circa 7/14/41; *Release Date:* 11/28/41
Director: Ray McCarey
(Carole appeared as "Gene Baxter," female lead)
Cast: George Montgomery, Shepperd Strudwick, William Tracy, Janis Carter, Robert Lowery, Basil Walker, Charles Tannen, Chick Chandler, Otto Han, Irving Bacon, Jayne Hazard, Edna Mae Jones, Charles Trowbridge
Notes: Royalties from the song "Uncle Sam Gets Around" by Leo Robin and Ralph Rainger were donated to the U.S.O. at Carole's request.

I Wake Up Screaming
Produced 20th Century–Fox Film Corporation, 82 minutes
Production: 7/21/41–8/25/41 and 9/5/41 retakes; *Release Date:* 11/14/41
Director: H. Bruce Humberstone
(Carole appeared as "Vicky Lynn," second female lead)
Cast: Victor Mature, Laird Cregar, Betty Grable, William Gargan, Alan Mowbray, Allyn Joslyn, Elisha Cook, Jr., Chick Chandler, Cyril Ring, Morris Ankrum, Charles Lane, Frank Orth
Released in U.K. as *Hot Spot*
Notes: Originally released *Hot Spot*, but after the popularity of *Photoplay*'s serialization of Steve Fisher's book, the film name was changed back to the book title.

1942

A Gentleman at Heart
Produced by 20th Century–Fox Film Corporation, 67 minutes
Production: circa 11/29/41; *Release Date:* 1/16/42
Director: Ray McCarey
(Carole appeared as "Helen Mason," female lead)
Cast: Cesar Romero, Milton Berle, J. Carrol Naish, Richard Derr, Rose Hobart, Jerome Cowan, Francis Pierlot, Chick Chandler, Steven Geray, Matt McHugh, Kane Richmond, Syd Saylor

My Gal Sal
Produced by 20th Century–Fox Film Corporation, 101 or 103 minutes
Production: 12/26/41–2/27/42; *Release Date:* 5/8/42
Director: Irving Cummings
(Carole appeared as "Mae Collins," second female lead)
Cast: Rita Hayworth, Victor Mature, John Sutton, James Gleason, Phil Silvers, Mona Maris, Walter Catlett, Frank Orth, Stanley Andrews, Margaret Moffatt, Libby Taylor, John Kelly, Curt Bois
Notes: Rita Hayworth replaced Alice Faye, who went on maternity leave.

It Happened in Flatbush
Previous working title: Dem Lovely Bums
Produced by 20th Century–Fox Film Corporation, 80 minutes
Production: circa 3/26/42; *Release Date:* 5/30/42
Director: Ray McCarey
(Carole appeared as "Kathryn Baker," female lead)
Cast: Lloyd Nolan, Sara Allgood, William Frawley, Robert Armstrong, Jane Darwell, George Holmes, Scotty Beckett, Joseph Allen, James Burke, Roger Imhof, Matt McHugh, LeRoy Mason, Pat Flaherty, Dale Van Sickel
Locations: Gilmore Field in Los Angeles

Orchestra Wives
Produced by 20th Century–Fox Film Corporation, 97 minutes
Production: 4/6–17/41–6/5/41; *Release Date:* 9/4/42
Director: Archie Mayo
(Carole appeared as "Natalie Mercer," second female lead)
Cast: Glenn Miller and His Band, George Montgomery, Ann Rutherford, Cesar Romero, Lynn Bari, Jackie Gleason, Virginia Gilmore, Mary Beth Hughes, the Nicholas

Brothers, Tamara Geva, Frank Orth, Grant Mitchell

Notes: Academy Award nomination for "I've Got a Gal in Kalamazoo" as Best Song

Manila Calling
Produced by 20th Century–Fox Film Corporation, 81 minutes
Production: 6/15/42–7/31/42; *Release Date:* 10/16/42
Director: Herbert I. Leeds
(Carole appeared as "Edna 'Eddie' Fraser," female lead)
Cast: Lloyd Nolan, Cornel Wilde, James Gleason, Elisha Cook, Jr., Martin Kosleck, Ralph Byrd, Charles Tannen, Ted North, Harold Huber, Lester Matthews, Louis Jean Heydt

1943

Show Business at War
Produced by 20th Century–Fox Film Corporation
Release Date: 5/21/43
Directed by Louis De Rochemont
(Carole appeared as herself)
Cast: Eddie "Rochester" Anderson, Louis Armstrong, Phil Baker, Ethel Barrymore, Robert Benchley, Jack Benny, Edgar Bergen, Irving Berlin, Joe E. Brown, James Cagney, Bing Crosby, Michael Curtiz, Linda Darnell, Bette Davis, Olivia de Havilland, Marlene Dietrich, Walt Disney, Irene Dunne, Deanna Durbin, W.C. Fields, Errol Flynn, Glenn Ford
Note: Film released also as *The March of Time*, Vol. IX, Issue 10; it was a multi-studio collaboration honoring the work of the stars assisting the war effort.

The Spirit of '43
Produced by a collaboration of National Screen Service, U.S. Department of the Treasury, Walt Disney Pictures, 56 minutes
Release Date: 1/7/43
Directed by Jack King
War propaganda film produced by Walt Disney Studios and 20th Century–Fox Film Corporation, 56 minutes
Combination of three short films and a cartoon: *The Spirit of '43* by Disney, using Donald Duck to explain how taxes and savings assist the war effort; *The House I Live In*, a short on tolerance with Frank Sinatra that won an Academy Award; *Women in Defense*, a short written by Eleanor Roosevelt and narrated by Katharine Hepburn; and *The Big Picture—Soldiers in Greasepaint*, a documentary narrated by Celeste Holm describing the role of actors and actresses entertaining troops, including Carole, Joe E. Brown, Merle Oberon, Ray Bolger, Paulette Goddard, Clark Gable, Bob Hope and Jack Benny.

The Powers Girl
Produced by Rodgers Productions Inc., 93 minutes
Production: 8/24/42–10/5/42; *Release Date:* 1/15/43
Director: Norman Z. McLeod
(Carole appeared as Kay Evans," second female lead)
Cast: George Murphy, Anne Shirley, Dennis Day, Benny Goodman and His Orchestra, Alan Mowbray, Jean Ames, Mary Treen, Rafael Storm, Helen MacKellar, Harry Shannon, Roseanne Murray, Jayne Hazard, Lillian Eggers
Released in the U.K. as *Hello Beautiful*

Wintertime
Produced by 20th Century–Fox Film Corporation, 82 minutes
Production: 3/15/43–6/15/43; *Release Date:* 9/17/43
Director: John Brahm
(Carole appeared as "Flossie Fouchere," second female lead)
Cast: Sonja Henie, Jack Oakie, Cesar Romero, Cornel Wilde, S.Z. Sakall, Woody Herman and His Orchestra, Don Douglas, Geary Steffen, Matt Briggs, Arthur Loft, Jean Del Val

1944

Four Jills in a Jeep
Produced by 20th Century–Fox Film Corporation, 89 minutes
Production: 10/18/43–xx/x/43; *Release Date:* 3/17/44
Director: William A. Seiter
(Carole appeared as herself)
Cast: Kay Francis, Mitzi Mayfair, Martha Raye, Alice Faye, Carmen Miranda, Betty Grable, George Jessel, John Harvey, Phil Silvers, Dick Haymes, Jimmy Dorsey and His Orchestra

Secret Command
Working titles: By Secret Command, Pilebuck
Produced by Terneen Productions for Columbia Pictures, 80 minutes
Production: 1/17/44–3/8/44; *Release Date:* 6/13/44
Director: Edward Sutherland
(Carole appeared as "Jill McCann," female lead)
Cast: Pat O'Brien, Chester Morris, Ruth Warrick, Wallace Ford, Barton MacLane, Tom Tully, Howard Freeman, Erik Rolf, Matt McHugh, Frank Sully
Notes: Academy Award nomination for Best Special Effects. This was the first production for Pat O'Brien and Phil Ryan's Terneen Productions.

Wilson
Produced by 20th Century–Fox Corporation, 154 minutes
Production: dates unknown; *Release Date:* 8/1/44
Director: Harry King
(Carole's scenes were removed from the final film)
Cast: Alexander Knox, Charles Coburn, Geraldine Fitzgerald, Cedric Hardwicke, Vincent Price, Thomas Mitchell, Ruth Nelson, William Eythe, Mary Anderson
Notes: Nominated for eight Oscars, including Best Special Effects, Film Editing, Directing, Writing, Cinematography, Best Actor, Music and Best Picture (won for Film Editing); won a Golden Globe for Best Acting.

1945

Having Wonderful Crime
Produced by RKO Radio Pictures, 69 minutes
Production: 4/25/44–7/1/44; *Release Date:* 4/12/45
Director: Edward Sutherland
(Carole appeared as "Helene Justus," female lead)
Cast: Pat O'Brien, George Murphy, Lenore Aubert, George Zucco, Gloria Holden, Richard Martin, Charles D. Brown, William "Wee Willie" Davis, Blanche Ring, Chili Williams
Locations: Malibu Lake, Del Monte, Carmel and the Lakeside Country Club for outdoor scenes

Hollywood Goes to War
Cast: Carole, Bob Hope, Betty Grable, Bing Crosby and several dozen others
Notes: Film is a combination of three wartime propaganda films: *Hollywood Canteen Overseas Special* (1944), *Mail Call* (1944) and *The All-Star Bond Rally* (1945), featuring dozens of entertainers of World War II with the troops and raising money for war bonds.

1946

Behind Green Lights
Working title: Precinct 33
Produced by 20th Century–Fox Film Corporation, 64 minutes
Production: 9/13/45–10/15/45; *Release Date:* 2/15/46
Director: Otto Brower
(Carole appeared as "Janet Bradley," female lead)
Cast: William Gargan, Richard Crane, Mary Anderson, John Ireland, Charles Russell, Roy Roberts, Mabel Paige, Stanley Prager, Charles Tannen, Fred Sherman, Don Beddoe, Bernard Nedell, Tom Moore

A Scandal in Paris
Working titles: Vidocq, Thieves' Holiday
Produced by Arnold Productions for United Artists, 97 or 100 minutes
Production: 10/8/45–11/26/45; *Release Date:* 7/19/46
Director: Douglas Sirk
(Carole appeared as "Loretta," second female lead)
Cast: George Sanders, Signe Hasso, Akim Tamiroff, Gene Lockhart, Jo Ann Marlowe, Alma Kruger, Alan Napier, Vladimir Sokoloff, Pedro de Cordoba, Leona Maricle, Fritz Leiber, Skelton Knaggs, Fred Nurney, Gisela Werbisek
Released in U.K. as *Thieves' Holiday*

It Shouldn't Happen to a Dog
Produced by 20th Century–Fox Film Corporation, 70 minutes
Production: 1/22/46–2/21/46; *Release Date:* 7/46
Director: Herbert I. Leeds
(Carole appeared as "Julia Andrews," female lead)
Cast: Allyn Joslyn, Margo Wood, Harry Morgan, Reed Hadley, Jean Wallace, Roy

Roberts, John Ireland, John Alexander, Whit Bissell, Charles Cane, Kathryn Card

1947

Out of the Blue
Produced by Eagle Lion Films, 86 minutes
Production: 2/25/47–4/5/47; *Release Date:* U.K. 10/11/47, Europe 4/48–11/48, U.S. 5/11/50
Director: Leigh Jason
(Carole appeared as "Mae Earthleigh," second female lead)
Cast: George Brent, Virginia Mayo, Ann Dvorak, Turhan Bey, Hadda Brooks, Alton E. Horton, Charles Smith, Julia Dean, Elizabeth Patterson, Richard Lane, Paul Harvey, Jerry Marlowe

1948

The Brass Monkey
Produced by Diadem Films and Eagle Lion Films for British-Lion Studios, 90 minutes
Production: circa 9/5/47; *Release Date:* 12/47, U.S. 10/11/48
Director: Thornton Freeland
(Carole appeared as "Kay Sheldon," female lead)
Cast: Carroll Levis, Herbert Lom, Avril Angers, Ernest Thesiger, Edward Underdown, Henry Edwards, Henry Worthington, Terry Thomas, Campbell Cotts, Jack McNaughton, Lyn Evans, John Salew
Released in U.S. as *Lucky Mascot*
Locations: Warner Bros./First National Teddington Studios, Teddington, London

Noose
Produced by Edward Dryhurst Productions and Associated British Studios and Monogram Studios, 76 minutes
Production: 12/26/47–3/1/48; *Release Date:* U.K. 8/1/48, Europe 4/50–6/50, U.S. 7/19/50
Director: Edmond T. Greville
(Carole appeared as "Linda Medbury," female lead)
Cast: Joseph Calleia, Derek Farr, Stanley Holloway, Nigel Patrick, Ruth Nixon, Carol van Derman, John Slater, Leslie Bradley, Reginald Tate, Edward Rigby, John Salew, Robert Adair, Hay Petrie
Released in the U.S. as *The Silk Noose*
Locations: Warner Bros./First National Teddington Studios, Teddington, London

1953

Screen Snapshots: Hollywood's Greatest Comedians
Produced by Columbia Pictures Corporation, 10 or 12 minutes
Release Date: 5/14/53
Director: Ralph Staub
Notes: Columbia production number 5858. Host Ralph Staub shows Glenn Ford clips from earlier radio shows, among them a the Jimmy Durante–Garry Moore "Blue Ribbon Radio" program recorded on June 5, 1943, at the Marine Corps base in San Diego on which Carole appeared.

1961

Stars Give All for Boys Overseas
Produced by Filmrite Associates and Official Films, 15 minutes
Narrated by Tom Hudson
Notes: Documentary discussing Hollywood's contribution to servicemen morale during World War II, including footage of Carole, Joe E. Brown and Jack Benny.

Appendix B: Radio Appearances

1940, Jan. 21, *Hillman Hour*, KFWB radio

1941, Dec. 4, with Walter Huston on Bing Crosby's radio show

1941, Feb. 15, HCN Radio, with Pat O'Brien and Donald Crisp, performing "Brother Orchid"

1941, September 24, "The Eddie Cantor Show" (New York City) with Joe DiMaggio, WEAF radio

1941, October 8, KMRT Radio program, Los Angeles

1941, October 17, "The Louella Parsons Radio Show," plugging *Hot Spot* with Grable and Laird Cregar

1942, April 10, CBS Playhouse production of "I Wake Up Screaming"

1942, Aug. 10, CBS WBBM radio "VOX Pop" show, at Fort Bliss, Texas, interviewing U.S. Army soldiers and soldiers from the Mexican army stationed in Juarez, Mexico, broadcast around the world via short wave; substituting for Parks Johnson, who was on vacation

1943, May 10, with John Garfield and Robert Paige, "Johnny Eager," KNX radio

1943, May 26, with Brian Aherne, "Soldiers with Wings" Program from West Coast Army Air Force Training Center, Santa Ana, KHJ

1943, June 5, Groucho Marx "Blue Ribbon Town" radio program, recorded at the Marine Corps Base in San Diego

1943, June 8, "Duffy's Tavern" Radio Program

1943, June 28, "Vox Pop," interviewing soldiers from Aleutian Campaign, with Warren Hull

1943, July 23, CBS Radio, "Playhouse," "Too Many Husbands"

1943, July 24, "Maritime Service Radio Show," on WABC, from Sheepshead Bay Training School

1943, July 27, "Frank Sinatra's Band Box," KNX, New York with Eileen Farrell and Cab Calloway

1943, July 29, CBS Radio, "Canteen," with Monty Woolley and the Andrews Sisters

1943, Aug. 3, Army Air Force Salute, WMCA

1943, Aug. 17, Radio Hollywood show with Paula Stone, WNEW

1943, Aug. 20, "Phillip Morris Playhouse," CBS Radio, "Love Crazy" with Jerry Lester

1943, Aug. 28, "Army Service Radio Program," WJZ

1943. Sept. 2, "Stage Door Canteen," with Bert Lytell, Paul Robeson, Lionel Stander, WABC

1943, Sept. 5, Jerry Lester program

1943, Sept. 19, "Reader's Digest" show

1943, Sept. 24, Ethel Colby Radio show, WMCA

1943, Sept. 24, Radio Broadway with Ethel Colby, WMCA

1943, Oct. 23, Command Performance radio program

1943, Nov. 8, Screen Guild Play, "George Washington Slept Here," WABC

1943, Nov. 25, NBC Radio Thanksgiving Program with Bob Hope, Jack Benny and other U.S.O. performers

1943, Dec. 11, "Command Performance" radio program

1943, Dec. 23, Bob Burns radio show, with Dick Haymes, redid scene from *Four Jills and a Jeep* (sometimes listed as a Dec. 16 appearance)

1943, Dec. 29, Blue Network, "Star for a Night"

1944, January 7, "Stage Door Canteen," recorded in U.K. during Raft trip

1944, February 21, "Screen Guild Play" "Design for Scandal," with Robert Young, WABC

1944, February 22, Bob Hope Show, WEAF Radio

1944, March 15, NBC Radio, with Eddie Cantor

1944, March 18, Groucho Marx program, WABC

1944, April 11, "Duffy's Tavern," Blue Network, WJZ, with Duffy's Band

1944, April 26, "Orson Welles' Almanac"

1944, June 24, "Command Performance"

1944, August 29, from military base New Caledonia, with Jack Benny, WEAF Radio

1944, October 1, Dorothy Kilgallen's "Voice of Broadway" program, WOR

1944, October 6, "Hollywood Canteen"

1944, October 7, "Armstrong Theater"

1944, October 14, KPFA Radio, "The Palmolive Party Show," with Barry Wood, Patsy Kelly and the Million Dollar Band

1944, October 27, 1944, New York Newspaper Guild First Anniversary Show, with Burl Ives, Gertrude Niesen and Dan Murphy, WMCA

1944, November 12, "Philco Radio Hall of Fame Show," guest host with Charles Boyer and Diana Lynn

1944, December 1, "Stage Door Canteen," with Bert Lytell, Victor Borge and Gregory Ratoff

1945, March 5, "The Jerry Wayne Radio Show," with Benny Goodman

1945, March 10, "Broadway News," with Radie Harris, WJZ

1945, April 8, "The Earl Wilson Show," Mutual Network with Paul Douglas

1945, November 15, "Command Performance"

1945, November 15, "The Rudy Vallee Show"

1945, December 3, "Vivacious Lady," with Jimmy Stewart, KNX Radio

1946, December 26, "Command Performance," starring with Frank Sinatra, Jimmy Durante and Clark Dennis

1946, March 16, "Continental Celebrity Club"

1946, March 20, Jack Smith program

1946, April 3, "Chesterfield Supper Club"

1946, July 11, Paula Stone radio show

1947, February 17, "Screen Guild Theater" production of "You Belong to Me," with Don Ameche

1947, May 22, "Lift Up Your Voices" with Tony Martin, Danny Thomas, the Benny Goodman Sextet, Victor Young's Orchestra, others, KECA

1947, July 22, "We the People," from the L.A. County Jail

1947, July 27, "Hollywood Tour"

Chapter Notes

Note: Columnists were syndicated. BC — Bennett Cerf, "Try and Stop Me"; BT — Bob Thomas, "Hollywood"; CL — C.J. Lejeune; CS — Charles G. Sampas, "Sampascoopies"; DK — Dorothy Kilgallen, "On Broadway"; DM — Dorothy Manners; EG — Edith Gwynn; EJ — Erskine Johnson, "Short Takes"; ES — Ed Sullivan; EW — Earl Wilson; HC — Harrison Carroll, "Hollywood Notes"; HR — Harry Crocker, "Behind the Makeup"; HH — Hedda Hopper, "Looking at Hollywood"; JF — Jimmy Fidler, "News of Hollywood"; JL — Jack Lait, "Broadway and Elsewhere"; JS — Jimmy Starr; LP — Louella Parsons; KM — Ken Morgan, "Ken Morgan's Hollywood Keyhole"; PH — Paul Harrison, "Harrison on Hollywood"; RC — Robbin Coons, "Hollywood Speaks"; VV — Virginia Vale, "Star Dust"; WM — Ward Morehouse, *New York Sun* theater critic; WW — Walter Winchell, "Notes of an Innocent Bystander," "New York Heartbeat" columns

Introduction

1. Kirk Crivello, *Film Fan Monthly*, November 1973.

Chapter 1

1. Sampson, Nance, County Coordinator, unpublished history of Fairchild, WI, 1972.
2. Dept. of Commerce, U.S. Federal Census, 1910, Eau Claire County, WI, map 59, p. 4-B.
3. Dept. of Commerce, U.S. Federal Census, 1910, Ramsey County, MN, map 137, p. 10-A.
4. U.S. Military Information Records, World War I Registration Card no. 25-2-5-A, June 5, 1917.
5. Dept. of Commerce, U.S. Federal Census, 1920, Eau Claire County, WI, map 136, p. 4-B.
6. Clara Ridste, "The Heartbreaking True Story of Carole Landis," *True Story Magazine*, October, 1948.
7. Ibid.
8. Dept. of Commerce, U.S. Federal Census, 1920, Fergus County, MT, map 104, p. 7-A.
9. Dept. of Commerce, U.S. Federal Census, 1920, Lake County, IL, map 263, p. 58-B.
10. *True Story*, October 1948.
11. Ibid.
12. Ibid.

Chapter 2

1. Dept. of Commerce, U.S. Federal Census, 1930, San Bernardino County, map 77, p. 5-A.
2. All Clara Ridste quotes in Chapter 2 from *True Story*, October 1948.
3. Dept. of Commerce, U.S. Federal Census, 1930, San Bernardino County, map 106, p. 9-A.
4. Nevada Star Journal (Reno), July 16, 1925.
5. Kirk Crivello, *Fallen Angels*, p. 86.
6. Ibid., p. 86.
7. Gary Carey, *All the Stars in Heaven*, p. 146.
8. Carey, op. cit., p. 86.
9. *True Story*, October 1948.
10. *Los Angeles Examiner*, April 20, 1938.

Chapter 3

1. *Los Angeles Evening Herald Express*, November 15, 1939.
2. Kirk Crivello, *Fallen Angels*, p. 86.
3. *Time*, June 17, 1940.

Chapter 4

1. *Marion Star*, September 12, 1941.
2. RC, October 1, 1937.
3. Kirk Crivello, *Fallen Angels*, p. 87.
4. Ibid., p. 87.
5. Roland Flamini, *Thalberg*, p. 271.
6. Tornabene, Lyn, *Long Live the King*, p. 230.
7. Kirk Crivello, *Fallen Angels*, p. 87.
8. *Chronicle Telegram* (Elyria, OH), July 6, 1948.
9. JS, November 18, 1937.
10. Barney Oldfield, interview with author.
11. *Los Angeles Times*, December 31, 1937.
12. *The Hollywood Reporter*, May 7, 1938.

13. Op. cit., May 2, 1938.
14. ES, November 3, 1938.
15. Op. cit., May 20, 1938.
16. LP, May 28, 1938.
17. *Coshocton Tribune*, May 22, 1938.
18. Ibid., May 20, 1938.
19. *Edwardsville Intelligencer*, August 16, 1938.
20. SS, August 14, 1938.
21. Dennis McDougal, *The Last Mogul*, p. 81.
22. HC, November 11, 1939.
23. *Hollywood Citizen News*, April 4, 1939.
24. *Motion Picture Herald*, June 17, 1939.
25. Bernard Rosenberg, and Harry Silverstein, *The Real Tinsel*, p. 29.
26. EJ, June 17, 1939.
27. JF, November 23, 1939.
28. *Los Angeles Times*, November 1, 1939.
29. JS, November 2, 1939.
30. ES, December 4, 1939.
31. *Hollywood Citizen News*, May 17, 1940.
32. *Hollywood Preview*, April 16, 1940.
33. HC, December 11, 1939.
34. *Zanesville Signal*, January 14, 1940.
35. VV, February 8, 1940.
36. *Los Angeles Times*, December 22, 1939.
37. Andy Edmonds, *Bugsy's Baby*, p. 75.
38. Barney Oldfield, interview with author.
39. SS, July 23, 1943.

Chapter 5

1. *Los Angeles Times*, February 29, 1940.
2. *Screen Guide*, June 1940.
3. *Hollywood Citizen News*, May April 30, 1940.
4. *Los Angeles Times*, April 23, 1940.
5. LP, May 4, 1940.
6. Dept. of Commerce, U.S. Federal Census, 1930, Los Angeles County, CA, map 96, p. 13-B.
7. JF, June 6, 1940.
8. Ibid., May 26, 1940.
9. *Daily Variety*, May 26, 1940.
10. *Edwardsville Intelligencer*, May 27, 1940.
11. RC, June 28, 1940.
12. Ibid.
13. "PING," *American Magazine*, January 1941.
14. SS, November 23, 1945.
15. EJ, March 16, 1946.
16. ES, November 3, 1938.
17. *Los Angeles Examiner*, July 31, 1940.
18. *Film Daily*, August 5, 1940.
19. HC, June 3, 1940.
20. *Sunday Times Signal* (Zanesville, OH), August 4, 1940.
21. *Lima News*, July 5, 1940.
22. *Time*, July 15, 1940.
23. *Gettysburg Times*, July 5, 1940.
24. *Film Daily*, August 15, 1940.
25. *Evening Herald Express*, February 7, 1941.
26. *Film Daily*, February 20, 1941,
27. Ibid.
28. *Life*, August 19, 1940.
29. Andy Edmonds, *Hot Toddy*, p. 295.
30. *Frederick News*, December 30, 1940.
31. *Nevada State Journal*, July 20, 1945.
32. *Marion Star*, September 5, 1940.
33. *Oshkosh Daily Northwestern*, September 5, 1940.
34. *Screen Guide*, September, 1940.
35. HH, October 16, 1940.
36. HR, November 13, 1940.
37. Op. cit., September 21, 1940.
38. *Los Angeles Evening Herald Express*, November 14, 1940.
39. *Los Angeles Herald Examiner*, November 21, 1940.
40. *Los Angeles Times*, March 15, 1941.
41. JF, February 9, 1941.
42. HC, March 17, 1941.
43. *Silver Screen Magazine*, June 1941.
44. LP, January 12, 1941.
45. SS, January 1, 1942.
46. JS, February 11, 1941.
47. *Motion Picture*, May 1942.
48. PH, January 18, 1941.
49. EJ, January 31, 1941.
50. Ibid., February 19, 1941.
51. LP, November 20, 1940.
52. KM, January 10, 1941.
53. *Photoplay*, December 1940.
54. SS, January 22, 1941.
55. Budd Shulberg, Budd, *Moving Pictures: Memories of a Hollywood Prince*, from *The Grove Book of Hollywood*, Christopher Sylvester, ed., p. 211.
56. Maurice Rapf, interview with author.
57. Donald Bogle, *Dorothy Dandridge*, p. 86.
58. Leonard Mosley, *Zanuck*, p. 243.
59. LP, January 22, 1948.
60. JF, May 29, 1942.
61. Ibid., June 3, 1942
62. Rex Harrison, *Rex: An Autobiography*.
63. John Austin, *More of Hollywood's Unsolved Mysteries*, p. 109.
64. Ibid., p. 110.
65. *Silver Screen Magazine*, November 1940.
66. JF, February 15, 1941.
67. *American Magazine*, January 1941.
68. Tom McGee, *Betty Grable*, p. 68.
69. PH, February 28, 1941.
70. *Modern Screen*, March 1941.
71. *Silver Screen*, March 1941.
72. *Movie-Radio Guide*, April 19, 1941.
73. Kyle Crichton, "Carole Landis—Determined Lady," *Colliers*, May 10, 1941.
74. *Screenland*, October 1941.
75. *Photoplay*, December 1941.
76. Op. cit.
77. JF, March 11, 1941.
78. Ibid., April 8, 1941.
79. EJ, April 11, 1941.
80. Op. cit., April 17, 1941.
81. Barney Oldfield, interview with author.
82. JF, March 5, 1941.
83. *Hollywood Reporter*, March 10, 1941.
84. SS, March, 12, 1941.
85. HC, March 29, 1941.
86. Op. cit., April 11, 1941.
87. JF, March 6, 1941.
88. *Los Angeles Times*, April 4, 1941.
89. HC, March 26, 1941.
90. JF, October 23, 1941.
91. SS, April 14, 1941.
92. HC, August 25, 1941.
93. *Screenland*, February 1942.
94. Barney Oldfield, interview with author.
95. *Film Daily*, April 21, 1941.

96. *Hollywood Citizen News,* April 30, 1941.
97. JF, March 25, 1941.
98. HC, April 10, 1941.
99. *Life,* June 30, 1941.
100. *Evening Herald Express,* April 24, 1941.
101. CC, April 24, 1941.
102. *Evening Herald Express,* April 24, 1941.
103. *Movie-Radio Guide,* April 19, 1941.
104. *Hollywood Citizen News,* April 23, 1941.
105. Ibid., July 1, 1941.
106. *Film Daily,* July 9, 1941.
107. *Los Angeles Times,* May 18, 1941.
108. Ibid., June 15, 1941.
109. *Hollywood Citizen News,* June 30, 1941.
110. *Film Daily,* June 20, 1941.
111. SS, August 13, 1941.
112. Ibid., July 21, 1941.
113. Ibid., August 4, 1941.
114. HC, August 6, 1941.
115. Op. cit., August 13, 1941.
116. Tom McGee, *Betty Grable,* p. 89.
117. *Film Daily,* October 17, 1941.
118. Ibid., November 21, 1941.
119. *Boston Globe,* October 1, 1941.
120. John Kobal, *Rita Hayworth,* p. 115.
121. Ibid., p. 56.
122. Barbara Leaming, *If This Is Happiness,* p. 54.
123. John Kobal, *Rita Hayworth,* p. 115.
124. SS, January 1, 1942.
125. Barney Oldfield, interview with author.
126. Ibid.
127. *Indiana Evening Gazette* (PA), October 3, 1941.
128. *Film Daily,* January 8, 1942.

Chapter 6

1. JF, May 3, 1941.
2. *Los Angeles Times,* October 17, 1941.
3. Carole Landis, *Four Jills in a Jeep,* p. 3.
4. *Edwardsville Intelligencer,* August 27, 1941.
5. Hays Office Release, February 1941.
6. JF, September 6, 1941.
7. *Los Angeles Times,* September 22, 1941.
8. WW, September 31, 1941.
9. *Life,* October 20, 1941 and November 3, 1941.
10. Op. cit., October 13, 1941.
11. JF, December 9, 1941.
12. Ibid., August 28, 1942.
13. EJ, April 2, 1943.
14. Cari Beauchamp, *Without Lying Down,* p. 348.
15. Tichi Wilkerson, and Marcia Borie, *The Hollywood Reporter,* p. 126.
16. *Los Angeles Examiner,* December 13, 1941.
17. LP, December 12, 1941.
18. *Los Angeles Times,* December 13, 1941.
19. Ibid., December 23, 1941.
20. Barbara Leaming, *If This Is Living,* p. 68.
21. *Motion Picture Herald,* April 18, 1942.
22. Lawrence J. Quirk, *Fasten Your Seat Belts,* p. 266.
23. Ibid., p. 272.
24. *Movie Star Parade,* April 1942.
25. Betty Boone, "Inside the Star's Homes," *Screenland,* January 1942.
26. SS, July 25, 1942.
27. JF, May 9, 1942.
28. *Los Angeles Times,* March 15, 1942.
29. *True Story,* October 1948.
30. *Los Angeles Times,* November 23, 1941.
31. *Look Magazine,* December 14, 1940.
32. Carole Landis, *Four Jills in a Jeep,* p. 6.
33. *Hollywood Citizen News,* March 2, 1942.
34. Barney Oldfield, interview with author.
35. SS, March 2, 1942.
36. Ibid., April 25, 1942.
37. JF, April 15, 1942.
38. *Lethbridge Herald* (Alberta, Canada), March 31, 1942.
39. *Edwardsville Intelligencer,* April 2, 1942.
40. *Los Angeles Times,* April 1, 1942.
41. *Evening Courier* (Decatur, IL), April 3, 1942.
42. SS, March 23, 1942.
43. JF, March 21, 1942.
44. WW, "New York Heartbeat," May 26, 1942.
45. *Newark Advocate* (OH), April 24, 1942.
46. *Hollywood Citizen News,* March 2, 1942.
47. Ibid., March 27, 1942.
48. *Los Angeles Times,* January 17, 1942.
49. SS, May 8, 1942.
50. Op. cit., June 20, 1942.
51. *Hollywood Citizen News,* June 4, 1942.
52. *Los Angeles Times,* June 29, 1942.
53. *The Chillicothe Constitution Tribune,* July 6, 1942.
54. JF, July 16, 1942.
55. *Los Angeles Examiner,* July 4, 1942.
56. SS, July 7, 1942.
57. *Hollywood Citizen News,* January 26, 1942.
58. RC, August 7, 1942.
59. *Film Daily,* December 18, 1941.
60. *Hollywood Citizen News,* August 4, 1942.
61. *Los Angeles Examiner,* August 4, 1942.
62. Ibid., August 13, 1942.
63. *Los Angeles Times,* September 10, 1942.
64. SS, October 12, 1942.
65. *Edwardsville Intelligencer,* April 14, 1943.
66. Carole Landis, *Four Jills in a Jeep,* p. 14.
67. *New York Times,* October 28, 1942.
68. Op. cit., p. 9.
69. Ibid., p. 29.
70. *Chillicothe Constitution Tribune,* November 4, 1944.
71. Op. cit., p. 32.
72. Ibid., p. vii.
73. *Stars and Stripes,* Fall 1942.
74. Ibid., p. 44.
75. *Gettysburg Times,* January 6, 1943.
76. David A. Johnson, "The Pre-Eagles," *Air Force Magazine: The Journal of the Air Force Association.*
77. Carole Landis, *Four Jills in a Jeep,* p. 65.
78. *Hollywood Citizen News,* December 15, 1942.
79. *Charleston Daily Mail,* November 29, 1942.
80. *Evening Herald Examiner,* December 15, 1942.
81. LP, January 18, 1943.
82. *Newark Advocate,* December 23, 1942.
83. *Coshocton Tribune,* January 9, 1944.
84. HC, January 18, 1943.
85. *Marion Star,* January 9, 1943.
86. Carole Landis, *Four Jills in a Jeep,* p. 126.
87. Jack Benny, *Sunday Nights at Seven,* p. 153.
88. *Lethbridge Herald* (Alberta, Canada), September 26, 1944.
89. EW, July 18, 1948.
90. Carole Landis, *Four Jills in a Jeep,* p. 75.

91. *Frederick News*, January 20, 1943.
92. *Soda Springs Sun*, February 17, 1944.
93. Ibid., January 16, 1943.
94. *Lethbridge Herald*, January 16, 1943.
95. *Los Angeles Times*, February 27, 1943.
96. Carole Landis, *Four Jills in a Jeep*, p. 158.
97. *Lethbridge Herald*, January 28, 1943.
98. Op. cit., p. 94.
99. LP, February 5, 1943.
100. *Edwardsville Intelligencer*, March 6, 1943.
101. *Los Angeles Times*, February 23, 1943.
102. *Screen Guides*, June 1943.
103. Ernie Pyle, *Senior Scholastic Magazine*, March 29, 1943.
104. LP, February 18, 1943.

Chapter 7

1. *Marion Star*, March 6, 1943.
2. *Los Angeles Times*, March 8, 1943.
3. LP, March 10, 1943.
4. *Screenland*, July, 1943.
5. HC, March 19, 1943.
6. Earl Wilson, *I Am Gazing Into My 8-Ball*, p. 36.
7. Executive Sessions of the Senate Permanent Subcommittee on Investigations of the Committee on Government Operations, Committee of Government Affairs, Joseph R. McCarthy, Chairman, March 25, 1954, Testimony of Edwin Seaver, p. 999.
8. *Los Angeles Herald*, March 21, 1943.
9. *Los Angeles Times*, March 21, 1943.
10. Ibid., April 2 and 3, 1943.
11. HC, November 10, 1943.
12. Ibid., March 10, 1943.
13. Ibid., April 4, 1943.
14. *Daily News*, May 21, 1943.
15. HC, May 19, 1943.
16. *Zanesville Signal*, May 30, 1943.
17. *Clearfield Progress*, July 3, 1943.
18. EJ, March 13, 1943.
19. Darrel Carnell, correspondence with author.
20. Stanley Frankel, *Frankel-y Speaking*, Ch. 6.
21. *Sunday Times Signal*, October 8, 1944.
22. *Los Angeles Times*, June 27, 1943.
23. *Life*, February 1, 1943.
24. *Screen Guide*, January 1943.
25. *Look*, June 29, 1943.
26. *Women's Home Companion*, July 1943.
27. HC, June 22, 1943.
28. *Evening Herald Examiner*, July 16, 1943.
29. *Los Angeles Times*, July 16, 1943.
30. LP, July 23, 1943.
31. *Hollywood Citizen News*, July 27, 1943.
32. Ibid., July 29, 1943.
33. *New York Times*, August 28, 1943.
34. HC, September 11, 1943.
35. LP, September 11, 1943.
36. *Troy Record*, September 10, 1943.
37. *New York Daily News*, September 21, 1943.
38. *New York Times*, September 22, 1943.
39. LP, September 24, 1943.
40. HC, December 15, 1943.
41. *Edwardsville Intelligencer*, September 23, 1943.
42. EJ, December 8, 1943.
43. *Coshocton Tribune*, January 9, 1944.
44. PH, December 10, 1943.
45. *Los Angeles Evening Tribune*, January 10, 1944.
46. *Film Daily*, March 17, 1944.
47. *Hollywood Citizen News*, May 5, 1944.
48. EJ, January 27, 1946.
49. Barney Oldfield, interview with author.
50. *Los Angeles Times*, November 26, 1943.
51. *Edwardsville Intelligencer*, December 20, 1943.
52. *Daily Kennebec Journal*, October 10, 1944.
53. *Zanesville Signal*, December 26, 1943.
54. *New York Times*, December 25, 1944.
55. *Screen Guide Magazine*, December 1943.
56. EJ, March 10, 1944.
57. *New York Times*, June 6, 1944.
58. Ibid., January 7, 1944.
59. *Los Angeles Times*, January 7, 1944.
60. *New York Daily News*, January 10, 1944.
61. Op. cit., January 15, 1944.
62. SS, February 2, 1944.
63. *The Hollywood Reporter*, January 26, 1944.
64. *Movies*, January 1944.
65. *Los Angeles Herald Examiner*, February 23, 1944.
66. *Los Angeles Times*, March 18, 1944.
67. *American Magazine*, March 1944.
68. EJ, May 18, 1944.
69. *Nevada State Journal*, July 25, 1945.
70. DM, April 30, 1944.
71. HC, June 29, 1944.
72. *Life*, June 26, 1944.
73. *Sunday Times Signal*, April 8, 1944.
74. LP, July 6, 1944.
75. *Dixon Evening Telegraph*, August 12, 1944.
76. Irving I. Fein, *Jack Benny*, p. 92.
77. *Wisconsin Rapids Daily Tribune*, July 14, 1944.
78. Barry Ralph, correspondence with author.
79. *Clearfield Progress*, November 17, 1944.
80. *Nevada State Journal*, July 22, 1945.
81. Jack Benny, *Sunday Nights at Seven*, p. 157.
82. LP, July 21, 1945.
83. Mary Livingston Benny, *Jack Benny*, p. 159.
84. "A Bouquet for Carole," *New York Times*, September 16, 1945.
85. Wiley O. Woods, Jr., *Legacy of the 90th Bombardment Group*, p. 129.
86. Bill Starke, letter to author.
87. *Los Angeles Times*, August 30, 1944.
88. Letter, Edgar Rice Burroughs to Jane Burroughs, courtesy ERB, Inc.
89. Fred Hohmann, correspondence to "Australia at War" website.
90. HC, September 21, 1944.
91. Copied from *Ladies' Home Journal*, August 1944.
92. Library of Congress, *The Evening Star* (Washington, D.C.), September 14, 1943.
93. *MAST*, November 1944.

Chapter 8

1. *True Story*, August 1948.
2. *Los Angeles Times*, October 1, 1944.
3. *Photoplay*, November 1945.
4. WW, October 12, 1944.
5. Ibid., January 31, 1945.
6. Ibid., January 15, 1945.
7. Ibid., January 14, 1945.
8. Tom Bowerman, letter to author.
9. All Ch. 7 stories detailing relationship between Carole and Jacqueline Susann are from Barbara Seaman, *Lovely Me*.

10. Jacqueline Susann, *Valley of the Dolls,* p. 00?
11. U.S. Federal Census, Lewiston County, MT, 1930, p. 4-B.
12. WW, May 8, 1952.
13. Wilson, Earl, *I Am Gazing Into My 8-Ball,* p. 33.
14. SS, January 8, 1945.
15. *Hollywood Citizen News,* February 1, 1945.
16. *New York Times,* March 20, 1945.
17. EJ, June 4, 1945.
18. DK, August 28, 1945.
19. HC, May 3, 1945.
20. *Los Angeles Times,* May 4, 1945.
21. SS, August 6, 1945.
22. JS, May 23, 1945.
23. *Herald Press,* May 26, 1945.
24. *Hollywood Reporter,* May 28, 1945.
25. *Los Angeles Times,* June 9, 1945.
26. *Dixon Evening Telegraph,* July 20, 1945.
27. *Los Angeles Times,* July 21, 1945.
28. LP, July 20, 1945.
29. *Dixon Evening Telegraph,* July, 24, 1945.
30. EJ, August 28, 1945.
31. *New York Times,* August 15, 1945.
32. LP, August 24, 1945.
33. JS, September 13, 1945.
34. JF, August 11, 1945.
35. *Nevada State Journal,* August 3, 1945.
36. WW, August 4, 1945.
37. DK, August 16, 1945.
38. DM, September 12, 1945.
39. DK, August 24, 1945.
40. LP, August 27, 1947.
41. *Silver Screen,* September 1947.
42. JS, October 4, 1945.
43. FM, October 11, 1945.
44. HC, October 25, 1945.
45. Ibid., December 3, 1945.
46. EJ, December 3, 1945.
47. *Hollywood Citizen News,* October 9, 1945.
48. Op. cit., February 4, 1946.
49. HC, November 24, 1945.
50. *Traverse City Record Eagle,* November 17, 1945.
51. *Daily Review,* November 15, 1945.
52. *Zanesville Signal,* November 15, 1945.
53. *Edwardsville Intelligencer,* November 15, 1945.
54. Op. cit., November 18, 1945.
55. *Lethbridge Herald,* November 19, 1945.
56. LP, October 13, 1945.
57. *Hollywood Citizen News,* November 9, 1945.
58. *Life,* January 7, 1946.
59. DK, December 10, 1945.
60. *Herald Press,* December 11, 1945.
61. LP, December 10, 1945.
62. JF, December 30, 1945.
63. *Traverse City Record Eagle,* February 20, 1946.
64. Ibid., April 25, 1947.
65. JL, August 9, 1945.
66. *Los Angeles Herald,* December 25, 1945.
67. BT, February 15, 1946.
68. JF, June 4, 1946.
69. A stratoliner was an early version of today's mobile camper homes.
70. BT, February 15, 1946.
71. Jeffrey Meyers, *Bogart,* p. 260.
72. HC, March 21, 1946.
73. *Silver Screen,* May 1946.
74. *Screenland,* May 1946.
75. GH, May 16, 1946.
76. *Silver Screen,* July 1946.
77. *Los Angeles Evening Herald Express,* July 17, 1946.
78. *Dixon Telegraph,* October 23, 1946.
79. SG, October 26, 1946.
80. The 1946 "kitten" story was referred to many times, the last of which was WW, July 15, 1948.
81. Barbara Leaming, *Rita Hayworth,* p. 239.
82. DK, December 26, 1946.

Chapter 9

1. JF, January 2, 1947.
2. *Mansfield News Journal,* January 6, 1947.
3. WW, May 18, 1948.
4. BC, January 10, 1947.
5. DK, January 14, 1947.
6. Ibid., February 1, 1947.
7. Ibid., January 18, 1947.
8. BT, January 23, 1947.
9. Lewis Yablonski, *George Raft,* p. 187.
10. Andy Edmonds, *Bugsy's Baby,* p. 83.
11. SG, February 5, 1947.
12. WW, February 12, 1947.
13. Ibid., February 15, 1947.
14. SS, March 5, 1947.
15. *Liberty,* July 19, 1947.
16. CL, September 27, 1947.
17. Alexander Walker, *Fatal Charm,* p. 55.
18. *Screen Guide,* December 1947.
19. *Reno Evening Gazette,* March 10, 1948.
20. Donald Bogle, *Dorothy Dandridge,* p. 115.
21. HH, April 28, 1948.
22. LP, January 22, 1948.
23. Alexander Walker, *Fatal Charm,* p. 141.
24. Ibid., p. 141.
25. LP, February 7, 1948.
26. DK, December 13, 1947.
27. *Dixon Telegraph,* March 12, 1948.
28. *Reno Evening Gazette,* March 10, 1948.
29. EW, April 24, 1948.
30. *Hollywood Reporter,* March 15, 1948.
31. SS, March 22, 1948.
32. Alexander Walker, *Fatal Charm,* p. 142.
33. DK, March 29, 1948.
34. EJ, April 8, 1948.
35. LP, May 13, 1948.
36. Ibid., June 17, 1948.
37. Ibid., May 14, 1948.
38. DK, May 26, 1948.
39. EJ, June 17, 1948.
40. LP, May 15, 1948.
41. WW, May 28, 1948.
42. Ibid., June 14, 1948.
43. Alexander Walker, *Fatal Charm,* p. 143.
44. Harrison conversation with Arthur Barbosa, quoted from Walker.
45. Carole and Harrison conversations with Arthur Barbosa, quoted from Walker.

Chapter 10

1. *Los Angeles Times,* July 9, 1948.
2. *Oxnard Press Courier,* July 6, 1948.
3. Alexander Walker, *Fatal Charm,* p. 145.
4. Ibid., p. 146.
5. *Chronicle Telegram,* July 8, 1948.

6. Op. cit., p. 146.
7. *Los Angeles Examiner*, July 7, 1948.
8. Rex Harrison, *Rex*, p. 206.
9. Alexander Walker, *Fatal Charm*, p. 151.
10. *Los Angeles Examiner*, July 6, 1948.
11. *Clearfield Progress*, July 6, 1948.
12. *Oxnard Press Courier*, July 6, 1948.
13. Op. cit., July 6, 1948.
14. *Chronicle Telegram*, July 8, 1948.
15. *Oxnard Press Courier*, July 6, 1948.
16. Op. cit.
17. *Independent Record*, July 6, 1948.
18. *Nashua Telegraph*, July 6, 1948.
19. *Los Angeles Time*, July 7, 1948.
20. *Mount Pleasant News*, July 8, 1948.
21. *Evening Herald Examiner*, July 6, 1948.
22. *Los Angeles Examiner*, July 7, 1948.
23. Alexander Walker, *Fatal Charm*, p. 152.
24. *Indiana Evening Gazette*, July 7, 1948.
25. *Traverse City Record Eagle*, July 6, 1948.
26. *Los Angeles Herald*, July 5, 1948.
27. *Springfield Daily News*, July 5, 1948.
28. *Bridgeport Telegram*, July 5, 1948.
29. *Time*, July 19, 1948.
30. Ibid.
31. *Chronicle Telegram*, July 8, 1948.
32. *Los Angeles Herald Tribune*, July 8, 1948.
33. *Daily Register*, July 6, 1948.
34. *Los Angeles Examiner*, July 7, 1948.
35. Ibid.
36. *Chronicle Telegram*, July 6, 1948.
37. *Independent Record*, July 8, 1948.
38. Register-Recorder County Clerk, County of Los Angeles, Death Certificate no. 11686, filed July 13, 1948.
39. *Chronicle Telegram*, July 8, 1948.
40. WW, July 12, 1948.
41. Alexander Walker, *Fatal Charm*, p. 157.
42. Lilli Palmer, *Change Lobsters and Dance*, p. 179.
43. *Clearfield Progress*, July 9, 1948.
44. *Los Angeles Times*, July 8, 1948.
45. *Los Angeles Examiner*, July 6, 1948.
46. *Indiana Evening Gazette*, July 7, 1948.
47. *Los Angeles Herald Tribune*, July 7, 1948.
48. *Independent Record*, July 8, 1948.
49. *Los Angeles Herald Examiner*, July 9, 1948.
50. All Harrison inquest testimony from the *Los Angeles Examiner*, July 9, 1948.
51. *Los Angeles Examiner*, July 9, 1948.
52. *Los Angeles Daily News*, July 9, 1948.
53. *Los Angeles Times*, July 9, 1948.
54. DK, July 24, 1948.
55. *Mount Pleasant News*, July 8, 1948.
56. *Dixon Evening Telegraph*, July 8, 1948.
57. Digby Diehl, *Esther Williams*, p. 165.
58. *Hollywood Reporter*, August 1948.
59. Last Will and Testament of Carole Landis Wallace, June 22, 1944, probate no. 284466
60. *Mount Pleasant News*, July 8, 1948.
61. *Waterloo Daily Courier*, July 11, 1948.
62. Digby Diehl, *Esther Williams*, p. 165.
63. *Waterloo Daily Courier*, July 11, 1948.
64. Ibid., July 11, 1948.
65. Roland Culver, *Not Quite a Gentleman*, quoted from Walker.
66. *Portland Press Herald*, July 11, 1948.
67. *Mansfield News Journal*, July 11, 1948.
68. *Oxnard Press Courier*, July 9, 1948.
69. Last Will and Testament of Carole Landis Wallace, probate no. 284436.
70. *Mansfield News Journal*, July 12, 1948.
71. Ibid., July 14, 1948.
72. *Indiana Evening Democrat*, July 14, 1948.
73. Op. cit., July 20, 1948.
74. DK, April 24, 1948.
75. *Indiana Evening Democrat*, July 19, 1948.
76. *Dixon Evening Telegraph*, March 21, 1949.
77. WW, January 23, 1949.
78. Ibid., July 13, 1948.
79. Ibid., July 15, 1948.
80. *Nashua Telegraph*, July 17, 1948.
81. *Oxnard Press Courier*, July 10, 1948.
82. Ibid., June 27, 1950.
83. *Dixon Evening Telegraph*, July 8, 1948.
84. *Chronicle Telegram*, July 6, 1948.
85. *Picturegoer*, August 14, 1948.
86. *American Weekly*, September 19, 1948.
87. *Motion Picture*, October 1948.
88. *Dixon Evening Telegraph*, July 7, 1948.
89. *Indiana Evening Democrat*, July 8, 1948.
90. *Los Angeles Times*, July 5, 1948.
91. *Dixon Evening Telegraph*, July 7, 1948.
92. SS, July 5, 1948.
93. *Los Angeles Examiner*, July 7, 1948.
94. The 1946 "kitten" story was referred to many times, the last of which was WW, July 15, 1948.
95. PH, October 4, 1941.
96. *Portland Press Herald*, July 7, 1948.
97. *Dixon Evening Telegraph*, July 8, 1948.
98. *Chronicle Telegram*, July 6, 1948.
99. *Dixon Evening Telegraph*, July 7, 1948.
100. *Los Angeles Times*, July 7, 1948.

Epilogue

1. DK, October 22, 1949.
2. LP, March 1, 1955.
3. Rachel Roberts, *No Bells on Sunday: The Rachel Roberts Journals*, Alexander Walker, ed., p. 256.
4. EW, July 2, 1953.
5. Op. cit., August 2, 1948.
6. EW, January 11, 1949.
7. DK, January 31, 1949.
8. EJ, March 26, 1950.
9. EW, November 14, 1949.
10. EW, November 10, 1950.
11. WW, February 4, 1951.
12. DK, April 11, 1952.
13. EW, February 23, 1953.
14. EW, March 7, 1953.
15. DK, July 6, 1953.
16. WW, October 11, 1953.
17. EW, December 22, 1953.
18. WE, February 6, 1955.
19. EW, November 6, 1955.
20. Elsi Maki, secretary to Mrs. Schmidlapp, interview with author.
21. BT, December 27, 1948.
22. CS, October 6, 1954.
23. JF, October 18, 1955.

Selected Bibliography

Public, Legal and Government Records

1920 Census, Illinois, Lake, Glenview, map 263.
1930 Census, Montana, Fergus, District 84, map 104.
1930 Census, Wisconsin, Eau Claire, Fairchild, map 135.
1920 Census, Wisconsin, Eau Claire, Fairchild, map 136.
1930 Census, California, San Bernardino, San Bernardino, map 77.
1930 Census, California, San Bernardino, San Bernardino, map 106.
1930 Census, California, Los Angeles, Los Angeles, map 96.
Register-Recorder County Clerk, County of Los Angeles, Death Certificate no. 11686, Carole Landis Schmidlapp, filed July 13, 1948.
Executive Sessions of the Senate Permanent Subcommittee on Investigations of the Committee on Government Operations, Committee of Government Affairs, Joseph R. McCarthy, Chairman, March 25, 1954, Testimony of Edwin Seaver, p. 999.
United States Naval Chronology, World War II, Naval History Division, GPO, Washington, D.C., 1955, Pacific Counterblow, the 11th Bombardment Group and the 67th Fighter Squadron in the Battle for Guadalcanal.

Books

Allyson, June, with Frances Spatz Leighton, *June Allyson*. New York: G.P. Putnam's Sons, 1982.
Altman, Diana. *Hollywood East: Louis B. Mayer and the Origins of the Studio System*. New York: Birch Lane Press, Carol,1992.
Anger, Kenneth. *Hollywood Babylon*. San Francisco: Straight Arrow Books, dist. by Simon & Schuster, 1975.
_____. *Kenneth Anger's Hollywood Babylon II*. New York: E.P. Dutton, 1984.
Arce, Hector. *Gary Cooper: An Intimate Biography*. New York: William Morrow, 1979.
_____. *The Secret Life of Tyrone Power*. New York: William Morrow, 1979.
Astor, Mary. *My Story*. New York: Doubleday, 1959.
Austin, John. *Hollywood's Greatest Mysteries*. New York: Shapolsky, 1993.
_____. *Hollywood's Unsolved Mysteries*. New York: Shapolsky, 1990.
_____. *More of Hollywood's Unsolved Mysteries*. New York: Shapolsky, 1991.
Bacon, James. *Hollywood Is a Four-Letter Word*. New York: Avon Books, 1977.
_____. *Made in Hollywood*. Chicago: Contemporary Books, 1977.
Baxter, John. *Hollywood in the 30's*. New York: A.S. Barnes, 1968.
Beaton, Cecil. *Memoirs of the '40s*. New York: McGraw Hill, 1972.
_____. *The Years Between*. London: Weidenfeld & Nicolson, 1965.
Beauchamp, Cari. *Without Lying Down: Francis Marion and the Powerful Women of Early Hollywood*. New York: Scribner, 1997.
Behlmer, Rudy. *Inside Warners Bros. (1935–1951)*. New York: Viking Penguin, 1985.
_____. *Memo from David O. Selznick*. New York: Viking, 1972.
Benny, Jack, and Joan Benny. *Sunday Nights at Seven: The Jack Benny Story*. New York: Warner Books, 1990.
Benny, Mary Livingstone, and Hilliard Marks, with Marcia Borie. *Jack Benny*. Garden City, NJ: Doubleday, 1978.

Berg, A. Scott. *Goldwyn: A Biography*. New York: Knopf, 1989.
Billman, Larry. *Betty Grable: A Bio-bibliography*. Westport, CT: Greenwood Press, 1993.
Blum, Daniel. *A Pictorial History of the Talkies*. New York: Putnam, 1973.
Bogdanovich, Peter. *Allen Dwan: The Last Pioneer*. New York: Praeger, 1971.
Bogle, Donald. *Dorothy Dandridge: A Biography*. New York: Amistad, 1997.
Bosworth, Patricia. *Montgomery Clift: A Biography*. New York: Harcourt Brace Javonovich, 1978.
Brownlow, Kevin. *Hollywood: The Pioneers*. New York: Knopf, 1980.
_____. *The Parade's Gone By*. New York: Knopf, 1968.
Calvet, Corinne. *Has Corinne Been a Good Girl?* New York: St. Martin's Press, 1983.
Capra, Frank. *The Name Above the Title: An Autobiography*. New York: Macmillan, 1971.
Carey, Gary. *All the Stars in Heaven*. New York: E.P. Dutton, 1981.
Carpozi, George. *The Gary Cooper Story*. New Rochelle, NY: Macmillan, 1971.
Chaneles, Sol, and Albert Wolsky. *The Movie Makers*. Secaucus, NJ: Derbibooks, 1974.
Conner, Floyd. *Lupe Velez and Her Lovers*. New York: Barricade Books, 1993.
Connors, Martin, ed. *Video Hound's Golden Movie Retriever*. Detroit: Visible Ink Press (a division of Gale Research), 1991.
Coward, Noël. *The Noël Coward Diaries*. Graham Payn and Sheridan Morley, eds. Boston: Little, Brown, 1992.
Crawford, Christina. *Mommie Dearest*. New York: William Morrow, 1978.
Crawford, Joan. *My Way of Life*. New York: Simon and Schuster, 1971.
_____, with Jane Ardmore. *A Portrait of Joan*. Garden City, NJ: Doubleday, 1962.
Crivello, Kirk. *Fallen Angels: The Lives and Untimely Deaths of 14 Hollywood Beauties*. Secausus, NJ: Citadel Press, 1988.
Crowther, Bosley. *Hollywood Rajah: The Life and Times of Louis B. Mayer*. New York: Henry Holt, 1960.
_____. *The Lion's Share: The Story of an Entertainment Empire*. New York: Dutton, 1957.
Croy, Homer. *Starmaker: The Story of D.W. Griffith*. New York: Duell, Sloan & Pearce, 1959.
Culver, Roland. *Not Quite a Gentleman*. London: William Kimber, 1979.
Davis, Bette. *The Lonely Life*. New York: Lancer Books, 1963.
_____, with Michael Herskowitz. *This N' That*. New York: Putnam Books, 1987.
DeMille, Cecil B. *The Autobiography of Cecil B. DeMille*. Englewood Cliffs, NJ: Prentice-Hall, 1959.
Diehl, Digby. *Esther Williams: The Million Dollar Mermaid*. New York: Simon & Schuster, 1999.
Donaldson, Norman, and Betty Donaldson. *How Did They Die?* New York: St. Martins Press, 1980.
Dunne, Dominick. *Fatal Charms and Other Tales of Today*. New York: Bantam Books, 1987.
Dunning, John. *Tune in Yesterday*. Englewood Cliffs, NJ: Prentice-Hall, 1976.
Eames, John Douglas. *The M-G-M Story*. New York: Crown, 1971.
Eels, George. *Hedda and Louella*. New York: Putnam, 1976.
Everson, William K. *The Films of Hal Roach*. New York: Museum of Modern Art, 1971.
Eyles, Allen. *Rex Harrison*. London: W.H. Allen, 1985.
Eyman, Scott. *Ernst Lubitsch: Laughter in Paradise*. New York: Simon and Schuster, 1993.
Fairbanks, Douglas Jr. *The Salad Days*. New York: Doubleday, 1988.
Farber, Stephen, and Marc Green. *Hollywood Dynasties*. New York: Delilah Books, 1984.
Fein, Irving A. *Jack Benny: An Intimate Biography*. New York: G.P. Putnam's Sons, 1976.
Feinman, Jeffrey. *Hollywood Confidential*. New York: Playboy Books, 1976.
Finch, Christopher, and Linda Rozencrantz. *Gone Hollywood: The Movie Colony in the Golden Age*. New York: Doubleday, 1979.
Finler, Joel W. *The Hollywood Story*. New York: Crown, 1988.
Flamini, Roland. *Thalberg: The Last Tycoon and the World of MGM*. New York: Crown, 1994.
Flynn, Errol. *My Wicked, Wicked Ways*. New York: Putnam, 1959.
Fowler, Will. *Reporters: Memoirs of a Young Newspaperman*. Malibu: Roundtable, 1991.
Frankel, Stanley, A. *Frankel-y Speaking About World War II in the South Pacific*. Stanley A. Frankel, 1992.
Freedland, Michael. *The Two Lives of Errol Flynn*, New York: William Morrow, 1979
_____. *The Warner Brothers*. New York: St. Martin's Press, 1983.
Garceau, Jean. *The Biography of Clark Gable*. New York: Little, Brown, 1961.
Giesler, Jerry. *The Jerry Giesler Story*. New York: Simon and Schuster, 1960.
Golden, Eve. *Platinum Girl: The Life and Legend of Jean Harlow*. New York: Abbeville Press, 1991.
Goodman, Ezra. *The Fifty Year Decline and Fall of Hollywood*. New York: Simon and Schuster, 1961.
Graham, Shiela. *Confessions of a Hollywood Columnist*. New York: Bantam Books, 1970.
_____. *Hollywood Revisited*. New York: St. Martin's Press, 1984.
Griffith, Richard, and Arthur Mayer. *Movies: The Sixty-Year History of the World of Hollywood*. New York: Bonanza Books, 1957.

Selected Bibliography

Guiles, Fred Lawrence. *Hanging on in Paradise.* New York: McGraw-Hill, 1975.
_____. *Tyrone Power: The Last Idol.* New York: Berkeley, 1979.
Gussow, Mel. *Don't Say Yes until I Finish Talking: A Biography of Darryl F. Zanuck.* Garden City, NY: Doubleday, 1971.
Hadleigh, Boze. *Celebrity Feuds.* Dallas: Taylor, 1999.
_____. *Hollywood Babble-On: Stars Gossip About Other Stars,* Secaucus, NJ: Carol, 1994.
_____. *Hollywood Lesbians.* New York: Barricade Books, 1994.
Halliwell, Leslie. *The Filmgoer's Book of Quotes.* New York: Signet, 1975.
_____. *The Filmgoer's Companion.* Fourth edition. New York: Hill & Wang, 1974.
Harris, Marlys J. *The Zanucks of Hollywood.* New York: Crown, 1989.
Harris, Warren G. *Gable and Lombard.* New York: Simon and Schuster, 1974.
Harrison, Rex. *A Damned Serious Business.* New York: Bantam, 1989.
_____. *Rex: An Autobiography.* New York: William Morris, 1975.
Haver, Ronald. *David O. Selznick's Hollywood.* New York: Knopf, 1980.
Heimann, Jim. *Out with the Stars: Hollywood Nightlife in the Golden Era.* New York: Abbeville Press, 1985.
Henderson, Robert M. *D.W. Griffith: His Life and Work.* New York: Ferrar, Straus & Giroux, 1972.
Higham, Charles. *Errol Flynn: The Untold Story.* New York: Macmillan, 1980.
_____, and Roy Moseley. *Cary Grant: The Lonely Heart.* New York: Harcourt Brace Jovanovich, 1989.
_____. *Hollywood at Sunset.* New York: Saturday Review Press, 1972.
_____, and Joel Greenberg, eds. *Hollywood in the 40's.* New York: Paperback Library, 1970.
_____. *Merchant of Dreams: Louis B. Mayer and the Secret Hollywood.* New York: Donald I. Fine, 1993.
_____. *Warner's Brothers.* New York: Scribner's, 1975.
Hirschhorn, Clive. *The Warner Brothers Story.* New York: Crown, 1979.
Hopper, Hedda. *From Under the Hat.* Garden City, NJ: Doubleday, 1952.
Hyams, Joe. *Bogie: The Humphrey Bogart Story.* New York: The New American Library, 1962.
Kanin, Garson. *Hollywood.* New York: Viking Press, 1967.
Katz, Ephraim. *The Film Encyclopedia.* New York: Thomas Y. Crowell, 1979.
Kobler, John. *Damned in Paradise: The Life of John Barrymore.* New York: Atheneum, 1977.
Keats, John. *Howard Hughes.* New York: Random House, 1966.
Keylin, Arlene, and Suri Fleischer, eds. *Hollywood Album: Lives and Deaths of Hollywood Stars from the Pages of* The New York Times. New York: Arno Press, 1979.
_____. *Hollywood Album 2: Lives and Deaths of Hollywood Stars from the Pages of* The New York Times. New York: Arno Press, 1979.
Kobal, John. *People Will Talk.* New York: Knopf, 1986.
_____. *Rita Hayworth: The Time, The Place, The Woman.* New York: W.W. Norton, 1977.
Lambert, Gavin. *The Making of Gone with the Wind.* Boston: Little, Brown, 1974.
_____. *Norma Shearer.* New York: Knopf, 1990.
Landis, Carole. *Four Jills in a Jeep.* Cleveland: World, 1944.
Langman, Larry. *Encyclopedia of American Film Comedy.* Garland Reference Library of the Humanities, vol. 744. New York: Garland, 1987.
Lasky, Betty. *RKO: The Biggest Little Major of Them All.* Englewood Cliffs, NJ: Prentice-Hall, 1984.
Lasky, Jesse L. *I Blow My Own Horn.* Garden City, NJ: Doubleday, 1957.
_____. *Whatever Happened to Hollywood?* New York: Funk & Wagnall, 1975.
Leaming, Barbara. *If This Was Happiness: The Biography of Rita Hayworth.* New York: Viking, 1989.
Levin, Martin. *Hollywood and the Great Fan Magazines.* New York: Harrison House, 1970.
Lewis, Arthur H. *It Was Fun While It Lasted: A Lament for the Hollywood That Was.* New York: Trident Press, 1973.
Loos, Anita. *Cast of Thousands.* New York: Viking, 1977.
_____. *Kiss Hollywood Good-bye.* New York: Grosset and Dunlap, 1975.
Madsen, Alex. *The Sewing Circle: Female Stars Who Loved Other Women.* New York: Birch Lane Press, Carol Publishing Group, 1995.
Maltin, Leonard. *Leonard Maltin's Movie & Video Guide.* New York: Signet Books, published by Penguin Group, 1993, etc.
Mann, William J. *Wisecracker: The Life and Times of William Haines, Hollywood's First Openly Gay Star.* New York: Viking, 1998.
Martin, Mart. *Did She or Didn't She?* New York: Citadel Press, 1996.
Marx, Samuel. *Mayer and Thalberg, The Make-Believe Saints.* New York: Random House, 1975.
_____, and Joyce Venderveen. *Deadly Illusions: Jean Harlow and the Murder of Paul Bern.* New York: Random House, 1990.
Mast, Gerald. *A Short History of the Movies.* New York: Macmillan, 1992.

McClellan, Diana. *The Girls: Sappho Goes to Hollywood*. New York: St. Martin's Griffin, 2000.
McGee, Michael. *Betty Grable: The Girl With the Million Dollar Legs*. New York: Vestal Press, 1995.
Meyers, Jeffrey. *Bogart: A Life in Hollywood*. New York: Fromm, 1997.
Miller, Don. *"B" Movies: An Informal Survey of the American Low-Budget Film 1933–1945*. New York: Curtis Books, 1973.
Mordden, Ethan. *Movie Star: A Look at the Women Who Made Hollywood*. New York: St. Martin's Press, 1983.
Morello, Joe, and Edward Z. Epstein. *Gable and Lombard and Powell and Harlow*. New York: Dell, 1975.
_____. *The "IT" Girl: The Incredible Story of Clara Bow*. New York: Delacorte Press, 1976.
_____. *Lana: The Public and Private Lives of Miss Turner*. New York: Dell, 1971.
Mosely, Roy, with Phillip Masheter, and Rex Martin. *Rex Harrison: A Biography*. New York: St. Martin's Press, 1987.
Mosley, Leonard. *Zanuck: The Rise and Fall of Hollywood's Last Tycoon*. New York: Little, Brown, 1984.
Niven, David. *Bring on the Empty Horses*. New York: Putnam, 1975.
_____. *The Moon's a Balloon*. New York: Putnam, 1982.
Palmer, Lilli. *Change Lobsters — and Dance*. New York: Macmillan, 1975.
_____. *The Red Raven*. London: W.H. Allen, 1976.
Parrish, James Robert, and Don E. Stanke. *The Glamour Girls*. New Rochelle, NY: Arlington House, 1975.
Parrish, James Robert, with Ronald L. Bowers. *The MGM Stock Company: The Golden Era*. New Rochelle, NY: Arlington House, 1973.
Parsons, Louella. *The Gay Illiterate*. New York: Doubleday, 1944.
_____. *Tell It to Louella*. New York: Putnam, 1961.
Ragan, David. *Who's Who in Hollywood: 1900–1976*. New Rochelle, NY: Arlington House, 1976, 1977.
Ramsaye, Terry, ed. *1936-37 International Motion Picture Almanac*. New York: Quigley, 1936.
_____, ed. *1944-45 International Motion Picture Almanac*. New York: Quigley, 1945.
_____, ed. *1947-48 International Motion Picture Almanac*. New York: Quigley, 1947.
Robinson, David. *Hollywood in the Twenties*. London/New York: Zwemmer/Barnes, 1968.
Rosenberg, Bernard, and Harry Silverstein. *The Real Tinsel*. New York: Macmillan, 1970.
Rubin, Martin. *Showstoppers: Busby Berkeley and the Tradition of the Spectacle*. New York: Columbia University Press, 1993.
Ruuth, Marianne. *Cruel City: The Dark Side of Hollywood's Rich and Famous*. Malibu: Roundtable, 1984.
St. Johns, Adela Rogers. *Love, Laughter and Tears: My Hollywood Story*. New York: Doubleday, 1978.
Schessler, Ken. *This Is Hollywood: An Unusual Movie Guide*. 10th ed., 11th ed. Redlands, CA: Ken Schessler, 1992, 1993.
Schickel, Richard. *D.W. Griffith: An American Life*. New York: Simon and Schuster, 1984.
Schulberg, Budd. *Moving Pictures: Memoirs of a Hollywood Prince*. Briarcliff Manor, NY: Stein & Day, 1981.
Seaman, Barbara. *Lovely Me*. New York: William Morrow, 1987.
Selznick, David O. *Memo from David O. Selznick*. Rudy Behlmer, ed. New York: Viking, 1972.
Selznick, Irene Mayer. *A Private View*. New York: Knopf, 1983.
Sennett, Mack, and Cameron Shipp. *King of Comedy*. Garden City, NYL Doubleday, 1954.
Sennett, Robert, S. *Hollywood Hoopla: Creating Stars and Selling Movies in the Golden Age of Hollywood*. New York: Billboard Books, 1988.
Shuster, Mel, comp. *Motion Picture Performers*. Metuchen, NJ: Scarecrow Press, 1971.
Sinclair, Andrew. *John Ford: A Biography*. New York: Dial, 1979.
Spada, James. *More Than a Woman: An Intimate Biography of Bette Davis*. New York: Bantam, 1993.
Spoto, Donald. *Blue Angel*. New York: Doubleday, 1992.
Springer, John, and Jack Hamilton. *They Had Faces Then: Super Stars, Stars, and Starlets of the 1930's*. Secaucus, NJ: Citadel Press, 1974.
Stenn, David. *Bombshell: The Life and Death of Jean Harlow*. New York: Doubleday, 1993.
_____. *Clara Bow: Runnin' Wild*. New York: Doubleday, 1991.
Swindell, Larry. *Gary Cooper: The Last Hero*. Garden City, NY: Doubleday, 1980.
_____. *Screwball: The Life of Carole Lombard*. New York: William Morrow, 1975.
_____. *Spencer Tracy*. New York: World, 1969.
Symons, Mitchell. *The Celebrity Sex Lists Book*. London: Andre Deutsch, 2002.
Thomas, Bob. *King Cohn: The Life and Times of Harry Cohn*. New York: G.P. Putnam, 1967.
_____. *Thalberg: Life and Legend*. New York: Bantam, 1970.
_____. *Selznick*. Garden City, NY: Doubleday, 1970.
Thomas, Tony, and Jim Terry. *The Busby Berkeley Book*. Greenwich, CT: New York Graphic Society, 1973.
Thomson, David. *A Biographical Dictionary of Film*. New York: William Morrow, 1976.

_____. *Showman: The Life of David O. Selznick.* New York: Knopf, 1992.
Tornebene, Lynn. *Long Live the King: A Biography of Clark Gable.* New York: Putnam, 1976.
Torrence, Bruce T. *Hollywood: The First 100 Years.* New York: Zoetrope, 1982.
Truitt, Evelyn Mack. *Who Was Who on Screen.* New York: R.R. Bowker, 1974, 1984.
Wakeman, John, ed. *World Film Directors, Volume One, 1890–1945.* New York: H.W. Wilson, 1987.
Walker, Alexander. *Fatal Charm: The Life of Rex Harrison.* New York: St. Martin's Press, 1993.
_____. *No Bells on Sunday: The Rachel Roberts Journals.* London and New York: Pavilion Books and Simon & Schuster, 1984.
Wallace, David. *Lost Hollywood.* New York: LA Weekly and St. Martin's Press, 2001.
Wallace, Irving, Amy Wallace, Sylvia Wallace, and David Wallechinsky. *The Intimate Sex Lives of Famous People.* New York: Dell, 1982.
Warner, Jack. *My First Hundred Years in Hollywood.* New York: Random House, 1965.
Warren, Doug. *Betty Grable: The Reluctant Movie Queen.* New York: St. Martin's Press, 1981.
Wayne, Jane Ellen. *Gable's Women.* New York: Prentice Hall, 1987.
_____. *Grace Kelly's Men.* New York: St. Martin Press, 1991.
Weaver, John T., comp. *Forty Years of Screen Credits, 1929–1969.* Metuchen, NJ: Scarecrow Press, 1970.
Webb, Michael, ed. *Hollywood: Legend and Reality.* Boston: Little, Brown, 1986.
Wiley, Mason, and Damian Bona. *Inside Oscar: The Unofficial History of the Academy Awards.* New York: Ballantine, 1986.
Williams, Ester, with Digby Diehl. *The Million Dollar Mermaid.* New York: Harcourt, 1999.
Wilson, Earl. *Hot Times: True Tales of Hollywood and Broadway.* Chicago: Contemporary Books, 1984.
_____. *I Am Gazing Into My 8 Ball.* Garden City, NY: Sun Dial Press, 1945.
Woods, Wiley O., Jr. *Legacy of the 90th Bombardment Group.* Paducah, KY: Turner, 1994.
Yablonski, Lewis. *George Raft.* New York: McGraw Hill, 1974.
Zierold, Norman. *The Moguls.* New York: Coward-McCann, 1969.
_____. *The World of Yesterday.* New York: Viking, 1943.
Zuckor, Adolph. *The Public Is Never Wrong.* New York: G.P. Putnam's Sons, 1953.

Materials from Newspaper Columns

Note: Columnists were syndicated.

BC — Bennett Cerf, "Try and Stop Me"
BT — Bob Thomas, "Hollywood"
CL — C.J. Lejeune
CS — Charles G. Sampas, "Sampascoopies"
DK — Dorothy Kilgallen, "On Broadway"
DM — Dorothy Manners
EG — Edith Gwynn
EJ — Erskine Johnson, "Short Takes"
ES — Ed Sullivan
EW — Earl Wilson
HC — Harrison Carroll, "Hollywood Notes"
HR — Harry Crocker, "Behind the Makeup"
HH — Hedda Hopper, "Looking at Hollywood"
JF — Jimmy Fidler, "News of Hollywood"
JL — Jack Lait, "Broadway and Elsewhere"
JS — Jimmy Starr
LP — Louella Parsons
KM — Ken Morgan, "Ken Morgan's Hollywood Keyhole"
PH — Paul Harrison, "Harrison on Hollywood"
RC — Robbin Coons, "Hollywood Speaks"
VV — Virginia Vale, "Star Dust"
WM — Ward Morehouse, *New York Sun* theater critic
WW — Walter Winchell, "Notes of an Innocent Bystander," "New York Heartbeat" columns

Periodicals and Newspapers

Ames Daily Tribune (Ames, Iowa), 1945–1948 archives
Appleton (WI) Post Crescent
Aracadia (CA) Tribune
Atchison (KS) Daily Globe
Bennington (VT) Evening Banner
Berkshire (MA) Evening Eagle
Berkshire County (MA) Eagle
Bradford (PA) Era, 1945–1948
Bridgeport (CT) The Post
Bridgeport (CT) The Telegram
Charleston (WV) The Daily Mail
Chronicle Telegram (Elyria, Ohio)
Clearfield (PA) Progress
Daily Kennebec Journal (Augusta, Maine)
Daily Register (Harrisburg, Pennsylvania)
Daily Review (Decatur, Illinois)
Dixon (IL) Evening Telegraph
Dixon (IL) Telegraph
Edwardsville (IL) Intelligencer
Evening Courier (Decatur, Illinois)
Frederick (MD) News
Gettysburg (PA) Times
Helena (MT) The Independent
The Hollywood Reporter
The Independent Record (Helena, Montana)

Indiana Evening Gazette (Indiana, Pennsylvania)
Iowa City (IA) Press Citizen
Lethbridge (Alberta, Canada) Herald
Lima (OH) News
Long Beach (CA) Independent
Los Angeles Daily News
Los Angeles Herald Examiner
Los Angeles Times
Lowell (Massachusetts) Sun
Mansfield (OH) Journal News
The Marion (OH) Star
The Mount Pleasant (IA) News
Nashua (NH) Telegraph
Nevada State Journal (Reno, Nevada)
Newark (OH) Advocate
Oshkosh (WI) Northwestern
Oxnard (CA) Press Courier
Reno (NV) Evening Gazette
Traverse City (MI) Record Eagle
Waterloo (IA) Daily Courier
Wisconsin Rapids (WI) Daily Tribune
Zanesville (OH) Signal

Magazines

Air Force Magazine: The Journal of the Air Force Association, Johnson, David A., "The Pre-Eagles"
American Cinematographer, April 1943
American Magazine, January 1941; October 1942; March 1943
American Weekly, August 18, 1948
Close-Up Magazine, December 1942; January 1943
Colliers Magazine, May 10, 1941
Complete Photographer Magazine, October 19, 1942
Confidential Magazine, August 1953
Family Circle, February 1942
Hollywood Magazine, April 1940; June 1940; May 1941
Homefront Digest, October 2001
Inside Story, August 1956
Liberty Magazine, July 19, 1947
Life magazine, June 17, 1940; August 19, 1940; April 7, 1941; June 30, 1941; July 21, 1941; October 13, 1941; October 20, 1941; November 3, 1941; November 10, 1941, February 16, 1942; May 18, 1942; July 13, 1942; August 3, 1942, August 17, 1942; February 1, 1943; April 19, 1943; May 3, 1943; June 21, 1943; February 19, 1945; October 22, 1945; November 5, 1945; January 7, 1946; January 28, 1946; June 9, 1947
Look Magazine, April 23, 1940; April 22, 1941; July 29, 1941; August 12, 1941; August 22, 1941; June 29, 1943; November 10, 1943; May 2, 1944
Modern Screen Magazine, March 1941; October 1941; April 1942; November 1948
Motion Picture Magazine, October 1940; October 1942; December 1942; June 1943; September 1943; April 1944; May 1944; December 1944; June 1945; July 1946; October 1948
Movie-Radio Magazine, April 19, 1941; December 12, 1942
Movie Show, November 1943; March 1944; May 1944
Movie Stars Parade, February 1941; July 1941; April 1942; June 1943; July 1943; January 1944
Movie World Magazine, August 1946
Movieland Magazine, June 1943; November 1944; October 1948; November 1948
Movies Magazine, July 1941; March 1942; May 1942; October 1942; November 1942; December 1943; January 1944
Newsweek Magazine, July 13, 1942; January 18, 1943; October 24, 1944; January 29, 1945; July 12, 1948
Photoplay, May 1940; June 1940; June 1941; December 1941; May 1942; February 1943; June 1943; August 1943; October 1943, November 1943; December 1943; August 1944; January 1945; February 1945; November 1945; November 1948
Pic Magazine, January 23, 1940
Picture Play, April 1940
Picturegoer, August 14, 1948
Saturday Evening Post, December 18, 1944; December 26, 1944, January 8, 1944, January 15, 1944
Screen Guide Magazine, June 1940; July 1940; August 1940; September 1940; February 1941; July 1941; November 1941; May 1942; July 1942; June 1943; December 1943; May 1945; Screen Guide, December 1947
Screenland Magazine, October 1941; January 1942; February 1942; July 1942; September 1942; July 1943; December 1943; May 1945; August 1946
Senior Scholastic, March 29, 1943
Silver Screen Magazine, July 1940; March 1941; August 1941; September 1941; March 1942; June 1942; Sep-

tember 1942, October 1942; December 1942; January 1943; July 1943; November 1943; May 1945; July 1946; September 1947
Stardom, February 1943; February 1944
Time magazine, February 15, 1940; May 13, 1940; December 15, 1941; August 31, 1942; January 18, 1943; March 8, 1943; March 29, 1943; March 3, 1944; January 22, 1945; November 26, 1945; March 4, 1946; August 19, 1946; July 18, 1948
Transmitter, Library of American Broadcasting newsletter, Volume 2, Number 1, Spring 2000
True Story Magazine, October 1948
Woman's Home Companion, July 1943

Internet Websites Used for Research

http://www.anthropoetics.ucla.edu (Carole Landis background)
http://www.afa.org/magazine (American Eagle Squadron)
http://www.armed-guard.com (Brooklyn Armed Guard Center)
http://www.audio-classics.com (*Duffy's Tavern*)
http://www.bombshells.com/grable (Betty Grable background)
http://apollo.carroll.com/franny/jslove.html (Carole Landis site) http://www.cr.nps.gov/nr/travel/aviation/mrc (March Field research)
http://www.crispy.com/benny (Jack Benny radio archives)
http://www.fourthfightergroup.com/eagles (Thomas C. Wallace)
http://www.frenkenstein.com/ww2 (Eagle Squadron history)
http://www.genordell.com/stores/lantern/FMPU (First Motion Picture Unit history)
http://www.geocities.com/Hollywood/Hills (Denny Jackson's Carole Landis Page; Betty Grable background)
http://www.glamourgirlsofthesilverscreen.com/landis (Carole Landis background)
http://www.history.acusd.edu (Hollywood Canteen; Betty Grable background; U.S. Naval battle background, World War II; U.S.O. during World War II)
http://www.history.navy.mil/faqs/faq72-1 (Sullivan brothers background)
http://www.home.st.net.au/~dunn (Australian U.S.O. travels)
http://www.ibdb.com (Schmidlapp Broadway history)
http://www.imdb.com (Internet Movie Database; movie statistics)
http://www.jackbenny.org (Jack Benny wartime experiences)
http://www.lkwdpl.org/wihohio/star-bel.htm (Belle Starr site)
http://www.loc.gov/exhibits/bobhope (Library of Congress; Bob Hope radio archives)
http://www.missionbf.tripod.com/USO (history of U.S.O.)
http://www.nps.gov/goga/clho/suba (San Francisco history, Sutro Baths)
http://www.onwar.com/maps/wwii (Pacific Theater maps)
http://www.otrsite.com/logs (Eddie Cantor radio show listing)
http://parlorsongs.com/bios/composersbios (Composer biographies)
http://www.san.beck.org (Movie reviews)
http://www.sfmuseum.org/hist9/bcoast.html (San Francisco history, music clubs)
http://www.stagedoorcanteen.net (Stage Door Canteen history)
http://www.surfnetinc.com/chuck/trio3m.htm (Republic Studio western serials)
http://www.swinginchicks.com/jacqueline_susann.htm (Jacqueline Susann — Carole relationship)
http://www.wsu.edu/~delahoyd/one.mill.b.c. (*One Million B.C.*)
http://www.ww2homefront.com (British War Relief Society)
http://www.90thbombgroup.org (90th Bomber Group, U.S.O. visit)

Video

Andrews, Maxene. *Over Here, Over There: The Andrews Sisters and the USO Stars in WWII*.
Hoberman, J. *42nd Street*. London, BFI Film Classics, 1993.
Pike, Bob, and Dave Martin. *The Genius of Busby Berkeley*. Reseda, CA: Creative Film Society, 1973.

Index

A.A.F. Anniversary Radio Program (radio program) 220
Abbott, Bud 108, 111
Abraham Lincoln (1930) 55
actresses, abuse at the hands of studio employees 88
Adler, Larry 152, 166, 167, 168, 178, 180
Adrian, Gilbert 31, 32
The Adventures of Sherlock Holmes (1939) 122
Adventurous Blonde (1937): filmography 264
Adventurous Blonde (1938) 38
Albertson, Jack 187
Alcatraz Island (1937) 38, 42, 45; filmography 263
Alexander, Catherine 23
Alfred Hitchcock Presents (military series) 110
All Around the Town (television show) 201
All That Heaven Allows (1955) 201
Allen, Gracie 108, 129; radio programs of 151
Allen, Joseph 120
Allgood, Sara 120
Ambassador Hotel 31
Ameche, Don 91, 99, 126
American Cancer Society 180
American Magazine (magazine) 69, 89, 163
American Society for the Prevention of Cruelty to Animals (ASPCA) 59
The American Theater Wing 117
American Weekly (magazine) 252
Amos 'n' Andy (radio program) 151
Amphytrion 38 258
Anders, Glen 149
Anderson, Eddie ("Rochester") 75, 94, 168
Anderson, Maxwell 228, 231, 238
Andres Restaurant 129
Andrews, Dana 71, 80, 82, 99, 126
Andrews, Grayce 23
The Andrews Sisters 113, 155
Angers, Avril 222
The Animal Kingdom 190

Anna and the King of Siam (1945) 210, 217, 218
Anna and the King of Siam (1946) 200, 201
Anne of a Thousand Days 228
Arbuckle, Roscoe 20
Arden, Eve 192
Arden, Robert 121
Armed Forces Radio Network 151, 177
Armidon, Phil 76
Armstrong, Robert 120
The Army Hour (radio program) 124
Arnaz, Desi 51
Arnold, Gen. Hap 109
Arnold, Stan 225
Arthur, Jean 192
Ascari, Alberto 215
Associated Filmmakers, Inc. 206
Astor, Mary 64
Austin, John 87
Averill, Anthony 46
The Awful Truth (1937) 51

Bacall, Lauren 208
Bacon, Lloyd 42
Bailey, Eleanor 50
Baker, George 56
Baldwin, Faith 44
Ball, Cleo 51
Ball, Lucille 51, 159, 218; morality of 22
Bankhead, Tallulah 149
Banton, Travis 102
Bari, Lynn 71, 102, 121
Barker, Lex 220
Barnes, Binnie 31
Barrie, Elaine 74
Barrie, Mona 43, 44
Barry, Elaine 122
Barry, Philip 190
Barrymore, John 74, 122
Bartel, Jean 192
Barthelmess, Richard 96

Barton, Lady Ellen 260
Basevi, James 163
Bates, Florence 72
Battle of Britain 148, 153
Bautzer, Gregson 50, 53, 73, 74, 121, 130, 200, 225; affairs with female clients 50
Baxter, Anne 99
Bayley, Eleanor 50
Beal, Frank 23
The Bear Café 20
Beaudine, William 261
Beckett, Scott 120
Beddoe, Don 200
Beery, Wallace 38; and death of Ted Healy 61
Behind Green Lights (1946) 198, 200, 207; filmography 270
The Belvedere 20
Benet, Steven Vincent 43
Bennett, Bruce 53
Bennett, Constance 129
Bennett, Joan 122
Benny, Jack 141, 152, 159, 165, 166, 167, 168, 170, 171, 177, 180, 193
Bergman, Ingrid 214; morality of 22
Berkeley, Busby 27, 28, 32, 35, 38, 40, 44, 45, 47, 48, 52, 61, 74, 87, 121, 210; alcoholism 32, 33; Army service 32; arranges for Carole's first studio contract 34; audition process 33, 34; automobile accident 33; breaks off engagement to Carole 48; as choreographer 32, 38; death 260; diminished status as musical director 50; marriages and divorces 33; residences 210; sexual themes in choreography 32; sued by Irving Wheeler 49; suicide attempt 210; as womanizer 32, 33
Berkeley, Gertrude 210
Berle, Milton 96, 98, 105, 108
Beverly Hills Hotel 98
Beverly Wilshire Hotel 73
Bey, Turhan 216, 227
Bieschke, Albert 167, 168
Billingsly, Glenn 162
Biltmore Hotel 31, 96
Bing, Herman 45
Biograph Studios 55
The Bishop's Wife 222
Bitzer, George W. ("Billy") 55
Blaine, Vivien 196
Blandick, Clara 31
Blondell, Joan 27, 75, 97, 129
Blondes at Work (1938) 37, 40, 42; filmography 264
Blood and Sand (1922) 102
Blood and Sand (1941) 102, 104, 106, 111, 122
The Blossom Sisters 131

Blue, Robert 197
Blue Ribbon Town (radio program) 150
Blyler, Jimmy 20
Body and Soul (1947) 218
Bogart, Humphrey 23, 44, 159, 160, 208
Bolden, Fannie Mae 230, 232, 233, 234, 238, 241, 253, 255
Bombshell (1933) 160
Bona, Damian 90
Bond, Ward 41, 71
Boone, Betty 114
Boston Globe (newspaper) 101
Bow, Clara 67
Bowerman, Tom, Gunners Mate 2nd Class 188
Bowers, John 262
Bowman, Lee 245
Box Office Magazine (magazine) 53
Boy Meets Girl (1938) 47, 160; filmography 266
Boyer, Charles 108, 112, 117, 159
Brand, Harry 124, 147, 233
Brandsma, Dr. Maynard D. 253
Branton, Geri 222, 223
The Brass Monkey (1948) 220, 222, 261; filmography 271
Brent, George 215, 216
Brewer, Alva Consuelo (Mrs. "Dolly" Hunt) 66, 67, 71
British-Lion Studios 215, 221, 226, 230, 250
British War Relief Society (B.W.R.S.) 90, 116
Brittingham, Det. Herbert W. 234
Broadhurst Theater 186
Broadway Melody of 1935 (1935) 38
Broadway Melody of 1938 (1937) 31, 32; filmography 263
Broadway Radio Box (radio program) 155
Broadway Serenade (1938) 50
Broccoli, Albert 61; and death of Ted Healy 61
Bromley, Sheila 47
Bronsonia Apartments 23
Brook Street Auto Camp 11
Brooklyn Armed Guard Center 187, 189
Brooks, Phyllis 180, 209
Brower, Otto 198, 200, 207
Brown, Ben (coroner) 236, 240, 241, 242
Brown, Clarence 77
Brown, Fred 20
Brown, Joe E. 129, 130, 143, 159, 180, 194
Brumbelow, Carrie 11
Brumbelow, Lucy ("Grandma") 11, 13
Brumbelow, Ronny 11
Bruner, June 166, 167, 168, 180
Brute Force (1946) 214

Bryan, Jane 42, 47
Bryan, Oscar 196
Bundles for Britain program 117
Burke, Billie 75, 97, 209
Burns, George 108, 129; radio programs 151
Burroughs, Edgar Rice 178
Busch, Niven 82
Butterworth, Charles 72, 192
Byrd, Ralph 127

Cadet Girl (1941) 99, 101, 102, 103, 105, 120; filmography 268
Cagney, James 47, 200
Calleia, Joseph 221
Calling All Girls (1939) 50
Calloway, Cab 155; Orchestra 192
Calvet, Corrine 86
Camp Callan 116, 130
Camp Cook 130
Camp Haan 116, 130
Camp Hunter Liggett 98, 99, 116, 130
Camp Shows, Inc. 119
Campbell, Alan 29
Campbell, Stanley 63, 64
Canova, Judy 115
Cantor, Charlie 151
Cantor, Eddie 32, 107, 129, 163, 188
Canutt, Enos ("Yakima") 54
Capone, Al 214
Capra, Frank: military service 110
Carmichael, Hoagy 72
Carnegie, Hattie 209
Carradine, John 102
Carroll, Harrison 95, 100, 149, 150
Carson, Jack 114
Carter, Janis 96
Casablanca (1939) 132
Cerf, Bennett 213
Chadwick, Helene 31
Chandler, Chick 158
Chandler, Eddy 41
Channel, Coco 188
Chaplin, Charlie 74, 76
Chaplin, Sydney 83
Charley Chan (movie serial) 157, 158
Chase, Charley 55
Chateau Elysee Apartments 23
Cheers (television program) 151
Chiang, Madame 148
China Clipper (1936) 160
Chiquita 71
Churchill, Winston 134
Churchill, Mrs. Winston 117
Circhton, Kyle 90
Ciro's Restaurant 45, 74, 98, 124, 194
Cleveland, Grover 80

Cliff House Restaurant 19, 21
Clinton, William Jefferson 260
Club Alabam 222
Clurman, Howard 88
Coakley, Tom 21
Cobb, Lee J.: military service 110
Cobb, Patrizia ("Buff") 200, 201, 210, 217
Coconut Grove Café 65
Cohn, Harry 103, 104, 159
Cohn, Roy 148
Colbert, Claudette 108, 204
Colby, Ethel 157
Cole, Ben 130
Collier's (magazine) 90
Colman, Ronald 117
Columbia Pictures Corporation 103, 104, 160, 161, 201
Columbo, Ross 16
Combs, Carl 97
Command Performance (radio program) 124
Como, Perry 193
Compson, Betty 42, 54
Compton, Joyce 41
Coney, Violet 44
Coney Island (1943) 130
Connolly, Bobby 27, 41
Connolly, Walter 45
Consolidated Film Laboratories 52
The Constant Husband (1955) 258
Conte Richard 194
The Continental Celebrity Show (radio program) 209
Conville, Frankie 131
Coogan, Jackie 93
Coons, Robbin 25, 68
Cooper, Gary 16, 180
Cooper, Gladys 233
Cooper, Jackie 251
Cooper, Melville 41, 45
Corrigan, Ray ("Crash") 53
Cort Theater 192
Costello, Lou 108, 111
Count Me In 192
Cowan, Lou 124
Cowboy and the Blonde (1941) 106
The Cowboys from Texas (1939) 54; filmography 266
Craven, Eddie 42
Crawford, Broderick 42
Crawford, Joan 50
Cregar, Laird 99, 102
Crichton, Kyle 94
Crivello, Kirk 2
Crocker, Harry 180, 194
Cronyn, Hume 214

Crosby, Bing 117, 119, 124, 125, 129, 159; radio programs 151
Crosby, Dixie Lee 117
Crossfire (1947) 70
Crowe, James Francis 65
Crump, Owen 109; military service 110
Cugat, Lorraine 260
Culver, Nan 233, 234, 238, 245, 255
Culver, Roland 225, 231, 233, 236, 245, 246, 255
Cummings, Irving 80, 112
Cummings, Robert 91, 95, 99, 180
Curtiz, Michael 45
Cushing, Georgette 260

Dames (1934) 32
Dance Hall (1941) 96, 97, 99, 106; filmography 267
Dandridge, Dorothy 29, 85, 88, 121, 222, 223, 258
Dane, Karl 261
Dane, Pat 260
D'Arcy, Alexander 51
Daredevils of the Red Circle (1939) 53; filmography 266
Darling, William S. 163
Darnell, Linda 88, 98, 102, 111, 130
Darwell, Jane 41, 120
Dastigar, Sabu: military service 110
Davidson, William B. 40
Davies, Marion 47
Davis, Bette 42, 72, 112, 117, 160, 213; promiscuity 113
Davis, Wee Willis 164
Day, Dennis 166
A Day at the Races (1937) 28, 222; filmography 263
Daymond, Maj. Gregory Augustus 148
de Havilland, Olivia 45
Delafield, E.M. 41
del Rio, Dolores 82
Del Ruth, Roy 31
Derr, Richard 105
DeSilva, B.G. 88
Devine, Andy 31
DiCicco, Pasquale 61, 62, 63, 73, 214; and death of Ted Healy 61
Dietrich, Marlene 98, 99, 108
DiMaggio, Joe 107
Dix, Richard 54
Dixon, Crawford 229
Dixon, Pert 260
Dmytryk, Edward 70
Do You Love Me? (1946) 209
Dolfina 20
Doll Face (scheduled, 1946) 193

Donahue, Woolworth 121
Donnelly, Ruth 42
Donohue, Woolworth 87, 185
Doolittle, Col. James ("Jimmy") 110, 143
Dorsey, Jimmy 157; Orchestra 157, 248
Dorsey, Tommy 21, 159, 211, 260
Douglas, Melvyn 111
Down Argentina Way (1940) 94
Downing, Judd 240, 241
Dozier, William 88
Drake, Betsy 261
Dream Girl 224, 253
Drieser, Paul 111
Drieser, Theodore 111
Drums Along the Mohawk (1939) 77
Duffy's Tavern (radio program) 151, 164
Dumont, Margaret 29
Dunham, Katherine 221
Dunn, Irene 217
Dunn, Malvina 37
Dunn, Steffi 57
Durant, Tim 76
Durant, Will 77
Durante, Jimmy 108
Durbin, Deanna 79, 213
Dvorak, Ann 216

Eagle-Lion Studios 214, 220, 224, 227, 255, 256
The Eagle Squadron 107, 134, 148, 153
Eberhart, Mignon G. 41
Edwards, Sarah 41
8th Air Force 148
Eilers, Bud 138
Eilers, Sally 138
Eisenhower, Gen. Dwight D. 143
Eisler, Hanns 201
El Capitan Apartments 23
El Morocco Club 192
El Rancho Vegas Hotel 196
Elizabeth, Princess 136, 137, 222
Elizabeth I, Queen 136, 137, 222
Ellington, Duke 21
Ellis, Kay 20
Ellis, Maj. Richard 139
Ellis, Robert 157, 158
The Emperor's Candlesticks (1937) 32; filmography 263
Enright, Ray 45
Entwhistle, Peg 261
Ernest Blecher Academy 93
Escape (1947) 220, 221
Esquire (magazine) 197
Ethyl Barrymore Theater 192
Ettinger, Edward 256
Evans, Herbert 31
Eythe, Bill 201

Fairbanks, Douglas, Jr.: military service 110
Fairbanks, Douglas, Sr. 114
Fairbanks, Mary 245
Fairchild, Lucius 3
Fairchild, Wisconsin: history 4
Falkenburg, Jinx 186
Fangio, Juan Manuel 215
Farmer, Francis 88
Farouk, King 223
Farr, Derek 221
Farrell, Charlie 218
Farrell, Eileen 155
Farrell, Glenda 37, 38, 42
Farrow, John 42
Fay & Gordon (dance team) 65
Fay, Frank 29; alcoholism 29; studio-arranged marriage to Barbara Stanwyck 29
Faye, Alice 89, 94, 98, 157, 213, 248
Feld, Fritz 45
Fellows, Judith 234, 238
Fenner, Charles 7, 8; death 259; divorces Clara Ridste 8
Fenner, Edward 8
Fenner, Floyd 8
Fidler, Jimmy 66, 82, 87, 89, 95, 106, 107, 121, 198, 207, 213, 216, 262
Fields, Gracie 117
The Fighting 69th (1940) 160
Film Daily (magazine) 99, 158
First Motion Picture Unit (F.M.P.U.) 109
Fischbeck, Harry 70
Fischetti, Charlie 214
Fisher, Mary Gale 76
Fisher, Steve 100
Fiske, William Meade Linsley: death 135
Fitzmaurice, George 32
Flagg, James Montgomery 34
Fleming, Rhonda 60, 89
Fletcher, Adele 153
Floyd, Lee 20
Fly-Away Baby (1937) 37, 38; filmography 264
Flynn, Errol 45, 65, 159, 212; as comic actor 45, 46
Flynn, Nora Eddington 212
Follow the Boys (1944) 163
Fontaine, Joan 159
Footlight Serenade (1942) 157
Foran, Dick 41, 43, 47
Forbes, Ralph 41
Ford, John: military service 110
Forest Lawn Memorial Park (Glendale) 243, 259
Fort Ord 98, 116
42nd Street (1933) 32
44th Fighter Squadron ("The Vampire Squadron") 176
400th Bomber Group ("The Moby Dicks") 175
Four Jills in a Jeep (book) 142, 147, 155, 160
Four Jills in a Jeep (1944) 138, 146, 147, 150, 155, 157, 160, 165, 248, 260; filmography 269
Four's a Crowd (1938) 45; filmography 265
Fox, Matty 97, 101
Fox, Paul Harvey 105
The Foxes of Harrow (1947) 217, 218
Foy, Bryan 44
Frances, Eleanor 91
Francis, Kay 41, 98, 117, 118, 131, 132, 136, 137, 139, 143, 146, 157, 158, 159, 165, 248, 260; illnesses 145
Frankel, Stanley 153
Frawley, William 120
Freed, Arthur 31
Freeland, Thornton 222
French, Eleanor 131
Frickert, Joseph 56
The Front Page (1931) 160
Front Page Woman (1935) 42

Gable, Clark 16, 23, 31, 108; military service 110
Gabor, Zsa Zsa 50
Gahagan, Helen 111
Gallagher, Carol 91
Gardner, Ava 50
Gardner, Ed 63, 151
Garfield, John 108, 112, 160, 218
Gargan, William 64, 200
Garland, Judy 31, 98, 125, 232, 251
Garson, Greer 159, 204
Gaynor, Janet 29, 31
General Services Studio 198, 203
A Gentleman at Heart (1942) 104, 105; filmography 268
George, King 136
George VI, King 222
Gershwin, Arthur 187
Gershwin, George 187
Geulich, Earl 152
The Ghost and Mrs. Muir (1946) 217
Gibbons, Cedric 31, 32, 74, 76, 82
Gieger, William 135
Giesler, Jerry 33, 248, 249, 256
Giler, Berne 64
Gilligan's Island (television series) 110
Gilman, Margelo 188
Gilmore, Virginia 121
Gilmore Racing Team 216
Girl on the Moon (1945) 199
Girls on Probation (1938) 47, 48; filmography 266

Gish, Dorothy 55
Gish, Lillian 55
Giuntoli, Agostino 20
Gleason, James 127
Goddard, Paulette 50, 114
Goetz, William 96
Goff, Ivan 76
Gold Diggers in Paris (1938) 45, 50; filmography 265
Gold Diggers of 1933 (1933) 32
Gold Diggers of 1937 (1937) 32
Golden Boy (1939) 102
Goldwyn Girls 32
Gone with the Wind (1939) 82, 102
The Good Earth (1937) 69
Goodman, Benny 211, 227; Orchestra 38
Gordon, James 10
Gottlieb, William 209
Gould, Joseph J. 200
Gould, Thomas C. 54
Grable, Betty 67, 86, 89, 91, 94, 95, 96, 99, 100, 102, 107, 108, 124, 129, 130, 157
Grable, Lillian 93
Graham, Sheilah 211
Gramlich, Charles 203, 204, 205
Grand Passion (1937) 27
Grant, Cary 52, 98, 108, 117, 121, 218, 220; homosexual relationships 42, 121
The Grapes of Wrath (1940) 85
Grauman's Chinese Theater 31, 64, 76, 97, 99, 149, 165
Gravey, Fernand 27
The Great Dictator (1940) 74
The Great Hospital Mystery (1937) 41
Green, Eddie 151
The Green Hornet Strikes Again (1941) 122
Greene, Harrison 40
Greene, Richard 208
Greenwood, Charlotte 91
Gretna Green Hotel 71
Gréville, Edward 221, 226
Griffith, D.W. 55, 56; alcoholism 55; as discoverer of talent 55
Guild, Nancy 205

Hakim, Raymond 88, 97, 108
Hakim, Robert 88
Hal Roach Studio 54, 109
Haley, Jack 91
Hall, Gladys 91
Hall, Jon 71, 77
Hall, Thurston 41
Halton, Charles 43
Hamilton, Margaret 42
Hampton, Lionel 40
Hardy, Oliver 39, 129

Harlow, Jean 160
Harris, Daniel 239
Harris, Helen 188
Harris, Phil 94
Harrison, Carey 220, 236
Harrison, Paul 82
Harrison, Rex 86, 87, 200, 208, 210, 246, 253, 254, 256, 257, 258, 261; affair and marriage to Kay Kendall 258; amorality 224, 227; arrives unannounced at Capri house July 5 233; attends Carole's funeral 245; background 217; blackballed by U.S. film industry 258; breaks off with Carole 231; burns letters from Carole 236, 237, 243; calls Capri house July 5 233; at Coroner's Inquest 240, 241; denies rumors of affair with Carole 237; divorces 217, 218; divorces Lilli Palmer 258; infidelity 217, 218; marriages 217, 259; marries Rachel Roberts 258; meets with press in Carole's driveway 236; in *My Fair Lady* 258; relationship with the press 218; residences 221, 225, 236; separation from Lilli Palmer 225, 255
Harron, Robert 55
Hartford, Huntington, III 121
Harvey, John 158
Harwood, Leo 23
Hasso, Signe 198, 201
Hatton, Raymond 54
Havelock-Allan, Anthony 218
Having Wonderful Crime (1945) 164, 165, 254; filmography 270
Hawaiian Paradise Café 48
Hawkins, John 161
Hawkins, Ward 161
Hawks, Howard 65, 200
Haymes, Dick 157, 197, 209, 211, 212, 218, 232, 243, 245, 250, 254
Hayward, Leland 230, 231, 238, 243
Hayward, Susan 39, 47, 49
Hayworth, Rita 20, 60, 89, 95, 104, 111, 112, 113, 123, 129, 212, 213, 223
He Couldn't Say No (1938) 40, 44; filmography 265
Healy, Ted 38, 40, 200; alcoholism 38; death 38
Hearst, William Randolph 116
Hearst's International Cosmopolitan (magazine) 44
Hecht, Ben 29
Hedda Hopper's Hollywood No. 2 (1941): filmography 267
Heflin, Van: military service 110
Hellinger, Mark 214
Helton Hall, Australia, military base 169
Hemingway, Ernest 77

Henderson, Charles 260
Hendry, Whitney ("Whitey") 33
Henie, Sonja 149, 208
Henry, William 98
Hepburn, Katharine 149, 213
Herbert, Hugh 38, 44, 45
Herman, Woody 149; Orchestra 149
Heydt, Louis Jean 192
Hill, George 10
Hill, Willie 10
The Hippodrome 20
Hitler, Adolf 135
Hively, Maj. Howard W. 66
Hodiak, John 205
Hogan, Marty 11
Holden, Jann 260
Holden, William: military service 111
Holloway, Stanley 221
Hollywood (magazine) 59
Hollywood Bowl 31
Hollywood Canteen 106, 113, 115, 131, 164, 165
Hollywood Canteen (radio program) 186
Hollywood Goes to War (1945): filmography 270
Hollywood Hotel (1938) 38, 49, 50; filmography 264
The Hollywood Preview (magazine) 59
Hollywood Professional School 93
The Hollywood Reporter (magazine) 112
The Hollywood Reporter (newspaper) 48, 162, 195, 219, 225, 243, 251
Hollywood Victory Committee 106, 109, 119, 148, 166
Holmes, George 123
Hope, Bob 111, 119, 125, 130, 159, 175, 180, 182, 186
Hopkins, Miriam 217
Hopper, Hedda 74, 223, 224
Horsey, Judge Charles Lee 196
Horton, Edward Everett 27
Horwin, Jerry 45
Hot Spot (1940) 105
Hotel Aviz 132
Hough, Donald 60
House Un-American Activities Committee (HUAC) 70, 148
How Green Was My Valley (1941) 85
Howard, Elizabeth 11
Howard, Leslie: death 120
Howard, N.C. 3
Hubbard, Maj. Glen 144
Hubbard, John 64, 71
Hughes, Howard 91, 160
Hull, Warren 122
Humberstone, H. Bruce 87, 99, 100

Hunt, Willis 65, 67, 70, 74, 91, 96, 101, 107, 122, 126, 159, 161, 230
Hunter, Ross 224, 253
Hussey, Ruth 124
Huston, John: military service 110
Hutton, Betty 88

I Wake Up Screaming (1941) 87, 89, 99, 101, 102, 103, 106; filmography 268
Imitation of life (1959) 201
The Invisible Menace (1938) 40, 42; filmography 264
The Iowa 20
It Happened in Flatbush (1942) 105, 120, 123, 127; filmography 268
It Never Rains 192
It Shouldn't Happen to a Dog (1946) 207, 209, 210, 211, 214; filmography 270
It's a Wonderful Life (1946) 102
Iturbi, Jose 200
Ives, Burl 186
The Ivy Bar 20

The Jack Smith Show 209
James, Frank 80
James, Harry 40, 211
James, Jesse 80
Jason, Leigh 215
Jay Whidden Orchestra 93
Jenkins, Allen 42, 45
Jerome Cowan 105
Jessel, George 185, 188, 192, 197, 199, 261
Joan of Arc (1946) 214
John Golden Theater 192
Johnny Belinda (1946) 214
Johnson, Erskine 69, 165, 226
Johnson, Parks 123
Johnson, Russell: military service 110
Johnson, Van 245
Jolson, Al 20, 129; radio programs 151
Jones, Det. Emmett 234, 235
Jones, Grover 56
Jones, Jennifer 128
Joslyn, Allyn 100, 207
Juneau, U.S.S. 162

Kaiser, Kay 148; Orchestra 98, 148
Kai-shek, Chiang 148
Kane, Courtney 198, 199, 226
Karloff, Boris 42
Kaye, Danny 192
Keeler, Ruby 33
Keeper of the Flame (1942) 149
Kelly, Grace 88, 128; amorality 22, 88
Kelly, Johnny 11
Kelly, Patsy 73, 75, 162, 186

Kendall, Cy 42
Kendall, Kay 259; death 258
Kennedy, Arthur: military service 111
Kennedy, Edgar 31, 39
Kennedy, John F. 116
Kennedy, Joseph 116
Kennedy, Tom 42
Kent, Atwater 233
Kibbee, Guy 33, 188
Kilgallen, Dorothy 186, 198, 199, 209, 212, 213, 224, 225, 226, 227, 242, 258
King, Sam 20
The King and I (1946) 218
The King and the Chorus Girl (1937) 27, 31, 32, 35; filmography 263
King Dinosaur (1955) 60
Kirby, Edward M. 124
Kirk, Myron 63
Kit Carson (1940) 71
Knowles, Patric 41, 45
Koslick, Martin 127
Krasna, Norman 27
Krueger, Kurt 194
Kruger, Alma 201
Krupa, Gene 40
Kuhlmann, Jo 260

L.A. Confidential (1997) 88
La Conga Club 57, 71
La Martinique Café 119
Lacy, Adele 34
Lacy, Madison 34
Ladd, Alan: military service 111
Lady in a Quandary (scheduled, 1942) 123
A Lady Says Yes 186, 187, 188, 190, 250
Laemmle, Carl 83
Lait, Jack 207
Lake, Veronica 88, 113
LaMarr, Hedy 74, 122, 201
Lamour, Dorothy 50, 115, 122
Lancaster, Burt 214
Landis, Carole 7, 8, 10, 12; affair with Rex Harrison 218, 220, 223, 224, 225, 227; in Africa 141, 142; alcohol level at time of death 238; alleged second suicide note 241; announces divorce from Horace Schmidlapp 224, 225; annulment of Irving Wheeler marriage 17; appears in stage productions 51; appraisal of estate 248, 249; arranged "first" meeting with Rex Harrison 218; arrival in Hollywood 22; athleticism 14, 60; attends Academy Awards ceremony 90; attends classes at night 51, 60; attends high school 14, 16, 18; attends movie previews 15, 16; auction of her property 249, 250; auditions for Busby Berkeley 33; auditions for D.W. Griffith 56; automobiles 66, 96; autopsy 236, 238; awards won by 147, 148, 159, 192, 193, 213; beaten by Pasquale DiCicco 61, 73; befriends soldiers 133, 138; in Bermuda 131, 132; better performances than co-stars 60, 89, 93, 100, 101, 128; birth 6, 7; body 234, 235; in Brazil 146; burial 247; burial site 246, 247; Calcraft Knitting Mills lawsuit 68, 69; call girl rumor 48; and "casting couch" 32; and censors 157, 201, 203; charity 163; and children 63; chooses stage name 19; claims against estate 249; Command Performances of (for British royal family) 136, 222; confusion regarding actual birth date 7; contract with Warner Brothers 34; Coroner's Inquest into Death 240; crowd at funeral 244, 245, 246, 247; dances with soldiers 168, 187; dating habits 63, 74, 76, 82, 87, 90, 97, 101, 108, 121, 122, 185; death 2, 232; death certificate 238; decides to commit suicide 231; divorces Horace Schmidlapp 225, 226, 227, 248, 256; divorces Irving Wheeler 52, 53; divorces Thomas Wallace 193, 194, 197; divorces Willis Hunt 74, 76; does own stunts 69, 70, 72, 73, 127; dropped by Warners 48; early "cheesecake" photos 24; early physical development 16; early schooling 14; elopes with Irving Wheeler 17; employment 18, 20; endorsements 105, 155, 180, 182, 256; ends sexual relationship with Darryl Zanuck 103; engagement to Busby Berkeley 48; engagement to Horace Schmidlapp 197, 199; engagement to Thomas Wallace 137; engagement to Willis Hunt 66; in England 133; extravagance 80; failed relationships 50; feelings for Rex Harrison 224; feud with Betty Grable 93, 94, 95, 100, 101, 107; fights with Willis Hunt 71, 73; filming in England 215, 220; finances 230, 248, 255, 256; first beauty pageant 16; first contract 26; first public performance 13; first studio work 24; "Flame Song" number 201, 202, 203; flying lessons 76, 80; friendship with Burgess Meredith 70, 74, 101, 107; friendship with Cesar Romero 96, 97, 98, 106, 149, 251; friendship with Diana Lewis 37, 44, 45; friendship with Dick Haymes 158; friendship with Mark Hellinger 214; friendship with Pat O'Brien 159, 160, 161; friendship with Tony Martin 101; friendship with Willard Parker 38, 42, 45; front-line visits 143, 145; funeral service 243, 244, 245, 246, 258; generosity 155; grave marker 247; helps take care of siblings 12; hobbies 80,

215; honeymoon in Cuba with Horace Schmidlapp 206; hospitalization 62, 63; illnesses 2, 108, 137, 138, 145, 165, 166, 171, 172, 174, 177, 180, 211, 234; inability to have children 239; independence 8, 14, 27, 37, 68, 90, 104, 106, 218; at Indianapolis 500 216; injured in filming 73; installs bomb shelter 79; invests in race team 216; in Ireland 137; and Irving Wheeler suit versus Busby Berkeley 49; judgment 62; large amount of early movie work 25; Last Will & Testament 248, 249; leaves letters at Culver house 231, 255; leaves studio to facilitate Wallace divorce 196; legally changes name 123; lesbian relationships 188, 189, 190; loses *Blood and Sand* role to Rita Hayworth 103, 111; loses *Doll Face* role to Vivien Blaine 196; loses *The Spider* role to Faye Marlowe 196; love of music 77; love of reading 77; marriage to Horace Schmidlapp 206, 208, 209, 213; marriage to Irving Wheeler, first 1; marriage to Irving Wheeler, second 17; marriage to Tom Wallace 138, 139, 140, 153, 155, 156, 159, 161, 162, 163, 165, 167; marriage to Willis Hunt 70, 71, 73; meets Horace Schmidlapp 190; meets Irving Wheeler 17; meets Rex Harrison 217; meets Tom Wallace 134; and men 1, 15, 51, 60, 91, 104, 229; military camp visits 80, 95, 99, 107, 108, 111, 116, 117, 119, 122, 124, 127, 131, 132, 136, 146, 148, 149, 151, 152, 154, 161, 165, 166, 167, 168, 170, 175, 180, 183, 187, 188, 189, 196, 214, 254; moves to Hollywood 22; moves to Nevada to divorce Tom Wallace 195; moves to San Francisco 18; on Nazi "hit" list 143; near-marriage to Busby Berkeley 210; negotiating to return to England 226; newspaper coverage of death 237, 250, 251; nicknames 67, 95; personal appearances 194, 211; personality 217; pets 79, 80, 98, 114, 257; physical attributes 69, 87, 89, 95, 127, 129, 217, 237; as pilot 106; and "PING" campaign 67, 68, 69, 71; potential radio host job offer 160, 163; problems with the "studio wives" 1, 48, 87, 88, 196, 209; publicity tours 107; racial tolerance 14, 222; radio appearances 107, 122, 124, 126, 127, 150, 151, 154, 155, 157, 160, 163, 164, 177, 180, 186, 209, 220; records promotional record 229, 230; recuperates in Australia 183; relationship with Busby Berkeley 34, 37, 45, 47, 49, 54; relationship with Cedric Gibbons 82; relationship with Dana Andrews 126; relationship with Darryl Zanuck 82, 85, 94, 105; relationship with fans 96; relationship with George Jessel 197; relationship with Gregson Bautzer 50; relationship with Hal Roach, Jr. 57; relationship with Horace Schmidlapp 192, 198, 200, 206, 215, 216, 218, 220; relationship with Jacqueline Susann 188, 189, 190; relationship with Kenny Morgan 52, 54, 57; relationship with Pasquale DiCicco 61, 73; relationship with Rex Harrison 251, 253; relationship with soldiers 171, 172, 173, 176, 177, 178; relationship with Willis Hunt 65; relationships with co-workers 209; relationships with ex-husbands 159, 161; reputation and rumors 22, 25, 35, 36, 47, 48, 54, 62, 82, 85, 87, 89, 100, 123, 210; residences 8, 10, 19, 23, 45, 52, 62, 65, 66, 73, 76, 78, 96, 114, 115, 130, 149, 152, 157, 159, 160, 162, 180, 185, 188, 191, 196, 197, 199, 200, 206, 208, 209, 212, 216, 220, 221, 224, 225, 228, 231, 233, 236, 238, 249, 256; with Rex Harrison in England 221, 222; roles 27, 28, 31, 32, 33, 37, 38, 40, 41, 42, 43, 44, 45, 46, 47, 51, 53, 54, 55, 56, 64, 70, 71, 74, 80, 91, 98, 99, 101, 104, 105, 112, 120, 123, 127, 146, 149, 160, 161, 193, 194, 198, 200, 201, 207, 211; rumored marriage to Kenny Morgan 57; rumors of affair with Harrison go public 218; rumors of note left for Rex Harrison 239; sale of Capri Drive house 248; in San Francisco 19; separation from Irving Wheeler 17; separation from Wallace, Thomas C. 185; separation from Willis Hunt 73; sexual reputation 26; shares Thanksgiving dinner with airmen 136; sighs 125, 126; signs with Hal Roach Studios 54; signs with Republic Studios 51; signs with 20th Century–Fox 76; sings 72, 89, 98, 101, 103, 112, 132, 136, 137, 161, 168, 170, 261; sings at St. Francis Hotel 21; South Pacific tour 166; stage appearances 186, 190; stalkers 63, 64, 203, 204; star on Hollywood Walk of Fame 261; suicide 232; suicide attempts 165, 211, 232, 233, 254; suicide note(s) 231, 232, 234, 239; supports young musician 227; tabloid press coverage 37, 48, 51, 57, 61, 64, 66, 68, 69, 74, 82, 86, 87, 88, 89, 94, 95, 100, 106, 107, 108, 112, 114, 121, 122, 123, 128, 141, 145, 147, 162, 165, 171, 180, 185, 187, 194, 195, 197, 198, 199, 200, 206, 207, 208, 210, 211, 212, 213, 215, 216, 218, 221, 223, 224, 225, 226, 227, 237, 239, 242, 247, 250, 252, 253, 258, 261, 262; theories about suicide 253; trading sex for work 32, 35, 48, 86, 87; travel conditions 141, 142; travels the country with Ravazza Orchestra 21; travels to Egypt with

Dorothy Dandridge as guest of King Farouk 223; travels to Europe with Dorothy Dandridge 223; tributes to 162; turns down *Somewhere in the Night* 205; ultimatum to Rex Harrison 230; unprejudiced nature 169, 184; visit from fan 96; volunteerism 87, 88, 106, 107, 111, 114, 115, 119, 120, 121, 124, 126, 129, 130, 131, 146, 148, 149, 153, 154, 155, 156, 157, 158, 159, 160, 162, 164, 165, 166, 180, 185, 186, 187, 188, 194, 196, 198, 209, 212, 220, 222, 227; wake 243, 244; Warner Brothers contract 32; wartime travel 2; watches air raids 145; wears old wedding rings 54; as writer 182, 183, 184; writes letters to soldiers' families 171; writes own fan response letters 214
Lane, Lola 38, 46
Lane, Priscilla 40, 43, 44
Lane, Rosemary 38, 45
Lang, Harry 240
Langford, Francis 77, 159, 180
Lansky, Meyer 214
Lardner, Ring, Jr. 29
LaRue, Jack 71
Lasky, Jesse 114, 208
Lastfogel, Abe 118
Latham, Mrs. Wales 116
Latin Quarter Restaurant 199
Laurel, Stan 39
Laurel & Hardy (movie serial) 55
Lawler, Anderson 42
Lawrence, Florence 55
Layman, John, Det. 234
Leave It to Blanche (1934) 217
Lee, Anna 166
Leeds, Herbert 127, 207
Leigh, Vivien 117, 217
Leonard, Audrey 43
LeRoy, Mervyn 27, 28
Lester, Jerry 155, 160
Let's Face It 192
Levene, Sam 111
Levine, Nat 52
Lewis, Carroll 222
Lewis, Diana ("Mousie") 37, 40, 44, 45, 140, 230, 244
Lewis, Mary 20
Liberty (magazine) 217
Life (magazine) 97, 153, 166, 205
Lilly, Doris 226
Lindsay, Howard 42
Lindsey, Margaret 46
Litel, John 38, 41, 42, 43
Little, Thomas 163
Little Women (1933) 77
Litvak, Anatole 121

Livingston, Bob 53, 54
Livingston, Mary 166, 193
Lloyd, Harold 55
Lockhart, Gene 44, 201, 203
Lockhart, Kathleen 44
Loew's State Theater 76
Logan, Stanley 41, 43
Lom, Herbert 222
Lombard, Carole: death 130, 166
The London Mirror (newspaper) 132
The Long Dark Hall (1951) 258
Look (magazine) 153
Loper, Don 160, 199, 201, 214
The Los Angeles Daily News (newspaper) 241
Los Angeles Examiner (newspaper) 111
Los Angeles Herald Examiner (newspaper) 240, 254
Los Angeles Philharmonic Symphony 78
The Los Angeles Times (newspaper) 60, 116, 123, 163, 185
Louis, Joe 212
Louis, Joe E. 188
Louise, Anita 54, 71
Love, Robert 239
Love, Honor and Behave (1938) 40, 42, 44; filmography 264
Loy, Myrna 122, 143
Luciano, Charles ("Lucky") 61, 73, 214
Lukas, Paul 159
Lynn, Jeffrey 46
Lynne, Carol 260
Lyon, Arthur 214, 224, 225, 226, 227
Lytell, Bert 155

MacArthur, Gen. George 174
MacDonald, Jeanette: sexuality 22
MacDonald, Marie 213
MacLane, Barton 37, 42, 162
MacMahon, Aline 41
MacMurray, Fred 152
MacVeagh, Jim 133, 136
Magnificent Obsession (1954) 201
Mamoulian, Rouben 102, 103, 105, 122
Mander, Miles 53
Manila Calling (1942) 120, 126, 127, 128; filmography 269
Mankiewicz, Joseph 205, 223
Manners, Dorothy 199, 239
Mannix, Edgar J. 15, 61
Mansfield, Irving 188, 261
Mansfield, Jayne 50
Manson, Charles 261
Mantz, Paul 70
March, Fredric 29, 31
Margaret, Princess 136, 137
Marion, Francis 109

Mark Hopkins Hotel 93
The Mark of Zorro (1940) 102
Markey, Gene 74, 76, 80, 122, 124
Marlowe, Faye 196
Marsh, Mae 55
Marshall, Bill 101
Marshall, George E. 71
Martin, Mary 68
Martin, Richard 164
Martin, Tony 101, 108, 121
Marx, Chico 28, 29, 108
Marx, Groucho 27, 28, 29, 150, 164, 213
Marx, Harpo 28, 29, 72
Marx, Helen 28
Marx, Zeppo 28
The Marx Brothers 28, 31
Marxer, W.L., Dr. 211
Mascot Pictures Company 52
Masquerade Party (television show) 201
Massey, Theodore 11
Mast (magazine) 182
Matson, Norman 44
Mature, Victor 56, 57, 58, 60, 71, 89, 112, 201
Mauborgne, Maj. Gen. J.O. 90
Mayer, Louis B. 15, 28, 31, 51, 85, 114
Mayfair, Mitzi 117, 118, 131, 132, 133, 136, 137, 139, 143, 146, 148, 157, 158, 159, 165, 260; illnesses 145
Maynard, Ken 53
Mayo, Virginia 215, 216
McBrien, William ("Bill") 133
McCarey, Ray 105, 120
McCarthy, June 70
McClain, John 64
McClintock, Patricia 260
McCool, William 23
McDonald, Frank 41
McDonald, Marie 130
McDonald, William Colt 52, 53
McGann, William 46
McHugh, Frank 44, 124
McKenna, Peggy 96, 97
Meet the Stars (1940) 96
Meet the Stars: Hollywood Visits the Navy (1941): filmography 267
Men Are Not Gods (1936) 217
Men Are Such Fools (1938) 40, 44; filmography 265
Menjou, Adolph 23, 29, 31, 64, 71, 72
Mercer, Johnny 38
Meredith, Burgess 70, 74, 101, 107
Merman, Ethel 188, 261
The Merry Macs 111
Metro-Goldwyn-Mayer Studios 15, 28, 51, 61, 90

Meyer, Johnny 129
Middleton, John 53
Military Maritime Service Show (radio program) 154
Miller, Ann 50
Miller, Glenn 120, 121; Orchestra 120, 121
Miller, Ivan 54
Miranda, Carmen 94, 96, 97, 157, 159, 193
Mr. Lucky (1942) 117
Mitchell, Grant 41
Mitchell, Thomas 43
Mitchum, Robert 70
Mocambo Café 45, 49, 66, 87, 122, 161, 218
Modern Screen Magazine (magazine) 252
Monogram Pictures Corporation 52
Monroe, Marilyn 37, 262
The Monterey 20
Montez, Maria 88, 102
Montgomery, George 96, 97, 99, 101, 106, 111, 120; military service 111
Montgomery, Harry 13
Montgomery, Robert 222; military service 110
Montgomery, Robert J. 247
Moon Over Miami (1941) 89, 90, 91, 93, 95, 99, 100, 106; filmography 267
Moore, Dickie 43
Moore, Owen 31
Moore, Pauline 91
Moore, Victor 159
Moran, Dolores 126
Moran, Earl 37
Moran, Peggy 37, 45
Morgan, Frank 32
Morgan, Harry 207
Morgan, Kenny 51, 52, 54, 63, 82, 90, 97
Morris, Bobby 187
Morris, Chester 162
Morris, Wayne 40, 43, 44
Morrisson, Charlie 130
Motion Picture Herald (magazine) 53
Motion Picture Magazine (magazine) 80, 252, 254
The Moulin Rouge 20
Movie Production Code 54
The Movie-Radio Guide (magazine) 90, 97, 153
Movieland Magazine (magazine) 229, 252
Movies (magazine) 162
Mowbray, Alan 27, 100
Muir, Florabelle 252, 254
Muni, Paul 52
Murphy, Dan 186
Murphy, George 31, 128, 131, 159, 164
Murphy, Owen 155

Murray, Arthur 126
Murray, Ken 74
Music Corporation of America (MCA) 112
Music Hall (radio program) 124
musicals, decline of popularity 50
Mutual Studios 206
My Gal Sal (1942) 89, 104, 106, 108, 111, 112; filmography 268
My Girl Tisa (1940) 86
Mystery House (1938) 42
Mystery Sea Raider (1940) 67, 70, 71; filmography 267

Nagel, Conrad 76
Naish, J. Carroll 102, 105
Naked Genius (1946) 192
Nance, Ira (deputy coroner) 241
Napier, Alan 201
Nazimova, Alla 102
NBC Radio Thanksgiving Program (radio program) 159
Neal, Stanley 206
Neilan, Marshall 31
New York Canteen 130
New York Daily News (newspaper) 141
New York Post (newspaper) 192
The New York Times (newspaper) 59
Newbarr, Frederick 241
Nicholas, Fayard 120, 223
Nicholas, Harold 120, 121, 223
The Nicholas Brothers 121, 223
Niesen, Gertrude 186
Nimitz, Admiral Chester W. 194
90th Bombardment Group ("The Jolly Rogers") 174, 175, 176, 177, 178, 180
99th Artillery Division 152
Niven, David 222
No More Vices (1948) 225
Nolan, Lloyd 120, 127, 205
Noose, aka *The Silk Noose* (1948) 219, 221, 226; filmography 271
Norris, Edward 72, 76
North, Sheree 260
Novak, Kim 128
Novak, Mickell 56, 64
Nye, Ben 244, 245

Oakes, Billy 216
Oakie, Jack 149
Oakley, Alexander L. 49
Oberon, Merle 125, 129, 159
O'Brien, George 229, 230
O'Brien, Mavourneen 160
O'Brien, Pat 33, 41, 47, 127, 159, 160, 161, 162, 164, 211, 243, 244, 245, 247
O'Brien, Terry 160

O'Connell, Hugh 43
O'Driscoll, Martha 91, 130
Of Mice and Men (1939) 55, 60
O'Hara, Maureen 209
O'Keefe, Dennis 31, 193
Oklahoma 192
Oldfield, Col. Barney 61, 94, 95, 104, 121
Oliver, Edna Mae 77, 78, 79, 114
Olsen & Johnson (comedy team) 47
Olson, Ole 4
Once Upon a Night 51
One in a Million (1936) 149
One Million B.C. (1940) 55, 56, 57, 60, 69, 76, 89, 100, 217; filmography 267
Orchestra Wives (1942) 120, 123; filmography 268
Oregon Dance Hall 20
Orsatti, Vic 51
Orson Welles' Almanac (radio program) 164
O'Sullivan, Margaret 29
O'Sullivan, Maureen 32
Our Gang (movie serial) 55
Out of the Blue (1947) 215, 216, 217, 220; filmography 271
The Outrigger Club 178
Over the Wall (1938) 40, 41; filmography 264

Palace Hotel 21; Restaurant 20
Palmer, Lilli 86, 217, 220, 222, 223, 224, 225, 227, 230, 231, 234, 236, 237, 239, 240, 242, 246, 254, 258, 259; attends Carole's funeral 245; ignores Harrison's affairs 219; lies about whereabouts weekend of July 4, 1948 230, 237, 242, 255
Palmolive Party Show (radio program) 186
Pals of the Saddle (1938) 53
Pan, Hermes 102
Pangborn, Franklin 31, 45
Paramount Pictures, Inc. 28, 51, 67, 70, 86, 91
Parents Magazine (magazine) 86
Parker, Dorothy 29
Parker, Willard (Worster Von Eps) 38, 42, 244, 245
Parsons, Louella 23, 40, 49, 86, 145, 153, 171, 185, 197, 198, 199, 206, 224, 226, 258, 259
Parsons, William 11
Pasadena Playhouse 56
The Patient in Room 18 (1938) 40, 41, 42; filmography 264
Patrick, Gail 54
Patrick, Nigel 221
Pearl Harbor (2003) 176
Pearman, Michael 116
Pennington, H.F. 126

Penrod's Double Trouble (1938) 40, 43, 44; filmography 265
The Perfect Specimen (1937) 45
The Perils of Pauline (movie serial) 52
Perlick, Bob 70
The Philadelphia Story (1942) 117
Phillip, Prince 222
Phillip Morris (radio program) 154
Phillips, Jean 67
Photoplay (magazine) 59, 82, 91, 153, 171, 185, 252
PIC (magazine) 59
Pichel, Irving 96
Pickford, Mary 55, 114
Picturegoer Magazine (magazine) 252
Pictureplay (magazine) 59
Pieces of Silver (scheduled, 1942) 123
Pierlot, Francis 105
Pilebuck (1944) 160, 161
Pinter, Francis 126
Pitts, Zasu 73
The Plays' the Thing 253, 254
Poling, Guy 260
Polonaise 192
Polonsky, Abraham 218
Polzak, Anton 4
Porter, Donald: military service 111
Porter, Ross 261
Powell, Dick 33, 38
Powell, Eleanor 31
Powell, William 32, 37
Power, Tyrone 96, 98, 102, 107, 111, 218, 220, 222
The Powers Girl (1943) 128, 131, 149; filmography 269
Praster, Robert 10
Préjean, Albert 221
Pressburger, Arnold 198, 203
Preston, Joey 227
Pride of the Yankees (1942) 102
The Prisoner of Zenda (1937) 51
Proctor, Kay 88
Purcell, Dick 41, 43
Purcell, Lou 20
Purcell's Jazz Club 20
Pyle, Ernie 70
Pyman, Bishop Fred L. 243, 246, 247; eulogy for Carole 246

Quigley, Charles 53
Quinn, Anthony 102
Quiz Kids (radio program) 124

Rachmilovich, Jacques 77
Raft, George 100, 101, 161, 214
Raguse, Elmer 59

The Rainbow Room 155
Rainer, Louise 32, 69
Ramsey, Waly 57
Rapf, Maurice 85
Rappe, Virginia 20
Ravazza, Carl 21, 22, 119; hires Carole 21
Raye, Martha 117, 118, 131, 132, 136, 137, 139, 143, 144, 145, 146, 157, 158, 165, 248, 260; awards given to 260, 261; death 260; marriage to Mark Harris 260; military funeral 261; volunteerism 260
Reagan, Ronald 39, 47; military service 111
Reagan, Rusty 226
The Red Mill 20
Reed, Donna 130
Reeves, George 262; military service 111
Reid, John 90
Renaldo, Duncan 54
Renner, Beth 27, 35
Reno (1939) 54; filmography 266
Republic Pictures Corporation 51, 55
Return Engagement 192
Rickenbacker, Eddie 198
Ridste, Alfred 5, 8, 11, 236, 237, 245; abandons family 6; allows Carole to re-marry Irving Wheeler 17; death 259; divorces Clara Ridste 7; marriage to Clara Zentek 5; meets Clara Zentek 5; Naval Air service 7
Ridste, Ann 11
Ridste, Clara 7, 10, 18, 25, 66, 77, 114, 123, 138, 139, 145, 147, 148, 149, 185, 236, 239, 243, 245, 246, 249, 255, 256; death 259; divorces Alfred Ridste 7; divorces Charles Fenner 8; employment 12, 13; illnesses 12; marries Charles Fenner 8; moves in with Charles Fenner 7; relationship with Charles Fenner 8; residences 8, 239; returns to Montana 7
Ridste, Dorothy 7, 8, 10, 13; birth 6
Ridste, Dorothy (Ross) 235, 244, 245, 246, 248, 249; children 63
Ridste, Jerome ("Jerry"): birth 6; death 6
Ridste, Lawrence Bernard 8, 10, 13, 245, 246; birth 5
Ridste, Lewis 7, 8, 10; accidental death 13; birth 6
Ridste family: in Minnesota 5; in Montana 5; in San Bernardino 9, 10; in San Diego 9, 10; in Wisconsin 6
Riley, Lewis A. 114
Rin Tin Tin (movie serial) 85
Ripley, Clements 43
Ripley's Believe It or Not (radio program) 151
Ritchie, Bob 107
RKO Radio Pictures, Inc. 91, 164
Roach, Hal, Jr. 55, 56, 57, 58, 59, 60, 64, 66, 71, 97, 109; military service 110

Roach, Hal, Sr. 55, 56, 58, 60, 67, 73, 109
Road Show (1941) 71, 72, 73, 74; filmography 267
Roberta 51
Roberts, Rachel 224; suicide 259
Robeson, Paul 155
Robinson, Edward G. 42, 100
Robson, May 31
Rogers, Buddy 200
Rogers, Charles "Buddy" 128; military service 110
Rogers, Ginger 32, 50, 159
Rogers, Roy 108, 111
Rogers, Will 55
Roland, Gilbert 114
Roll, Ernest S. (deputy district attorney) 242
Romance in Paris (1937) 27
Romance Is Sacred (U.K., 1937) 27
Romeo & Juliet (1936) 77
Romero, Cesar 52, 96, 97, 98, 105, 106, 121, 123, 130, 149, 211, 243, 244, 245, 247; post mortem letter to Carole 251, 252
Rooney, Mickey 98
Roos, Bo 248
Roosevelt, Franklin 118
Roosevelt Hotel 21
Rose, Hobart 105
Rose, Mauri 216
Rosen, Robert 218
Rosenbloom, "Slapsie" Maxie 155
Rosenstein, Sophie 37
Rosenthal, Joseph 194
Ross, Diane Carol 245, 246
Ross, Evelyn 252
Ross, Lt. Lanny 166, 168
Rosson, Harold 32, 200
Route 66 (television series) 110
Royal Hawaiian Club 20
Rubin, Jan 199
Runyon, Damon 42
Russell, Rosalind 45, 115, 213
Ruth, Baby 20
Rutherford, Ann 120
Ryan, G. Bentley 53, 74
Ryan, Phil 160
Ryan, Sue 187

St. Clair, Malcolm 84
St. Francis Hotel 20, 21, 22
St. Johns, Adela Rogers 29
Sakall, S.Z. 149
Samuel Goldwyn Studios 32
San Francisco Chronicle (newspaper) 194
Sanders, George 201, 205; aloofness 203
Santa Anita Park 31, 58
Sardi's Restaurant 48, 63

Saturday Evening Post (magazine) 147, 160, 161
Savoy Hotel 222
Saylor, Sid 53
A Scandal in Paris (1946) 198, 200, 201, 205, 211; filmography 270
Schaggs, Allen 10
Schenck, Joseph 65, 85
Schlow, Eugene 41
Schmidlapp, Carl 191
Schmidlapp, Charlotte R. 191
Schmidlapp, Emelie 191
Schmidlapp, Emma 191
Schmidlapp, Heinrich (H. William) 191
Schmidlapp, Jacob G. ("Jack") 190, 191
Schmidlapp, Jean 191
Schmidlapp, Jean Maxwell 191
Schmidlapp, Lawrence Maxwell 191
Schmidlapp, Louis 191
Schmidlapp, W. Horace, Jr. 190, 193, 194, 197, 208, 209, 211, 212, 214, 225, 238, 245, 247, 256, 259, 260; birth 191; as Broadway producer 191; contests pre-death financial agreements with Carole 249; death 260; exploits Carole for plays and movies 206, 207; family 198; family estate(s) 190, 191; family history 191; last conversation with Carole 253; marries Patricia McClintock 260; as Miss America judge 192; at Princeton 191; reaction to Carole's death 236; tabloid press coverage 260; travels with Katherine Dunham 221, 222
Schmidlapp, W. Horace, Sr. 191
Schmidlapp, William 191
School for Husbands (1937) 217
A School for Scandal (1930) 217
Schroeder, Carl 57
Schultz, Dutch 214
Schwab, Charles W. 191
Scott, Fred L. 246
Scott, Mary 130
Scott, Randolph 42, 80, 82, 101, 121
Scott, Vera 260
Screen Guide (magazine) 64, 74, 95, 146, 160, 220
Screen Snapshots: Hollywood's Greatest Comedians (1953): filmography 271
Screenland (magazine) 90, 210
Seabright, Roy 59
Seaman, Barbara 188
Seaver, Edwin 147
Secret Command (1944) 162; filmography 270
Seiler, Lewis 44
Seiter, William A. 157
Seltzer, Frank 68

Seltzer, Jules 57, 67
Selznick, David O. 23, 28, 29, 31
Sennett, Mack 55, 83, 98
71st Fighter Group 148
Seymour, Harry 63
Sharpe, David 53
Shaw, Artie 21
Shaw, Wini 166
Shearer, Douglas 31, 32
Shearer, Norma 28, 114
Sheridan, Ann 38, 41, 42, 67, 68, 159, 186, 210
Sherman, George 52
Shirley, Anne 128
Shore, Dinah 107, 119, 220, 256
Show Business at War (1943): filmography 269
Shubert, J.J. 186, 188, 192
Shubert, Lee 192
Shuftan, Eugene 201
Shurr, Louis 51, 54, 55
Sieg, Richard C. 240
Siegel, Benjamin ("Bugsy") 65, 214
Sigal, Dave 63
Silbert, Bernard 225
Silver Screen Magazine (magazine) 79, 88, 197, 210, 221
Silvers, Phil 157, 248
Simon, Simone 71, 88
Sinatra, Frank 155
Singleton, Penny 44
Sirk, Douglas 198, 201
Sis Hopkins (1941) 82
6th Armored Division 149
Skolsky, Sidney 62, 69, 94, 100, 194, 213, 216, 253
A Slight Case of Murder (1938) 40, 42; filmography 265
Smart, Pat 260
The Smart Blonde (1937) 37
Smight, Jack, military service 110
Smith, Al 161
Smith, Alexis 222
Smith, Jack 209
Smith, Joan 213
Smith, Kent: military service 111
Smith, Thorne 64
Smoot, Wil 11
So Different Café 20
Sokoloff, Vladimir 201
Somerville, Lt. Atwell W. ("Slim") 175
Somewhere in the Night (1946) 205
The Song of Bernadette (1943) 163
Song of the Islands (1942) 157
The Sons of the Pioneers 111
South Pacific 192
Sperling, Milton 85, 86, 100

Spewack, Bella 47
Spewack, Sam 47
The Spider (scheduled, 1946) 194, 196
Spider Kelly's Bar 20
Spielman, Fred 187
The Spirit of '43 (1943): filmography 269
The Squeeze-In Club 20
Stack, Robert 76
Stage Door Canteen (radio program) 155
Stahl, John 217
Stanwyck, Barbara 29, 31, 98; bi-sexuality 29; studio-arranged marriage to Frank Fay 29
Star for a Night (radio program) 160
A Star Is Born (1937) 28, 29, 31; filmography 263
Starke, William ("Bill") 176, 181
Starr, Belle 80, 82
Starr, Jimmy 57
Stars and Stripes (newspaper) 133
Stars Give All for Boys Overseas (1961): filmography 271
State Fair (1945) 197
Steadman, Vera 31
Stein, Jules 112, 113
Stella Dallas (1937) 31
Sterling, Robert: military service 111
Stevens, Craig 222; military service 111
Stevens, George: military service 110
Stevens, Onslow 70
Stevenson, Edward 164
Stewart, B.M. 248
Stewart, James ("Jimmy") 143; military service 110
Stewart, Laura 248
Stewart, Martha 193
Stone, George 72
Stone, George E. 41
Stone, Paula 155
Stop, You're Killing Me (1952) 42
Storey, June 130
The Stork Club 155, 161, 193
Storm in a Teacup (1937) 217
The Story of G.I. Joe (1945) 70
The Strange Woman (1954) 201
Strawberry Blonde (1942) 103
Strickling, Howard 61
Stromberg, Hunt 208
Strudwick, Shepard (Shepard, John) 101
Sturgis, Jean Maxwell Schmidlapp 206
Sturgis, Preston 200
Sullivan, Albert 162
Sullivan, Ed 57, 69, 118, 119
Sullivan, Francis 162
Sullivan, George 162
Sullivan, Joseph 162
Sullivan, Madison 162

Sullivan, Wallace 45
The Sullivans (1944) 162
Sun Valley Serenade (1941) 157
Sunset Towers Apartments 65, 159, 199
Susann, Jacqueline 187, 188, 189, 190, 197, 198; death 261; as writer 261
Sutherland, Edward 161, 164, 244, 245
Sutro, Adolph 19
Sutro Baths 19, 21
Sutton, John 99
Swerling, Jo 102
Sydney, Sylvia 256

Taft, William Howard 190
Tait's Bar 20
Tales of Manhattan (1942) 123
Tamiroff, Akim 201
Tarkington, Booth 43
The Tarnished Angels (1958) 201
Tate, Sharon: death 261
Taylor, Robert 31, 98; military service 110, 143
Temple, Shirley 251
Terhune, Max 53
Terhune, William 73
Thalberg, Irving 15, 28, 114; death 28, 29; health 28
Thesiger, Ernest 222
13th Air Force 176
38th Bomber Group 171
Thomas, Bob 207, 208, 261
Thomas, Collette 217, 224
Thompson, Alexis 97
Thompson, Carlos 259
Three Blind Mice (1938) 91
The Three Mesquiteers (1936) 52, 53
The 365 Club 20
The Three Stooges 38
333 Club 222
Three Texas Steers (1939) 51, 53; filmography 266
Tierney, Gene 82, 88, 89, 99, 102, 217
Tilton, Martha 166, 167, 168, 170, 171, 176, 182
Tin Pan Alley (1941) 94
Tinker, Mercia 259
The Tivoli Café 20
Todd, Mabel 45
Todd, Thelma 73; beaten by Pasquale DiCicco 73; death 62; marriage to Pasquale DiCicco 61; murder 61, 73
Tone, Franchot 74, 76, 82, 130
Toots Shor's Restaurant 212
Top Flat (1936) 73
Topper (1937) 55, 74
Topper Returns (1941) 69, 73, 74, 75, 76, 97; filmography 266

Topper Takes a Trip (1939) 74
Topping, Dan 149
Topping, Henry J. ("Bob") 185, 220, 261
Torchy Plays with Dynamite (1939) 37
Torchy Runs for Mayor (1939) 37
Tracy, Spencer 74, 149
Travis, June 41
Trevor, Claire 42
Trocadero Café 31, 45, 49, 63, 66, 122, 162, 163, 218
True Story (magazine) 252
Tucker, Sophie 20, 31
The Turkish Café 20
Turnabout (1940) 64, 66, 69, 71; filmography 267
Turner, Lana 31, 46, 67, 82, 95, 98, 142, 185, 213, 220, 260, 261
Twelve O'Clock High (1949) 85
20th Century-Fox Studios 41, 51, 76, 82, 85, 86, 87, 89, 90, 91, 94, 95, 96, 98, 99, 105, 111, 128, 146, 147, 155, 163, 194, 195, 196, 197, 198, 200, 205, 206, 207, 209, 211, 212, 218, 220, 226, 233, 234, 236, 240, 243, 245, 247, 248, 256, 260
The 21 Club 192
25th Liason Squadron 183
Twilight Zone (television series) 110

Under the Roofs of Paris (1930) 221
Unfaithfully Yours (1948) 223, 225
Universal Studios 91, 201, 214
Untamed Women (1952) 60
U.S.O. 118, 132, 214; first clubs open 118; history 118

Vale, Virginia 60
Valentino, Rudolph 102
Vallee, Rudy 45; radio programs 151
Valley of the Dolls (1967) 261
Valley of the Dragons (1961) 60
Van Auken, John 3
Van Dyke, Woodridge Strong 253
Variety (newspaper) 251
Varsity Show (1937) 33, 37, 38; filmography 263
Velez, Lupe 232, 251, 253, 254, 262; sexuality 22
Vernon Kellogg, S.S. 153, 154
The Victory Caravan 117, 128, 129
Villa Carlotta Apartments 23
Vitagraph Studios 206, 222
Von Briesen, Ada 33
Vukovich, Billy 215

Wald, Jerry 45, 84
Walker, Alexander 224, 239
Wallace, Jean 207

Wallace, Thomas C. 145, 147, 148, 153, 155, 156, 157, 159, 160, 161, 162, 163, 165, 167, 185, 193, 194, 200, 248; asks Carole to marry him 135; marriage to Carole 139; meets Carole 134; wartime service 135
Walling, Joe 133, 136
Wallis, Hal 44
Walter, Lena 11
Walthall, Henry B. 55
Wanger, Walter 96
Waring, Fred, and His Pennsylvanians 38
Warner, Harry 113
Warner, Jack L. 44, 109
Warner Brothers Pictures, Inc. 27, 32, 33, 34, 38, 41, 43, 45, 48, 51, 54, 67, 72, 83, 110, 117, 126, 210, 234, 236
Warners Hollywood Theater 72
Warrick, Ruth 160, 162
Washoe Pines Dude Ranch 196
Wasson, Florence (nee Jones) 96, 97, 166, 211, 234, 239, 241, 244, 245
Wasson, Lou 96, 241, 244, 245
Watson, Elizabeth 13
Watson, Howard 10
Wayne, John 52, 53, 54, 65
Weeks, Anson 21
Weidler, Virginia 124
Welles, Orson 164
Wellman, William 29, 31, 70
Westmore, Perc 40
Wetzler, Sidney 35
What Price Glory (1952) 86
Wheeler, Irving 17, 18, 27, 35, 49, 52, 53; annulment of marriage to Carole 17; elopes with Carole 17; marries Carole second time 17; separation from Carole 17
When Were You Born? (1938) 46; filmography 265
While the Patient Slept (1935) 41
White, Robertson 41
Whittell, Josephine 164
Whoopee! (1930) 32
Wickersham, George Woodward (U.S. attorney general) 190
Wilcoxon, Henry 70
Wilde, Cornell 127, 149
Wiley, Mason 90
Wilkerson, Edith Gwynn 225, 243
William Morris Talent Agency 118
Williams, Chili 213
Williams, Esther 242, 243
Wilson (1944): filmography 270
Wilson, Cami 260
Wilson, Earl 141, 147, 192, 225, 259, 260
Wilson, Elizabeth 217
Wilson, Marie 42, 47

Winchell, Walter 67, 107, 123, 129, 185, 187, 198, 225, 227, 239, 250, 260
Winning Your Wings (1942) 109
Wintertime (1943) 149, 155; filmography 269
Withers, Jane 115, 208
Witherspoon, Cora 44
The Wizard of Oz (1939) 42, 50
Women Are Like That (1938) 40, 41, 160, 161; filmography 265
Women's Home Companion (magazine) 153
Wong, Anna May 46
Wood, Barry 186, 209
Wood, Prunella 192
Wood, Sam 28, 29
Woode, Margo 207
Wooley, Monty 155
Wray, Fay 71
Wright, Cobina 91
Wright, James 139
Wrigley, Dewey 70
Wurtzel, Ben 102
Wyler, William: military service 110
Wyman, Jane 27, 44, 214

Yank in the R.A.F. (1941) 107
Yates, Herbert 52
Young, Frank 59
Young, Loretta 68, 88, 91, 97
Young, Polly Ann 72
Young, Robert 32, 222
Young, Roland 75
Young Mr. Pitt (1942) 148
Younger, Cole 80

Zanuck, Darryl 61, 76, 77, 80, 82, 83, 84, 85, 87, 88, 89, 91, 94, 96, 99, 102, 103, 104, 106, 111, 120, 121, 122, 123, 129, 146, 149, 158, 160, 162, 186, 193, 194, 196, 197, 198, 200, 203, 205, 207, 209, 217, 218, 220, 224, 225, 226, 244, 245, 256, 258; affairs 121; afternoon sessions 85, 86; appears at Coroner's Inquest 240; controls Coroner's Inquest 240, 242; exploits Carole's death 247, 248; forces Rex Harrison to return to Lilli Palmer 226; military service 109; releases Carole 212; retains portion of Carole's earnings 123, 124; sexual additions 85, 86, 88; suspends Carole 205; uses Carole 255; as writer 107
Zanuck, Susan 84
Zanuck, Virginia Fox 162
Zanzibar Club 192
Zasa Café 20
Zentek, Agnesika ("Agnes") 4
Zentek, Clara Lillian 5; marriage to Alfred Ridste 5; meets Alfred Ridste 5

Zentek, Francesca Lillian Gronowska ("Frances") 4
Zentek, Harry 4
Zentek, Ludvig Louis 4
Zentek, Maria 4
Zentek, Martha 4
Zingeheim, Peter 4
Zucco, George 164

www.ingramcontent.com/pod-product-compliance
Ingram Content Group UK Ltd.
Pitfield, Milton Keynes, MK11 3LW, UK
UKHW050542150426
5217IPUK00026B/2034